PRINCES AT WAR

ALSO BY DEBORAH CADBURY

PRINCES AT WAR

THE BITTER BATTLE INSIDE BRITAIN'S ROYAL FAMILY
IN THE DARKEST DAYS OF WWII

DEBORAH CADBURY

PublicAffairs
New York

PublicAffairs books are available at special discounts for bulk purchases in the U.S. by
corporations, institutions, and other organizations. For more information, please contact
the Special Markets Department at the Perseus Books Group, 2300 Chestnut Street, Suite
200, Philadelphia, PA 19103, call (800) 810-4145, ext. 5000, or e-mail special.markets@
perseusbooks.com.

First published in Great Britain in 2015 by Bloomsbury Publishing Plc
ISBN: 978-1-4-088-4524-0 (UK hardback)

Designed by Jack Lenzo

Text set in Garamond

A catalog record for this book is available from the Library of Congress.
Library of Congress Control Number: 2014957933
ISBN: 978-1-61039-403-1 (hardcover)
ISBN: 978-1-61039-404-8 (e-book)

First Edition

10 9 8 7 6 5 4 3 2 1

To Julia, Pete and Jo,
with love

CONTENTS

DRAMATIS PERSONAE

The leading royal princes and their wives have several titles and for ease of reference these are set out below.

HOUSE OF WINDSOR

George VI (r. 1936–52)
Known as **HRH The Duke of York** 1920–36
Born as Prince Albert (1895)
Married Lady Elizabeth Bowes-Lyon
who became **Queen Elizabeth** (1936–52)

HRH The Duke of Windsor (1936–72)
who was Edward VIII (January–December 1936)
Born as **Prince Edward** (1894)
known as David or 'D' by his family
Married Wallis Simpson,
known as the Duchess of Windsor (1937–86)

HRH The Duke of Gloucester (1928–74)
Born as **Prince Henry** (1900)
Married Lady Alice Montagu-Douglas-Scott,
known as HRH the Duchess of Gloucester (1935–2004)

HRH The Duke of Kent (1934–42)
Born as **Prince George** (1902)
Married Princess Marina of Greece and Denmark,
known as HRH the Duchess of Kent (1934–68)

Notable German descendants of Queen Victoria during the Second World War

HOUSE OF HESSE

Prince Philipp of Hesse (1896–1980), great-grandson of Queen Victoria

Married **Princess Mafalda**, daughter of King Victor Emanuel of Italy

Prince Christoph of Hesse (1901–43), great-grandson of Queen Victoria

Married Princess Sophia of Greece and Denmark

HOUSE OF SAXE-COBURG

Charles Edward, Duke of Saxe-Coburg & Gotha (1884–1954)

Grandson of Queen Victoria

Additional characters: friends or associates of the Duke and Duchess of Windsor

Betty Lawson-Johnston

American high-society friend of the Dukes of Kent and Windsor, married to British businessman and philanthropist, Ormond Lawson-Johnston

Charles and Fern Bedaux

Charles Bedaux: American citizen, millionaire entrepreneur, associate of the Duke and Duchess of Windsor

Axel Wenner-Gren

Swedish citizen, millionaire creator of the Electrolux Company, owner of the world's largest yacht and friend of the Duke of Windsor

Ricardo Espírito Santo Silva

Portuguese host to the Duke of Windsor, banker and, according to British intelligence, suspected of laundering German funds looted from captive countries

Friends or advisers to George VI

Sir John 'The Snake' Simon

Home Secretary 1935–7
Chancellor 1937–40
Lord High Chancellor 1940–5

The Viscount Halifax, 'The Holy Fox'

Foreign Secretary 1938–40

Ambassador to Washington 1940–6

Neville Chamberlain, 'The Old Umbrella'

Prime Minister 1937–40

Franklin D. Roosevelt and Eleanor Roosevelt

President and First Lady of the United States 1933–45

And finally

Winston Churchill

Prime Minister 1940–5, 1951–5

PROLOGUE

2o May 1910. The streets below Windsor Castle were filled with crowds wait-ing for a sight of the gun carriage. Every window, roof top and ledge was commandeered to watch King Edward VII's coffin complete the final stage of its journey. The late king, a once wayward youth, had become a popular mon-arch, 'the Uncle of Europe' whose contribution, especially in foreign diplomacy was respected. Thousands had passed silently by the king's body when it lay in state in Westminster Hall. Even larger crowds watched the magnificent royal procession along the funeral route in London. The streets of Windsor offered a last chance for a glimpse of the great monarch who was to be buried as he had lived, in unimaginable splendour, accompanied on his way by many of the crowned heads of Europe. The solemn and carefully stage-managed event would unite royal relatives from across Europe in a unique pageant.

Nine years had elapsed since the death of Queen Victoria and yet her all-pervasive influence had continued with a momentum of its own through her descendants. In her later years the great matriarch had tried to maintain royal power through the dynastic marriages of her forty-two grandchildren. Her grandchildren and great-grandchildren from her marriage to her beloved Prince Albert of Saxe-Coburg formed a 'galaxy of Emperors, Kings, Princes, Grand Dukes and Dukes'.[1] By 1910, this dazzling constellation counted among their number the heirs to the British throne as well as the German Emperor, the 'Tzar of all the Russias', and cousins, uncles and aunts married into the royal houses of Norway, Greece, Spain, Denmark, Romania, Belgium, Portu-gal, Bulgaria and a myriad of princely dynasties. To the people in the streets they were the celebrities of their day. Photographs of royalty were included in family albums as a talking point, royal visitors to England were followed in newspaper reports, and on 20 May many of these commanding figures would be in the streets of Windsor.

The royal train steamed into Windsor station from London. Edward VII's coffin was lifted onto a gun carriage and slowly the cortege, almost hidden from view by the accompanying Blue Coats, carried the King through the thronging streets to St George's Chapel. Behind the procession of Blue Coats came nine of Europe's monarchs, mounted on horseback, resplendent in military or ceremonial dress. To onlookers this appeared to be where absolute power resided, among the glittering plumed heads of Europe, difficult to distinguish among all the feathers and finery of their elaborate costumes. The new British king, George V, led the monarchs, followed closely by his cousin, the Emperor of Germany, Kaiser Wilhelm II, on a white horse. Behind came seven other sovereigns and their entourages: the late king's son-in-law, King Haakon VII of Norway, his brothers-in-law, George I of Greece and Frederick VIII of Denmark, his nephew-in-law, King Alfonso XIII of Spain, and more distant cousins, King Albert I of Belgium, King Manuel II of Portugal and Tzar Ferdinand of Bulgaria. The kings were followed at a measured distance by thirty of Europe's princes, many of them relatives, such as the late king's nephew, Prince Charles Edward, Duke of Saxe-Coburg. Among them was the doomed heir to the Austro-Hungarian throne whose name was yet to make its mark in history: Archduke Franz Ferdinand.

The royal relations had come to pay their respects to the late king and also to take their place among the princely superstars. Even without the great matriarch that united many of them by blood, in 1910 the British monarchy was important, standing at the pinnacle of society in the largest empire the world had ever seen. The British Empire's 11 million square miles spanned almost a quarter of the surface of the planet. Its 400 million subjects inhabited the subcontinent of India, the scorching deserts of Africa, the great forests of Canada, the distant outback of Australia, and even far flung coral islands scattered across the Pacific Ocean. Britain's Navy straddled the globe, her ships, steel, cotton, textiles, were sold across the world and fuelled the teeming prosperity of the country.

The heir to this extraordinary legacy, the late king's grandson, fifteen-year-old Prince Edward, recognised what he would later call 'the golden thread' of his inheritance from his earliest years. He marched up the hill behind George V with his brother, fourteen-year-old Prince Albert, both princes dressed in their naval-cadet uniforms and required to show a dignity beyond their years on that hot day in May. Even for the confident Prince Edward, 'it was all rather overpowering', bringing an awareness of the very public role that he would soon be required to fulfil.[2] His mother, the new Queen Mary, considered her confident oldest son well placed to meet the expectations upon him, but his grandmother, Queen Alexandra had her doubts, warning that he could dominate his brothers and sister, 'laying down the law & thinking himself far superior to the younger ones.'³

Prince Edward's dominance appeared to have had an effect on Prince Albert, who had failed to blossom in his older brother's shadow and became shy and nervous, suffering from a debilitating stammer from the age of eight. Bertie, as he was known in the family, felt he compared unfavourably to Prince Edward and developed an almost excessive admiration of his older brother, while he himself shrank from view. He took 'refuge . . . in silence' knowing that any blighted attempt at speech might condemn him further.⁴ He would rather wait in a darkening room than face the daunting task of asking palace staff to light the gas lamps.⁵ His one sustaining comfort stemmed from his position as the second son: he was sure that he would always be able to avoid the limelight that shone so brightly on his older brother. On the day of his grandfather's funeral he had the support of his younger brother and sister, Prince Henry and Princess Mary. George V and Queen Mary's youngest two sons, Prince George and Prince John stayed away.

The gun carriage passed by the floral tributes which covered the grass outside the chapel. The royal procession followed behind at a stately pace, winding its way up the hill, past the Round Tower, into the courtyard and slowly filled the chapel. The mourners could not know as they took their places in the inside that they were marking a watershed in history. This was the high tide of royal power, the last blazing show of era that had begun to fade. Many of those commanding dignitaries lined up in the carved wooden pews that day were poised on the threshold of momentous change. The words from the burial service rang out across the chapel, reminding those present that all eventually 'must come to dust'.

Within just a few years this glittering company would be divided by war and revolution; four empires were destroyed and several royal houses were thrown from their kingdoms. Kaiser Wilhelm II would abdicate his throne, his reputation demolished for the part he played in precipitating the First World War. Queen Victoria's favourite granddaughter, Alexandra, the Tzarina of Russia, and her husband, Tzar Nicholas, their son and four beautiful daughters were brutally murdered. The King of Portugal, Manuel II was exiled from his country in 1910, as would be Alfonso XIII of Spain in 1931. The assassination of the Archduke Franz Ferdinand in 1914 fired the starting gun of a 'Great War' so terrible that the generation who lived through vowed there would never be war in Europe again.

But in spite of the tumultuous upheavals of world war and revolution that had parted many of their relatives from their thrones, the British monarchy survived intact. It emerged at the end of the First World War in 1918 with a new name, 'Windsor'—replacing the German name of 'Saxe-Coburg'—and at the helm of an expanded empire, swollen with a further 1,800,000 square miles. George V and Queen Mary were popular and their eldest son, Edward, the Prince of Wales, showed much promise, having all the necessary qualities in abundant supply to create a popular and successful monarch.

As the young Prince of Wales embarked on tours of the empire in the 1920s he was greeted by rapturous crowds keen to welcome the son of the British king. With his blonde good looks, his modernising approach and easy charm the heir to the throne became famous, his image recognisable across the empire. He was a man who knew his way in the world—he was idolised by the working classes for championing the cause of the under-privileged and was at the same time every young girl's romantic day dream. The path chosen for him by fate and the role he had created for himself seemed perfectly united: he was the prince who embodied a shining new future. The British royal family, that symbol of the unity of the country and empire, appeared as strong an edifice as the towering walls of Windsor Castle. Nothing and no one, it seemed, had the power to damage this fabled dynasty or topple the occupant from the British throne.

PART ONE

·····················

DECEMBER 1936–SEPTEMBER 1939

1

CIRCUMSTANCES WITHOUT PARALLEL

··

'I meet you today in circumstances that are without parallel in the history of our Country . . . '

—George VI, 12 December 1936, Accession Council

Thursday 10 December 1936. For 40-year-old Prince Albert, Duke of York, the distressing moment was almost upon him. It was a short drive through Windsor Great Park to reach Fort Belvedere from Royal Lodge. That morning a fog lingered in the Thames valley, lifting slowly to reveal the crenellated skyline of the rambling, turreted lodge. The Fort had been built as a folly but retained the forbidding air of a castle, in spite of Edward VIII's lavish recent refurbishments. It had become the king's 'enchanted anchorage', where he felt most himself, away from the formality of Buckingham Palace or Windsor Castle and surrounded by his choice of friends.[1] The Duke of York had not been welcome there, even in the final few days when he had tried repeatedly to talk to his brother. The press were camped outside the drive, flashbulbs poised to snatch glimpses of the princes' lives for a worldwide audience who all knew that the British monarchy was being rocked to its foundations. Inside the grounds the commotion at the gates suddenly receded. The car door was opened for him and the duke was led through a dark hallway to an elegant octagonal room.[2]

Forty-two-year-old King Edward VIII was already waiting when the Duke of York arrived promptly at 9.30 am. For a man who was about to give up the throne he seemed to the duke to be 'perfectly calm'.[3] His older brother's composure was remarkable, never deserting him in public, even at a momentous time such as this. The Duke of York noted that their two younger brothers, Prince

Henry, the Duke of Gloucester, and Prince George, the Duke of Kent, had not yet arrived. The ceremony would have to wait until, as officials from Downing Street had requested, all four royal brothers were present.

On Edward VIII's writing table, the Duke of York could see five or six copies of the Instrument of Abdication laid out for signature by the king's red leather dispatch box, along with several copies of the King's Message to Parliament and each Dominion Parliament. The documents had to be signed by each brother, as one transferred a kingdom and empire to the other, witnessed by the next two in line. A few officials had already gathered and there was the 'dignified, dull murmur' of hushed conversations, a politeness that belied the strength of feeling in the room.[4]

Less than a year had elapsed since King George V had died. The Duke of York shared his mother Queen Mary's bewilderment and shock that the monarchy was being plunged into its deepest crisis in generations. He viewed the abdication papers 'with revulsion.'[5] Queen Mary too was grief-stricken that her oldest son, who had been brought up to understand 'the Monarchy was something sacred', the sovereign bearing an obligation to put 'Country before everything else', could wish instead to marry a divorced woman already in possession of 'two husbands living'.[6] The 'Great Silence' of the British press on the new king's private life had ended abruptly just days earlier at the beginning of December. The shaming tittle-tattle of 'the king's matter' was splashed in headlines that reached the furthest outposts of the empire. Suddenly the monarchy was degraded, perhaps even destroyed. If the king should abdicate and it fell to the Duke of York to take over, 'a change of this nature might shatter public confidence' warned the *Mirror* on 4 December. 'Similar situations in the past have arisen in Foreign Countries—the result has generally been that the armed forces have had the last word.'[7] But in the octagonal room that morning there was no hint in Edward VIII's bearing of the great strain he was under or the lack of sleep of the previous night as he had waited until the small hours for the hurriedly drafted documents to arrive from Whitehall.

A few moments later, the third brother, 36-year-old Prince Henry, Duke of Gloucester, was shown into the room. The third son of George V and Queen Mary was an army man, slightly taller than the Duke of York and with the erect bearing of those accustomed to military drill. Gloucester was not close to his oldest brother but had expected him to do his duty and had found the events of recent weeks disturbing. 'Everything seems different,' he had confided to his mother from Balmoral earlier in the autumn.[8] Gloucester recognised the time-honoured role required of a monarch. His father had understood his position as the figurehead for Britain and Empire but his brother was breaking all the rules. The last few days had been pandemonium. But Gloucester too appeared unmoved as he prepared for the unpleasant duty of witnessing his oldest brother's signature.[9]

As the incoming monarch, the Duke of York knew he would have to rely heavily on the Duke of Gloucester to provide support in the daunting task ahead of restoring confidence in the monarchy. But his brother did not inspire confidence. Like his father he had a keen interest in ceremonial occasions and was conscientious about details of dress and uniform, but he did not appear to be blessed with the many other skills so badly needed for life in the public eye. Gloucester was often cast as the least intelligent of the brothers, who wanted nothing more than a quiet life in the army. It was well known he was most at ease in the company of his drinking friends and that their escapades were at times excessive.[10] Yet this was the man who was about to be elevated to the next adult in line for the throne. The Duke of York wanted to feel the strength of reliable help from his brother Henry, but could he count on his support?

The fourth and youngest brother, the hedonistic and glamorous 33-year-old Prince George, Duke of Kent, was still missing. 'George *would* be late,' remarked Edward VIII, trying to lighten the mood.[11] His lateness was in character. To the Duke of York, Kent was unpredictable, volatile, flamboyant in ways quite alien to his older and much more sober brother, a princely playboy to whose irresistible good looks a series of women, possibly men too, had surrendered. Kent appeared to have no sense of duty or boundaries; his closeness to his oldest brother was, to date, the pivotal guiding force in his life. How Kent would respond to his favourite brother's departure was unguessable. As the new head of the family, it would fall to the Duke of York to keep his brothers in order and do all he could to enlist their support to face down the crisis. But he simply didn't know if he could rely on Kent to play his part.

The Duke of York could not be certain he could even trust himself. In his eyes, his oldest brother had always possessed a star quality that he felt he lacked. At dinner with the prime minister just two nights previously York had fallen silent as Edward VIII was the 'life and soul' of the party. His fitness to rule seemed self-evident. The king had dazzled his dinner guests as he talked of labour problems in South Wales and every conceivable subject.[12] The Duke of York believed he could never match his legendary older brother and knew there were grave concerns over whether he could replace him. For years he had lived with the constant unspoken reproach of failing to live up to people's expectations of royalty. He appeared to many as the dull brother, reticent to a fault, perhaps even unstable. If the public knew him at all they knew him by virtue of a medium that did not flatter him.

The Duke of York's first speech on the wireless at the closing of the British Empire Exhibition on 31 October 1925 had appeared to condemn him, announcing to all and sundry that this was a prince unfit to lead. It had been one of the largest exhibitions ever held, a triumphant showcase for the world's greatest empire which stretched over a quarter of the globe. From every corner of the earth people had come to admire and celebrate. Thousands had filled the Wembley stadium in north London. Ten million more, an invisible host, were listening for his voice on the wireless. When the exuberant bands and parades had finished, and the crowds fell silent, the world waited expectantly as the 29-year-old Duke of York stepped up to the microphone. But his voice quite failed him. He opened his mouth; no sound came. The long silences, the agonising delivery of garbled sounds and half words transfixed the audience. The duke, representing the Crown with all its associated grandeur, appeared to be incapable of articulate speech. For the Duke of York the humiliation was unforgettable.

In the eleven years that followed he wrestled with the problem. He had suffered from a stammer for so long that it seemed an intrinsic part of his personality. If the unwanted spasms started in muscles of his mouth and jaw, his throat could close and he was lost; a helpless figure of ridicule, quite unable to control his speech on cue. His father's exhortations to 'Get it out, boy!' had been no help. Nor were a succession of voice experts. Within six months of the ordeal at Wembley the duke engaged Lionel Logue, an Australian speech therapist who was building a reputation through his speech defect practice at 146 Harley Street. Logue had had success treating veterans of the Great War suffering from shell shock before he came to England and had developed a series of practical techniques to help his patients.[13]

The Duke of York had had eighty-two appointments at Logue's London flat in Bolton Gardens or in Harley Street over the next fifteen months. Logue's methods were unorthodox; they had practised breathing, tongue twisters, intoning vowels, even gargling—and the duke appeared to find his voice. On a state visit to Australia in 1927 he spoke well, his speech defect seeming under control. But with the heavy duties that now lay ahead, the Duke of York feared unpredictable setbacks. His stammer could reduce him utterly. He had a constant dread, difficult to face, that the fault lay in his mind and not in some more easily remedied mechanical dysfunction.[14] Was his very obvious inability to express himself hiding more subtle and deeply ingrained flaws? And how could a man who was not even master of his own speech possibly step forward as the king, a symbol of leadership at the helm of the greatest empire in the world?

For the Duke of York, the trauma of the sudden exposure, trapped in the searching lights of the world's press following the storm of interest created by his brother, was excruciating. While his brother, the abdicating king, was known the world over, he had managed to stay in the background. Pictures were hastily found of the new heir to the throne. The new ruler of a vast realm was unrecognisable. Lacking anything else to say, and to distract their readers from the thought that something might seriously be wrong, the press played the family card. 'We Four', 'We Happy Four', smiled from the pages of the papers: the awkward duke, his wife, Elizabeth, Duchess of York, and his pretty daughters, the princesses ten-year-old Elizabeth and six-year-old Margaret.

Overnight the family had become public property. His wife was shown holding her favourite Welsh corgi on a picnic blanket, looking warmhearted and motherly as she played in the garden with the dark-haired princesses in identical dresses also with pet corgis. She looked comely, not chic, but to the duke's eyes utterly wonderful.

When he arrived in London on 9 December as the heir to the throne, even as the crowd gathered outside his home at 145 Piccadilly to shout 'Long live King Albert . . . ', the future king was a man on the edge of a precipice. For months he had seen the danger approaching and now the dreaded event was becoming reality. He was trapped, swept up in a confusion of expectations and demands. The punishing strain of the past week combined with the appalling prospect ahead proved more than he could bear. The Duke of York had maintained his dignity in public as he navigated through London crowds but by the time he had reached his mother, Queen Mary, at Marlborough House, he could no longer cope. His words failed as he tried to explain everything that had happened. Like a child, the future King of Great Britain, Emperor of India, Head of the Church of England and Commander in Chief of the Armed Forces, wept on his mother's shoulder for an hour, caught up in private grief beyond a mother's consolation.[15]

But now in the octagonal room the brothers were at a point of no return. In a matter of hours, the Duke of York would be king and there was no way of stopping it. Unless of course, as the papers speculated that morning, the king had 'an eleventh hour change in his decision', unable to give up the role he was born for.[16]

King Edward VIII's apparent calm in the Octagonal Room was deceptive, something of a reflex action after weeks of indecision. He felt as though his entire life, 'the ordered sheltered existence that I had known since birth—had blown up and was disintegrating'. For him the crisis had come to a head with a 'violence' that plunged him into a 'state of siege'.[17]

As Prince of Wales he had been idolised, the face of the empire captured in posters and newsprint as one of the most photographed celebrities of his time. He was shorter than his brothers but exuded the confidence born of a lifetime's assurance that he held the highest status, a birthright that utterly guaranteed his standing in the world. One friend of the family recalled his mother's pride in her oldest son, 'who had so long charmed the whole world' and proved himself 'a master technician of his rare and difficult trade'.[18] For a generation of women the unmarried prince was the most eligible bachelor in history, his intoxicating royal charms immortalised in the dance-hall song: 'I've danced with a man, who's danced with a girl, who's danced with the Prince of Wales.' In January 1936, after the death of his father, he had inherited not just a throne but twenty-five years of loyalty and devotion built up during his extensive travels across the empire. As he waited for his youngest brother in the octagonal room just 325 days into his reign, his downfall seemed so mind-numbingly precipitous it was as though his emotions had not yet had a chance to catch up with events.

Edward VIII felt he had been hustled into this position with undignified speed by 'his' Prime Minister Stanley Baldwin once he told him on 16 November that he wished to marry Wallis Simpson. The king was enthralled by her; for him a life of service to the State 'would be an empty thing' without her beside him.[19] They had been introduced in 1931 by his mistress, Lady Thelma Furness, and gradually he came to appreciate Wallis's 'forthrightness' and refreshing independence. She read four newspapers each day and 'advanced her own views with vigour and spirit'. In his eyes her conversation was invariably 'deft and amusing'. Standing behind his parents' golden throne when she was presented at court, he had been struck by 'the grace of her carriage' and her intrinsic glamour.[20] Untouched by stuffy English establishment culture, she exuded that inborn American sense of freedom and she made him feel free. Wallis was exciting. By the time he became king he was convinced he had found the one woman he could not live without.

Stanley Baldwin took a different view. The king was the Supreme Head of the Church of England which did not permit the re-marriage of divorced people who had living ex-spouses. Wallis had divorced her first husband, Winfield Spencer, a US Navy aviator, in 1927 and in 1936 was in the process of divorcing her second, Ernest Simpson, a shipping executive. Baldwin reasoned that the British public would not tolerate a divorced 'Queen Wallis'. To Edward VIII, the prime minister appeared like 'the Gallup Poll incarnate' as he pontificated on the moral outlook of people across the empire and other insuperable obstacles, his fingers snapping with such frequency it appeared to him like an orchestral accompaniment to his theme.

During November 1936 Edward VIII also felt the 'shadowy, hovering presence' and looming disapproval of the Archbishop of Canterbury, Cosmo Lang, the Anglican Church's most senior prelate.[21] For the archbishop, the idea of the king marrying a divorced woman was utterly shocking; a scandal of a most deplorable kind. The Church had never recognised divorce. No British monarch in history had suggested marrying a divorced woman. Fanned by both the church and the state, the king's wish to marry rapidly escalated into a constitutional crisis. In fireside chats of mounting tension, Baldwin had puffed his pipe, 'his massive head wreathed in a cloud of smoke', recalled the king, and patiently, cannily, with consummate skill, out-manoeuvred him. Too late, the king realised he had played into the prime minister's hands when he gave his consent for his request to marry to be put before Cabinet and the prime ministers of the Dominions of Canada, Australia, New Zealand, South Africa and the Irish Free State. On 2 December Baldwin relayed the responses to Edward VIII. There was no support for the British king's proposal. The sanctity, honour and prestige of the monarchy was on the line. Baldwin delivered to the king in unequivocal terms his 'advice'. The king had a choice: either the throne or Mrs Simpson. He could not have both.

The modernising King Edward chafed at the prime minister's 'advice' and reeled at the constitutional stumbling that required he must follow it in all matters. 'Now the word "advice" . . . has a special meaning when used in relation to the Sovereign,' he wrote later. 'Whenever the prime minister *advises* the king he is using a respectful form of words to express the will and decision of the Government.' Not only was the king 'bound to accept such "advice"', but he could not seek 'advice' elsewhere.[22] By 3 December the king felt the need of an escape route to avoid Baldwin's constitutional crisis. He had a new plan: to appeal to the nation in a radio broadcast in which he would speak from the heart. He would wait overseas for the country's verdict. With the ease of organising a picnic, his staff had planes at the ready, hotels booked in Switzerland and a generous supply of money from Coutts Bank.[23] He planned to tell the world of his great love for Wallis. Let the people choose whether he should return from abroad with his choice of bride.

Baldwin was appalled. He pointed out to the king that this would require going over the heads of his ministers, 'a thoroughly unconstitutional procedure'.[24] If the king took this step and failed to follow his advice, Baldwin and his Cabinet might be forced to resign. The country would be split, asked to choose between the king and parliament. The king's desired course of action could put the political neutrality of the monarchy at risk.

The king felt tortured by moments of unbearable doubt. His future, once secure, suddenly seemed 'wraithe like' and uncertain. In the previous few days he had longed to talk it over with Wallis, but she had left England to avoid the worst of the furore and was staying with her friends, Herman and Katherine Rogers, on the French Riviera. Edward VIII was desperate to see her: without her he felt incomplete. He lived for the moment when he could hear her voice. Palace lines were kept clear for her use. His day was ruled by the chance of speaking to her, his agitation spiralling out of control if there was any delay. The king could only be calmed by one consuming thought: what would 'the most wonderful woman in the world' tell him to do?

When finally on 7 December Wallis announced she would withdraw from the situation the king interpreted her actions with profound emotion. She was prepared to sacrifice their love to prevent him giving up the throne. How could he possibly give her up? All he had to do was sign the documents to open the door to a living paradise with the woman he loved.

At 10 am Prince George, Duke of Kent, was shown in to the Octagonal Room. The youngest prince, with his film-star looks and champagne charisma, was, on this morning, uncharacteristically subdued. The Duke of Kent was generously endowed with the very kingly qualities that appeared to be lacking in the sombre Duke of York and the unprepossessing Duke of Gloucester, and he had always been closest to his oldest brother. It was a measure of their warm friendship that for many years his own special room was permanently reserved for him at the Fort, known as 'Prince George's Room'.[25]

Christmas card of Fort Belvedere, from the Prince of Wales to his friends Betty and Ormond Lawson-Johnston in 1933 (PRIVATE COLLECTION OF MRS LAWSON-JOHNSTON)

Kent had cancelled all his appointments and 'tried again and again' to see the king during his agonised 'self-imposed isolation' bunkered up at the Fort in the last few weeks. He wanted to reach his brother before he made an irrevocable decision. Eventually unable to keep away, Kent had turned up at the Fort 'uninvited and unannounced' on Tuesday 8 December.

'"What the dickens are you doing here?" said Edward VIII.

"Whether you want to see me or not I have come," replied Kent.'[26]

Kent understood the agony of mind his oldest brother was going through even though he had been held at bay. The king's interest in Mrs Simpson was all-consuming. Every available minute had been spent with her and he had seen little of him.

Kent had only met the king at public functions and 'had not been allowed to exercise any influence over him'.[27] The king had seemed ecstatic and isolated from reality on 19 November when he told Kent that he intended to stay as king *and* marry Wallis. Kent was stunned. 'What will she call herself?' he gasped. 'Call herself?' replied the king. 'What do you think—Queen of England of course. She is going to be Queen. Yes and Empress of India. The whole bag of Tricks.'[28]

For a short while it almost seemed possible. Over the unforgettable week-end of 5 and 6 December there had been an outpouring of support. A 'King's Party' had emerged from the endless quicksands of Westminster, nurtured by the famous backbench MP Winston Churchill, whose friendship with the 'P of W', as he called him, dated back to the 1920s and who had once predicted that Edward VIII's name 'would shine in History as the bravest and best loved of all sovereigns who have worn the island crown'.[29] Although out of office, Churchill still had a powerful voice and influential friends and was in possession of a warm heart where they were concerned. He argued for the king, rallying his high-powered friends to his cause.

Kent could see the 'King's Party' was taking shape rapidly in the hands of the press. With the support of Churchill's ally, Max Beaverbrook, who owned the *Express* group there was an unexpectedly large hoorah for the king. In the hands of the press Kent's brother was transformed into a heroic 'David' making a dignified stand against the 'Goliath of Church and State for love'.[30] Large crowds gathered outside royal residences waving banners in his support, united in rousing singing of 'God Save the King' and 'Land of Hope and Glory'. The national anthem was played early in news halls and cinemas to catch the public mood. In New York audiences cheered when images of the king and Mrs Simpson were shown on newsreels. In London graffiti appeared on walls: 'Stand by the king'. 'Our England loves its king,' pronounced the *Daily Mirror.*[31]

Would his headstrong oldest brother exploit the 'King's Party'? The press spelled out the implications. If the king married Mrs Simpson, explained the *Mirror* on 4 December, Baldwin would be obliged to resign. The king would need to 'seek an alternative Government to support him . . . the issues involved would require a General Election . . . The King's Party would appear . . . the country would be sharply split in two . . . ' The *Mirror* even contemplated the prospect of a 'Royal Dictator-ship' where the king 'driven by fury of cir-cumstance' could attempt to govern without Parliament. 'In these days of per-sonal dictatorships (consider the present European scene), that is not completely impossible.' The man in the street was interviewed and uninformed opinion was united by the sentimental cry: 'let our king be happy'.[32] All this would be better than abdication which was 'simply the greatest tragedy that could befall England'. 'Tell us the facts, Mr Baldwin,' stormed the *Mirror* on 5 December. 'The country will give you the verdict.'[33]

When Kent was finally admitted into the king's hallowed sanctuary at the Fort on Tuesday 8 December he found his brother in a state of exhausted anguish, his decision to leave all but final. The king's flagging hopes had been revived at the weekend with the outburst in his favour. Churchill had reasoned with Baldwin that the king must not be presented with an ultimatum and hounded into a decision. Edward VIII felt he had seen the backbench MP 'in his true stature'. When Churchill talked about the monarchy, 'it lived, it grew, it became suffused with light'. For him, there was a principle at stake.[34] 'The hereditary principle' should not be left to the 'twisting, crooked tricks of the Government'.[35]

The king had received a letter from Churchill that showed how ardently he had taken up his plight in a campaign which he outlined with spirited military bluster: 'News on all fronts. No pistol to be held at the king's head,' Churchill began. The king must be given more time and he had 'no doubt that this request for time will be granted . . . *On no account must the king leave the country* [Churchill's italics]. Windsor Castle is his battle station (poste de commandement) . . . ' Finally he reassured the king: 'Good advance on all parts giving prospects of gaining good positions and assembling large force behind them.'[36]

But events spiralled against the king after the weekend. Churchill was howled down in the House of Commons on Monday 7 December, dismissed as the man whose judgement had once again let him down. 'In three minutes his hopes of return to power and influence are shattered,' observed one MP.[37] To many he appeared finished politically, ruined by his ill-advised support. The serious papers, too, argued strongly for abdication. When Kent met his brother on Tuesday 8 December, it was beyond doubt that the king could not marry Wallis *and* keep his throne. He had to choose.

Kent soon found there was nothing he could say that would induce his brother to give up Mrs Simpson. 'As I made up my mind two years ago, why should I change it now,' Edward VIII repeated to Kent.[38] He seemed unable fully to grasp the position he was in or to comprehend the future. Being cloistered at the Fort with the king was like being in 'bedlam', according to one witness, the king agitated, chain-smoking, stressed beyond reason.[39] Kent heard the devotion in his brother's voice as he spoke on the phone to Mrs Simpson. He only had time for her; his great imperial inheritance was worthless. Kent confided later that day to Dugdale, Baldwin's parliamentary secretary, that he had talked with the king 'for a longer time than he had enjoyed for over two years. Whilst he deplored the situation and expressed in most emphatic terms his opinion of Mrs Simpson, he said that in his view nothing would move the king in his determination to abdicate at once.'[40] Not even the king's closest brother could avert the catastrophe.

The Duke of York meanwhile knew only that his youngest and oldest brothers had been ensconced together with the prime minister and various officials.

Was it possible that the whispers from various factions at the time, some of which suggested that the crown should pass not to him but to Kent contained a vestige of truth? It was rumoured that the prime minister wished to alter the succession to bypass Edward VIII's unsuitable second and third brothers, the Dukes of York and Gloucester, so that the youngest, with his regal attributes and natural ability, could inherit the throne.[41] Might not the abdicating king, in the face of uncertainty, have an interest in seeing his favourite brother on the throne? Was it possible that Kent had talked of such a drastic step? In the Octagonal Room that morning, the Duke of Kent certainly looked and sounded like a king. Could he be trusted to support the incoming monarch?

With Kent's arrival the formalities could commence. For those in the room an air of unreality took over as the instrument for ridding the throne of its monarch, never before enacted throughout England's long centuries of royal rule, was set in motion. The time had come for the very modern Edward VIII to put his signature upon the pages of history. The king moved forward to the writing table.

Nothing in his father's reign had prepared Albert, Duke of York for such a calamity. Although painfully aware of his own weaknesses as a prospective monarch, he was also familiar with his oldest brother's failings and felt he must atone for them.

Edward VIII had appeared to approach the role of king like a spoilt child at a party: the presents were all magnificent but they were the wrong ones. His laziness and unwillingness to co-operate was widely rumoured in court circles. Documents of State were returned unread. Representatives of august institutions as diverse as the Quaker Society of Friends and the Bank of England were instructed that they must address the king together. He offended the Church by his failure to attend services regularly or take communion on Sundays. The Duke of York, conscientious and hardworking, knew that people now looked to him to put these matters right.

More important still, his brother had blundered in foreign policy, a serious failing at a time of rising international tension. York knew their father had occasion to reprimand his oldest brother in June 1935, when he was still the Prince of Wales, following his speech to the British Legion in which he had expressed a desire 'to stretch forth the hand of friendship to the Germans' without reference to official British policy.[42] Adolf Hitler's rapid consolidation of power in

Germany since he became Chancellor in 1933 was casting an ominous pall over Europe. The Führer's passionate speeches made promises to the German people that threatened boundaries, challenged treaty obligations and endangered peace. By 1935, when his brother expressed his pro-German view, the German dictator had acquired total power as Head of State, Supreme Commander of the Armed Forces, as well as Chancellor. He had just reintroduced conscription in Germany and announced the official constitution of the German air force in direct contravention of the Treaty of Versailles signed after the First World War.

Apparently blind to the danger of Hitler's ruthless ambitions, Edward VIII continued to signal his pro-German views openly, ignoring their late father's warning, as though he had the authority to influence foreign policy. At an official function early in his reign, the king made a point of singling out the German Foreign Minister and feting him with a lengthy exchange in German, while other diplomats were impolitely kept waiting. This kind of encouraging signal to Germany from Britain's monarch had been duly noted by foreign governments across the world.[43]

The Duke of York could see that even his brother's selection of friends drew attention to his pro-German sympathies. His equerry, Major Edward 'Fruity' Metcalfe, had been featured in the *Tatler* on 30 May 1934 at a Blackshirt dinner organised by his brother-in-law, Sir Oswald Mosley, the founder of the Fascist movement in England.[44]

Fun-loving Fruity was far closer to Edward VIII than the traditional palace staff who might have guided the king more soberly through the labyrinthine complexities of his new role. The Duke of York knew that it was not for the British monarch to impose his own opinions on foreign affairs. Too clearly, York saw his older brother's misguided behaviour and took it upon himself to do better. He felt his responsibility keenly. 'I hope that time will be allowed me to make amends for what has happened,' he told the prime minister.[45]

The Duke of York did not know that the telephone at the Fort was already a symbol of the extent of the distrust that had sprung up between the monarch and his ministers. But he did know that of all the errors his brother had made in his first year, there was just the one fatal thing that he could not survive. *She* was the unseen presence in the octagonal room that morning. *She* was the catalyst who had brought the four brothers to this catastrophic watershed.[46] 'Mrs S' had reduced his older brother to a point where he would sit there before them and sign away his birthright.

New evidence shows that in the days before the abdication, the Home Secretary, Sir John Simon, known to his colleagues as 'the Snake', or even 'the

THE BLACK SHIRT DINNER

LADY RAVENSDALE AND COUNT PAUL MUNSTER

COUNTESS MUNSTER AND MAJOR METCALFE

LADY PETRIE AND SIR OSWA MOSLEY

CAPTAIN LUTTMAN-JOHNSON, CAPTAIN SIR THOMAS ROBINSON, MR. R. D. BLUMENFELD AND MR. J. LEES-MILNE

SIR JOHN SQUIRE, SIR CHARLES PETRIE AND MAUD, LADY MOSLEY

The January Club Dinner, which was a Black Shirt gathering, took place at the Savoy, and was notable for a very interesting debate between Sir Oswald Mosley, the originator of the Fascist movement in England, and Sir Charles Petrie, the famous historian and author of "The History of Government" and many other books, including "Mussolini." As might be expected, therefore, the debate was of a quite definitely serious nature. Sir Oswald Mosley is a brother-in-law of both Lady Ravensdale and Major "Fruity" Metcalfe, who married Lady Alexandra Curzon. Lady Cynthia Mosley was the third daughter of the late Lord Curzon of Kedleston, and, like her husband, a former Labour Member ; and Miss Aitken and Mr. W. Joyce, as will be noticed, were amongst those who strictly preserved the correct Black Shirt atmosphere. Literature and journalism were prominently represented by Sir John Squire, who is in the group with Sir Oswald Mosley's mother, and Mr. R. D. Blumenfeld

MR. W. JOYCE, DR. R. FORGAN AND MISS M. AITKEN

Photos: Sw

Edward VIII's equerry, Major Fruity Metcalfe, (TOP CENTRE) at a Black Shirt dinner, the *Tatler*, 30 May 1934 (*TATLER* [TBC])

Snakiest of the lot', made arrangements for the British government to bug the king's calls from the Fort to Mrs Simpson, who was on the continent.[47] In the eyes of senior ministers the monarch had lost his wits under her beguiling influence. He was taking advice from Mrs Simpson, and not his ministers, as he was constitutionally obliged to do. In tapping the king's calls to Mrs Simpson, the Home Secretary hoped to stay one step ahead of the wayward monarch. The relationship between the king and his ministers had broken down.

Sir John Simon's order to bug the king's calls was sent to Sir Thomas Gardiner, Head of the British Telephone Service: 'The Home Secretary asks me to confirm . . . that you will arrange for the interception of telephone communications between Fort Belvedere and Buckingham Palace on the one hand and the Continent of Europe . . . '. This order was deemed so sensitive that it has been buried in a Whitehall vault for seventy-five years and has only recently seen the light of day. (THE NATIONAL ARCHIVES)

'The domination of the King's mind by her mind was a matter of general comment,' recorded Captain Thomas Dugdale, Baldwin's parliamentary private secretary, who accompanied the prime minister on his visits to the Fort in the final week.[48] She was widely credited as the brains behind his campaign to marry her and keep the throne. As every possible option raised by the king to retain his throne and marry Mrs Simpson was painstakingly ruled out by Baldwin, she had urged him to appeal to the country over the heads of his ministers. He was after all the king, 'the adored Apollo', the admired 'Prince Charming', the man who had justly won the love of the Empire. His popular appeal would sway the country. He must hold out for his rights, Wallis reasoned.

Even when abdication became inevitable, ministers found Mrs Simpson urged the king to demand certain conditions before his departure 'with great persistency', recorded Dugdale. 'Most important of all in her eyes, that there should be adequate financial provision . . . to set up a rival court, to exercise influence,—in fact to achieve her obvious ambitions.'[49] Was it possible that the king was in love with a 'gold digging adventuress'?[50] Just how profitable the set-up was for Mrs Simpson was surmised by the Chancellor of the Exchequer, Neville Chamberlain, who considered that 'she had already ruined him [the king] in jewels and money'. How much more harm could she do? Captain Dugdale came to a harsh conclusion: she was 'selfish, self-seeking, hard, calculating, ambitious, scheming and dangerous'.[51]

Edward VIII's pen moved noiselessly over the paper, as he signed 'Edward R.I.' for the last time. Each paper was clearly headed 'Instrument of Abdication'. The king did not even stop to read it. He knew its contents intimately. His casual air that morning as he signed away his birthright matched the coolness he had shown in his approach to the responsibilities of kingship. When the king had finished writing he stood up and yielded the chair to the Duke of York. It was his turn to sign, and then each of his brothers in order of precedence; first Gloucester, and then Kent.

For the Duke of York, watching his brothers sign was 'a dreadful moment and one never to be forgotten'.[52] The whole fabric of monarchy might 'crumble under the shock and strain of it all . . . '[53] The abdication was causing widespread anti-monarchy feeling. He was aware of the activities of James Maxton, chairman of the Independent Labour Party, who caught the mood of many when he argued in favour of sweeping away the institution. 'It would be the will of the mass of the people,' argued Maxton, 'to replace the monarchy with a more stable and dignified form of government of a republican kind . . . '[54] York did not feel equipped to step into the shoes of a man widely perceived as the most popular in the British Empire. The task ahead seemed oppressive.

He knew his wife, Elizabeth, viewed the prospect with 'horror and emotion'.[55] All week she had been ill in bed with flu. Privately she was 'terrified' for him. The unspoken fear, never acknowledged but always shaping her thoughts, was that her husband was now cast in a role for which he was eminently unsuited. The strain would be more than he could bear and she would lose him.

Nothing of this was even alluded to at Fort Belvedere. Politeness and courtesy prevailed. There was an air of goodwill. The ex-king stepped outside the octagonal room to take in the cold morning air, with the relief of a swimmer 'surfacing from a great depth'.[56] The four brothers shook hands and parted without fuss or rancour.

Queen Mary set the tone for the royal family's response in a public statement in which she spoke of the 'distress which fills a mother's heart when I think that my dear son has deemed it to be his duty to lay down his charge'. Women were crying in the street, sharing in her grief, as Queen Mary emerged from Marlborough House dressed in black, her funereal ensemble softened only by the black fur trim. A snapshot appeared of the faces of Princess Elizabeth and Princess Margaret peering anxiously from the top window, watching their grandmother leave with great solemnity through a respectful crowd.[57]

A sense of awed shock also pervaded the House of Commons, as Stanley Baldwin delivered his account of the momentous drama against the sound of stifled sobs from one or two MPs in the packed galleries. But in the debate that followed not all MPs wished to express their respect.

'Mrs Simpson has a social set, and every Member of the Cabinet knows that the social set of Mrs Simpson is closely identified with a certain foreign Government and that the Ambassador of that foreign Government . . .'

Mr Gallacher, the Communist MP for West Fife, was shouted down, his sentence incomplete.[58] It was the first public statement that lent sup̄ disturbing rumour that the real reason Mrs Simpson w̄ from the throne, but from the country, was that she an affair with Hitler's new ambassador to Britain, Jo Gallacher was silenced before the words had left his m left unchallenged, the accusation still hanging in the air.

For the incoming king the accounts in the press of the events in the House could only add to the degradation of the monarchy. Was it possible that there was any truth in the wild allegations? Beneath the gentle sounds of polite court gossip ran a vein of red-hot whispering suggesting that she was involved with Von Ribbentrop. This graceless 43-year-old Nazi with a receding hairline, expanding waistline and narrowing lips, did not look the part of a celebrity lover but the former whisky and champagne salesman now enjoyed a position of great power. He had won the trust of Adolf Hitler and understood how much the Führer wanted Britain's agreement as he pursued a policy of rearmament and the acquisition of *Lebensraum* or 'living space' for the German people. The new German ambassador to Britain was said to be adept at turning on his own unique brand of icy charm for the leading lady in Edward VIII's circle. Mrs Simpson had received invitations to the most important events at the German Embassy. She had been courted and flattered with many gifts of flowers from Ribbentrop. In an interview with the FBI, one distant royal relation, Charles Alexander, Duke of Württemberg, later claimed that Ribbentrop sent Wallis seventeen carnations every day: 'The seventeen supposedly represented the number of times they had slept together.'[59]

Ministers knew that Wallis had taken it upon herself to facilitate a meeting between Ribbentrop and the former Prince of Wales at Lady Cunard's, prompting the Under Secretary for Foreign Affairs, Anthony Eden, to despair that such diplomatic gaffes made 'parliamentary government impossible'.[60] The suspicion that Wallis might even be acting for the Nazis was aroused when the Foreign Office intercepted messages from Ribbentrop, who saw in the political manoeuvres to stop Wallis becoming queen 'a desire to defeat those Germanophile forces which had been working through Mrs Simpson . . .'[61] The Duke of York had had several private meetings with the prime minister during the abdication week but whenever Baldwin was questioned about 'Mrs Simpson's dossier' and whether it shed any light on such claims, he always denied it.[62]

The atmosphere remained charged in London. Vast crowds gathered in the centre of the city following Baldwin's announcement as though expecting further shocks. People crammed into Downing Street and were only cleared at ten in the evening when the police put up a cordon. A few minutes later several hundred Fascists, who supported Edward VIII, ran down Whitehall from Trafalgar Square brandishing newspapers.

Winston Churchill rallied to the side not of the new king but the departing king. He went to the Fort on 11 December to look over his last speech. After their lunch together Edward VIII ceased to be king, and the fact that the moment passed with no significant ritual to mark the occasion moved Churchill. While they had been idly chatting something unique had occurred. The royal heritage, that unbreakable bond between a king and his subjects, had been severed. The unseemly speed with which the king had been forced out of office into exile brought to Churchill's mind the execution of Charles I in 1649. As he left the Fort, he was quietly murmuring the words from a famous political poem by Andrew Marvell on the death of Charles I, tapping with his stick to dramatise the words and underline his feeling that justice had not been done:[63]

> He nothing common did or mean,
> Upon that memorable scene . . .

That evening Windsor Castle was quiet and dark as the ex-king, now renamed His Royal Highness, the Duke of Windsor, crossed the large quadrangle and made his way up an ancient stone staircase to the Augusta Tower. Technicians from the BBC were waiting and he took his position behind the microphone.

'At long last I am able to say a few words of my own . . . ' he began. He explained that he would 'now quit altogether public affairs' and declared his allegiance 'with all my heart' to the new king. Then came the famous words which would define his short reign: 'I have found it impossible to carry the heavy burden of responsibility and to discharge my duties as king as I would wish to do, without the help and support of the woman I love.'[64] The world listened, spellbound, to hear the sovereign who would give up his throne for love, taking in the inflections in his voice as he spoke of 'the woman I love', and the heart-thumping break at the final 'God save the king' speaking of his profound emotion. And so began the myth of the greatest love story of the twentieth century, although many who witnessed the event were of the impression that an unknown American woman on the wrong side of forty with a questionable pedigree had just stolen the king of England.

Before the exhausted ex-king set sail for the continent he made his polite farewells to his family, formally bowing like a subject to the Duke of York. Only the Duke of Kent broke through the stifling politeness of it all as he shouted out in pain on seeing his oldest brother go: 'This is quite mad . . . It isn't possible! It isn't happening.'[65]

The former king had chosen the cliffs of Dover as his Christmas card that year but later that night on board HMS *Fury* the dim outline of the 'White

Walls of England' shrank swiftly from view in the darkness until the cliffs were a mere thread of white on the black water.[66] The duke was at sea. He seemed unconcerned, drinking brandy with the crew as his old life slipped away from him.

At 11 am on 12 December 1936, the Duke of York made his way to St James's Palace to his Accession Council. He looked worn, concerned that his voice, so hesitant and odd, would let him down. Not to be in charge of his words at such a time, never sure if his carefully constructed sentences would seem normal or whether the whole speech would disintegrate, was a terrifying ordeal. The eyes of the Privy Counsellors were on the new king.

He started slowly. 'I meet you today in circumstances that are without parallel in the history of our Country,' he began. 'With my wife and helpmeet by my side, I take up the heavy task that lies before me . . . '

The relief in the room was palpable. The ancient ritual was accomplished. Tradition was upheld. The Duke of York chose the name 'King George VI' to imply a continuity he hardly felt with his father's regime. Pathé newsreels trumpeted the proclamation of the new king in the cinemas. Across the empire, prayers were offered to God to support the new 'King's Majesty, to replenish him, enrich him and strengthen him'.

But behind the scenes, the new George VI was inconsolable. 'This is absolutely terrible . . . I never wanted this to happen; I'm quite unprepared for it,' he poured out his heart to his cousin, Lord Louis Mountbatten. 'I'm only a Naval Officer, it's the only thing I know about,' he lamented.[67] Quite apart from the burden of his new role as monarch, he could scarcely be sure he would be able to manage his own brothers. His uncle, Lord Athlone, witnessed the 'dear old boy' endeavouring to take control on his very first night with an ill-judged outburst against the dukes of Gloucester and Kent. 'He fairly went for his brothers,' observed his uncle, 'saying: "If *You Two* think that, now that I have taken this job on, you can go on behaving just as you like, in the same old way, you're very much mistaken!" he cautioned. "*You Two* have got to pull yourselves together."'[68]

Before him, the daunting prospect of his coronation loomed. He had not felt the need to consult Logue for some years, but now always hovering over him was the thought of all the public appearances with the obligatory speeches that would be an inescapable part of his life. Ever since his stammer began, such occasions were almost unendurable. His fear was that at some important function, attempting to deliver a beautifully chiselled speech, words would not come. Worse, the words that would leave his lips could be tortured, twisted sounds. He would stand in anguish talking rubbish, his jaw clicking out of control. Panic would set in. At the very worst it could even end in an epileptic fit, his dignity in tatters, apparently unfit to be king. He knew that this was whispered about him; certain factions continued to speculate whether they had the right man on the throne. Lionel Logue recognised the acute nervous strain his former patient might be experiencing and wrote to offer his services once more.[69]

In his Abdication Broadcast on 13 December the Archbishop of Canterbury took it upon himself to draw attention to the new king's weakness. 'When his people listen to him they will note an occasional and momentary hesitation in his speech,' announced Cosmo Lang. 'But he has brought it into full control and to those who hear it, it need cause no sort of embarrassment, for it causes none to him who speaks'.[70] The archbishop was trying to offer his support, but to the sensitive George VI, by drawing attention to his speech defect, he might just as well have trumpeted to the empire that the new king was unfit to rule.

2

A VERY FULL HEART

·······································

'It is with a very full heart that I speak to you tonight . . . '

—George VI on his coronation day, 12 May 1937

In the New Year of 1937, just twenty days into the new king's reign, the public were faced with another salacious royal scandal, this time centred on Prince George, Duke of Kent. Who is Mrs Allen? The *Daily Express* tantalised its readers in a story that embraced in one sensational package further royal transgressions including possible adultery and the dubious science of 'head-reading'.[1]

The conscientious new king, struggling to set improved standards of royal behaviour, woke up on New Year's Day to read in the papers that the 'Duke of Kent and Woman Friend have their Heads "Read"'. The recently married duke was decorating the front pages of the papers alongside a woman of exciting beauty: the very much married Mrs William Allen, who flaunted her film-star looks and come-to-bed eyes in a flimsy lace dress centrally placed on the front pages too. Evidently the king's stern directive to his brothers on his first night had not even lasted three weeks.

Mrs Allen was revealed as Paula Gellibrand, otherwise known as 'Britain's most painted woman', the society model and mannequin whose exquisite beauty had featured in advertisements across the empire.[2] Kent's warm relationship with her was noted, along with her two previous marriages. The implications were clear. Was Mrs Allen to be the next Mrs Simpson?

The findings of the London phrenologist Miss Evelyn Bool were laid before the public. The *Daily Express* was at pains to reassure its readers that Miss Bool herself was a grey-haired and bespectacled woman who sat amidst her skulls and charts in an office up a narrow stairway off Ludgate Circus in central London. Miss Bool had ruffled Kent's hair and massaged his scalp to explore his

WHO IS Mrs. ALLEN?

Wife Of Rich Ex-M.P.

FRIEND OF THE DUKE AND DUCHESS OF KENT

By WILLIAM HICKEY

"Who is Mrs. Allen?" people asked yesterday when they read the Daily Express report of the Duke of Kent's visit to a phrenologist.

The appointment was booked for him by a Mrs. Allen, who also appeared in the picture of him leaving after the reading.

Some thought that "Mrs. Allen" was a pseudonym. One newspaper described her as a well-known peeress.

This was wrong. She is Mrs. Allen—Mrs. William Allen, wife of a wealthy business man who was formerly M.P. for West Belfast and is an authority on the peoples of the Near East.

As Miss Paula Gellibrand—"the Gellibrand"—she was London's most beautiful mannequin in 1922, and was painted by many famous artists.

As the Marquise de Casa Maury she became one of the best-known figures in the social circle in which the Duke and Duchess of Kent move.

The recently married Duke of Kent was decorating the front pages of the papers with a woman of exciting beauty, Mrs William Allen. (*DAILY EXPRESS* 2 JANUARY 1937) 'head contours' and could reveal that, apart from his pronounced 'language bump', he was a man of exquisite taste, a great appreciator of art and beauty, 'a real English head . . . fine brains, Dresden China quality'. But not even Miss Bool, every detail of her appearance proclaiming a woman of good repute, could quite dispel the feeling among the public that this 'phrenology' was a naughty new game: an excuse for amorous exploration.

The story ran for days in the New Year of 1937 with worldwide interest inflamed under such headers as 'Royal English Family agog over Duke's Escapades' or 'Ex Duke's Brother now Under Fire'.[3] The *News Review* went further, listing a string of other striking beauties in the duke's life, including the talented redhead Edythe Baker, who shared his passion for jazz piano and was famed for her 'bluesy touch'. On Broadway and in London's West End she had won hearts with such hits as 'My Heart Stood Still' and 'One Damn Thing After Another'. Although originally involved with the Prince of Wales, according to the *News Review* in 1937 she was 'even dearer' in the duke's affections than Mrs Allen—and recently divorced.[4] How many potential Mrs Simpsons were there waiting in the wings?

The story revived all the old concerns about the Duke of Kent and his many peccadilloes that had vexed his parents over the years. Since the mid-1920s Prince George had indulged in a life of extremes as the archetypal royal bad boy. Previously the press had politely looked the other way as the dashing young prince apparently broke the law, had a string of inappropriate liaisons, was threatened with blackmail and even put his life at risk. But in the wake of Mrs Simpson, the gloves were off. The press were no longer tongue-tied when it came to royal indiscretions. The old King George V had tried, and appeared to have failed, to awaken in the young prince an awareness that he was 'a servant of the country'. It was down to the new king now, as head of the family, to try to succeed where his father had not.

The transformation of Prince George from an artistic and sensitive child to the thrill-seeking celebrity royal of the roaring twenties had taken place after the death of the fifth and youngest brother, Prince John. John suffered from epilepsy and some form of mental illness and, as his condition deteriorated, he had been moved to a separate household at Wood Farm on the Sandringham Estate, his weakness viewed as a source of shame to be hidden from view. Prince George had remained fond of his affectionate youngest brother. It was after his death in 1919 that Prince George began to change, revealing an unruly and hedonistic streak. Utterly bored by his father's career choice for him, tucked away at Dartmouth in the Royal Navy, Prince George had joined forces with his oldest brother at the heart of a racy high-society set. They shared the same taste for thrills and pleasure and Prince George jumped right in at the deep end. It did not take him long to discover he had an all-consuming interest in sex.[5]

He acquired a long list of glamorous and famous lovers. The stunning banking heiress Poppy Baring was an immediate favourite. There was talk of marriage in 1927, until George V found out and expressed his disapproval. A string of starlets were happy to entertain him, all dewy-eyed, curvaceous and irresistible. He had fun with actress and singer Jessie Matthews, and with the American Florence Mills, warm and sultry from cabaret. Many debutantes too required his attention, including Margaret Whigham, later the Duchess of Argyll, and Lady Alexandra Curzon, who is said to have—temporarily—broken Prince George's heart by marrying the Prince of Wales's best friend, Edward 'Fruity' Metcalfe.

The hedonistic youngest prince savoured every ravishing excitement that presented itself. Men or women; he did not discriminate. His alleged affair with Noël Coward led to audacious behaviour; 'dressed and made up as women', walking the streets of London, they were arrested for 'suspected prostitution'.[6] There were further claims of affairs with the future spy Anthony Blunt, his royal cousin, Prince Louis Ferdinand of Prussia as well as a number of young men all blonde and foreign. They all apparently, engaged in sessions forbidden by law with the irresponsible Prince George.[7] Inevitably it led to blackmail and at least once, according to the diplomat and journalist Sir Robert Bruce Lockhart, substantial sums were paid to recover Prince George's love letters to a male friend in Paris.[8]

By the late 1920s, Prince George's search for thrills found a more dangerous expression through the beautiful Kiki Preston, an American expatriate and heiress in Kenya. She was part of the Happy Valley set, a group of British and Irish aristocrats known for their drug use who had settled in the Wanjohi valley. Kiki, 'the girl with the silver syringe', took heroin, cocaine and morphine, dispatching her private plane for supplies whenever she ran out. The prince, who was enthralled yet again, is thought to have also become dependent on morphine and cocaine.[9] Rumours began to spread that Kiki had an illegitimate son in 1926 by Prince George who was put up for adoption—rumours which have continued to this day. The Prince of Wales, for once acting the role of responsible older brother, began to go to great lengths to keep the two lovers

apart. Kiki was unable to end her drug addiction but he found a discreet country retreat in 1929 and forced his youngest brother to comply with the watchful
ministrations of the nursing staff. It is a measure of their closeness that the
Prince of Wales could act as jailor to his wilful youngest brother and slowly
restore him.

When Prince George surfaced from his older brother's care, he was apparently
cured of his drug addiction, though little else. He lived with the Prince of Wales
at York House, St James's Palace, on the Mall and now began a happy period
with few responsibilities to dampen his spirits. A handsome, eligible royal prince
could enjoy an enchanted world of the immensely rich and the immensely talented. As an arts lover Prince George drew Hollywood stars, such as Douglas
Fairbanks, Junior, who counted the prince as his 'chief royal friend', into his
charmed circle as well as the actors Laurence Olivier and John Gielgud, the
American songwriter and composer Cole Porter, the actress and singer Beatrice
Lillie and the brilliant brother and sister dance team, Fred and Adele Astaire.[10]

One of the women in this dazzling crowd in the early 1930s was Betty
Lawson-Johnston, dubbed by the press as one of London's most stylish hostesses. Her husband, the philanthropist Ormond Lawson-Johnston, enjoyed
great wealth through his Scottish forebears, who built the family fortune as the
creators of the popular drink Bovril, and also were connected by marriage to
the American Guggenheim family, one of the richest in the world. The Lawson-
Johnstons enjoyed a jet-set life from their homes in New York, London and
Cuba and Betty regularly graced the society pages, her friendship with the
royal brothers adding significantly to her column inches.

While other hostesses 'were pulling innumerable wires' to have the Prince
of Wales as dinner guest, wrote one of New York's leading gossip columnists,
'Cholly Knickerbocker', otherwise known as Maury Paul, 'the Prince was having one of his secretaries *command* Betty Lawson-Johnston to give a small intimate event at her London residence in Cadogan Place for himself and a few
of his close friends'. But Betty Lawson-Johnston had other ways of pleasing
the Prince of Wales. Knowing his taste for all things American, she was a ver-
itable Macy's delivery service, her gifts including the latest 'pop-up' toaster,
place mats, charming napkins, even a desk. The Prince of Wales had a 'deep
rooted admiration for the diminutive and soignee Betty', according to Maury
Paul.[11] American *Vogue* took note of every change in the elegant tailoring of
Mrs Lawson-Johnston: 'her new emerald-and-diamond necklace shaped into a
small collar,' observed the editorial, 'required modifications to the neckline of
all Betty's dark blue dresses.'[12]

Prince George's undated letters to Betty in the early 1930s capture his easy, carefree style and reflect their growing friendship. At first he wrote formally to 'Mrs Lawson Johnston' thanking her for the social and charitable events that she arranged and her appreciative comments on his few public appearances. George evidently took no more pleasure in public speaking than his older brother, the Duke of York. 'I <u>was</u> frightened,' he told Betty, 'but it all went off on the night.'[13] Soon George's letters reveal more intimate soirées with 'dear Betty'. 'I enjoyed our evening so much,' he wrote thanking her on one occasion. 'We should never have gone out really . . . Hoping to see you again and again. Very many thanks. With love. Yrs. George . . .'[14]

But the society event that transformed Prince George's life took place in September 1933, at a luncheon arranged by a different hostess, Lady Emerald Cunard. Prince George's attention was held by one guest there with a strikingly cool self-assurance: Princess Marina. Her bearing and poise exuded a confidence that was perhaps hardly surprising: through her father, Prince Nicholas of Greece, she was related to the Danish, Greek and British thrones and through her mother, the Grand Duchess Elena Vladimirovna of Russia, to the Russian imperial family. She was accompanied by her older sister, Olga, who was married to Prince Paul, the Regent of Yugoslavia. Marina's dark good looks combined with her regal self-control made her appear unobtainable. The prince was captivated but clearly 1,000 years of royal blood was not to be approached carelessly. She made every woman in the room seem ordinary, even Wallis. When Marina returned to London in the spring of 1934, the prince was one of her first visitors at Claridge's.[15]

Prince George did not do things by half measures. That summer Princess Marina was staying in Yugoslavia at her sister and brother-in-law's country residence, a large shooting lodge by the Bohinj lake set in stunning alpine scenery not far from the Italian border.[16] On impulse the prince borrowed his oldest brother's plane and set off with his equerry to find her. The young man who emerged from the plane was tall, good-looking and 'irresistible' according to his good friend, the Conservative MP, Henry 'Chips' Channon.[17] And indeed, Marina, whatever she knew about his past, found she could not resist him. Their engagement was announced on 28 August 1934. In anticipation of the marriage, George V honoured his youngest son with a new title: the Duke of Kent.[18]

Betty Lawson-Johnston was one of the first to know the good news. Writing on 4 September from the villa at Bohinj, the Duke of Kent could not conceal his excitement. 'My dear Betty . . . When I told you at Cowes that I was

George and Marina, from their Christmas card to Betty and Ormond, 1935
(THE PRIVATE COLLECTION OF MRS LAWSON-JOHNSTON)

coming out here I had <u>no</u> idea I was going to be engaged—I am so happy and she could not be more sweet & lovely—I am <u>very</u> lucky. This is just one line as I have so many letters but I just wanted to tell you how delighted I am as you've always been such a wonderful friend to me . . . It's sweet of you to want to give me such a lovely present—I couldn't appreciate it more . . . '[19]

Word spread fast in Britain of the exotic foreign princess. When Kent returned to London he confided to Betty his worries over the press interest. 'I hate to see all the time "the Royal Lover"!' he unburdened himself. 'It's terrible and the one thing it shouldn't be before the marriage!' Kent thanked Betty for her letters and press cuttings. 'I've written 53 letters today & am going off my head!'[20] He was just about to meet his exotic Greek princess at Victoria Station. Thousands were waiting to catch a glimpse of their fairy-tale romance. Crowds lined the streets and petals were strewn in front of their car all the way to York House at St James's Palace.[21] The natural glamour of both Princess Marina and the Duke of Kent seemed magnified when they were together and they became 'that dazzling pair', according to Chips Channon.[22]

As preparations began for a spectacular wedding ceremony in Westminster Abbey, there were many who felt the disappointment keenly. Edythe Baker, once 'the special girlfriend' of the handsome prince according to Douglas Fairbanks Junior, was recently divorced and rumoured to have taken a sizeable payoff 'to bow out of her royal relationship gracefully'.[23] Fairbanks did not speculate on whether Kent was the reason for her divorce. Others, too, had to give up hope, such as the American glamour girl Sandra Rambeau, who claimed she had received generous diamond tokens of the prince's admiration.[24] Even Kent's oldest brother felt cut adrift. 'It seemed to me sadness began to envelop him,' observed Wallis Simpson. 'He and his younger brother were very close, and the bonds of blood were strengthened by an unusual kinship of spirit.'[25] She recognised the Prince of Wales was losing an 'anchor to his personal life' and felt he disappeared 'before my very eyes into uncertainty'.[26]

The Kents' marriage on 29 November 1934 had all the splendid pageantry expected from a royal wedding. Some 2,000 guests were in Westminster Abbey to witness this ancient rite and when the bride walked towards the altar through air made dense with fanfares and choral music, all eyes were on her: a rare creature dressed in white and silver which shimmered in the light, diamonds blazing.[27] A honeymoon lasting several months passed happily and in the spring the Kents returned to their new home at Belgrave Square. The duke was now a married man with responsibilities and commitments. A baby was on the way. His life had changed fundamentally. The playboy had grown up, hadn't he?

Faced with the headlines of his youngest brother's exploits with Mrs Allen in January 1937, for George VI it was hard to believe that Kent was taking the crisis in the monarchy seriously. His careless antics were all the more thoughtless since Marina had only just given birth to their second child, Princess Alexandra, who was barely a week old. Their first child, Prince Edward, was fifteen months old. The *News Review*'s comments on the Kents' marriage, repeated in newspapers across the world, created the impression of wounding divisions. Marina no longer cared to devote so much time to being at the centre of the social whirl, whereas the beckoning magic of the high life still enraptured her pleasure-loving husband.[28]

The Duke of Kent's playboy image contrasted sharply with the standards George VI set for himself. Although he too had had affairs before marriage, with the West End star Phyllis Monkman and a married Australian beauty, Lady Loughborough, among others, such dalliances held no serious interest for him once Lady Elizabeth Bowes-Lyon entered his life.[29] As a nineteen-year-old debutante, Lady Elizabeth, the pretty daughter of Scottish aristocracy, had had a great many admirers in the summer of 1920 when she had met the 24-year-old Duke of York. It had not taken the duke long to feel sure of his feelings and, in spite of his shyness, he had found the courage to propose to her three times before she finally said yes. For him, her acceptance after a prolonged courtship was 'the most wonderful happening in my life'.[30] His marriage proved emotionally richly rewarding for the Duke of York and his loyalty was beyond question. Their mutual friend Osbert Sitwell later commented it was nothing less than 'genius on the part of George VI' to have found so perfect a queen.[31]

His youngest brother was different. Behind the respectable façade of marriage there appeared to be a playboy still, one who continued to feel some solidarity with his oldest brother. The Kents stayed away from Sandringham during Christmas 1936. 'I'm so miserable about it all (the abdication),' the Duke of Kent confided in his brother-in-law Prince Paul, 'I feel rotten, cold and nervy and altogether bloody.'[32] In provocative mood he pushed the king for permission to visit the Duke of Windsor in Austria in January. The king declined, anxious about the continued press interest, still insecure in his position as monarch and concerned that his youngest brother might let him down. The change in Kent after the abdication was evident to those who met him. He was 'a nervous wreck', observed Sir Robert Bruce Lockhart, 'capable of doing anything'.[33]

The abdication had also unsettled Prince Henry, the Duke of Gloucester by suddenly elevating him to high office. Until the new king's oldest daughter, Princess Elizabeth, a sensible and serious ten-year-old, was eighteen it fell to Gloucester to become Regent and safeguard the throne for her, should anything happen to the king himself. George VI had to trust Gloucester to take over whenever he left the country or in any emergency. But Gloucester had not been marked out for such responsibilities. With two brothers before him in the line of succession, his parents had not foreseen such an eventuality.

George VI was aware of the reasons why his parents had not wanted to rely on Prince Henry. His school reports failed to find the right words to disguise his lack of spark or intelligence. Prince Henry was rapidly outshone at prep school, St Peter's Court, by his gifted youngest brother, the Duke of Kent, despite an age gap of three years. The disappointing feedback from his tutors at Eton continued, causing both parents to worry for his future. 'Do pray try & work harder & use your brains more . . . ' Queen Mary had admonished.[34] But Prince Henry did not see the point. Being confined indoors to a desk made no sense when football was on the agenda. His letters home invariably described sporting events, once again inviting parental reproof. 'All you write about is your everlasting football of which I am heartily sick . . . ' wrote Queen Mary.[35] This proved to be no discouragement; his next letter home was equally full of the matches he had played. By the time Prince Henry set out for a short spell to Trinity College at Cambridge University, his Eton masters had him well schooled not just at football and cricket but also polo, riding and any form of hunting: indeed all the sporting accomplishments necessary to the life of a gentleman. What need was there of books? After all, his father was a successful monarch who took little recourse in books.

George V concluded that his third son, with his 'shrewd common sense' according to his Eton masters, and team spirit, should join the army, not the Royal Navy like his brothers. The seventeen-year-old prince was so lacking in confidence when he applied to the Royal Military College at Sandhurst in 1918, he thought he might fail the entrance examination.[36] But to his delight he was accepted and after his training he served in the prestigious King's Royal Rifle Corps before joining the 10th Royal Hussars.

Prince Henry was prepared to follow the traditions valued by his father, despite sometimes displaying a truculent streak that prompted harsh words.[37] In the 1920s, while his oldest and youngest brothers were leading the high life from York House, it had fallen to Prince Henry to visit many far-flung corners of the empire that no one else had the time for, earning him in recognition of his arduous duties the additional title of 'the Duke of Gloucester'. Britain's immense empire in the Far East, embracing India and stretching south to Australia and New Zealand, was coming into conflict with imperial Japan, which also sought to extend its territory. In 1926 the Foreign Office considered it wise to mark the death of Emperor Taisho of Japan and the succession of his son, Emperor Hirohito, with a special mission of friendship. It fell to the Duke of Gloucester to fulfil this obligation by conferring on the new Emperor Hirohito the ancient honour of the Most Noble Order of the Garter as his father, George V, had done for the emperor's father, and his grandfather, Edward VII, had done for the emperor's grandfather. Emperor Hirohito spoke warmly of the 'traditional friendship between the two nations', reported *The Times* on 3 May 1929 and the duke in turn was presented with Japan's highest decoration, the Gold Collar of the Order of the Chrysanthemum.[38] The honouring of the new emperor passed without mishap as did the countless courtesy calls along the way in Egypt, the Aden Settlement, Ceylon, Singapore, Malaya, Hong Kong, Japan and Canada.

Building on this, the following year further imperial salutes and bows required the Duke of Gloucester's presence in another potential trouble spot, this time in Addis Ababa, Abyssinia, where he was to fly the English flag in defiance of growing Italian interest in the region. Ostensibly his mission was to honour another emperor, Haile Selassie, 'the King of Kings, elect of God,

Conquering Lion of Judah and Emperor of Ethiopia', with yet another title, the Grand Cross of the Royal Victorian Order.[39] Once again, Gloucester was treading in family footsteps. His great-grandmother, Queen Victoria, had thrilled Haile Selassie's predecessor with royal greetings conveyed to Africa on a phonograph. Gloucester's mission to Abyssinia was deemed a success but he confided to his mother that he remained 'terrified of making a fool of myself or other people'. This did not stop his parents sending the young prince on a six-month tour of New Zealand and Australia in the autumn of 1934 to represent his father at the centenary celebrations in Victoria.

When he returned from Australia in the summer of 1935, Gloucester joined his parents at Windsor Castle and at last had the opportunity to pursue more personal interests. It was time for 35-year-old Gloucester to find a bride and kindly relatives alighted on one strong contender: Lady Alice Montagu-Douglas-Scott. The daughter of Scotland's wealthiest landowner, John Montagu-Douglas-Scott, 7th Duke of Buccleuch, whose ancestry could be traced back to Charles II, Alice's family had known the royal family for generations and she had met the royal princes on many occasions.[40] The 33-year-old Lady Alice, unusually for the time, had delayed marriage and travelled the world, most recently returned from a safari in Kenya. She soon received an invitation to join the queen's brother, the Earl of Athlone, and his wife at the racing at Ascot.

The Duke of Gloucester's swift courtship, untroubled by press interest or even much romance, formed a marked contrast to that of his oldest brother. 'He was terribly shy,' Alice recalled. 'He did not shower me with flowers because he did not do things that way', but none the less she felt she had 'always had an instinct that one day we would marry'. They shared an enjoyment of the outdoor life and that June they met frequently out riding and walking in Windsor Great Park. One day in August, just before the start of the grouse season, Gloucester managed his proposal of marriage. 'There was no formal declaration on his part,' observed Alice. 'I think he just muttered it as an aside during one of our walks; nor was there any doubt about my acceptance.' At thirty-four, she felt she 'had had a good innings . . . '[41]

Lady Alice met with instant approval in royal circles: she was sympathetic and her appreciation of country pursuits endeared her to her like-minded husband. She was also modest, with such a marked lack of interest in fashion that when she was invited to Balmoral she had to borrow a dress because she had nothing sufficiently smart. For her wedding in the chapel of Buckingham Palace she commissioned Norman Hartnell, a couturier who was gaining a reputation for dressing stars such as Marlene Dietrich and Merle Oberon, and was transformed in a shell-pink satin gown. Her marriage in November 1935 completed the royal princes' betrothals—each had found a strong, independent-minded spouse. Except one: the prince of Wales.

George VI knew that the Duke and Duchess of Gloucester preferred a quiet life, enjoying the early years of their marriage out of the limelight. Lady Alice was very keen to start a family and Gloucester wanted to rejoin his regiment. But with Edward VIII demoted to a duke, Gloucester was raised above the former king in rank. George VI had to be able to count on him. Although Gloucester was not a natural performer, royal commentators considered that 'like the Duke of York he is a tremendous tryer . . . '[42] For many this was not enough. He 'has neither the sophistication of the Prince of Wales, nor the seriousness of the Duke of York' wrote another.[43] There was criticism of his stiffness at public functions, a lack of charm and small talk that was 'stale'.[44]

For George VI, the question troubling him was could his two younger brothers, the one wayward but exceptionally gifted, the other neither wayward nor gifted, rise to the challenge ahead.

Apart from managing his younger brothers, in the early months of his reign George VI also found himself thrown into conflict with his oldest brother over the terms of the abdication. When the Duke of Windsor left British shores, quite suddenly he was a man with none of the reassuring baggage of life: no country, no family, no occupation. He chose Schloss Enzesfeld, a castle near Vienna in Austria, the home of Baron Eugene de Rothschild, as his temporary destination. To facilitate the smooth passage of Mrs Simpson's divorce he would wait for her in a different country. They could not see each other until the divorce was final but they had the telephone, and for many hours each day and half the night the lines became red hot as they tried to remake their world with words alone. Money and position were the central issues and Windsor found his bride-to-be was not shy of fighting her corner. She wanted the duke to hold out for the best deal possible. Above all, 'the extra chic' of the title 'Her Royal Highness' was essential, she told Windsor on 14 December, '—the only thing to bring me back in the eyes of the world'.[45] To be merely a duchess was not enough. Wallis loathed the idea of 'joining the countless titles that roam around Europe meaning nothing'.[46]

Wallis was no soft-centred female deploring her fate. Behind the smart clothes and figure-hugging satins was a determined woman: strong, razor-sharp, almost masculine, empowered by a total belief in herself. A modest haven in obscurity was not what she had in mind. She wanted to be seen as royal, her status expressed in her title beyond doubt and acknowledged in every curtsey. At the very least, she expected to be put on a level with her royal sisters-in-law, perhaps even viewed as a potential queen. She was, after all, the woman who had captured the King of England and she would fight to retrieve some vestige of what had been promised.

Inspector Evans of Scotland Yard who was providing police protection to Mrs Simpson overheard her talking to the duke at midnight on 14–15 December. 'If they don't give you this thing I will return to England and fight it out to the bitter end,' Wallis said to Edward. 'The Coronation will be a flop compared to the story that I shall tell the British press. I will publish it in every paper in the World so that the whole World may know my story. Your mother is even persecuting me now. Look in all the Sunday papers you will see what she has done. On the front page of every paper is a black bordered notice stating that she has never seen or spoken to me during the past 12 months . . . Concentrate on the legal side now. That is the side that counts . . . '[47]

If the Duke of Windsor, after giving up his throne, was shocked at her tone, there is no record of it. He admired her forceful personality and that strain of pure confidence that ran through her veins. In spite of the ill-will centred on her she remained inviolable, not easily intimidated; a strength perhaps learned in her childhood when she and her widowed mother, Alice, were dependent on the whims of a wealthy uncle for financial security. The Duke of Windsor blamed himself for adding to her suffering. He felt 'grievously responsible for the trouble and sorrow that my love had brought down upon her head'.[48] He knew she felt hounded out of England and there had been little relief when she reached the Rogers's villa at Cannes in southern France where she had received letters of hatred and even death threats. 'Had you been living 200 years ago means would have been found to rid the country of you,' claimed one anonymous writer. 'It has fallen to my lot as a patriot to kill you. This is a solemn warning. I will do so.'[49] His future bride was being hunted down like an animal, press men camped outside watching every move.

There seemed no end to the humiliation he felt she endured for his sake. Even the Archbishop of Canterbury took it upon himself to criticise the Windsors in a speech before Christmas. The duke stood condemned from the pulpit for 'craving private happiness', and seeking it 'in a manner inconsistent with the Christian principles of marriage'. The very hostesses who had encouraged his liaison with Mrs Simpson were publicly admonished. 'Let those who belong to this circle know that today they stand rebuked by the judgment of a nation . . . ' pronounced the archbishop.[50] Wallis and her friends faced a backlash of anger as opinion turned against them. Lady Emerald Cunard, Lord Brownlow, who had escorted Wallis to the south of France, and others found themselves swiftly sidelined.[51]

After leaving England, the Duke of Windsor turned to George VI for help. He telephoned the palace frequently expecting to speak to his brother, his demands increasingly strident as he came under pressure from Wallis. It was important to the duke for her to be welcomed into the royal fold and elevated to 'Her Royal Highness' on marriage. But George VI felt undermined by the duke's calls; his advice was not wanted, his forceful pleas for Wallis unwelcome. Their reversal of roles was hard to adjust to, his affection as a brother in conflict with his new position as king. George VI was unable to give the reassurances the duke wanted and asked officials to intervene to stop the calls.

At the Rogers's villa in the south of France, Wallis felt the pain of her diminishing status. She was a woman blamed, disgraced, even reviled. Who was still standing with her and who could she count as her friends? Offers of help came from unexpected quarters. One of Europe's wealthiest entrepreneurs came to her assistance: the adventurer and big-game hunter Charles Bedaux. Bedaux had built up his business empire creating his own version of time-and-motion study to speed up production in the workplace. The 'Bedaux System' had been adopted in Europe and America and had earned him such a fortune that he was now the proud owner of a magnificent French castle, the Château de Cande, near Tours south-west of Paris, which he and his wife, Fern, put at Wallis's disposal. On hearing of the newly renovated art deco interiors, bathtubs that could fill with hot water in barely a minute and grounds large enough to keep the press at bay, Wallis could see the advantages of Bedaux's château over the Rogers's villa. It was only once she moved to the Château de Cande that she felt able to surface from her isolation and write to respected friends of her prospective new husband such as Betty and Ormond Lawson-Johnston.

Tuesday March 16
Chateau de Cande

Darling Betty

Please forgive my too long silence, but I know you'll understand. What it has been all these awfully sad months and the post looking always like a mountain. I did get your wines but have not had a letter from you . . . I am glad to be away from Cannes which is really very dull as I was not going

out and taking part in the gay side, a few quiet dinners with friends . . .
This is a lovely quiet place with grounds to walk in and an 18 hole private
golf course. If you and Ormond ever wanted a little change—why not
come over for the weekend. You know I would adore to see you . . . I miss
all my friends so very much and you must really discount some of the stories you hear about some of what I termed my acquaintances . . . [52]

Betty evidently found she was not able to visit, but Wallis did not give up.
'Betty dear . . . I am so sorry you did not come here for Easter,' Wallis wrote
on Easter Sunday. 'I would have loved it so. I had no idea naturally that you
would be in France . . . if you feel like coming for a rest before all the great festivities and the American intrusion send a wire . . . '[53] Wallis sensed her friends
were hesitant about making contact. She was sure the undeniable glamour of
being an HRH would rectify that and restore her social position, but despite
the duke's demands, no comforting letter arrived from London confirming her
status on marriage.

That spring divisions deepened between the royal brothers. George VI was
dismayed to find that the Duke of Windsor appeared to have misled him
about his very substantial savings at the time of the abdication. Before he left
England Windsor had extracted from the king the promise of an annual pen-
sion of £25,000. But he also took with him twenty years of wealth accumulated through the Duchy of Cornwall as Prince of Wales which amounted to
a large sum, estimated at between £850,000 and £1.1 million. These savings
were intended to ease the expenses of kingship when he ascended the throne
and provided the duke a handsome annual income of between £60,000 and
£80,000—a fact which he failed to mention when he gave up the throne. To
compound the brothers' problems, the duke had inherited a life interest in the
royal properties at Sandringham and Balmoral and now demanded that George
VI buy this back. Harassed officials trying to resolve these difficulties found
the government unwilling to pay the ex-king any more money given his large
resources, not to mention the ill-will that arose through his lack of straight
dealing. Almost incredibly, officials poring over the paperwork found that the
duke had settled a very significant portion of his savings on Wallis herself.

The duke, however, retained a forceful ally in one member of the parliamentary Civil List Committee. Winston Churchill, once again, was on hand with
soothing reassurance. 'How very wise and prudent, Sir, you have been in all
that you have done since leaving England,' he wrote to the duke on 24 March
1937. He explained that as a member of the committee he would endeavour

to seek 'proper provision' for His Royal Highness, as a representative of '"the Honour and Dignity of the Crown"'.[54] He also wrote to the chancellor, Neville Chamberlain, pointing out that although Windsor 'possessed a large capital sum, which I gather is from £800–950,000—a large part of which was at one time settled on the lady, though I believe she has renounced all but £10,000 a year . . . ' none the less, he hoped that Windsor could keep all his savings and £25,000 a year in return for handing over his inherited life interest in the royal estates.[55] And to help settle on this, he put subtle pressure on George VI by explaining how much he would wish, should any member ask a question in the House, to say 'that the matter has been settled within the Royal Family on a basis of natural affection and good will'.[56]

Neville Chamberlain saw things quite differently. Churchill was 'a bandit' and a 'pirate', he confided to his sister, Hilda, who was effectively using the risk of publicity to blackmail the king into agreeing to 'swindling arrangements'.[57] If Labour party members or the press were aware of the duke's huge savings accumulated as Prince of Wales this could put pressure on the Civil List Committee to reduce all pensions and perhaps even ignite debate about the future of the monarchy in a modern democracy. In Chamberlain's view, which was likely to have the support of George VI, the Duke of Windsor, aided once again by Churchill's poor judgement, was using the threat of exposure to ensure a disproportionately generous settlement for himself.

George VI became increasingly agitated as his coronation approached on 12 May and knew that no good would come of public exposure of the large sums the duke had accumulated as Prince of Wales. But Wallis, believing that she and the duke were being victimised, advised him to threaten the king. If George VI's 'filthy treatment', in which he turned his brother into 'an outcast' continued, she thought the duke should 'let the world know'.[58] She confided her despair to society photographer Cecil Beaton when he visited the Château de Cande in April. She wanted him to know that at the height of the abdication crisis she had been willing to withdraw and end her relationship with the king rather than let him sign away his throne. She had urged him not to stand down. Baldwin held papers signed by her in which she was willing to stop her divorce with Mr Simpson. The weeks since the abdication had been so tough, she told Beaton, 'that it had been difficult for her not to give way and hang herself on one of the many pairs of antlers in the room in which we sat'.[59]

But such moments of despair did nothing to mitigate the intensity of her desire to secure a better deal. News spread of the family rift, which became quite overt when the Duke of Windsor learned that George VI agreed with his ministers, who argued that the royal family should not attend his wedding in June since it was not supported by the Church of England. Even the Duke of Kent, his long-standing favourite, would not be there. Kent had been permitted to make a brief visit to see Windsor in Austria in February, and under the watchful eye of *The Times* correspondent, the two brothers had toured Vienna's great landmarks and the rich art treasures of the city, before slipping back to Enzesfield Castle for private talks.[60] But Kent too was persuaded to stay away from the wedding. Their cousin, Louis Mountbatten, also did a U-turn and withdrew his offer to act as best man. With mutual friends forced to take sides over the course of April, many members of the old court found a polite reason to decline—even loyal friends such as the Lawson-Johnstons.

It was painful for Wallis to see reports in the society pages and court circular of her former London life. Buckingham Palace and Windsor Castle were being adapted for its new occupants, including the provision of a nursery department for the two princesses. Social events too were reported, such as an evening party held by Mrs Lawson-Johnston in Cadogan Place at which 'the Duke and Duchess of Kent were the chief guests . . . '—not herself. She was stuck in the middle of nowhere and obliged to appear pleased to be with the love of her life, while all the fun was happening elsewhere.[61]

I n London as Coronation Day approached, rumours began to escalate that the new king could not take the strain. His mental and physical health was deemed so fragile that it was alleged the coronation would be too much for him.[62] Some claimed that like his youngest brother, Prince John, he suffered from epilepsy or another strange malady that would oblige him to live as a recluse. Papers such as the *Sunday Chronicle* denied the 'malicious, cruel and unfounded' allegations concerning the health of the king.[63] But this hardly silenced the concern which had grown ever since the archbishop highlighted the problem of the king's stammer the previous December. Even the king was full of doubt as to whether he would rise to the occasion. As pressure mounted during April, he turned once more to his therapist, Lionel Logue.

The informal sessions in Logue's apartments were no longer possible. Logue had to go to the king. Arriving at Windsor Castle on 19 April, he could see at once the strain his former patient was under. The king was a 'gallant fighter', he noted, determined to do his level best, but he was carrying too great a load. 'Give him too much work and it impacts on his weakest part—his speech,' he noted in his diary. 'If overworked, he will crash and they will only have themselves to blame.'[64] George VI was all too often frustrated with his efforts and held back by his fears, as shown powerfully in the film, *The King's Speech*. The two men became absorbed in intense preparations but there were painful setbacks, the king irritable with unending pressure. Rehearsing with the microphone on one occasion, the king was quite unable to form the words and angry with himself at having spoiled 'the bloody record'.[65]

Elizabeth hid her anxiety for her husband, her calming presence alone enough to make a difference. On the Sunday before the ceremony, prayers were said for them both in churches up and down the country. The archbishop came to Buckingham Palace to give them his blessing and together they prayed for kingdom and empire. The king and queen saw the coronation as a dedication of their lives to the highest order. This was to be no mere glittering show but the first day of their life's work, whatever the task demanded. For the archbishop, their simple private prayer, calling for the strength and spirit to inform their new roles was full of spiritual meaning. They all recognised the enormity of the task. 'I was much moved and so were they,' the archbishop said. 'Indeed there were tears in their eyes when we rose from our knees.'[66]

Well before dawn on 12 May 1937 the king was woken by a strange noise nearby on Constitution Hill. 'I . . . had a sinking feeling inside,' he wrote. The long-awaited day had arrived to the unwelcome sound of tests on loudspeakers near the palace at three in the morning followed by the noise of bands and troops getting into position. 'Sleep was impossible,' he realised. Nor could he eat, in spite of the long day ahead. As daylight broke the waiting was nerve-wracking.[67]

Later that morning in Westminster Abbey, Henry 'Chips' Channon observed the grand setting for what he called 'a feudal, capitalistic show'. He was dazzled by the 'red, the gold, the gilt, the grandeur', as he waited amongst the MPs. The north transept for him 'was a vitrine of bosoms and jewels and bobbing tiaras . . . ' When the procession finally started he noted that the Duchess of Gloucester 'looked so lovely' that for an instant he mistook her for Princess Marina. Behind them was Queen Mary, 'ablaze, regal and overpowering', followed by the queen, who was smiling and 'much more bosomy'. Finally came the slight figure of George VI himself, strained and subdued, and almost hidden by dignitaries bearing the heavy gold symbols of office.[68]

For George VI, the ancient ritual was richly endowed with sacred meaning and the seriousness of the occasion meant a great deal to him as Head of the Church of England. The highlight of the ceremony, the anointing of the king, was a sacramental sign of being symbolically set apart for a purpose and equipped with the grace to tackle the task ahead. The Sceptre with the Dove endowed him with peace, the Sceptre with the Cross brought mercy, the ring symbolised his marriage to the nation and the orb surmounted by a cross acknowledged a world subject to Christ.[69] For nearly one thousand years kings and queens had been crowned in Westminster Abbey and George VI was in a tense state of concentration to make sure he made no mistake.

The great majesty of the occasion was almost accidentally undermined by the clergy, not the king. The bishops who were to hold out the words for him could not find the correct page in the Order of Service. The archbishop offered his own copy, but 'horror of horrors, his thumb covered the words of the Oath', the king wrote later. The Lord Great Chamberlain 'nearly put the hilt of the sword under my chin trying to attach it to the belt'. Finally the critical moment arrived when the archbishop was to put St Edward's Crown on the king's head. The archbishop relied upon a red thread as a marker to help him lower the crown into the right position. But the thread was nowhere to be seen. The king could not be sure the seven-pound crown was secure as he rose to move towards the throne. Almost immediately he felt a tug on his gown and realised one of the bishops was standing on it. 'I had to tell him to get off it pretty sharply.'[70] But the king was now beyond nerves, protected by a sublime feeling, almost like a religious experience. He told the archbishop later 'that he felt throughout that Someone Else was with him'.[71]

The ceremony was a triumph. Many who watched were moved by the solemnity and commitment of the king. Churchill famously leaned across to his wife, Clementine, and commented, 'You were right. I see now the "other one" would not have done.' With the weight of centuries of royal tradition at his back, the king retraced his steps slowly down the long aisle, feeling the tremendous relief of managing 'the most important ceremony in my life'.[72] But he could not yet relax. The most dreaded point of the day had yet to come: the coronation broadcast.

The king had rehearsed for weeks yet still there was no way of approaching the microphone with confidence. Logue was waiting to help him, in a quiet room on the first floor of the palace overlooking the quadrangle. But for all their efforts, a mishap with the stage management nearly ruined the king's composure. As the National Anthem finished, there was a heart-stopping pause. Millions listening across the empire had reason to fear the rumours were true. But it was nothing other than an error of timing as the king took his place before the microphone a few seconds too late. 'It is with a very full heart that I speak to you tonight . . . ' he began.

The Duke and Duchess of Windsor listened to the momentous proceedings of the day from the Château de Cande. 'The words of the service rolled over me like an engulfing wave,' Wallis wrote later. 'I fought to suppress every thought, but all the while, the mental image of what might have been and should have been kept forming, disintegrating and re-forming in my mind.'[73] Even the king's broadcast, despite moments of slow and hesitant delivery, was judged to be a success. There was no chance now of 'Queen Wallis'. In fact, even her transition to 'Duchess' was not going smoothly since no vicar could be found to perform the Windsors' wedding service. The clergy were taking their cue from the Archbishop of Canterbury and would not officiate at the marriage of a divorced woman with living husbands. It was Bedaux's ingenuity that resolved the impasse. He knew there was no problem that could not be sorted with money. He travelled to England and tracked down a vicar in Darlington who was prepared to put aside his scruples, the Reverend R.A. Jardine. For a fee of $6,000 he would marry the Windsors. His wallet replenished, the Reverend Jardine set off for France.[74]

A week before the wedding, at a Cabinet meeting of 26 May 1937, the question of Wallis's elevation to 'Her Royal Highness' was raised. Baldwin and Sir John Simon had been closely concerned with the matter and knew that George VI and others in the royal family felt strongly that Wallis was to blame for the crisis in the monarchy and conferring an 'HRH' upon her would degrade the institution further. Legally, however, this was a somewhat vexatious issue. Of Wallis's prospective sisters-in-law, Marina was a princess by birth as a member of the Greek royal family, but the two Scottish brides, Elizabeth and Alice, had both been elevated on marriage to the status of princess and styled as 'Her Royal Highness'. Neither the king nor his ministers wanted to promote Wallis to an HRH but on what legal basis could she be singled out for exclusion?

The wily Sir John proposed the solution to his Cabinet colleagues. Seventy years previously, Queen Victoria had issued letters patent in which royal status, including the title 'HRH', could only be enjoyed by royal relations who are 'in succession to the Throne'. When the ex-king abdicated, he had given up his right of succession and with it his right to the title 'HRH', both for himself, and his spouse and future children. 'There had never been a case of a lady receiving the title of "Royal Highness" when not marrying someone in direct succession to the Throne,' Simon reasoned.[75] However the king was keen to ensure that his brother could 'continue personally to enjoy the title of "Royal Highness"', but did not want to extend the designation to his wife. The Cabinet was in agreement. Consequently letters patent would be issued as soon as possible, formally elevating the duke to 'HRH', but not the duchess. It was left to the duke's trusted legal adviser, Walter Monckton, who had earned a reputation for great tact and discretion during the abdication crisis, to convey the decision to the Windsors in person.

Cecil Beaton returned to France the day before the wedding to take the photographs for *Vogue*. He had to fight his way through 'swarms of journalists and their vans and motorcycles outside the gates', but inside it was hard not to feel the Windsors' humiliation. With no court, few friends and no family, the Windsors' fall from grace was painfully exposed before the 200 waiting journalists—who explained away the mere handful of guests with phrases such as 'invitations confined to those who have been with them during the past months'. Inside the château, Herman Rogers was manning the phones and dealing with press queries and Beaton felt aware of the presence of Fern Bedaux who 'persisted in saying inconsequential things' while Charles Bedaux 'hovered about'. The famous florist Constance Spry, armed with a carload of flowers, was trying to create an ambience. But her magnificent displays in capacious rooms devoid of guests only served to underline the emptiness.

Cecil Beaton found Wallis 'was showing the strain'. This was not the memorable day she had envisaged with the château full of important guests, the atmosphere sparkling, the occasion an obvious success. Instead she was harassed, supervising last-minute arrangements. Was this how her future would be, deserted by friends, an outcast, her glamour fading, her vibrance gone, trying hard to smile?

The photographic session began with the duke alone. Beaton was struck by his underlying melancholy, 'tragic eyes overruling the impertinent tilt of his nose'. When Wallis was ready for photographs of them both together there were further interruptions and she found it hard to conceal her irritation. The duke apologised as though it were his fault. The session was underway when unwelcome news arrived. The mood changed for the worse. 'It was painful,' wrote Beaton. He felt he could hardly say, 'please look pleasant . . . ' It was Wallis who snapped out of it first, reminding the duke 'we're having our pictures taken'.[76]

The bad news was likely to have been that conveyed by Walter Monckton, who also arrived the day before the wedding bearing a letter from George VI explaining that there would be no 'HRH' for Wallis. To see the humiliation set out in black and white by his brother struck the duke 'like a wound in battle' according to his biographer, Frances Donaldson. 'It altered him as a gunshot might have done', as though inflicting a mortal pain that would blight the rest of his life.[77] His brother was damning him. *He* was impotent. He could not give Wallis what he knew she really wanted: a royal title. He was unable to conceal his feelings from his best man and loyal ally, Fruity Metcalfe, making it clear he wanted nothing more to do with his family. His sense of injustice could only be soothed if he disowned them completely. Baffled and hurt he returned unopened to the Duke of Kent a stunning wedding gift of a Fabergé box.

And so the Duke of Windsor and the woman he loved were married, somehow; the sprinkling of guests and friends, feeling a little awkward, tried to work out what was missing. Cecil Beaton had the answer: it was love. Neither bride nor groom seemed enveloped by love's great mystery; rather they appeared held by some private torment that could never be righted. He noted that Wallis, in spite of a garnishing of huge sapphires and wearing a baby-blue couturier dress, 'looked especially unlovable, hard and calculating' while the duke looked 'essentially sad'.[78]

As though by way of compensation for the emotional void, the Windsors' baggage for their honeymoon was replete with every conceivable material comfort. The duke and duchess left Cande with 266 pieces of luggage, of which 189 were trunks.[79] The honeymoon for the romance of the century began with a short stop in Venice and then on to Wasserleonburg Castle, set in the enchanting mountain landscape of the Austrian Tyrol.

Wallis's letters to Betty Lawson-Johnson create a picture of the world's most famous honeymoon couple in which more time was spent in the office than the bedroom. Her correspondence proudly denoted her new married status, each letter complete with their logo, 'WE', capped with a crown.

'It is lovely to be here in this peaceful lovely spot,' Wallis told Betty in July, 'even though the house is not in the best of repairs the scenery is too divine and the weather.' They had decided to have picnics, she said, and not bother 'teaching dumb Austrian servants—who are more at home yodelling than cleaning . . . We have spent most of the honeymoon at the desk—you could never believe the amount of telegrams and letters we're seeing . . . from the time of the wedding alone and our post averages 300 letters per day . . . '[80] Her letter on Thursday (August) the 12th from Schloss Wasserleonburg was equally revealing of Wallis's preoccupation with her friends while the duke went out hiking alone.

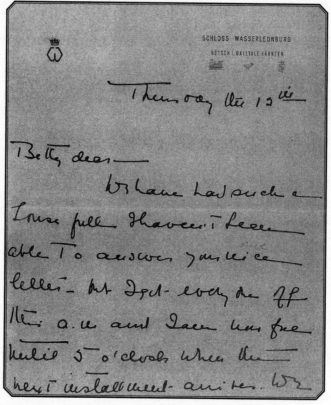

Honeymoon letter from Wallis to her friend Betty Lawson-Johnston, 12 August 1937 (THE PRIVATE COLLECTION OF MRS LAWSON-JOHNSTON)

Betty dear—We have had such a house full I haven't been able to answer your nice letter—but I get everyone off this am and I am now free until 5 o'clock when the next installment arrives. We would love to have you and Ormond come to see us if you could arrange to come for the 2nd and 3rd of September as we are off after that to visit in Hungary and Czechoslovakia and must have 2 days to see to the packing etc . . . The Duke is awfully well and full of energy which he gets rid of by climbing all the mountains in sight . . . [81]

The visitors filled a terrible void that was waiting for them when the castle was empty and they were left alone. Boredom and frustration confronted them in every room. Wallis could not let go of the trauma of the recent weeks, constantly reworking it in her mind, and this led to 'interminable post mortems' about the abdication.[82] Her sense of loss was palpable. Why had he given up the throne? Why had he not stood up to the British officials? Why had he ignored her eleventh-hour wish to withdraw? Now she was trapped. Her prospects had fallen with giddy speed from one-time Queen of Britain to the most hated woman in the world. *His* weakness, *his* actions had reduced them to this.

Even the loyal Duke of Kent found he was unable to visit them. He and his family were staying with Prince Paul at Bohinj just a short distance from the Windsors at Wasserleonburg in southern Austria. The Duke of Kent's plan to pay his brother a visit ended in further hurt. Marina felt uncomfortable about acknowledging the new Duchess of Windsor, especially in the face of implacable advice from the Queen Mother that it was inappropriate for her as a member of the royal family to do so. Windsor would not see his younger brother unless their wives could also meet. The king's attempt to intervene was overruled by Queen Mary forcing the Kents to withdraw with polite excuses.

Wallis felt marooned. The sun terraces with their spectacular views, the pillared walkways, the scenic enchantment of the location; all this underlined the fact that she was with the wrong man. According to the Duchess of Windsor's most recent biographer, Anne Sebba, she took comfort in secretly writing to her former husband. 'I think of us so much, though I try not to,' she confessed to Ernest. She acknowledged it was her hunger for security and wealth that had caused the trouble; that side of her nature had dominated over the other. Surrounded by the luxury that the duke provided, she wrote 'if we could only have done these things'. Her letters were tender and full of longing for the life with him she had given up. 'Wherever you are, you can be sure that never a day goes by without some hours thought of you & for you & again in my . . . prayers at night. With love, Wallis.'[83]

But it was not long before a welcome distraction glided smoothly into the driveway at Wasserleonburg in a gleaming Rolls-Royce. Out stepped Charles Bedaux, full of tempting ideas about how to revive the ex-king's career and win respect. Bedaux understood all too well the duke's seething anger towards his younger brother. He had a plan that would lift his spirits and enable him to present the duchess to the world by his side with her rightful royal status. Bedaux proposed that the duke and duchess undertake a tour of Nazi Germany. The duke would appear on the world stage in front of the press, at the heart of Europe's most thriving economy, and champion the cause of the working man as he made a special study of German labour. Meetings would be arranged for their royal highnesses to talk to the senior Nazi leadership. The duke would have his own self-styled platform and find his own voice as a popular leader for the common man. Edward seized this new lifeline and he and Bedaux spent the weekend mulling over arrangements.[84]

Bedaux's next stop was a health spa at Bad Reichenhall in Germany, near the border with Austria and just 125 miles north of the honeymoon castle. Bad Reichenhall was very conveniently sited close to Hitler's Eagle Nest retreat near Berchtesgaden. Equally convenient were the visitors to the spa at Bad Reichenhall. Hitler's personal adjutant, Captain Fritz Weidemann, was one of those who checked in for treatment. Weidemann agreed to set up a meeting between Bedaux and Dr Robert Ley, the Nazi leader of the *Arbeitsfront* or German Labour Front.

Even for a man of Bedaux's rugged pedigree, the meeting in Dr Ley's home in Berlin was an uncomfortable experience. The exchange did not start well. When the head of the German Labour Front emerged at the top of the stairs he appeared well fortified with schnapps and required help from his staff to manoeuvre his bulky frame down the stairway. The man who confronted Fern and Charles Bedaux at the bottom of the stairs represented the ugly face of the Third Reich. He was thick-set, thuggish and argumentative: character traits that appeared to have qualified him for a rapid rise through the Nazi party although his reputation for corruption, embezzling of funds and womanising was known even to Hitler.

The two tough men squared up. For Dr Ley, the former sovereign of Britain and Empire was a big fish to hook. The wedding and the abdication had been followed closely in Germany. Ley was eager to curry favour with Hitler and insisted the duke must attend a number of Nazi political functions. Bedaux wanted the duke to have opportunities to meet working men and knew that the trip should appear politically neutral. Ley could not see his point. The dispute threatened to erupt in violence.

Accounts vary as to what happened next. It is widely held that both men recognised a good deal. Bedaux was relieved of £50,000. Ley agreed to set in motion the arrangements for the duke's trip including tours of German labour. And on 1 July the German Bedaux company, which had been seized by the Nazis, reopened for business. Other sources suggest that Charles Bedaux did not benefit financially and claim even the idea of Windsor's trip came from the duke himself.[85] But the close conjunction of these events before the duke's trip suggest that Bedaux was trying to cash in on his new royal friendship.

Ley and Bedaux were not the only ones who stood to benefit from the love-lorn duke. Reverend Jardine's career also prospered. The vicar acquired an agent in Los Angeles, embarked on a series of talks and had special cards designed promoting himself as 'The *Duke's* Vicar'. While back in Wallis's home town of Baltimore, her former childhood residence in East Biddle Street also had a makeover: it was now 'A Shrine to Love'. For little over a dollar, any visitor seeking to enhance their sexual powers could sink back into the very bath in which Wallis had once lain and hopefully soak up her mythic potency.[86]

3

ENMITY AND FEAR

....

'We see over parts of the world the shadows of enmity and of fear . . . '

—George VI, Christmas Speech, 1937

Apart from the internal crisis in the monarchy, an even greater threat to king and empire was looming through the expanding Third Reich. In the cinema at Buckingham Palace this growing danger was on plain view to George VI in the flickering Pathé newsreels. He saw Adolf Hitler shouting to the exultant crowds driven almost hysterical from being at one with their leader. The louder and more preposterous he became, the more they seemed lost in the drama of the moment; they were there, at Valhalla, their dark-haired demoniacal figurehead the mouthpiece of those ancient German gods. In vast squares, surrounded by the ominous and ubiquitous swastika, Hitler defiantly mastered what Winston Churchill later described as 'the dark and savage furies latent in the most . . . ruthless and ill-starred race in Europe'.[1] Peering at the grainy newsreels, it was impossible to know what was in the mind of the dictator except that it did not look good for Europe.

The voices sounding the alarm were not those of His Majesty's ministers. Churchill's continued clarion cry fell on deaf ears. Still in his wilderness years, he repeatedly warned of German rearmament when Hitler introduced German conscription, built an air force to rival that of Britain's RAF and re-equipped his armies. The king knew Churchill was seen as a troublemaker and warmonger, a man who had casually squandered goodwill with his ill-judged support for his brother during the abdication crisis as well as his intransigent alignment with those who resisted any kind of reform in India. For his new prime minister, Neville Chamberlain, like his predecessor, Stanley Baldwin, who retired two weeks after the coronation, Churchill was a man to be kept out of government, conveniently held at bay painting and writing in his peaceful Kent home at Chartwell. In Baldwin's view it was as though when Winston Churchill was born, all the fairies swooped down and gave him everything a mother could wish for her son: 'imagination, eloquence, industry, ability . . . ' But the last fairy saw he had too much and withdrew one crucial skill: judgement. For the Conservative leadership, Churchill was doomed, his prodigious attributes forever squandered rushing headlong down the wrong path.[2] The king, intimately acquainted with the weaknesses of his older brother and the support Churchill gave him, could understand this point of view.

For the king, 68-year-old Chamberlain was a safe pair of hands, bringing all the reassuring confidence borne of a line of distinguished politicians stretching back to the time of his great-grandmother. Chamberlain's father, 'Great Joe', described by Churchill as 'the man who made the weather', was a giant in Liberal and Unionist politics in the late nineteenth century. Neville Chamberlain believed he could reason with the dictator. The dictator would listen to reason. And the king was listening to his prime minister who enjoyed the support of the British government, the governments in the commonwealth and the British people in pursuing appeasement.[3] War was morally abhorrent. 'Never again' was the common cry since the Great War. Appeasement made strategic sense too, protecting Britain and empire by avoiding conflict with imperial Japan and fascist Germany and Italy.

The uncertainty was where this would lead. Churchill would not be silent. Britain, irresolute, undecided, adrift, and impotent, was losing precious time, he warned. Its greatness was being wasted for the 'locusts to eat'. King, country and empire were at stake. British cities could be bombed. Should such a man be taken seriously? Before he came to power, Hitler had written of a 'Thousand Year Reich' whose vast frontiers would stretch across the continent. But to many it was inconceivable that he would endeavour to realise the conquest of Europe. The international situation was deeply worrying. War was unthinkable. And yet it had to be thought about.

Against this volatile background, with its nightmare machinations of diplomacy that confounded even Britain's great political dynasties, George VI was horrified to learn in late September 1937 that his older brother was wading into the fray. Windsor kept very quiet about his proposed private tour of Germany until the eleventh hour. Quite apart from the Foreign Office, even his friends such as Winston Churchill were kept out of the loop. The ex-king was breaking his promise to keep a low profile. In his abdication speech he had promised 'to quit altogether public affairs' but now, without consultation, he was quite prepared to court the very regime that threatened Europe. Even more troubling for the king and queen, they discovered that the Duke and Duchess of Windsor planned to follow their trip to Germany with a tour of the States. The idea of the ex-king using his royal platform to launch himself as an informal roving 'ambassador' promoting his and Wallis's interests with no regard to official views was disturbing. With the threat of war hanging over Europe, the king did not want his older brother building his own following in America and was anxious about his motives. Fears that the Duke of Windsor was acting from self-interest and gathering support for a comeback could not be dismissed.

But the former king was listening to Wallis, not officials at home. After their honeymoon at Schloss Wasserleonburg in Austria, he and Wallis had toured Europe, settling in the luxurious Hotel Le Meurice in the centre of Paris while they searched for a more permanent home. Unlike the king, the duke rejected the advice of all those who might steer him through the labyrinth of international diplomacy, except his wife. Correspondence with Betty Lawson-Johnston from Hotel Le Meurice is revealing of the Windsors' life in Paris.

'Betty dear—what an angel you were to send the lovely flowers and at first I thought you were here, so telephoned the Ritz,' Wallis began in a letter on 30 September 1937. 'Very hectic place for us just now with so many people coming from England to see the Duke . . . '4 A few weeks later, as she tried to arrange a visit for Betty, she asked her friend to give advance warning of her dates, as 'we are fairly booked up with so many people of all <u>sorts</u> and <u>descriptions</u> coming over and we should want our time free for you . . . ' (Wallis's underlining).5

So who were these visitors of 'all <u>sorts</u> and <u>descriptions</u>'? There are some colourful theories. Biographer Charles Higham, in *Trading with the Enemy*, claims that MI6 files in the Ministry of Defence show at least one bizarre encounter in the Hotel Le Meurice that summer. In Higham's account Charles Bedaux arranged a secret meeting between Hitler's deputy, Rudolf Hess; his personal secretary, Martin Bormann; the Duke of Windsor and Bedaux's friend, the actor Errol Flynn. Among the topics of discussion was how to build an alliance between Germany and Britain with Windsor volunteering introductions to like-minded British aristocrats.6 But the intelligence files in support of these claims have not surfaced. A more probable version has Charles Bedaux arriving at Hotel Le Meurice with Hitler's adjutant, Captain Weidemann, who brought the schedule for the Windsors' trip to Germany.7

Whoever came to visit the duke and duchess as they finalised arrangements for their German tour from the rooftop restaurant of Hotel Le Maurice taking in the glamour of night-time Paris, there can be little doubt they relished the international platform that Charles Bedaux was creating for them. And after their hurtful expulsion from the royal family, what the duke desired above all was recognition for his wife. She had been denied a throne, but he could still make her feel like a queen, if only for a short time.

Adolf Hitler and his Foreign Minister, Joachim von Ribbentrop, savoured the prospect of a tour of Nazi Germany by Britain's ex-king. Of all the pieces moving swiftly across the chessboard of European diplomacy, the former king turning up in the heart of Berlin was an unexpected bonus. Hitler had known of the duke's pro-German views for some years, not least through the duke's own relatives. A German grandson of Queen Victoria, Charles Edward, Duke of Saxe-Coburg, a member of the Nazi party and the Brownshirts, had agreed to spy for Hitler as early as 1936. Mingling unobtrusively with the royal family when they mourned the passing of George V at Sandringham, the Duke of Saxe-Coburg had extracted from the untried new king, Edward VIII, much useful information for the Führer.

The Duke of Saxe-Coburg's report of January 1936, marked '*Strictly confidential. Only for the Führer and Party Member v Ribbentrop*', provided Hitler with an intimate portrait of the British king.[8] Edward VIII saw a German–British alliance as 'an urgent necessity', claimed Saxe-Coburg, and was quite prepared to take matters into his own hands rather than work through his ministers. 'The king is resolved to concentrate the business of government on himself,' he said. When Saxe-Coburg had pressed Edward VIII on this point, suggesting that a meeting between Baldwin and Hitler was desirable, he found the king had a strong desire to take the lead on this policy. 'Who is king here? Baldwin or I? I wish myself to talk to Hitler, and will do so here or in Germany. Tell him that please . . . ' The British king was 'looking forward with pleasure' to meeting Hitler's deputy, Rudolf Hess, and various non-official links were also discussed. The two cousins identified 'the peculiar mentality of the Englishman' as a possible obstacle to achieving an Anglo-German peace agreement and concluded that 'the sincere resolve to bring England and Germany together' should not be made in public too early.[9] It was this kind of talk that helped to fuel the belief among the Nazi leadership that a British monarch had some power and influence over British policy.

Saxe-Coburg's report complemented an account also written on the first day of Edward VIII's reign by Hitler's German ambassador in Britain, Leopold von Hoesch. While still the Prince of Wales, he had confided his 'complete understanding' of German aspirations' to the German ambassador, recognised the case for German conscription and complained of 'the too one-sided attitude of the [British] Foreign Office'.[10] Just six weeks into Edward VIII's reign in March 1936, German columns streamed over the Rhine to a riotous reception from the cities in the region. The occupation of the Rhineland was Hitler's first act of aggression in foreign policy since he came to power three years previously. According to von Hoesch, Edward VIII went to great lengths to ensure that the British government would not go to war over this and told his ministers 'complications of a serious nature are in no circumstances to be allowed to develop'.[11] This was confirmed by the London correspondent of the *Berliner Tageblatt*, Dr Stutterheim, who wrote that 'the king is taking an extraordinarily active part in the whole affair . . . the king won't hear of there being a danger of war'.[12]

Joachim von Ribbentrop, who had taken over as German ambassador to Britain in the autumn of 1936 and witnessed the abdication, was convinced Edward VIII had not been forced from his throne because of Wallis Simpson. 'The whole marriage question was a false front,' he told Hitler. Baldwin schemed to get him off the throne, he claimed, because of his open support for Germany.[13] Even as an ex-king he could still be very useful with his huge groundswell of support in his home country, although quite how this piece should be played was still not clear. Was he a king or a pawn? Ribbentrop knew that for the purposes of this forthcoming trip he was to appear every inch a king. Although the Windsors' tour was a private invitation by Dr Ley, all the Nazi leadership including his cousin, the Duke of Saxe-Coburg, were to play their part in spreading the adulation thickly.

It was indeed a regal Wallis who stepped on to the platform at Friedrich-strasse station in Berlin on 11 October 1937, dressed in an exquisitely tailored blue suit, ready to be her gracious best, the duke at her side. Pathé caught the moment they emerged from the station into a large crowd that had gathered determined to see this unique couple: a king who had thrown away the greatest throne in the world for love, and the woman herself, who must possess some magical quality. Dr Ley, the head of the German delegation, wearing his brown Nazi uniform and for once not drunk, delighted them both by deferring to her as 'Her Royal Highness'. But the majestic air that Dr Ley had aimed for was destroyed completely by the crush of two thousand people. Any sense of the dignity of a royal occasion was thrown to the winds as the Windsors were engulfed and Dr Ley steered them hurriedly to his waiting Mercedes. He squeezed into the back seat beside them and ordered the car to get away at top speed, at some discomfort to the SS guards on the running board. Sirens blazing, they made their way to the Kaiserhof Hotel.

At the palace in London, George VI could watch his brother's progress in *The Times* where the bare facts were stated: a hearty reception in Berlin, bouquets for Wallis, and working men at a Wagnerian concert honouring them with Nazi salutes and singing both German and British national anthems.[14] The following day it was more smiles and handshakes as Ribbentrop feted their Royal Highnesses over dinner.[15] By 14 October the duke and duchess were entertained by General Goering, who gave his visitors a special tour of Karinhall, his large hunting estate north-east of Berlin.

Goering's benign 'Father Christmas' look was the perfect foil for his major occupation as commander in chief in charge of the *Luftwaffe*, and in charge of speeding up rearmament. The fact that he had also founded the Gestapo, or secret police, was also well hidden behind his plump rosiness and generally munificent air. As the duke talked in fluent German with Goering, Wallis took in an impression of the vast residence: the gym in the basement complete with a massage apparatus, the small army of maids in smocked peasant dresses, the Rembrandt over the four-poster bed and other lavish art treasures. There was a pause in the smooth flow of German conversation when the duke spotted Goering's map of Germany showing Austria as part of the Reich. Goering's face wrinkled with amusement, observed Wallis. The Austrians would want to be part of the Reich, he said. The moment passed, the statement left unchallenged.[16]

Over the course of two weeks the Windsors visited the Krupp weapons factory at Essen, which was already making panzers and U-boats, and saw one of the few elite Führer Academies in Germany for training young Aryans as future leaders.[17] Gradually they made their acquaintance with those closest to Hitler, including his minister for propaganda, Joseph Goebbels, who saw in the duke's lack of official escort and his keen interest in German labour a modernising and accessible ex-king who was a '*eine Personlichkeit*'—a great man. 'What a delight to talk to him . . . We discussed a thousand things,' he gushed in his diary. 'With him an alliance would have been possible . . . What a shame. What a terrible shame.'[18]

The highlight of the Windsors' trip was a meeting with Hitler at his mountain hideaway at Berchtesgaden near the border with Austria. It was reported in papers across the world with pictures showing Wallis resplendent, all Gloriana, her adoring ex-king in tow, and Hitler almost rubbing his hands in glee, his often despondent expression transformed. There was much handshaking and mindfulness of royal rank. The Windsors gave Nazi salutes. Wallis took tea with Hitler's deputy, Rudolf Hess, while the duke was ensconced privately with Hitler. The records of their conversation have never been found, though Hitler too concluded that 'his abdication was a severe loss for us . . . If he had stayed, everything would have been different.'

If the Windsors were worried about the coolness of the official British response to this tour, once again Churchill was on hand with reassurance. 'I am told that when scenes of it (your tour) were produced in the news reels in the cinemas here your Royal Highness' pictures were always loudly cheered,' he wrote on 28 October. The visit, he thought, had passed off 'with distinction and success' and he wished them well for their American tour, convinced they would get a reception 'from that vast public which no Englishman has ever had before'.[19] They were prophetic words, but not quite in the way any of them imagined.

The arrangements for the American tour were in the hands of Charles Bedaux who was anxious to ensure an equally majestic reception for the couple. He asked officials in Washington to acknowledge Wallis as 'Her Royal Highness' and styled the duke as the 'Head of the Peace Movement'. He presented the ex-king as a man 'who has always been keenly interested in the lot of the working man' and who aimed to 'devote his time to the betterment of the life of the masses'. Bedaux hoped an official invitation would follow and that the Windsors' tour would have the prominence of a state visit. But when he arrived in New York on 1 November, he was surprised to find more than a hundred press men waiting—and they did not appear to be on message.

First there was the irritation of an outstanding tax bill of $48,976, presented to Bedaux himself by the Internal Revenue Service with indecent haste. Next he found that far from falling in with his view of a peace-loving duke on a visit to America to champion the masses, the questions from the press cast his mission in an unpalatable light. Why was the duke mixed up with 'a swarthy little French immigrant' whose rags-to-riches story was dubious at best. Bedaux may have one of the highest incomes in the United States but how could he justify his labour-management system when it exploited workers to the limit? The idea that the duke was seriously interested in working conditions was humbug. In reality he was touring the country 'as a salesman and trade representative for a business efficiency system', declared the *New York Daily News*. To round off the reception, Bedaux was presented with a lawsuit of $250,000 from a former lover, Louise Booth, a lady whose blowsy well-used charms, and titillating story of sex in Central Park with two men simultaneously, completed the image of the whole trip being a second-rate money-making promotion imbued with the flyblown glamour of yesterday's men.[20]

The next day the duke's visit was roundly denounced, ironically the opposition starting in Wallis's home town. The Baltimore Federation of Labor pointed out that the Windsors were visiting Nazi Germany 'under the personal guidance of Dr. Ley, the man who ordered and ruthlessly directed the destruction of all German free trade unions: the man who was personally responsible for the imprisonment and slaughter of honest, courageous, God-fearing free men'. The Baltimore Federation took note that the duke and his wife had continued their studies of labour problems 'in conference with Adolf Hitler, the world's most notorious foe of democracy and freedom of conscience'. Worse, their study in the States would be with Bedaux, whose adaptation of the original Taylor labour-management system was 'vicious'. Finally, Wallis herself while living in Baltimore had never shown 'the slightest concern nor sympathy for the problems of labour or the poor and needy!'[21] Within hours trade-union movements across the country echoed the rallying cry. As the attacks on Bedaux and the duke escalated, the Windsors were obliged to cancel their trip.

For Bedaux personally there was worse to come in the form of a betrayal of his own manager of Bedaux America, Albert Ramond. Seizing the moment when his boss was under fire, Ramond mounted a coup from within, demanding he should take over as chief. With hostility spiralling, Bedaux handed control to his manager and fled the States. In hot pursuit was a bill from the Internal Revenue Service for a further $202,718. The shock was too great and Bedaux collapsed in hospital in Munich only to learn that he was also required to sign over control of Bedaux Germany to the Nazis. The glare of publicity had been the last straw. Far from being his route to the pinnacle of society, Bedaux's association with Windsor had cost him $60,000 for the wedding alone and proved the catalyst that destroyed the golden goose in America. All that Bedaux claimed to have received in return for his trouble was a case of a dozen bottles of cognac.[22]

But behind the scenes the episode was equally damaging to the duke and duchess. Wallis put a brave face on it when she wrote to her friend Betty on 27 November: 'we feel we made a wise decision about the US,' she said.[23] Beneath the bravado, the high hopes they entertained that the duke could make a comeback and carve out a niche for himself on a world stage were badly shaken. For years as prince and as king, he was used to being feted, embassy doors flung wide open with welcoming hospitality. But now these same doors were slamming shut.

American friends were on hand to provide an escape from the world's press. A letter survives from Betty Lawson-Johnston's daughter, Jane, to Wallis dated 30 December 1937 revealing the secret arrangements she was making to help the Windsors slip to Cuba. Jane provided every comforting detail that a woman like Wallis might wish to know.

> Wallis dear . . . I've combed Havana and have seen every available house . . . but in all honesty I couldn't find anything which didn't have infinitely more glaring defects than our own humble shanty. On re-reading both your letters, our house seems to combine, as nearly as possible, most of your requirements, with the possible exception of adequate quarters for one or two of your servants . . .

Jane proposed alternative housing for their staff and the Country Club for guests. She had discreetly arranged for Maison Glace in New York to send any delicacies that they wished for and had detailed advice for their wardrobes. Only the tourists would stoop to garish colours and straw hats, she explained. Pastel shades were suitable for the country and dark prints or tailored suits for the town.

> For evening—almost anything, from cretonne to lames and velvets. (The men always wear black ties except on rare super official occasions.) Bring a fur or velvet evening wrap for it gets quite chilly after sun down. And don't forget to stock up with plenty of stockings for the climate is hard on them . . .

She assured Wallis about the fashionable social scene.

> The old casino is going full blast and there are entertaining night clubs where one can get the legitimate version of the Rumba! We've a new forty-six foot cabin cruiser which you can have whenever you want her for fishing and cruising. The tarpoon fishing on the south coast is considered <u>tops</u> by the experts . . . It looks as though <u>everyone</u> is coming to Cuba . . . so it should be entertaining from the 'social' angle . . .

And finally she provided peace of mind on the press.

> Since your coming has become an actual possibility we haven't breathed it to a living soul, not even Mother. So please don't worry, at least from this end, about 'leaks' . . . You'll find all the foreign correspondents as well as

**Best wishes
for Christmas and
the New Year**

Wallis   Edward

Christmas card from the Windsors to the Lawson-Johnstons, 1937 (THE PRIVATE COLLECTION OF MRS LAWSON-JOHNSTON)

the local gentlemen (?!) of the fourth estate more than friendly and sympathetic to you both. After the first barrage you won't be hounded to pieces by them either . . . [24]

While the Duke of Windsor was adjusting to his lack of position, the Duke of Gloucester was coming to terms with his high rank. The king did not wish for him to continue his army career as a soldier; he had to be available for royal duties. Although the Duke and Duchess of Gloucester loved travel, they found there were limitations on this too. Anxiously churning in his mind everything that could go wrong, the king concluded that his deputy must be based in Britain on hand to help with any unforeseen danger. Neither he nor the duke should be out of the country at the same time and this should continue until Princess Elizabeth reached the age of eighteen in 1944. When the Duke of Gloucester received an offer to go to Australia as royal governor-general for two years, insuperable objections were found, Gloucester's private secretary, Sir Godfrey Thomas, offering the most bizarre. 'Suppose some crazy communist shot the king,' he reasoned; as Regent, the Duke of Gloucester would instantly be needed in London. So the Gloucesters settled down to create a home of their own not too far from London in Northamptonshire, favouring a sixteenth-century house near Broughton on account of its proximity to some of the finest English hunts.[25] Despite suffering a miscarriage, the Duchess of Gloucester was keen to support her husband and increased her official load as well as taking on her first patronages.

While the Duke of Gloucester was endeavouring to meet the expectations placed upon him, the king continued to find Kent troublesome. Kent was in an unusual position of influence on the Continent, in part due to the remarkable legacy of the prodigious matriarch of the family, his great-grandmother Queen Victoria. She had taken a keen interest in the marriages of her children and grandchildren at the end of the nineteenth century, extending blue-blooded family connections across the royal houses of Europe. Kent and his brothers had relatives on the European thrones of Norway, Denmark, Belgium, Romania, Sweden, Hungary, Spain and others. But of all the brothers, Kent had the greatest number of connections in this princely network through his marriage. Marina, as a royal princess in her own right, unlike the aristocratic Scottish brides Elizabeth and Alice, was also related to many of these same thrones as well as to the Greek royal family. The Duke of Kent, equipped with this rich heritage as well as his ambassadorial charm, was uniquely placed not just to help George VI gain insights into the view from Europe, but also to carry out a little continental diplomacy of his own. Was he using these links to represent the interests of the British royal family or for his own purposes?

Close readers of *The Times*, which faithfully reported each royal foreign tour, would see that Kent travelled regularly to Europe to see his wife's sisters. Marina's middle sister, the stunning beauty Elizabeth, was married to a German aristocrat, Carl Theodor, Count of Toerring-Jettenbach, and their two families met several times a year. The Toerrings were wealthy and there was no shortage of pleasurable European diversions: skiing holidays in the Bavarian Alps, visiting the Toerring country seats, exploring the Salzburg Festival or travelling on the Orient Express.[26] Frequently these trips ended up at the hunting lodge in Bohinj in Yugoslavia where the Kents had become engaged, staying with Princess Marina's oldest sister, Princess Olga, and her husband, Prince Paul, the Regent of Yugoslavia.[27] Prince Paul and the Duke of Kent, both passionate art lovers, found they had much in common and became very close friends. Luxuriously idle weeks passed each summer with their young families enjoying the beauty of the Yugoslav countryside.

The Times also revealed Kent's meetings with his own German relatives. There was one grandson and two great-grandsons of Queen Victoria who were playing a growing role in Nazi diplomacy. The grandson, Charles Edward,

Duke of Saxe-Coburg, continued to brief Hitler about England after the abdication. The great-grandsons, Philipp and Christoph Hesse, were from a different princely dynasty, the 'von Hessen' family, which had once dominated central Germany around Kassel and whose most famous descendant was Princess Alix, the last tsarina of Russia. Prince Philipp of Hesse and his younger brother, Christoph, were close in age to the Duke of Kent and met at formal family events as well as socially, visiting art galleries in London, enjoying racing events and staying at the magnificent Hesse estate in Kronberg, Germany.[28]

Like the Duke of Saxe-Coburg, the Hesse princes joined the Nazi party. Philipp became a member of the SA, or Brownshirts, and his brother Christoph joined the SS. Both brothers also made royal connections through their marriages, continuing the tradition of their great-grandmother. In Princess Mafalda, daughter of the King of Italy, Victor Emanuel III, Philipp of Hesse made a particularly fortunate choice. Her gentle nature and charm was well known and had inspired Puccini to dedicate his opera *Turandot* to her.[29] Prince Christoph of Hesse fell in love with Princess Sophia of Greece and Denmark, a cousin of Princess Marina. But it was not the protective eye of a British matriarch keeping tabs on these marriages, rather Hitler himself, who wasted no time in spotting the splendid opportunities that arose from the German princes' prestigious connections. A link to the Italian royal household and the Fascist regime of Benito Mussolini was especially timely. In October 1936 Germany and Italy signed the Rome–Berlin Axis, the first step in building a closer alliance, and Hitler soon found he had tremendous respect for Prince Philipp of Hesse.[30] The German prince became part of his inner circle and trusted as go-between liaising with the Italian and German leadership. Prince Christoph also prospered under the Nazis, rising in Goering's intelligence division, where his many tasks of espionage extended to bugging the phones of the Windsors when they were in Austria.[31]

Although the Hesse brothers' careers prospered, their position as part of the British royal family remained in place. Intriguingly there is a photograph of a portrait of Philipp of Hesse in Betty Lawson-Johnston's collection, perhaps an indication of how he was an accepted part of their circle at this stage.

George VI was aware that the Duke of Kent was in a unique position to develop family ties. But could he be trusted in the way he used them? In the immediate aftermath of the abdication, Kent had been 'tiresome' in his continued support for his oldest brother, amongst his other headline-grabbing transgressions. For the king, still precarious on his throne, ever watchful for disasters ahead, could there be a possibility that Windsor might exploit his youngest brother's connections to develop unofficial channels of communication? Windsor and Kent's former long-standing solidarity was not readily dismissed. Windsor's desire to win back public adulation and regain his international platform was now painfully exposed. The palace staff, observed Sir Ronald Lindsay, British ambassador to America, 'are seeing ghosts and phantasms everywhere'.[32]

I n December 1937, another fear returned to stalk the king, faithful as a shadow, almost beyond endurance, further destroying his peace of mind. Letters arrived at the palace from all parts of the empire urging George VI to broadcast a Christmas message. Still haunted by his older brother's ability to outshine him with ease, the very idea of a Christmas Day broadcast filled him with dread. George VI agonised and shrank from the decision, hoping that he could avoid it. The usually light-hearted spirit of Christmas was sunk in gloom, intruding on the sanctuary of Sandringham where for years he had been able to escape public attention. Now BBC engineers at the press of a button could put him on a world stage, where his stammer was on display for anyone to construe as they pleased. 'Speech from the throne by George VI,' Goebbels wrote gleefully in his diary in October. 'It's enough to make anyone stutter.'[33] For him, the king's disability, like the advanced years of his leading ministers, was a glaring symbol of a weak regime.

Lionel Logue agreed to join the king for Christmas Day and in early December George finally acquiesced, fearing that not to broadcast might also be seen as a sign of weakness. Logue was met by the royal chauffeur at Wolferton station in Norfolk and was touched by the warmth of the reception he received from the royal family. As 3 pm approached, the king and Logue went together to the broadcasting room, a place which invariably invoked memories he would rather forget. The microphones and red light were in position, waiting. Outside they could hear the engineers in the adjoining room. The king rehearsed his speech; those few words that he had read time and again and yet still could not be sure that he could say them out loud. He lit a cigarette. Finally the red light flickered. The king found the words, suddenly, too fast. 'Many of you will remember the Christmas . . . ' Long pause. 'Broadcasts of former years . . . ' he began. He paid tribute to his father and, in his desire to avoid establishing a tradition, pointed out he could not aspire to take his place. He thanked his audience 'for the love and loyalty' he had received from every quarter of the empire. 'We have promised to try to be worthy of your trust and this is a pledge that we will always keep.' For many of his listeners across the empire, his sincerity and strength of feeling shone through the oddly formed sentences and long pauses. But the Christmas spirit of peace and goodwill that he hoped 'will in the end prevail' was not to last.

The first crisis erupted with no warning during 11 March 1938. The alarm began to sound in the late morning. The phones in the Foreign Office were ringing insistently. There was a rumour of the movement of German troops in Bavaria near the southern border with Austria. Officials in Germany denied it. By lunchtime a party was in full swing at 10 Downing Street. Almost farcically, Neville Chamberlain, his leading ministers, even Churchill, were entertaining the Ribbentrops when a message arrived that the Germans had entered Austria. The news reached the palace, bringing an afternoon of excruciating anxiety. By the evening reports were grim. The Austrian government stepped down. German storm troops were marching in Vienna. The police keeping order were wearing swastika armbands. The Nazi flag flew over the Chancery. Even the music on the wireless changed from Viennese waltzes to Hitler's favourite storm troopers' song. The Führer had moved by stealth to embrace a German-speaking country for the Reich, many of its citizens welcoming the *Anschluss* or union. By midnight Austria was part of Germany.[34]

It was hard to know what might happen next. The task had been accomplished with such lightning speed. Full of nervous tension, the king was oblivious to anything but the latest developments. He could read the chilling sequence of events in the papers the following day. Austria's leading cities were 'entirely in the hands of Nazis,' reported *The Times*, 'who were surging about in enormous masses and shouting interminably several slogans, including anti-Jewish ones'.[35] It had all been too easy. Independent Austria was dead.

In London, people watched in alarm as the German army entered Austria on 12 March and Hitler embarked on a triumphal tour. George VI soon learned that Chamberlain and his ministers remained convinced that appeasement was the right course of action despite the dictator's clear aggression. The king gave his wholehearted support, but for the first time even Chamberlain's most passionate admirers, such as MP Henry 'Chips' Channon, were deeply shaken. 'Is Winston, that fat, brilliant, unbalanced, illogical orator, more than just that?' he confided to his diary. 'Is he perhaps right, banging his head against an uncomprehending country and unsympathetic government?'[36]

Just six weeks later there was a new flashpoint: Czechoslovakia. Hitler wanted the Sudetenland, a wide strip of Czechoslovakia that bordered Germany (and Austria) and was home to 3 million German speakers. German troops were reported on the Czech border. In a matter of hours the Czech army mobilised. Troops gathered 'in unannounced numbers on either side of the frontier', reported *The Times*. The atmosphere was 'critical'.[37] Over the weekend of 22 May, the world held its breath once more. Europe seemed suddenly catapulted to the very brink of war. Lord Halifax, the Secretary of State for Foreign Affairs, steered a path through the diplomacy.[38] Telegrams flew between European embassies. Halifax hinted to the Germans that if they attacked Czechoslovakia, Britain would support France. The world waited.

It was against this tense international backdrop that the king and queen embarked on their first state visit overseas. On 19 July they sailed on HMS *Enchantress* to France. It was a critical show of solidarity aimed at underlining the strength of Anglo-French relations.[39] The press was won over as the king and queen reviewed troops at Versailles and watched a flypast of the French air force. Crowds gathered and warmed to them. It was as though the whole of France was suddenly in love with the British royal family. To the French, like a flag, they stood for peace and security as the king talked of co-operation, happiness, and the common purpose of the French and British governments. On camera, George VI's handsome features and slim figure looked stately, and his speeches, no matter how poorly delivered, invariably stood for integrity and reason. Queen Elizabeth, dressed in white mourning following the loss of her much-loved mother, hid her grief. Together they embodied on that shining summer visit the hope that all was well, and that the posturing and threats from darker forces would not prevail.

But the uneasy summer erupted in crisis in September. Once again, Europe was shuddering on the verge of war. The king's ministers brought him the urgent unfolding news. Hitler demanded the Sudetenland. Czechoslovakia would not cede any territory. France promised to march if Czechoslovakia was violated. Britain had promised to support France. It looked as though the delicate balance that kept Europe's peace might crumble, when Neville Chamberlain asked to have a meeting with Hitler. Flying for the first time in his life at the age of sixty-nine, the prime minister came face to face with the Führer at Berchtesgarten. 'It is one of the finest, most inspiring acts of all history,' wrote an admiring Chips Channon on 14 September, capturing the mood of the times. 'History must be ransacked to find a parallel.'[40]

In London, war seemed a certainty. Gas masks were distributed; even the king was fitted with one. Trenches were excavated in London parks. The air-raid system was tested, its ominous deep wail like some primeval warning echoing across the land. Basements were appropriated to turn into shelters. Cordons diverted the traffic as anti-aircraft guns were positioned on Horse Guards Parade and Westminster Bridge. The talk was all of war: no longer if, but when. Scenes of war-torn Flanders and the Somme, buried by time, now resurfaced. Was this really about to happen all over again?

For the king the nervous strain became acute. He had seen the theatrical spectacle in May as the Nazi high command, bloated with success, had descended by train on Mussolini's Italy. The newsreels showed the all-powerful dictator in the splendour of Rome where giant swastikas and flags were unfurled above unending military parades. Here he was again in September at the Nuremberg Rally celebrating the creation of Greater Germany, the gigantic square at Nuremberg filled with an orderly multitude, arraigned in neat columns, awaiting his word. The king could read about the Führer's speech, dramatically staged under a huge dome of converging searchlights, as he told his vast audience, 'I know that I can trust you blindly and you can blindly trust me . . . ' The immense assembly before him roared back its delight: 'We will follow our leader. We will follow our leader . . . '⁴¹

George VI articulated his worst fears in a letter to his mother on 27 September. Was it possible that his clever, sober ministers were, after all, dealing with a lunatic? He told her the latest proposal from Chamberlain to Hitler, which would give in to his demands for the Sudetenland and agree to a timetable for peace. 'If Hitler refuses to do this then we shall know, once and for all, that he is a *madman*' (George VI's italics). 'It is all so worrying, this awful waiting for the worst to happen,' the king went on.⁴² George VI was eager to do what he could. Chamberlain advised against him sending a personal telegram to Hitler.

The House of Commons was packed on 28 September. Black Wednesday. The fleet was at the ready. The auxiliary air force was prepared. The atmosphere in the House was charged. Everyone expected war. Queen Mary, a sombre, dark figure, made an unprecedented visit. On the eve of battle, she wanted to report the events in the House directly to the king. Chamberlain talked for an hour explaining the painstaking detail of the negotiations; the raised hopes, the hopes dashed. Hitler's mobilisation. The aggression of the dictator. The longer he talked the more it seemed there was no way out.

Even as Chamberlain was speaking, a note was passed from Foreign Office officials to Sir John Simon, now Chancellor of the Exchequer. Simon struggled to get the prime minister's attention. There was a beat as Chamberlain looked at its contents, his solemn expression unchanging. 'Shall I tell them?' he whispered to Simon. Simon nodded. Was there a reprieve? Chamberlain outlined how he had telegraphed the dictators that morning seeking one more meeting.

Finally, he read from the piece of paper. He and Mussolini were invited to Munich the next day. There *was* a reprieve.

The House erupted. The unbearable tension and anxiety exploded into hope and euphoria. Peace was surely saved? The world would not march to war. Civilisation was secure. The prime minister who had stayed unswervingly on the path of peace 'seemed the reincarnation of St George', observed Chips Channon.[43] Queen Mary, too overwhelmed to speak, went straight to the palace to tell the king.

'Neville, the Man of our Age' stepped out of his plane, returning from Munich on 30 September 1938. He walked up to the waiting microphones, that fateful sheet of white paper fluttering in the wind. He had a settlement; a prelude to a bigger settlement for peace. The crowds roared their ovation, his exit from the airport delayed as his car was engulfed, many trying to open the vehicle's doors and shake him personally by the hand. The king invited him to Buckingham Palace. Jubilant throngs lined the route, 'indifferent to the heavy rain,' reported *The Times*, 'their hearts full of relief'. It took almost two hours to travel the short distance from Heston Aerodrome to central London. In the hysteria of the moment, even the rainbow that appeared dramatically over Buckingham Palace as the rain stopped and the prime minister's car eased into the courtyard 'was hailed by some as an omen', continued *The Times*, as though the very heavens confirmed the promise of peace. Crowds surged to the palace railings and 'motorists sounded their horns in chorus'.[44] Then, shoulder to shoulder, Chamberlain emerged on the balcony beside the king and queen. Everyone was ecstatic. It was 'peace with honour' and 'peace for our time'. The next day Hitler took the Sudetenland. He had promised he would demand no more territory.

The reprieve was felt across the world, the news filtering to distant outposts of empire including the lush green valleys of south-west Kenya, where the Gloucesters were visiting relatives of Alice. The Gloucesters understood the hideous pressure on the king and queen during 'this horrid European situation'—as Alice called it.[45] She had 'dreaded seeing the dust of an approaching motorbike', fearing news of war.[46] Several times they had been on the brink of returning to London. Now Gloucester wrote to his mother to express his relief that 'another Great War has been averted'. After the recent headlines, it seemed a miracle to travel home across a still-peaceful Europe, taking time to stop in Paris, at the request of the prime minister.

Chamberlain wanted the Gloucesters to call on the Windsors in an attempt to gauge the public reaction. The king hoped to find some way of repairing the family split although he was anxious about his brother returning so soon. The queen, too, objected, according to Walter Monckton, because she feared that Windsor's 'attractive vital' presence in the country would undermine her husband.[47] But Windsor, restless and bitter, lobbied to return. Perhaps with a little help from the duchess, the American papers got hold of the story. As the threat of war receded, the press shone the spotlight on lighter topics. The royal drama of the king and the 'beggar maid from Baltimore' regained its appeal. 'To curtsey or not to curtsey,' asked the *New York Times*, 'that is the question now dividing British society.' Could 'Her Grace of Windsor' become 'Her Royal Highness' and return happily to Fort Belvedere after all?[48]

The Windsors were on their best behaviour when they met the Gloucesters in Paris. It was smiles all round for the camera, the only slight faux pas that Alice was upstaged by the ever chic Wallis in the Paris restaurant, having only safari clothes with her. The king kept a close eye on public reaction following the meeting and was taken aback by an outburst of hostile letters to the Gloucesters. The British public were not yet ready to forgive. 'I have heard from all sides that there is a strong feeling amongst all classes that my brother should not return here even for a short visit with the Duchess of Windsor,' the king wrote to Neville Chamberlain. 'This is the moment for you to write and tell him that it would not be at all wise for him to contemplate such a visit . . . I think that you know that neither the Queen nor Queen Mary have any desire to meet the Duchess of Windsor and therefore any visit made for the purpose of introducing her to members of the royal family obviously becomes impossible.' He thanked the prime minister for making his 'good offices' available for a matter of 'such an intimate nature' and expressed the view that 'my brother would take this decision in a more kindly manner from you than from me!!'[49]

Within weeks, events occurred in Germany which cast the success at Munich in a different light. On 9 November, a wave of anti-Semitic violence erupted across Germany as members of the SA paramilitary and citizens launched attacks on Jewish families. On *Kristallnacht* or 'Night of the Broken Glass' the synagogues burned from Vienna to Berlin, 7,000 Jewish businesses were destroyed, 30,000 Jews were sent to concentration camps. Ninety-one Jews lost their lives.

'A Black day for Germany,' thundered *The Times* on 11 November 1938. 'The scenes of systematic plunder and destruction have seldom had their equal in a civilized country since the Middle Ages.'[50] Germany was shamed before the world; its government had failed to intervene to stop the violence. No one could be left in any doubt that this was a regime that encouraged the persecution of the Jews.

The king's worry that madness lay at the heart of the Nazi leadership was painfully underlined in *The Times*. In German propaganda, Mr Churchill was transformed into 'Public Enemy No-1'. The pretext for the wave of violence across the Reich was the murder of a German diplomat at the German embassy in Paris by a young Jew, Herschel Grynszpan, who was avenging the treatment of his parents. According to German propaganda, Churchill was linked to this Paris murder and there was 'a straight line from Churchill to Grynszpan' with both at the heart of an international conspiracy of Jews and Freemasons.[51] *The Times* in those two days caught the insanity, cruelty and violence at the heart of the regime. Winston Churchill launched a major attack on the government. The prime minister's policy was based on the assumption he was dealing with rational, reasonable men. *Kristallnacht* was a warning. What price had been paid to avoid war? Churchill was sure of the answer. The British had a bleak choice between 'War and Shame'. If they chose Shame they will 'then have War thrown in a little later'.[52]

But the British people, their government, and the king continued to support appeasement. War had to be averted at all costs. The Windsors, obliged to remain in France, made the best of it as they rented a magnificent villa, Château de la Croë, at Cap d'Antibes, in one of the most prestigious parts of the French Riviera near Cannes. Wallis spent lavishly, re-creating a royal palace of their own where she and the Duke of Windsor could hold court. There would be no mistaking the royal ambience. Every detail would proclaim it. The perfume of luxury would permeate everything from the silver and the china to the gold-plated swan-shaped bathtub. The grounds of the mansion swept to the Mediterranean Sea and Wallis delighted in hosting grand receptions there. Invitations went out to all their friends and supporters.

The Windsors in their lavish refurbishment of La Croë had fashioned a tempting paradise for visitors and also, unwittingly, something more sinister— which soon came to the attention of German intelligence. The house stood alone hidden by trees that created dense shadow. Sunlight made the grand forecourt and raised pillared entry stand out against a dark background: perfect for the assassin. The proximity to the coast made it possible for any hit squad to arrive by boat, approach the house unseen and take up a position under cover of woodland. The unwary visitor, greeted by the English butler and looking forward to the lavish hospitality afforded by the sixteen staff, could be in close range of a sniper's bullet.[53]

Several of Hitler's inner circle ran their own security staff but the order is most likely to have come from the offices of Heinrich Himmler who had consolidated great power in Nazi Germany as chief of the German police and also taken over the Gestapo from Goering. Working for him was Reinhard Heydrich, head of the Nazi intelligence service, a man who even Hitler was prompted to describe as 'the man with the iron heart'. His deputy was Walter Schellenberg, who showed a talent for foreign intelligence and counterespionage and was promoted rapidly. But it was not the Windsors who were the focus of interest.

Winston Churchill had been invited to stay.[54]

No matter how grave the international scene, the Duke of Kent, it seems, could not usher in a New Year without a little pleasant distraction with one of his glamorous women friends. 'Going abroad Tuesday could you come in Monday around 6.30 as much want to see you . . . ' he telegrammed to Betty Lawson-Johnston on 1 January 1938, signing himself affectionately, 'love Georgie . . . '[55] There is no evidence they had an affair, but despite Marina's restraining presence, George found time to maintain his wide circle of admirers. Whatever her feelings about Mrs Allen, Edythe Baker, Mrs Lawson-Johnston and the many beautiful confidantes of her husband, Marina was the sole of discretion. In public the Kents presented a united front, with the duke invariably finding the right words to reassure his wife. When they were in Athens in January 1938 for the wedding of Marina's cousin Paul, Crown Prince of Greece, Kent delighted his audience in one speech by declaring that 'Greece has given me a wife . . . [whose] influence over me is as incalculable as the Hellenic influence over civilisation . . . '[56]

The Kents' travels across the Continent gave them a bird's-eye view of Europe's threatened boundaries, the fear of the expanding Third Reich casting an ominous shadow over the lives of Marina's close family. It was hard for Marina not to feel a sense of foreboding for her mother, Princess Nicholas, who wished to remain in Athens, following the death of her husband, Prince Nicholas, in February 1938.[57] As the solemn royal group assembled for his funeral, their home country in south-east Europe seemed vulnerable. From Greece just across the deep blue of the Ionian Sea in the Mediterranean lay Mussolini's Italy and his disturbing imperial ambitions. Marina was worried, too, for her sister, Princess Olga, and Prince Paul in Yugoslavia. Following the annexation of Austria, Greater Germany now stretched to the Austrian border, just 70 miles from their traditional summer retreat at Bohinj.

In the summer the Duke and Duchess of Kent attended another royal reunion in Eastern Europe at the funeral of Queen Marie of Romania, a grand-daughter of Queen Victoria. During the Kents' visit one curious incident was reported by the press of the neighbouring country of Hungary, which prompted investigation by the British Foreign Office. 'The throne of Hungary needs a king,' urged the Hungarian journal *Politika*. 'The Hungarian nation would most gladly elect HRH the Duke of Kent to the throne of Hungary.' The idea was to promote peace in Europe by extending the British parliamentary system into Eastern Europe. Had the Duke of Kent, once considered for the British throne, encouraged such an idea? He was evidently anxious to distance himself from any involvement in the matter. Foreign Office files reveal the response of the Duke of Kent's private secretary, John Lowther: 'the only action that the Duke of Kent had taken was to put the copy which had been sent to him in the wastepaper basket,' he said.[58]

Was the Duke of Kent advancing his own agenda within the well-travelled clique of royal cousins and relations? He visited Poland and Austria in 1937, Greece and Romania in 1938 and Yugoslavia and Germany repeatedly. The Duke of Windsor visited France, Austria, Germany and was on friendly terms with the royal house of Savoy of Italy. At many of these events they had meetings with their cousins in Fascist regimes. George VI could see that Prince Philipp of Hesse had risen so high in the ranks of Nazi leadership that during the Sudetenland

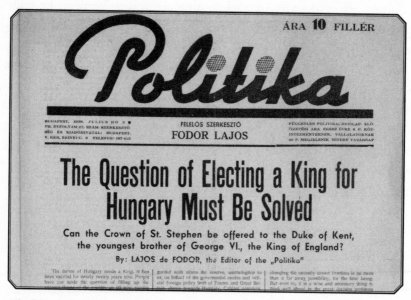

The Hungarian journal *Politika* asked, should the Duke of Kent become King of Hungary? (THE NATIONAL ARCHIVES)

crisis he appeared in newsreels on tour with Hitler as part of the inner clique.[59] Philipp was older and thinner but it was unmistakably him with the receding hairline, standing respectfully behind Hitler with Goering and Himmler as they celebrated the German bloodless victory and Britain was bent to Hitler's will.

The king saw an opportunity that would enable his youngest brother to develop his career well away from European troubles. Kent could take on the post that he had asked Gloucester to decline: Governor-General of Australia. It was a brilliant decision that would give Kent a great responsibility representing the Crown overseas and also allow the king to take advantage of Kent's winning charm. The appointment would not start for another year, but even so, for the Kents it was a major upheaval. Their smart London home in Belgrave Square was a treasure trove of exquisite works of art and furniture; all this had to be put in storage or packed for transport. Their neighbour, Chips Channon, was quick to point out how much the Kents would save. 'As far as I know,' he said, 'neither Melbourne nor Sydney has a Cartier, or a Rochelle Thomas or a Ross Harris for you to spend thousands in . . .'[60]

Over Christmas of 1938, as the royal family gathered at Sandringham, it was still possible to believe that there would be no war. George VI was relieved there was no Christmas speech. He did not want to set a precedent and there was a sense that the worst might be over. The welcome reprieve continued through January and February. In early March, the prime minister was seen in the 1936 Club, jovial and relaxed. With each day of British rearmament, he said, the threat from both the Soviet Union and Germany was lessened. He was beginning to have confidence that he had taken the right course.

It was not to last. The crisis that began to unfold on 14 March marked a watershed. At Buckingham Palace each new fragment of news built to a disturbing picture: the Czech government was resigning; the Czech president was travelling to Germany; questions were being asked in the House as German tanks were rolling over the Sudetenland border virtually unopposed. Suddenly it was clear: Germany was seizing the rest of Czechoslovakia. The next day, German troops were in the capital, Prague, and Czechoslovakia as a country was wiped off the map of Europe. Everything that had been agreed at Munich was overturned. The policy of appeasement was demolished. That symbol of hope, the white sheet of paper fluttering in the breeze that Chamberlain held up so proudly on his return from Germany, was torn up.[61] Chamberlain outwardly appeared calm. The king knew he was broken-hearted.

Not to be outdone by Hitler, Mussolini prepared to seize Albania. This little Mediterranean country held a big strategic position. Albania shared borders with Greece and Yugoslavia and was an important beachhead to that large area of south-east Europe called the Balkans. Mussolini wanted to annex Albania, just as Hitler had annexed Austria. On 7 April every Albanian port was under fire, and within hours succumbed to the might of the Italian invasion force. The King of Italy was crowned King of Albania and Mussolini boasted of a great Italian triumph. On May 22 the Fascist threat was further underlined as the two dictators signed an alliance in which Italy and Germany would aid the other if war was declared: the 'Pact of Steel'.

Marina's sister and brother-in-law in Yugoslavia were becoming cornered. After the invasion of Albania, Yugoslavia had a second border with Italy as well as German troops in neighbouring Austria. Prince Paul turned to the British Foreign Office for help, but none was forthcoming. He felt under pressure to accept the Italian dictator's invitation to Rome, swiftly followed by an invitation to Germany to meet Hitler. Prince Paul tried to counter Fascist bullying with politeness, courtesy and strict neutrality, but the stress was taking its toll. 'The news shows a little improvement,' the Duke of Kent confided to Betty Lawson-Johnston on 16 April. 'With so much armed force about one hesitates if guns should go off by mistake.'[62]

It was 5 May 1939. The king and queen had good reason to be anxious as they boarded the *Empress of Australia* for their first official visit to Canada and America. In a climate of impending war they had to step on a world stage as symbols of solidarity between the world's greatest democracies. The king had to give several important speeches, each one painstakingly rehearsed with Logue before departure. A minefield of diplomatic pitfalls lay ahead. Their trip might be seen as an ill-disguised political attempt to persuade neutral America to support any European war. The Jewish community might take offence at British policy. Above all, would they themselves be seen as a dull substitute for the ex-king who the American people had already taken to their hearts?[63] As the Prince of Wales, he had been feted in America and, despite the debacle following Bedaux's efforts, still enjoyed a large following. 'Friends of the Duke of Windsor in America', an organisation launched on 20 January 1939 to mark the anniversary of his succession as Edward VIII, brought together his admirers who aimed to defend him 'against ill-natured attacks upon his character' and nominated him 'Ambassador at Large for Democracy and Peace'.[64] The 'David who has dared to face the Goliath of Tradition' was seen by some as the perfect envoy.[65]

In Britain, Prince Henry was to represent George VI in his absence as Senior Counsellor of State. It was a heavy responsibility for Henry who, as he once put it, felt anxious 'to keep my wicket up and just take the edge off the bowling until the star turns are ready to go in'. This was exactly how he felt at this moment too—and he had his work cut out. The king and queen were just four days into bracing Atlantic winds when the Duke of Windsor attempted to upstage them. After a visit to the First World War battlefield at Verdun, he broadcast an evocative plea for world peace on NBC America. Millions of Americans could hear the British ex-king appeal to them 'as a soldier of the last war', praying 'that such a cruel and destructive madness shall never again overtake mankind'. Millions heard his good speaking voice ring out promoting his pacifist line in which he deplored the use of such terms as 'encirclement' or 'aggression' that he felt inspired 'dangerous political passions'.[66] The *New York Times* later defined it as one of the 'historic broadcasts of 1939'.[67] But in Britain Windsor did not collect quite the applause he was looking for. The BBC declined to air his statement. At the palace, even his old ally, the Duke of Kent, did not support him. 'Everyone is furious he should have done it just after you left,' Kent informed the king.[68] With the explosively volatile international situation, Windsor's efforts to grab the limelight were ill-judged.

George VI and Queen Elizabeth arrived late in Canada on account of the icebergs to a cautious welcome in French-speaking Quebec. As they toured the country the news from home was bleak. Gloucester, an army man, conveyed the facts succinctly to his brother. Hitler 'will soon be doing something about Danzig', he told him in mid-May. The Germans wanted the free city of Danzig and the surrounding corridor of Polish land which held a strategic position on the Baltic Sea. Gloucester thought that Hitler was unlikely 'to do anything rash [about Poland] till the autumn harvest has been gathered', but he was worried about Spain. The Spanish Civil War had just ended and while the Italians were leaving the country, 'the Germans are not for the present' he warned the king. Then he had concerns about the Far East where the Japanese, who had invaded China in 1937, were making things 'very difficult for us' in Shanghai. For a man whose schoolwork had been a disappointment, his observations were not too wide of the mark. Gloucester was also troubled about a more personal matter regarding his own brother-in-law, Walter Scott, 8th Duke of Buccleuch, who held high office as the king's Lord Steward. Buccleuch made no secret of his pro-German views and his indiscretions prompted one magazine, *The Week*, to accuse Gloucester himself of being 'in the hands of the Germans'. Gloucester was concerned and reassured the king that he was taking action. 'I am having a talk with Walter,' he explained, and intended to suggest that 'he does not go over [to] Germany again, while he is Lord Steward . . . as my brother-in-law, not until things become a <u>lot more</u> peaceful.'[69]

In public George VI and Elizabeth hid their worries. Word began to spread across Canada of a well-informed and conscientious king and his charming queen. When they reached Ottawa 100,000 people waited in the central square. An impromptu walk among thousands of veterans, some overcome with emotion, had an electric effect. By the time they reached America, it was clear that any fears they had over their reception were misplaced. 'Never have I seen a crowd such as linked the whole route between Union Station and the White House,' Mrs Roosevelt wrote in her diary. The king particularly valued the day he spent with Roosevelt in his private home at Hyde Park. The president spoke frankly late into the night, the king making notes of all the points they covered, his confidence growing with the insights of the older statesman.[70] In one month the king and queen were seen by more than 15 million people and when they returned to London on 22 June 1939, 50,000 crammed into the Mall to cheer and applaud them. King George VI was becoming the figurehead he had feared he could never be.

In their absence the Duke of Kent was briefed about one more assignment in Europe before he took up his position in Australia. The wedding in the Italian city of Florence of Princess Irene of Greece and the Duke of Spoleto of central Italy was one of the most glittering royal events of the summer season in Europe. The date was set for 2 July and the lengthy guest list from the royal houses of Europe included Queen Victoria's descendants from thrones great and small. Foreign Office records show that the Duke of Kent was not particularly keen to go but agreed to do so if 'the Secretary of State thought that it would be useful politically . . . '[71] Lord Halifax, a politician whose shrewd cunning had earned him the nickname 'the Holy Fox', owing to his incongruous passion for both fox hunting and theology, could detect some advantage in closer liaison between the Italian and British royal families. Foreign Office staff put some thought into anticipating any indelicate circumstance that might arise. Following Mussolini's conquests, the King of Italy had also been proclaimed Emperor of Abyssinia and King of Albania. While Kent could join in any toast, diplomatic protocol required he must on no account find himself in a position where he had to *propose* a toast to the Italian king and acknowledge these ill-gotten titles.[72]

It was as though the people of Florence had not heard of the prospect of war. Time stood still on a day of radiant sunshine for the spectacular royal wedding. The streets were abundantly decked with flags and bunting, the colourful crowds in celebratory mood ready to cheer each royal party who descended on the city. And European royalty descended on Florence in large numbers in their exquisite finery as though there was no imminent danger. Princess Marina, stunningly dressed in a slimline white dress with a short-sleeved jacket, her handsome white-uniformed husband beside her, had a chance to see her mother and her sisters as well their relatives from many other European houses.

Mingling among the guests keeping an eagle eye for any opening that might lead to information was the German prince, Philipp of Hesse. He particularly hoped for a quiet word with the Duke of Kent. The envoys watching over the proceedings somehow managed to miss exactly when in the two-day festivities that July the two cousins were able to find a discreet opportunity for a frank exchange of views. Perhaps disarmed by the atmosphere of the wedding, or perhaps determined to ensure that his cousin was under no illusions about the danger, the Duke of Kent revealed enough of the British position that when Hesse returned to Germany he demanded an appointment with Hitler.[73]

At the House of Commons in London, almost unbelievably, members of parliament debated adjourning until early October. Churchill was the first to return to his 'theme song', as Chips Channon observed, that dictators 'help themselves to a country' while the British House is in recess.[74] By 14 August he was in France briefing himself about French military defences and meeting their generals before he planned a few quiet days painting in the French Riviera, taking the chance to catch up with the Duke of Windsor at La Croë.[75]

Churchill's repeated warning of the Nazi danger had not only served to keep him in the wilderness of British politics, but also turned him into a Nazi target. Quite how German intelligence knew that Churchill would be at La Croë that August is not known, although the Windsors had a large staff, so it is possible the news was leaked. Churchill was unaware that his movements were of interest as he wrote home happily to his wife, Clementine, reporting his impressions of his travels. In Paris he met General Georges of the French army and together they inspected French defences at the Maginot Line on the border before Churchill moved on to visit family relations in Dreux.[76]

He was about to embark on his journey south when, according to his former bodyguard, Walter Thompson, he received a warning from French intelligence. Churchill was not a man to fret about personal safety. He had already suffered life-threatening physical ailments and combined with his fondness for a drink was surprisingly casual about his own mortality. But such was the seriousness of the threat on this occasion, he took notice.

On 22 August he sent a cryptic telegram to Thompson, now working as a grocer in London. Without explanation, he asked Thompson to meet him at Croydon Aerodrome at 4.30 pm on Wednesday. At the airport, Thompson thought there was a certain grimness in his face. Churchill was preoccupied to the point of being offhand and Thompson felt 'treated as a servant'.[77] It was only later, in the privacy of his country home at Chartwell in Kent, that Churchill revealed he had received a warning 'on the highest authority that the Germans were about to assassinate me'. He asked his former bodyguard if he would come back and protect him and explained that undercover Nazi agents were also in Britain. 'I rarely take notice of threats,' he told Thompson. 'But I have something to do.'[78]

Churchill learned of the assassination plot at La Croë on a fateful sunlit morning when Europe woke up to the startling news of a Nazi-Soviet non-aggression pact. Across the continent people felt double-crossed by the Russians. War and the partition of Poland seemed unstoppable. Ribbentrop was already in Moscow to seal the alliance.

Philipp of Hesse was still trying to reach Hitler. Days had passed since the Florence wedding and Hitler held him at arm's length. Hesse was finally allowed into the Führer's inner sanctum at the Berghof late on 23 August and confided everything that he had heard from the Duke of Kent. Above all he wanted Hitler to understand that a German attack on Poland would bring Britain into the war and lead to the ruin of Germany. Hitler had to recognise that this was no British bluff. If Kent had overstepped the mark and gone beyond his cautious Foreign Office briefing talking to his cousin in Florence, at least his message was spot on. Philipp of Hesse conveyed the stark warning that any move on Poland would not result in an isolated 'local war'. It would be the start of World War II.[79]

But Hitler was not listening to bearers of inconvenient truths. Ribbentrop was the man of the moment who had won his confidence with his stunning non-aggression pact with the Soviet Union. During his discussion with Hesse, Ribbentrop rang from Moscow heady with victory. The agreement with the Soviet Union was now signed. Germany was safe. Britain would not take on Germany now. Hesse was dismissed, the Duke of Kent's warning among many that were tossed to one side.

In London, George VI arrived at the palace from Balmoral and was plunged into the crisis. Neville Chamberlain informed him that Cabinet had already discussed the Nazi-Soviet pact and nothing was changed: Britain would stand by its pledge to Poland. The king's first thought was that he should appeal personally to Hitler, without delay, before the world was overtaken by calamity.

But Chamberlain dismissed the idea. He himself wrote to Hitler, warning 'of the grave consequences for humanity' which may follow and emphasising the 'steadfast attitude and intention of the British Government'.[80]

In Westminster, the heat had gone out of the House of Commons. It was all too late for remedy; world leaders, apparently empty ciphers, were swept along in something so much larger than themselves. An air of unreality prevailed as those persistent threats from Europe's heavyweight dictators, so carefully, so hopefully bandaged over for so long, began to crystallise into the imminent danger of war. Chamberlain and Halifax looked exhausted. There was an ominous quiet; a resigned acceptance. Churchill, face in his hands, knew the whole House understood war was now inevitable.[81]

The irrevocable had happened. People seemed different, all now trapped in some fatal, cataclysmic unknown. With furious energy the entire country was caught up in feverish preparations. A wave of volunteering swept the nation as people hurried to help with defence, evacuation, the creation of first-aid units, tractor driving and a million other necessities. By 31 August around the capital alone more than a hundred machines were excavating earth to fill sandbags. Miniature mountains of sand or earth appeared overnight and squads of men were transforming the familiar contours of London with sandbag walls. Temporary shelters were put up while work continued round the clock on the excavation of more permanent ones. Those with no shelters dug trenches. Air defences erected in London's parks looked incongruous among the deckchairs and flower beds. There were giant searchlights and huge barrage balloons lying in bizarre shapes as they were secured in position. Anti-aircraft units took up positions around the metropolis. Traffic lights were screened with hoods and white lines painted on pavements for guidance in blackouts. An unending parade of children, knapsacks on their backs, gas masks to hand, crammed into the capital's railway stations as much-rehearsed evacuation plans turned into reality. Everywhere windows were boarded up or blacked out, even criss-crossed with sticky tape as protection against the blast. At Buckingham Palace, staff organised the blackout of more than 700 windows and sandbags were banked up in the courtyard.[82]

The Dukes of Gloucester and Kent rallied to the king's side at the palace, the Kents returning from their summer holiday with Princess Olga and Prince Paul at Bohinj. In the face of certain war, the three brothers presented a united front. Both younger brothers were keen to share the king's load. 'I have seen more of them in the last week than I have during the year,' the king wrote to his mother on 28 August.[83] The Duke of Gloucester was photographed at the king's side as he visited the War Office and other government offices. The three brothers went together unannounced to morning service at Westminster Abbey, a quiet statement of composure and solidarity.[84] Throughout the country people waited. Suddenly Shakespeare's England, 'this sceptred isle . . . set in the silver sea', seemed very small and vulnerable. How long before German planes darkened the sky?

But Britain's ex-king remained in France, beside the sparkling Mediterranean Sea, unwilling to return home unless his demands were met. He remained with Wallis as, one by one, his small court of admirers said their goodbyes, the sounds of war difficult to hear when frothy white waves were crashing on golden sand. He remained what he called 'a citizen of the world' when he took it upon himself to send a personal telegram to Hitler on 29 August, urging him not to fight, and to the King of Italy begging him to use his influence to avert catastrophe.[85] He remained immovable when loyal Walter Monckton managed to reach him on the phone to tell him the king was sending his private plane to bring him home.[86]

There was one thing only that would induce him to return, the duke confided to Fruity Metcalfe, the last remaining friend and official at his side. 'I refuse to go *unless* we are invited to stay at Windsor Castle and the invitation and plane are sent personally by my brother.'[87] George VI would not meet these conditions. Even on the brink of world war, like a medieval king caught in a family feud, the brother who had always outshone him haunted him from overseas.

The duke was still at his villa on the Riviera on 1 September when Poland was invaded by Germany. When *The Times* phoned him for comment, he dismissed it. 'Oh! Just another sensational report.'[88]

That night in London there was a blackout, intended to hide the sprawling, glittering city and its river, silver in the moonlight, in 'complete and utter darkness', as its citizens awaited Hitler's next move.[89]

PART TWO

SEPTEMBER 1939–AUGUST 1940

4

IN THIS GRAVE HOUR

....

'In this grave hour, perhaps the most fateful in our history . . .'

—George VI, 3 September 1939

It was not long before the king realised that a new word had been minted to describe the particular kind of hell unleashed on Poland: *Blitzkrieg*, or lightning war. The newspapers he read outlined in vivid terms how Germany's military arsenal was let loose simultaneously by air, land and sea. During the darkness hours of 1 September 1939 the heavy guns from a German warship pounded the port of Danzig on the Baltic coast. Miles to the south-west, sleepy Polish villages woke up to the full destructive might of the *Luftwaffe*. Stuka dive-bombers rained terror on Polish positions, shelling anything that moved. Quietly massed in the forests along the Polish border were the panzers and armoured cars of the German army. At 5 am they began streaming into Poland with orderly efficiency.[1]

Elizabeth joined George VI from Scotland, tired from the night train, her presence a tremendous comfort. She was sad to leave the princesses behind at Birkhall near Balmoral. Her oldest sister, Rose, was solemnly entrusted to do her best for them should anything happen to herself and the king. They waited for news together at the palace in those first anxious days of September, 'hoping and praying, that a solution will be found', wrote Elizabeth.[2]

The prime minister did not declare war immediately. George VI learned they were delayed because the French were not yet ready. Then a wild hope spread around Whitehall that Italy would intervene and peace might yet be saved.[3] Chamberlain was stunned to find the mood was for war in the House of Commons. Anger was mounting at the delay. But no declaration of war came.

By the evening of 2 September London was in the grip of a thunderstorm. Buildings were nearly obliterated from view in the torrential rain. People hurried from the deluge, their shapes distorted, almost surreal in the gloomy light. From the Buckingham Palace windows, the world outside seemed to echo the confusion in Westminster. Polish people had endured two days of merciless destruction while they had stood by. The speed of events was appalling. Reports indicated the Polish air force had taken crippling losses.

Finally the king learned a decision had been reached at Number 10. The British ambassador, Sir Nevile Henderson, would deliver an ultimatum to the German government at 9 am the next day. If the German government did not give orders by 11 am to withdraw from Poland, Britain would be at war.

Sunday 3 September dawned glorious and church bells rang out across the land. The country was still at peace. The storm had passed and under summer skies that peace was tangible, the very essence of Sunday tranquillity in England before the war. 'Every moment was an agony,' wrote Queen Elizabeth, treasuring each precious second before 11 am. 'My last cup of tea in peace! My last bath at leisure; and all the time one's mind working on many thoughts.'[4] All over Britain people gathered by their wireless sets waiting for the news. The prime minister was due to broadcast to the nation shortly after the eleven o'clock deadline. George VI had hardly slept the night before.[5] Everything seemed unreal. He and Elizabeth waited for the broadcast in his sitting room. It is impossible to find words, she wrote later, 'to convey even an idea of the torture of mind that we went through'.[6]

Eleven o'clock began to strike.

'This is London,' announced the BBC presenter. 'You will now hear a statement by the prime minister.'

There was no pause; no interruption; no last-minute reprieve.

As the prime minister spoke, his querulous voice seemed disconnected from the fateful words. Hitler would not withdraw from Poland, said Chamberlain, ' . . . and consequently this country is at war with Germany.'

The king's first feeling was one of relief, according to the war diary that he began that week. The 'incessant worry' he had felt since Munich gave way to resolution. Hitler's violence had led the world to the 'edge of the Abyss'. Now Hitler 'had taken the plunge with the knowledge that the whole might of the British Empire would be against him'.[7]

He realised Elizabeth had tears pouring down her cheeks.[8] There was little time to comfort her. The strange and penetrating whine of air-raid sirens cut through the prime minister's familiar voice, bringing home the new reality.

It was hard to know what to expect. Would the clear London skies suddenly become overcast as German bombers reaped destruction as in Poland? The king and queen, holding their gas masks, made their way down to the palace base-ment that had been hurriedly converted into an emergency shelter, wondering how the enemy could attack so soon.[9] We felt 'stunned and horrified', the queen recalled, 'waiting for bombs to fall'.[10]

Lionel Logue was on standby, waiting in some trepidation knowing he would soon be needed. The call from the palace came at midday and he set off from his home in south London through the transformed streets. He found the king looking distinctive in his admiral of the fleet's uniform but nothing could conceal his anxiety. It was George VI's first wartime speech. Even for a man with his deep sense of purpose, it was a tremendous ordeal. How was he to lead the nation towards whatever unknowable terrors lay ahead? There was just time for Logue to look over the speech and make a few adjustments that he knew would help the king. At this, of all moments, failure could not be counte-nanced. Friends and enemies would hear him. The return of his stammer was a private terror that had to be banished from his mind. All too soon it was time. Just before 6 pm Logue was with the king in the broadcasting room. Both men were waiting for the red cue light. Nervously the king began.

'In this grave hour, perhaps the most fateful in our history, I send to every household of my peoples, both at home and overseas, this message . . . ' His voice was hesitant, his tone was flat, the words came at an uneven pace, but none the less, the king stuck to his message. He set out why the country had been forced into conflict: to challenge the dangerous code which permits a state 'to disregard its treaties and its solemn pledges; which sanctions the use of force, or threat of force, against the sovereignty and independence of other States. Such a principle, stripped of all disguise, is surely the mere primitive doctrine that Might is Right . . . ' If this became established, 'the peoples of the world would be kept in the bondage of fear' and all hopes of peace, justice and liberty would be ended. 'For the sake of all that we ourselves hold dear, and of the world's order and peace, it is unthinkable that we should refuse to meet the challenge. It is to this high purpose that I now call my people at home and my peoples across the Seas, who will make our cause their own . . . We can only do the right as we see the right, and reverently commit our cause to God.'

The stirring words of George VI resounded around the homes and offices of Britain. People fell silent, awed at the immensity of what lay ahead, responding to his rallying call, arguably all the more rousing despite his delivery, because the intensity of feeling was still plain. Across the world the cry was heard. The

Dominions were not signatories to the British guarantees to Poland but none the less, the Pacific Dominions declared war on Germany at the same time as Britain. Australia, too, was of one mind: 'One king, one flag, one cause.' New Zealand swiftly followed. South Africa and Canada joined the war after some debate a few days later.[11]

The reluctant king, now thrust hesitantly into the prominent role of Supreme Commander in Chief of the Army of an empire at war, found the sound of the sirens even worse at night, penetrating the darkness, forbidding sleep. Tired and disorientated, he and Elizabeth retraced their steps to their shelter in the small hours of 4 September. The certainties of the peacetime world were slipping away fast. The king knew his ministers had tried everything in their power to prevent war. There was no alternative. But it was impossible to imagine what lay ahead.

The king learned with some surprise that the man whose judgement had been viewed as suspect for so long had a position of real executive power as First Lord of the Admiralty: Winston Churchill.[12] This would be a critical role from the outset as British ships across the world became the target of U-boats. Others in Westminster shared his apprehension. Winston was 'very rhetorical and very emotional', according to Samuel Hoare. 'He strikes me as an old man who gets tired very easily.'[13] Across the fleet the news spread like wildfire: 'Winston is back.' Churchill himself felt an uplifting sense of detachment. 'The glory of Old England, peace-loving and ill-prepared as she was, but instant and fearless at the call of honour, thrilled my being . . . '[14]

In Berlin at the Reich chancellery, the Führer was astonished at the declarations of war from Britain and then France. 'It was plain to see how stunned he was,' wrote Hitler's press chief, Otto Dietrich.[15] Many in the Nazi leadership blamed Ribbentrop, who right to the last fuelled Hitler's fantasy that Britain would not fight. Philipp of Hesse had been just one of many who warned Hitler. Goering too had pushed for a negotiated settlement but was unable to counter Hitler's intransigent belief that he could invade Poland with impunity.

Ribbentrop had lived through a week of extremes. He had been feted by his revered Führer over the German pact with Moscow only to be banished from his presence when the British affirmed their support for Poland in late August. Mussolini, too, made it clear the Italians would not fight, a view that Ribbentrop had not expected. Ribbentrop cowered in his banishment, ill with anxiety as he turned over in his mind how to get back into Hitler's inner circle. His sense of wellbeing was so intimately linked to Hitler's approval that his exclusion brought on physical symptoms and emotional outbursts that were frightening enough to keep his subordinates out of the way. But when Germany invaded Poland and the democracies failed to act, he appeared redeemed in the Führer's eyes. Soon he was once more stoking up Hitler's fantasies and thirsting for war. Yet again there was a U-turn when Britain's ultimatum finally arrived. Goering simmered with rage. The war was 'Ribbentrop's doing', he told Goebbels years later. It was a view he had in common with the British ambassador, Nevile Henderson: 'I realised that no one did more than [Ribbentrop] to precipitate war,' he wrote. 'There is no hell in Dante's Inferno bad enough for Ribbentrop.'[16]

In villages across England the autumn ritual of bringing in the harvest was underway. At Barnwell in Northamptonshire the weather was close and the Duke of Gloucester found he could not count on the usual local support. It was not long before he too learned of his new role in the army as Chief Liaison Officer of the British Expeditionary Force or BEF. The duke and duchess's private plans to continue trying for a family had to be put on hold. Alice was to remain in England and was already involved in the creation of a Hospital Supply Depot at Barnwell, part of a network of medical relief across the country preparing for the invasion. Her husband would be at a secret location in France under the command of Lord Gort, the commander in chief of the British Expeditionary Force.[17]

The Gloucesters spent their last few hours together on 14 September in the army barracks at Camberley in Surrey. The intrusion of military formality made personal goodbyes impossible. Senior officers' gas masks were fitted and tested in a special sealed chamber. Official photographers and cinema operators began to gather to record their departure. Finally Gloucester's chauffeur, Prater, arrived to take him to Portsmouth.[18] 'My beloved Alice,' Gloucester wrote to her later, 'I did hate leaving you yesterday so very much that I could hardly keep a straight face.'[19] When he was sufficiently composed to turn around to wave, she was already out of view and soon the comforts of home were just a memory as he became involved in work in France.

What happened next did not auger well for the Duke of Gloucester's trip to France. The duke was in a long convoy from Cherbourg. The blackout was all-enveloping; the rain obscured vision still more. It was not long before the fourth car piled into the third, the fifth—with the duke and Lord Gort inside—crashed into the fourth. With sickening inevitability, the sixth and seventh rammed into the pile-up from behind. The duke wrote to the king and his wife to reassure them that his bruises were minor. This mishap did not dampen his enthusiasm. Gloucester set himself the goal of touring all the troops in the most advanced locations. He wanted to see the men's problems for himself, familiarise himself with British defences and keep the king informed of his observations.

The king had a loyal ally. In five weeks his brother travelled almost 4,000 miles. A diary from one of his staff (almost certainly his equerry Captain Howard Kerr) highlights the early teething problems. Apart from difficulties with the excitable French drivers in the blackout, there were curious local customs to adapt to. At their temporary headquarters in the Château de la Blanchardière at Le Mans, the French guard insisted they 'blew an appalling fanfare on their trumpets' whenever the commander in chief, Lord Gort, arrived or departed. French food was inevitably a problem. 'Ate an oyster in "family way." B— Awful.' As for French officers, the imposing General Georges came to visit, 'a smart looking old boy with about 28 medals!' After a cursory inspection of the guard of honour General Georges appeared more interested in lunch. It wasn't just the French who caused problems. One British officer in Nantes, a Colonel Barnes, appeared 'completely "poggled" at all times', wasted much time looking for his glasses 'which were dangling from his "starboard ear"', and totally 'bogged' the billeting—failing to provide sleeping quarters for arriving troops.[20] Despite the inevitable setbacks, Gloucester made the most of it. 'We are a most cheery party,' he told his mother, 'and everybody gets on well together.' The weather was lovely 'and it seems impossible that we are at war with anybody'.[21]

In his letters to the king Gloucester was discreet about staff failings. Regarding the billeting debacle in Nantes he commented merely 'we were not at all pleased with everything we saw'. When it came to essential matters he kept the king informed: the drainage on some pillboxes at the front was poor and the troops could be held up for want of vehicles, he observed.[22] The king thanked Gloucester, pointing out that it was hard to get news from the War Office which was frantically busy, but his letters 'tell me just what I want to know'.[23] Following a second car accident, Gloucester was keen to make sure his brother was aware 'I was not driving the car on either occasion'. The king soon learned of one serious complaint about life in the BEF from his brother. 'If Hitler is as

much in the dark as regards our movements as we out here are,' wrote Gloucester, 'he cannot know <u>very</u> much, if anything!!'[24]

Enthusiasm was somewhat less in evidence with the king's youngest brother.
The Duke of Kent's plans to go to Australia had to be hastily abandoned. Building on his diplomatic skills, he was assigned to the intelligence division of the
Admiralty, arriving at his post in Rosyth, north of Edinburgh, just before war
was declared, but he found it hard to adjust to long hours in an office.[25] His
cousin, Lord Louis Mountbatten, was commanding his own destroyer, HMS
Kelly, and tackling daring exploits on the high seas, and Gloucester was in the
thick of things in France, while he did little more exciting than contemplate the
mounting pile of papers on his desk.

Kent's letter to the king of 7 September provides a vivid snapshot of the
last-minute preparations in the Admiralty in Scotland. The commander in
chief's offices 'are old huts, relics of the last war', Kent explained. The ramshackle sheds leaked and were placed immediately next to oil tanks which had
no protection, 'so one bomb will not only destroy tanks but blow the offices
sky high!' Reports were coming in thick and fast from ships and coastguards
of submarine sightings, but they were mostly false alarms. Despite the fact that
the Home Fleet 'went off on a wild goose chase' they had managed to sink a
few submarines. No one had any accommodation, although Kent had been
invited to stay with Vice-Admiral Bertram Ramsay, who had been brought
back from retirement by Churchill to help deal with the threat to Britain's
coastal defences. The sociable Kent found him 'nice' but bafflingly unforthcoming, since he hardly said a word. The whole experience was 'like going to
school again', he confided to the king. He started looking around for a house of
his own; at the very least, Marina could join him.[26]

Marina was alone in London and when Chips Channon visited his neighbour's house on 5 September, he thought her eyes were a little tear-stained. In
preparation for their expected move to Australia, the Kents' London home in
Belgrave Square was stripped bare. The duchess sat in her private sitting room,
empty save for a couple of chairs. 'It was a sad little talk,' observed Chips. Marina,
surrounded by packing cases and dust sheets, was in transit as though suddenly
an alien, her thoughts oppressed by fears for her own family.[27] She was close
to her sisters, Olga and Elizabeth, but now these relationships were strained.
Elizabeth and her German husband, Count Toerring, had become the enemy
overnight, along with her cousins, including Christoph of Hesse's wife, Sophia.
Olga had confided the extreme pressures she and Prince Paul faced in Yugoslavia

where they were courted by the Nazi regime. Kent was pleased to learn that the king had invited his wife to stay at the palace where he knew she would have the comfort of family around her. 'Thank you so much for asking her,' he wrote on 7 September, grateful for his brother's thoughtfulness at such a time.[28]

As Kent adapted to life in the Admiralty, he left the office for inspections of Scottish defences. The Ministry of Supply were advising him where to visit, he told the king, but 'the Ministry of Information can't make up their minds whether I'm still to be shrouded in mystery or <u>not</u>! I think not! but they seem very muddled.'[29] At Britain's famous shipyards on the Clyde he observed a serious shortage of guns and trained men. The convoys were finding it a tough job looking after the ships, he reported. 'They have no idea of station keeping & straggle all over the place & run into the escort!' He saw the battleship HMS *Queen Elizabeth*, her great hull looming above them, newly painted in grey but none the less, he thought, 'a terrible target'. Further north he visited Invergordon where guns were being mounted and oil tanks removed away from the town to reduce the risk during an air raid. Everywhere he went along the coast he faced the bleak, unchanging view of the North Sea, the horizon stretching away for ever over dull grey waters. 'This is a gloomy place,' he confided to the king, '& the damp is terrible.'[30]

He missed the fun of his London life. Before the war, his appointments diary was invariably filled with a delightful schedule of balls, luncheons and visits to the theatre. Now, as he adapted to his Admiralty timetable, he let off steam in his private correspondence to Betty Lawson-Johnston.

Dearest Betty

Thank you for your letter. I'm sorry not to have answered before but I've been up here & have had little time. I work in an office all day! Not in my Line but it is interesting work—tho' I don't really have enough to do—I hope to change that but I had to start with something & this was the best they could suggest. I'm taking a house up here so at least my wife will come up for a little but the children will stay in the country where it is safe—What a b———y mess this all is—& what a change of plans for me & you and everyone. It is disappointing about Australia as I had done so much to get ready for it but now it is all wasted—I don't know when I'll be in London again and feel very cut off up here . . .

I have given up Belgrave Sq . . . It was lucky I didn't manage to sell Coppins—& so at least we have somewhere to go. One hesitates to think of all the misery & waste & destruction this war will lead to—and then what. How can anything ever be settled again? . . . I am depressed up here & hate being cut off from everything and don't feel I'm being at all useful.[31]

Within the royal family, the king's greatest concern was what to do with his oldest brother, the Duke of Windsor. His attitude to the European catastrophe was indifferent, almost cavalier. He hardly seemed bothered about the war; certainly there were no tears or planned heroics. He and Wallis remained abroad, savouring the last of the Mediterranean summer with long days lounging by the swimming pool at La Croë. On 3 September the duke was summoned to the telephone to take a call from the British ambassador in Paris. He returned to the pool where Fruity Metcalfe and Wallis were soaking up the sun. 'Great Britain has just declared war on Germany,' he said. 'I'm afraid in the end, this may open the way for world Communism.' His words were abruptly punctuated with a splash as he dived into the water.[32]

Windsor chose this, of all times, to pressurise the palace to meet his requirements for his wife. He refused to return unless he and the duchess were received by the king and queen, and his wife received by his family. Even Fruity Metcalfe was shocked to learn of the duke's demands. There is a war on, he reminded Windsor. Women and children were dying 'while *you* talk of your PRIDE'.[33] Officials at the palace took a similar view and an impasse was reached between the brothers. It fell to Churchill to find an expedient solution. Taking advantage of his position at the Admiralty, he simply asked Mountbatten to divert HMS *Kelly* to Cherbourg to bring the wayward duke home.

When the Windsors finally docked at Portsmouth on 13 September 1939 the duke was still secretly hoping for a reconciliation. He had been away for three years and felt uncertain of the response he might receive. As they came in to land in the inky blackness of Portsmouth harbour, moment by moment the humiliations piled up. Once again, Churchill had tried to muster some semblance of dignity for the former king, but it was not enough. A local guard of honour with tin hats stood to attention while a brass band played the National Anthem, although it was the short version, not the full version reserved for the king, the duke noted. A length of red carpet was hurriedly produced, at the end of which it was clear that no family had come to welcome him, not even his favourite, the Duke of Kent. There were to be no glittering palaces, no welcoming warmth for the ex-king and his lady. Nor was there a waiting royal car and chauffeur to whisk them off to the privacy and comfort of Fort Belvedere. Instead a functionary in the shape of Walter Monckton was sent to explain the cold realities of the situation.

There had been much anxiety in court about the prospect of the return of the duke and duchess. Elizabeth sought the advice of her mother-in-law about the best way of dealing with 'Mrs S'—her disdainful nickname for her sister-in-law. Queen Elizabeth knew how easily the ex-king undermined her husband and devoted herself to protecting George from the stresses of his demanding role as wartime leader, her serenity and ready smile a witness still in every war-time photograph. 'Her gracious smile has always been infectious,' announced the *Daily Mirror* on 12 September as Elizabeth toured ARP defences in South London. 'Today its an *example* to us all. Turn to pages 8 and 9 *and smile with them.*' The queen, wearing her powder-blue dress, holding her gas mask, at her husband's side, was an inspiration. 'A gloomy face never won anything, least of all a war,' the *Mirror* told its readers.[34]

Queen Elizabeth was convinced the king would suffer if his older brother returned. She told Queen Mary that she had no wish to receive the duchess, but was prepared to do so, if it was deemed necessary. It is likely that Queen Mary took the lead in setting the family line that the Windsors would not be welcome in any of the royal palaces. For years her oldest son had revelled in his superior position, but now she rallied to the defence of her second son. She would not receive the Duke and Duchess of Windsor. Arrangements were made for them to stay with Fruity Metcalfe and his wife, Lady Alexandra. It was left to George VI to meet Windsor alone.

Even without Wallis, he found his first encounter with his oldest brother since the abdication a trial. They met on 14 September in Buckingham Palace and as Windsor entered the room the king could see at once he looked well and had lost none of his magnetic charm. George VI had taken on the role of king in this splendid palace but his brother, exuding his customary, almost swaggering confidence, appeared to belong there. This was the brother whose very presence could make him feel inferior. Windsor invariably managed to reignite deep feelings of vulnerability in his brother and summon the most painful of childhood experiences where Bertie was always compared unfavourably. The duke told the king that he had already seen Winston Churchill. 'I expected that he had as he was very confident about himself,' the king noted, '& as to what he was going to do now that he was home.'[35]

The king was not by nature malicious or vindictive and did not want to prolong any rift but the duke's behaviour since his abdication had heightened his concerns. Windsor's self-made platform in Germany and his planned trip to America in 1937, his broadcast at Verdun in 1939, his showy 'second court' in France: all this suggested a man who would steal the limelight if he was back in England. Was he, or rather she, influencing the press even now? The *New York Times* took a favourable view of the duke's return. 'If three years ago, the head of the British Empire had not given up his throne it may well be that Hitler in 1939 would have shown more hesitation in precipitating a general war . . . '[36] Did American journalists seriously believe his brother would make a better job as king? Even perhaps avert war?

Oblivious to the way in which his own actions compounded their difficulties, the Duke of Windsor showed no sign of remorse. On the contrary, 'he seemed to be thinking only of himself', observed the king. He had always had a starring role and felt entitled to it; he expected a post that would command respect. The king took note that the duke failed to enquire after their mother, but did ask what his younger brothers were doing.[37] He wanted a similar gallant role for himself and, given a choice between working for the Regional Commissioner in Wales or with the army in France, he preferred Wales, doubtless envisaging himself on a tour of Home Commands around Britain, a dashing figure, rallying the troops, sure to impress Wallis.[38]

The king felt uneasy after the interview. Something about their exchange had raised a crucial issue of trust in his mind. If the duke remained in England he would be bound to upstage his brothers and lose no opportunity to display Wallis in front of the army; while she would almost certainly base herself in London and cause trouble. But if he worked in France, could he be trusted with military secrets? The king 'was very disturbed and walked up and down the room', observed Leslie Hore-Belisha, the Secretary of State for War. None of his forebears had been crowned while the previous monarch was still alive. 'Mine is not only alive, but very much so!'[39]

It is possible that the king was aware that his brother could turn to like-minded members of the aristocracy for backing. Less than two weeks into the war, the Duke of Westminster held a pro-peace meeting at Bourdon House, his Georgian residence in Mayfair in central London. As the richest man in England who owned large parts of London, the Duke of Westminster had much to lose from any bombing of the capital.[40] He was joined by a roll-call of peers, many from the House of Lords or who wielded power through their wealth or their links to the Conservative party, including the Marquis of Tavistock, Lord Noel-Buxton and Lord Harmsworth, whose brother, Lord Rothermere, ran the *Daily Mail* group. The pacifist members of the gentry could count on significant support. Some contemporary estimates indicated more than a third of the country was still in favour of peace, whatever the cost.[41]

The 8th Duke of Buccleuch also attended the anti-war meeting on 11 September 1939. It is not known whether Buccleuch, as Lord Steward in the King's Household, informed George VI of the pro-peace intrigues among the aristocracy but it is clear that when George VI met Hore-Belisha and General Sir Edmund Ironside, Chief of the Imperial General Staff (C.I.G.S.), on 16 September, his view had toughened against his brother. The duke and duchess must return to France, he insisted. The king confided to his mother that General Ironside did not 'mince matters' when it came to getting 'David's job settled'.[42] (The royal family called Windsor by his last name, David or 'D'.) Ironside 'put it to me very strongly' that in the British Military Mission in France, 'D would get access to the secret plans of the French'. Ironside was convinced he would pass them on to his wife. The king replied with a solemn warning. The generals in France 'must not tell D, or show him, anything really secret'.[43]

Saturday September 16th.

I saw H-B. & Ironside again after lunch, & the C.I.G.S. put it very strongly to me that in the British Military Mission in France, D would get access to the secret plans of the French, who would pass them on to his wife. He did not trust her. I replied tell Howard-Vyse that he must not tell D or show him anything really secret.

The points I made were :-
I. He & his wife must return to France.
II. Not to be attached to Commands at home, or inspect troops.
III. Not to be attached to a Corps in France.
IV. Not to be shown secret documents in the B.M.M. in Paris.

The king was concerned that his oldest brother David or 'D', was a security risk. Extract from his war diary, 16 September 1939 (THE ROYAL ARCHIVES © HER MAJESTY QUEEN ELIZABETH II)

Unaware of the scrutiny of his role, before the Duke of Windsor left for France he returned to Fort Belvedere, that little piece of England he had once called his home. Under his care, his staff had tended the lawns, trimmed the verges and shaped the conifers but now, as he and Wallis approached, the grounds were sadly neglected, the gardens rampant with weeds. The house had a forlorn air; the closed shutters accentuated the feel of a fortress. There were no signs of life; no housekeeper to shake down the furnishings and fling wide the windows. This was the house which he regarded as his creation, where he had held court and felt most himself, the central figure amongst his entertaining friends. Now the interior was dark, with not a vestige of its former gaiety; the shrouded furniture witness to a silence that forbade intrusion. It sent a clear message. England was no longer home. For Wallis, the neglect of their private home and her husband's smouldering anger at their treatment underlined what she saw as their 'little cold war with the palace'. She told her hostess, Lady Alexandra Metcalfe, that she had had enough of England and 'saw no reason ever to return'.[44]

Despite his isolation in Scotland, Kent gleaned all the salacious details of their visit and was quick to share the gossip with Betty. His letter of 22 September 1939 reveals that by this time he had aligned himself completely with the king. 'What about David and Wallis—' Kent wrote indiscreetly to Betty. 'Apparently his interview at BP [Buckingham Palace] consisted only of talking about himself! Thank God tho' they've left the country as its very tricky having him here & you never know what they're up to—I wonder if you saw them or heard any dirt about them? . . .'[45]

Britain lay as yet untouched by destructive German forces but the daily news from Poland gave the king a vivid impression of what was to come. 'It is so bewildering sitting here waiting,' he told his mother, 'but Elizabeth and I both go out and see what is going on.'[46] The nerve centre for information gathering was the Map Room in the Cabinet War Rooms, the government's hurriedly formed secret underground shelter in the heart of Westminster. In a thick fog of smoke, before the 'beauty chorus' of coloured phones, officials worked round the clock in their makeshift basement quarters to understand the state of the battle. The king found everyone 'very busy and . . . difficult to get hold of', but each day a summary was typed for himself and the military chiefs.[47] In the first two weeks of war it made grim reading.

The epic bravery of the Poles counted for nothing in the face of the German military might. The Polish air force was shattered. Civilians were rounded up and executed in their thousands. The ever-advancing German troops formed a raw red line on the horizon as villages were razed to the ground. By mid-September, the capital, Warsaw, was under siege. Then came the killer blow.

On 17 September the mighty Soviet Red Army invaded Poland. The 465,000-strong Soviet force rolled across its undefended eastern border. Poland was being crushed, divided in two between the mighty armies of the Nazis and the Communists. But still the Poles would not surrender and Warsaw continued its forlorn defence. 'It is all an amazing puzzle,' George VI entered in his war diary on 24 September. 'Many strange things have taken place.'[48] The Poles had fought magnificently but were unable to withstand the Nazi onslaught. And now looming uncertainly over Europe, casting a giant shadow from the east, was the threat from Stalin's Red Army. The mighty Russian bear seized control of eastern Poland. Both the German and Italian dictators were publicly anti-Bolshevik. How would they respond to this dangerous Soviet threat? And why had Britain been left alone? 'We must wait and see,' the king wrote anxiously.[49]

Fears ran riot across Europe about the power of the Soviets. 'Can still hardly believe that this is war and what is the outcome to be?' Kent wrote to Betty on 22 September, '& now with Russia coming in—one doesn't know what may happen. If only your country would come in <u>now</u> instead of waiting about & not making any sense—that would put heart into everyone & get all the neutrals and probably Italy in for us . . .'[50] There was a fear that the Fascists and the Bolsheviks together would destroy European civilisation.[51] It was hard to know which was the greater long-term menace. The merciless brutality of the Nazis in western Poland was matched by reports of mass executions in eastern Poland and the arrest and deportation of educated citizens. Soon the claws of the Soviet bear stretched north-east of Poland along the Baltic coast, as the Soviets insisted that their troops were stationed in Estonia, Latvia and Lithuania.

Would Britain fare any better with panzers and motorised divisions streaming in from her ports, the skies black with *Luftwaffe* planes? The king visited RAF Fighter Command at Stanmore and Bomber Command, based at Uxbridge at the start of the war, where he found the officers very shy in his presence, unable to say much. 'I must see them alone in future,' he noted. When he visited the army in Aldershot he found 'very few of the troops lived in the barracks for fear of air attack'. They were in tents under clumps of trees or in billets in the villages. So much would rest on these young shoulders.[52] 'There are no large movements of German troops etc. to the west yet,' he reassured his mother on 24 September.[53]

While the king could see British preparations for himself, far less was known about the French defences. The French could exude an air of secretiveness with their ally at the best of times, but the Duke of Windsor, as a major-general with the British Military Mission, was able to gain access to sectors of the French front. According to historian Michael Bloch, Windsor's observations held potential value for the British. French generals put great faith in their legendary Maginot Line, a remarkable system of fortifications built since the First World War along France's German border and widely believed to be impenetrable. Windsor noted, however, that 'the Maginot line does not seem to be an insuperable barrier' and, once broken, the roads were open to Paris. He identified specific points of weakness, crucially in the densely forested valley of the River Meuse in northern France. In places, 'there is a very narrow field of fire, and the entanglements could easily be approached up to within a few yards . . . there are no anti-tank defences.' He even described the low morale of the French and the in-fighting between their generals.[54] Unfortunately, on the British side there was no system in place to manage the duke or to recognise the worth of his observations. It was not long before he was straining at the leash for a more prominent position. He did not see himself tucked away on the French lines inspecting underground bunkers, but in a starring role, firing up the British front line and inspiring patriotism as he had as Prince of Wales in the Great War.

Windsor soon found a suitable pretext, which Gloucester duly reported to the king. 'He says he is not impressed by the French way of looking after a sector of these pill boxes & wants to compare it with ours,' wrote Gloucester, adding that if Windsor was not permitted to come he would argue 'he is not being given a chance to do his job properly'.[55] But when Windsor did get his chance to visit British troops on 18 October he misjudged the situation. The ex-king who had once been Supreme Commander-in-Chief of the Armed Forces simply could not humble himself to act according to the rank of major-general. The Duke of Gloucester watched his older brother with mounting alarm. 'To my horror I saw David taking the salute in spite of the Commander in Chief [Lord Gort] and Dill being present.' As an army man, he knew protocol was being breached. But Gloucester could see no diplomatic way to intervene, since his brother kept pushing himself forward. A smiling, tanned and gallant Windsor failed to ask about defences, but for line after line took the salute, the commander in chief increasingly disgruntled. Lord Gort finally brought the charade to an end.[56]

News of this errant behaviour reached the royal family. The king was uneasy. With the sinking of the battleship HMS *Royal Oak* just a few days earlier morale was low. His persistent fear that Windsor would upstage him and undermine his own authority as Commander of the British Army got the better of him. The king confided his annoyance to Gloucester, adding 'it will not happen again'.[57]

It wasn't long before Windsor detected what he called '"back door intrigue" against me' and complained to Churchill. He explained that he had recently discovered 'an order issued by the king behind my back, which in effect imposes a ban on my entering areas occupied by British troops'.[58] He was so angry about this he wanted to come back and confront the king in person, and appealed to Churchill for advice. But, for the first time, Churchill would not take his side. What was at stake was so immense that personal considerations were irrelevant. Churchill himself felt 'a kind of uplifted detachment from human and personal affairs'. The duke's ignoble stance was anathema to him.[59]

'Having voluntarily resigned the finest Throne in the world . . . it would be natural to treat all minor questions of ceremony and precedence as entirely beneath your interest and dignity,' Churchill wrote to the duke on 17 November. He appealed to his friend to rise above his petty grievances. 'By ignoring and treating with disdain all those small matters, your royal Highness would place yourself in an unassailable position, and clothe yourself in impenetrable armour. At a time like this when everybody is being ordered about, and millions of men are taken from their homes to fight, it may be for long years, and many others ruined, it is especially necessary to be defended in one's spirit against external misfortunes . . . '[60]

But Churchill's wise words failed to find their mark. The duke frequently slipped back to Wallis in Paris and she fuelled his grievances. If he was kept away from the British troops in France, she pointed out, the soldiers would assume he did not care about them. The Windsors would lose hearts and minds. She confided her feelings of injustice to Walter Monckton, complaining that they were trapped and ill-treated, and threw herself into counteracting these slights with her voluntary work for the French Red Cross, Section Sanitaire. There was no shortage of press interest in Wallis wearing a neatly fitting uniform and a big smile: the war heroine packing food parcels and taking medical supplies to the front.

Brooding and angry at the perceived slights against him, Windsor once again reached out to his circle of acquaintances to confide his hurt. According to Anthony Cave Brown's study of Sir Stuart Menzies, otherwise known as 'C', the head of British intelligence, this time Windsor turned to none other than the ex-kaiser of Germany himself.[61]

The ex-kaiser, a grandson of Queen Victoria, was viewed by Windsor's father George V as history's 'greatest criminal known'. Near the end of the First World

War he had been forced to abdicate his throne and had slipped ignominiously into the Netherlands. He bought a seventeenth-century estate near Utrecht and lived the life of quiet country squire, managing the grounds and obsessively chopping down trees, as though he had never wielded power, never seen the French battlefields and was in no way responsible for the young men of Europe who had died in their millions. Unlike his nephew, Philipp of Hesse, he was never part of Hitler's inner circle, although one of his sons, Prince Auwi, was an ardent supporter of the Nazi party. After the defeat of Poland the ex-kaiser's personal adjutant, General von Dommes, wrote to Hitler to congratulate him on the success of the *Blitzkrieg*. The kaiser and his family 'remained loyal', he told Hitler, and indeed the kaiser had one son and eight grandchildren serving in the German armed forces.

If this was the man from whom the Duke of Windsor sought advice, the correspondence between the two has never seen the light of day. An alternative theory has Charles Bedaux as the source for the German ambassador to The Hague in the Netherlands, Dr Julius von Zech-Burkersroda.[62] Either way, it is beyond doubt that Zech-Burkersroda was soon writing to Ribbentrop's second in command at the Foreign Office, Ernst von Weizsäcker. 'Through personal relationships I might have the opportunity to establish certain lines leading to the Duke of Windsor . . . ' he began.[63]

Hitler talked of Germany's desire for peace on 6 October before the Reichstag. He gloated over the success of the German *Blitzkrieg*: 'in all of history there has scarcely been a comparable military achievement'. Why should any war be fought in the West, he asked? He denounced Churchill and claimed that Germany only sought peace. England was to blame for seizing 'the first opportunity in order to resume the fight with Germany'.

These words did not sound like a sane man conducting complex hostilities and at an evening meeting with Chamberlain at the palace this was confirmed. As Chamberlain spoke, the growing gloom underlining the ominous feelings associated with Hitler, the king learned something of the dictator's headquarters. Chamberlain's description had come from a Swedish intermediary, Johan Dahlerus, who had recently met Hitler and Goering. Both men wanted to stop the war, claimed Dahlerus. Hitler had been 'in the clouds' while Goering was a worried man. Goering had looked out of the window and said, 'I am a soldier. What I have seen in Poland I don't wish to see anywhere else.' Hitler was

Monday October 9th

I saw Winston Churchill later, to tell him of my visit to the Fleet. He seemed very sleepy, stifling yawns or trying to, or perhaps it was boredom!! He was also very busy making drafts of the reply to Hitler. He wanted a much sterner reply, but I said do leave the door open at this stage. Hitler can't be having it all his own way at home. Winston is difficult to talk to but in time I shall get the right technique I hope.

Extract from the king's war diary, 9 October 1939. 'I saw Winston Churchill . . . He seemed very sleepy, stifling yawns . . . or perhaps it was boredom!! He was also very busy making drafts of the reply to Hitler. He wanted a much sterner reply, but I said do leave the door open . . . Winston is difficult to talk to, but in time I shall get the right technique I hope.' (THE ROYAL ARCHIVES © HER MAJESTY QUEEN ELIZABETH II)

disconnected from reality. Forgetting that he was at war with England, he suggested British negotiators could come to Berlin.[64] It sounded as though Laurel and Hardy were in charge and that anything terrifying or bizarre might happen.

Nothing could shake Chamberlain's conviction that the German leadership could not be trusted with peace treaties. Britain was fighting for the defence of freedom, he declared as he rejected the peace opening on 12 October. 'To surrender to wrong doing would spell the extinction of all hope.' Ribbentrop dismissed Chamberlain in a gloating speech from Danzig as he launched a tirade on the 'war guilt' of England.[65]

During the autumn of 1939 Hitler's attack in the West was expected at any moment. Constant rumours, with the attendant rush of anxiety, became a part of daily life. Churchill told the king a heavy air attack on Britain was more likely than a land attack on France.[66] A Yugoslav report warned of a parachute attack on an English east-coast port as a prelude to a seaborne expedition.[67] The king's distant cousin, King Leopold III of Belgium, was told by his diplomats in Berlin that the western attack was about to be launched through the Low Countries of Belgium and the Netherlands. King Leopold was so certain of his intelligence that he set off in the blackout, driving through the night to The

Hague, to warn Queen Wilhelmina of the Netherlands. Both countries had declared their neutrality. On 7 November, the King of Belgium and Queen of the Netherlands offered to mediate between the British, French and the Germans. King Leopold, a great-grandson of Queen Victoria's Uncle Leopold, appealed directly to George VI. The British government remained firm. Was all of Europe to buckle under Hitler's megalomaniac whim: *Blitzkrieg*, bombs falling, cities pulverised until they were white-hot bonfires? In spite of the threat, made all too real by media photographs of Poland, George VI replied on behalf of his ministers explaining why Britain had to fight on. His conviction was unwavering. 'The old reason for our being at war with him still holds good,' he wrote in his diary.[68]

The king and queen continued with their duties with quiet determination. On 28 November, they led the opening of Parliament. The ancient symbolic ceremony in the House of Lords chamber formed a marked contrast to Hitler's address to the Reichstag. There was no frenzied applause or extravagant emotion. In keeping with the national mood, the event was simple and dignified; no royal coach, no ostentatious display.[69] When he had spoken the king took the queen's hand and together they walked back down the chamber to a waiting car.

As the winter set in there was a growing unease in Britain that Chamberlain was not prosecuting war effectively. The phoney war was confusing. No attack had come in the West. Although the Navy and merchant shipping faced enemy fire at sea, the land war always seemed to be happening somewhere else. At the end of November 1939, Finland, in northern Europe on the Baltic Sea, faced the might of the Red Army as 450,000 Soviet troops poured over its border with the Soviet Union. But all was quiet on the western front.

After Hitler's dramatic attack on Poland annihilating the country with brutal swiftness, and England's response, stumbling into war, honouring its treaty with Poland but doing nothing to help militarily, came a period of relative calm. The expected *Blitzkrieg* did not come. Across Britain long golden autumn days saw the harvest in, normality returned, the evacuees went home. There was no war. 'Everything goes on here the same,' the Duke of Kent told Prince Paul that December. 'It seems years since war started—and the boredom is immense, three months without anything really happening.'[70] Wallis put it more succinctly, expressing her ennui: this was the 'Bore War'.

The king wanted to dispel the growing complacency and unite his far-flung subjects with a sense of purpose for whatever the next year might bring. Even with Logue's constant support, the Christmas speech remained an ordeal but he recognised its importance, this year especially. He praised the work of the

Royal Navy, the Royal Air Force, and the British Expeditionary Force. Like everyone else, George VI wondered what was to come. Europe was drawn into unknowable horror. England was a small offshore island in the sights of unscrupulous and powerful opponents. Was hope even possible? In a clear voice he finished with a poem which resounded across the world. 'I said to the man who stood at the Gate of the Year, "Give me a light that I may tread safely into the unknown." And he replied, "Go out into the darkness, and put your hand into the hand of God. That shall be to you better than light, and safer than a known way." May that Almighty Hand guide and uphold us all.'[71]

His words had a deep impact on his listeners. The Duke of Gloucester was one of thousands who heard the king's speech from their Spartan army quarters. He had a new radio—a gift from the king; 'the best one we have here,' Gloucester told him.[72] Like so many of the men in France that Christmas, he felt the desolation of waiting away from home for the attack in a foreign country. The roads were like glass. Clothes were never dry. Everyone seemed to have the flu. The wind could only come from the Arctic, freezing fingers, noses, eyes, everything: and no cure until wrapped in the warmth and comfort of home.

Letters were passed around the family and sent on to Gloucester. Alice enjoyed her stay, the king wrote from Sandringham. 'Without Mama, it was rather a relief this year, and the ball room evenings were confined to two,' he confided. 'We did well with the shooting and got over 3,000 head.'[73] Queen Mary wrote from Badminton, where she was joined by George and his family. She had tried hard to re-create the Christmassy atmosphere of Sandringham. 'The tree looked lovely in the big Hall with presents on tables as at Sand. My tea to the village and evacuee children was a great success, 150 of them—first tea in servants hall, then presents in big Hall followed by carols . . . Best love Harry darling . . . I am ever Yr devoted Mama, Mary.'[74]

Early in January once again, bad news. 'That tiresome man Hitler has done something to cause the cancellation of all leave for the present,' Gloucester told Alice. 'It affects Holland, Belgium and the French as well.'[75] Once again, the invasion was imminent. Once again, troops braced themselves for their worst fears. Once again, anxious look-outs scanned the wintry scene, waiting, eyes searching through bare trees across a frosted landscape for any sign of movement on the horizon with the familiar feeling of foreboding.

5

INTO THE UNKNOWN

'Give me a light that I may tread safely into the unknown . . . '

—George VI, 25 December 1939

January of 1940 was the coldest for forty-five years. There were snow storms and ice storms across the country. Trying to unwind in a stinging east wind at Sandringham in Norfolk, the king could not allay his fears for his troops in France as the 'war of nerves' continued unabated. 'I'm so glad you are able to stay on at Sandringham,' Kent wrote sympathetically from Scotland on 6 January, 'as I am sure it will do you so much good after London.' Kent had missed his elder brother Albert, but he added: 'Mama would have been upset I think if we hadn't gone there—we had a quiet Xmas and Mama enjoyed herself even to the paper hats we had to wear one night at dinner!'[1]

When the king returned to London in mid-January, all was familiar, the streets as yet unspoiled by war. Long stretches of the Thames were frozen, a white sheet of ice threading through parts of London. At the palace many treasures had been moved into safe storage but the gracious rooms and ornate interiors confirmed that he presided over a rich and secure heritage as his ancestors had done. There were repeated scares that Germany would invade the Netherlands and Belgium or the Balkans, George VI wrote in his war diary, each one with the attendant feelings of alarm. But no attack was forthcoming. Through the window the skyline was the same. People looked carefree: mothers with prams, walkers with dogs, occasionally children skating by. The very air seemed distilled by centuries of peace. There was nothing to indicate how rapidly the enemy could change all this into another Warsaw.

George VI knew that his War Cabinet faced growing criticism. The Allies had done little to help the Poles whose country was now wiped off the map.

Finland too was getting precious little support. 'The Finns are doing well,' Kent continued, 'but I wonder how long they can last without a great deal more help.'[2] The newspapers were full of the 'indomitable spirit' of the vastly out-numbered Finns as they battled for their country from the frozen shores of the Arctic Ocean to the Baltic Sea in the south. Around 150,000 Finns took on over a million Soviet troops, but the Finns could fight on skis and 'were making rings around Russian soldiery' declared *The Times* on 4 January.[3] In raids of epic daring, they emerged at furious speed from frozen landscapes camouflaged in white, swooping on cumbersome Soviet lines, machineguns blazing and hurling a new type of petrol bomb which acquired the nickname 'the Molotov cocktail'. These silent ski troops were dubbed 'White Death' by the Soviets. Once injured and immobilised, a man would freeze to death; tens of thousands of Soviets died. The British government had not yet taken action. Could the Finns hold out?[4]

For the Duke of Windsor, who made a short visit to London without the king's permission in early January, the Winter War highlighted his conviction that the Soviets were a far greater threat than the Fascists. Ugly details of Sta-lin's regime filtered through the news reports. 'Russian high command . . . is reported to have been purged,' announced *The Times* editorial on 4 January. Soviet soldiers were once roused by God and country but now 'Stalin has "liq-uidated" these ideals'.[5] In Windsor's view, Europeans should unite against the Soviet menace.

Windsor found support for the idea that it was not too late to negotiate peace with the Germans from his old friend, the once 'devoted tiger', Max Aitken, Lord Beaverbrook. Under his leadership the *Daily Express* had grown to become the bestselling paper in the world. 'The first Baron of Fleet Street,' as he was known, was also half-hearted about the 'phoney war', or 'sitzkrieg', with the Germans, a view he shared with Walter Buccleuch, the king's Lord Stew-ard, as well as other prominent aristocrats such as the Duke of Westminster.[6] Beaverbrook was in scurrilous mood when he met the ex-king at the home of his lawyer, Walter Monckton. It did not take long before Windsor was predict-ing the likely fall of France and urging the case for Britain to make peace with Germany. Beaverbrook impetuously backed his old friend, urging him to 'get out of uniform, come home, and after enlisting powerful City support, stump the country, in which case he predicted that the Duke would have tremendous success'.[7]

Walter Monckton, sober as a judge, grave with the responsibility of steering the adventurous duke from excitingly wayward paths back to the straight and narrow, warned Windsor later that their conversation was not only preposterous, but also high treason. In front of Beaverbrook, he confined himself merely to mentioning that should the duke live in England, taxes would be payable, which rapidly decided Windsor on another, less frightening course.

Once back in Paris at the Military Mission, the weight of Monckton's warning receded. Bruised by his reception in London where he had failed to make any progress on the personal grievances close to his heart, it appears that Windsor was once again indiscreet. By 27 January Julius von Zech-Burkersroda, the German ambassador to the Hague, was in a position to write to State Secretary Baron von Weizsäcker in Berlin with an accurate account of the duke's recent trip. Windsor was dissatisfied, explained Zech, 'and seeks a field of activity . . . which would permit him a more active role. In order to obtain this objective he was recently in London. There, however, he achieved nothing and is supposed to be disgruntled over it.' Windsor was being frozen out, observed the German ambassador accurately, adding that this 'fronde forming around W . . . might acquire a certain significance'. Weizsäcker at once saw the potential of this line of communication and passed Zech's report to Ribbentrop, who was always eager for any scrap of information that might curry favour with Hitler.[8]

Ribbentrop did not have to wait long. Less than a month later, there was more news from the 'Duke of W' and this time it went well beyond his personal gripes. Windsor had attended a recent Allied War Council meeting to discuss plans for neutral Belgium. The neutral countries were posing a serious problem for the Allies. While Belgium protected her neutrality in order not to provoke the Germans, Allied troops could not enter the country to prepare defences, but instead had formed a line of defence along the French-Belgium border. The Allied War Council discussed its strategy should Germany invade Belgium. According to Zech, Windsor reported that the military argued the line should be held at the Belgian-French border, 'even at the risk that Belgium should be occupied' by the Germans. Political leaders at the Allied War Council 'are said to have at first opposed this plan'. Windsor, doubtless wearing the invisible credentials of 'being in the know', created the impression that the weight of the meeting swung behind the military view: the Allies would not occupy Belgium if the Germans invaded.[9]

Historians have pointed out that in fact the Allied plan was the reverse. If the Germans attacked, Allied troops would move into Belgium to defend it at all costs. Was Windsor involved in some clever unauthorised double-bluff of his own making? Or was he merely misinformed? Either way, George VI's prediction had proved correct. By being prepared to discuss not just his grievances, but also the content of the Allied War Council meeting with the enemy, or those that could make contact with the enemy, he had crossed a new line. Ribbentrop, delighted to have established such a prestigious source of information passed the report from Julius Zech to Hitler himself.[10]

The Duke of Gloucester dealt with the war of nerves by throwing himself into the preparations. In one week alone he travelled many hundreds of miles visiting army bases across France. At Rennes, he inspected the storage facilities for the mounting stacks of ammunition and supplies. At Nantes he visited workshops for vehicle maintenance and repair. The port of Le Havre was preparing for the repair of guns and tanks. At Marseilles he met troops on their way to the Middle East.[11] The bitter chill remained as the mistral howled up the Rhone valley depressing spirits; 'about the coldest I have ever known,' Gloucester told Alice. 'I think I hate this country and war more than ever. It is such an awful waste of everything.'[12]

Hearing of his brother's low spirits, the king was quick to reply with encouragement. 'Gort tells me that your report on what you saw at Marseilles & other places has been most useful,' he told him on 9 March 1940. The king had urged Gloucester to leave GHQ and gain experience in the forward area in northern France at the Belgian frontier and now he counselled Gloucester to apply himself. 'You must work at the job yourself to make it a success.'[13]

Gloucester joined the command of Major-General D.G. Johnson who was responsible for the defences around Lille, not far from the Belgian border with France. Soon Gloucester's letters covered every aspect that George VI might wish to know, from the length of time needed to build communicating trenches to each pillbox to the shortage of trained officers.[14] While Gloucester invariably threw himself into the physical challenge, his brother-in-law, Lord William Scott, the younger brother of Walter Buccleuch, who was in attendance found the training exercises for the battle ahead were something of an ordeal. They could last all night and brought back all the discomforts of drills during the First World War.[15]

The king was also aware of his youngest brother's frustrations. Tours of Scottish naval dockyards and civil defences were relieved by occasional diplomatic tasks, such as meeting the inspirational Polish prime minister in exile, General Wladyslaw Sikorski.[16] But the duke confided to Prince Paul that his job at the Admiralty was 'an awful waste of time'. He went to see Chamberlain to ask if he could find him something 'I could do, which . . . would be really useful to the country'.[17]

Kent rented a home, Pitlever House near Rosyth, and the duchess came to stay when she could for private breaks together in spite of the all-enveloping war. This was less easy when the king, keen for the royal family to show a united front, approved the appointment of the Duchess of Kent as commandant of the Women's Royal Naval Service (WRNS known as the Wrens) and the Duchess of Gloucester to be an air commandant in the Women's Auxiliary Air Force (WAAF).[18] *The Times* court circular soon carried references to their busy schedules, although in the interests of security the details were vague. The Duchess of Kent visited naval establishments 'on the south east coast today' or 'in a north-east port'. Marina preferred to remain out of uniform like the queen, but Churchill would have none of it. She was compliant, obeying his order, but the beautiful duchess balked at the idea of being encased in military garb and invariably appeared with a few discreet accessories: high heels, jewels, or even a low-cut collar. The press took a great interest even if the glamorous duchess was just visiting a cabbage patch and talking to Wrens about their 'Dig for Victory' campaign.[19]

As Marina took on her first appointments as an air commandant in early March, the Winter War in Finland was reaching a brutal climax. The world had been witness to the weakness of the Red Army over the winter, but Stalin would not be made a fool of. With the spring thaw, he launched a new Soviet offensive to crush the Finns. The exhausted Finns were unable to hold out against an endless re-supply of Soviet troops without Allied support— which failed to arrive in time. At the palace the king found the prime minister 'very worried' when they met on the evening of 12 March 1940. Chamberlain explained that he was about to send eight bombers, with the promise of more to follow, on condition that the Finns did not surrender to the Soviets. But it was all too late.[20]

At Buckingham Palace the next day it was impossible to get through to the Foreign Office until 1 pm, 'as all the lines were engaged by the foreign press I suppose', noted George VI. Finally he and Elizabeth learned the rumours were true: the Winter War was over. The Foreign Office confirmed the Finns had surrendered to the Soviets on far harsher terms than anyone had suspected. A large swathe of land, critical industrial concerns, immense saw mills and power stations: all this now passed into Soviet ownership. Would they be used against Scandinavia, or even against Britain? The Finnish surrender 'has come as a shock to us', he confided to his diary on 13 March 1940, '& I am sure . . . it will be said that the democracies have failed again to protect a small nation against the power of aggression.'[21]

However honourably his ministers conducted themselves as gentlemen, it was not enough. Whichever way they turned seemed wrong. It was as if he was standing on the very threshold of chaos. Was it possible he was witness to the complete disintegration of everything Britain stood for? At a meeting with Sir John Simon, the chancellor, he found these feelings were shared. The whole country, said Simon, 'had a feeling of frustration that our ideas had not gone right' and that neutral countries felt Britain could not help them. For both men, Britain was suffering 'because we were honest & honourable in our deal-ings with Neutrals' while Germany 'had put the fear of God into them'.[22] In the sanctuary of his private sitting room, listening to the wireless and studying the map of Europe, it was hard for the king to picture what might happen next. German propaganda provided a continual rush of ominous threats. There were troubling reports of German merchant ships being adapted to carry troops. German vessels, large and small, on the high seas might be kitted out as trans-ports. But which port was the target? Any number of neutral countries could be liable to a capricious and brutal attack—perhaps Britain herself.[23] 'I am very worried over the general situation,' George VI wrote. 'Anything we do, or try to do, appears to be wrong and gets us nowhere . . . '[24]

The Duke of Windsor was under no such strain. The boundaries of Europe were changing. The foreboding of a bigger land war was in the air. But this was the time that the Duke of Windsor strolled into Cartier in Paris, precious stones jangling in his pockets. He was not thinking of war, but Wallis. His devotion undimmed, he wanted the stones refashioned to make a truly dazzling creation, something very large and showy: an exotic diamond clip, adorned with rubies, sapphires and emeralds in the shape of a flamingo. This was the one thing he could do for Wallis, and he would do it. She loved exciting new designs in a modern cut.

Norway, Belgium, Denmark, the Netherlands—perhaps even France: who knew where the next threat might fall. The world was at war, chaos ruled, but whatever direction the war took the Windsors' position was unique. There was every reason to feel relaxed in the hushed and discreet surroundings of Cartier Paris as the duke discussed the shape of the jewel on 4 March with their design-ers.[25] It was a complicated shape with tail feathers and he did not want any part of it digging into Wallis if she leaned over, making it awkward to wear. A solu-tion was found: delicate retractable legs. Cartier, delighted to do business with a former King of England, obliged.

Easter of 1940 was calm; eerily calm. There were no crises, the king noted in his diary. There was even time to forget the strain of the phoney war and ride out with the princesses into Windsor Great Park following the familiar paths through ancient trees covered in a delicate tracery of tender spring growth. It was just like the precious pre-war days: the king with his family, 'we four'. But it was not to last.

On Tuesday 9 April he and Elizabeth were listening to the wireless at 8 am. The dispassionate voice of the BBC newsreader invaded the space with words that were hard to take in. Germany had attacked the neutral countries of Denmark and Norway. German troops were in Copenhagen, the capital of Denmark. The enemy navy was at sea in force. The War Cabinet had already met at 6.30 and would meet again at noon. Norwegian ports were under attack.[26]

The king went to the War Rooms of the Admiralty later that day to see the positions of the British battle fleet for himself. The rooms were crowded and smoke-filled, the atmosphere hot and stale. The telephones did not stop ringing as officers tried to keep up with the movement of the fleet. The picture was confusing but it was hard not to feel that Britain had been outwitted once again. Denmark was unable to defend herself, having little more than a police force. The Danish king, Christian X, and his government had already capitulated. It took barely two hours. In Norway, the best information pointed to a stark conclusion: the key ports were already in German hands despite the efforts of the British Navy. All around him was frantic activity but for the king there was a constant nagging worry that Germany had been able to succeed in taking the Norwegian ports 'because we were too righteous' against an aggressor 'that stuck at nothing'. George VI listened to the BBC news at 6 pm and again at 9 pm hoping for a clearer picture. He felt the frustrations of the situation deeply. 'I have spent a bad day,' he confided to his diary that night. 'Everybody working at fever heat except me.'[27]

George VI had last seen his 'Uncle Charles', King Haakon VII of Norway, on a wintry day in London in late November 1938, at the funeral of his wife, Maud, the youngest daughter of Edward VII and Alexandra of Denmark. Before the day was out he learned that his 68-year-old Uncle Charles was in flight from Oslo. What he did not know was that Hitler himself had given instructions that the monarch must not escape.[28] German warships had entered the fjord at Oslo with a team of Gestapo agents on board under instruction to capture the Norwegian king and senior government officials. Fierce resistance by the Norwegians at Oslo gave King Haakon and his government time to flee. A Nazi supporter and Norwegian politician known as Vidkun Quisling, who had been painstakingly courted by German diplomatic staff reporting to Ribbentrop, now saw his moment. He seized power in Oslo and broadcast a message declaring himself prime minister of Norway.

Uncle Charles was thrown into the worst crisis of his life. A German ultimatum ordered him to install a Nazi puppet government, with Vidkun Quisling at its head. Should he fail to do so, the alternative would be far worse for Norway. At a momentous meeting in impromptu headquarters 125 miles north-east of Oslo, the King of Norway spoke gravely to his ministers. German retribution if thwarted did not need to be underlined. His brother, King Christian of Denmark, had surrendered, but King Haakon took a different view. If the Norwegian cabinet wished to appoint Quisling, then he would abdicate, he said, but he could never meet the German demands. 'It would conflict with all that I have considered to be my duty as King of Norway.'[29] King Haakon's passionate conviction made a deep impression. In spite of the danger to their country, the cabinet supported the king.

That night the Norwegian government's stand against their Nazi invaders was broadcast. Norway would resist the German attack as long as possible, whatever the consequences. The *Luftwaffe* sought revenge and bombed the village of Nybergsund where the king was staying. Haakon and his son fled into the surrounding country, deep in snow, heading for the northern coast. George VI felt as though the whole world 'is looking at us now waiting for our counterattack on Germany in Norway'.[30]

As Norway faced the Nazi onslaught, the Duke of Gloucester found it 'very trying' waiting in France, he confided to Alice. There was deep frustration in the British Army guarding the French-Belgian border but the appalling prospect of a German *Blitzkrieg* unfolding simultaneously on the Low Countries could not be dismissed. Gloucester told Alice that he expected the order to drive into Belgium to pre-empt a German invasion there. Despite the fate of neutral Norway, he found it very worrying that Belgium and the Netherlands still clung to neutrality in order not to provoke a German attack. King Leopold of Belgium, a friend of Gloucester's from school days, would not permit Allied troops to enter his country and prepare defences. For Gloucester this was a perilous kind of safety. 'These small neutral countries are most awful fools as they must see that Germany will eat them up one by one,' he wrote to his wife.[31]

By the end of April the king found the news from Norway 'all very depressing'. He knew the situation was dire, far worse than the public realised, the Germans in control of most of the country.[32] King Haakon and members of his cabinet were beaten back to the northern tip of Norway within the Arctic Circle. He and his son took refuge in a log cabin in the forest with the local rifle association for their protection. The evacuation of British troops in early May heightened divisions in the War Cabinet. 'Winston still seems to be causing a good deal of trouble according to the PM,' George VI wrote in his diary on the weekend of 30 April. Chamberlain blamed Churchill for critical delays in landing more troops in central Norway because he was worried about losing big ships. 'The PM is having another talk to Winston tonight laying down what he can and cannot do . . . '[33]

But ironically as news of the Norwegian campaign became widely known, the anger of MPs and public turned on Chamberlain, and not Churchill, who was primarily responsible for the campaign. For all his efforts, Chamberlain was increasingly under fire, cruelly transformed by his critics into 'the Old Umbrella', a relic from another age, known by his signature umbrella. The prime minister faced a hostile House on 7 May 1940, as one member after another stood up to vent their fury at his handling of the war. In a moment of high drama, Leopold Amery, Conservative MP for Birmingham South, rounded on his leader and condemned him, echoing the famous words of Cromwell to Parliament centuries before. 'You have sat too long here for any good you have been doing. Depart, I say, and let us have done with you. In the name of God, Go!'[34]

But Chamberlain did not offer his resignation to the king when he saw him that evening. The prime minister had the strained air of a man buckling under a burden too big to carry. He still 'spoke with a smile', noted the king, and hoped to continue by creating a coalition with the Labour party. George VI believed in his prime minister and disliked the way the government and the press were subjecting him to a 'stab in the back' at such a time. He offered to appeal to the Labour party to unite behind Chamberlain on his behalf.[35] But on 8 May there was a vote in the House of Commons in which it was clear that he was dismissed as yesterday's man, of no more use than the nickname given him by his critics. Quietly, rigidly, stiff upper lip unwavering, 'the Old Umbrella' walked out of the House, looking 'bowled over' according to one of his loyal allies. But the cheers of his supporters were drowned out by the humiliating chant, 'Go in God's name, go!' echoing around the chamber and still audible as the doors closed behind him.

George VI felt the vacuum in leadership the following day when the question continued to dominate Parliament. It was a bright and sunny May day, but for the king, impossible to relax. He waited impatiently for news. Now of all times was no moment for indecision. His prime minister still hoped to head a national coalition; or if not him, his like-minded friend and colleague, Lord Halifax. The king's loyalty to his prime minister was unshaken and he and Elizabeth felt that he was being hounded unfairly. Over this issue they were united, Elizabeth recognising what she called Chamberlain's 'wisdom and high purpose' in staking so much to try to prevent war.[36] Now that events had turned against him his treatment was shameful.

At 4.15 pm on 9 May Chamberlain summoned Lord Halifax and Churchill to Downing Street. The leadership issue was discussed and once again remained undecided. Later that day, Chamberlain renewed his offer to Labour to collaborate in a national coalition led by him. The answer was a resolute no. 'An unprofitable day,' the king wrote in his diary.[37] The indecision that had become the prime minister's hallmark continued to the last and was rapidly overtaken by events as Hitler pressed his advantage.

Events did not wait for Chamberlain. Before dawn on 10 May 1940, out of the night, German tanks and infantry emerged across 150 miles of the border into the Low Countries. Through the darkness, across peaceful land, the front blazed with flame and gunfire and all the accompanying horrors of war throughout Belgium, the Netherlands and Luxembourg. From above, German bombers dived over airfields, communications and military targets, unleashing terror.

To the north in the Netherlands an airborne assault took the Dutch by surprise. In the small hours, high above sleeping coastal towns, the *Luftwaffe* hummed overhead, disappeared into the night sky over the North Sea and circled back to bomb the Dutch airfields. They were swiftly followed by German planes dropping 5,000 paratroopers over the leading industrial port of Rotterdam and other cities, their parachutes gliding down silently over strategic sites. The paratroopers were under orders to seize bridges and airfields and then move to The Hague, the Dutch seat of government, to seize the royal family and leading ministers. To the east the German Eighteenth, Sixth and Fourth Armies blasted into the Netherlands and Belgium. In Brussels the anti-aircraft fire was deafening and the Belgian army hurried to the counter-attack, destroying bridges to slow down the enemy.

At 5.30 am Lord Gort received the alert that the attack on the western front had begun. The signal went out for a million Allied soldiers to go forward into Belgium. In anticipation that the Germans would attack France through Belgium, three French armies and the British Expeditionary Force were massed along the French-Belgium border. The vast operation 'Plan D' as these armies moved north to defend Belgium sprang into action. Western Europe had begun its long descent into hell.[38]

The Duke of Gloucester woke that night to the sounds of war. The skies were alive with aircraft and in the distance intermittent gunfire and the scream of air-raid sirens disturbed the night. 'Blast Hitler!' he wrote to Alice.[39] He had been due to go on leave, but 'Hitler has done me down again' he told her. He was back at GHQ at Arras, having returned to Lord Gort's command on 2 May. Even at this distance, 100 miles from Brussels, the sound of bombing brought home the reality of the western front.

As all hell broke out across the Channel, late in the afternoon in London, Chamberlain, the humiliating Commons defeat still fresh, went to the palace and tendered his resignation. It was a difficult task. Chamberlain was a broken man. 'I . . . told him how grossly unfairly I thought he had been treated,' the king wrote, '& that I was terribly sorry that all this controversy had happened.' But in the restorative peace of the elegant palace room, in an air of unhurried calm, both men were able to discuss in a rational way who should be the next prime minister. 'I of course suggested Halifax,' continued the king. For him, Halifax was the obvious choice; trustworthy, a man of sound judgement, a safe pair of hands. George VI was very disappointed to learn that Halifax was not keen. 'Then I knew that there was only one person who I could send for to form a Government who had the confidence of the country and that was Winston.' Chamberlain confirmed that 'Winston was the man to send for'.[40]

For George VI this was not an easy choice. Temperamentally the two men formed a striking contrast. Churchill with his commanding personality displayed all those regal attributes expected of a monarch. He appeared impetuous, undaunted by any challenge, almost a law unto himself, giving cause for his detractors on occasion to refer to him as a 'gangster' or 'pirate'.[41] The king, who could be diminished utterly at the prospect of a speech, felt he could never be comfortable in the company of such a man. For years the two had held different views. Before the war, the king had favoured appeasement, while Churchill had ridiculed it. It was hard to shake off the feeling that he thirsted for war. During the first air raid over London, Churchill's bodyguard, Walter Thompson, had found him 'staring up into the sky like a warhorse scenting battle'.[42] Britain's war horse exuded an almost cavalier sense of fearlessness. And there was also a question over his judgement. George VI was aware of Churchill's support for his brother which continued even now. Could he really trust such a man? How was he ever going to get on with this pushy politician? Chamberlain, safe and solid as silver, was to be replaced by this emotional maverick in Britain's hour of great need. 'Only in very exceptional circumstances would he consent to WSC's being made PM,' the king had allegedly confided to President Roosevelt in Washington.[43]

Churchill was in the Admiralty at 6 pm on 10 May 1939 when a message arrived summoning him to the palace. He drove along the Mall, a two-minute journey. Newspaper placards proclaimed the horror: 'Paris raided', 'Brussels bombed', 'Lille bombed' and even 'Bombs in Kent'.[44] There was no crowd or press waiting at the palace gates, the leadership crisis and the 'quiet conversations' of the previous day eclipsed by what Churchill saw as 'the splintering crash of this vast battle'. He was swiftly taken to see the king.

Their exchange that evening in Buckingham Palace was oddly light-hearted, George VI perhaps unable to believe in the very words he was saying.

'I suppose you don't know why I have sent for you,' the king said to Churchill.

Churchill responded to his tone, replying in a teasing manner. 'Sir, I simply could not imagine why.'[45]

The king laughed and asked him to form a government. Whatever his private reservations, George VI was determined to be open-minded, noting in his diary that Churchill was 'full of fire & determination to carry out the duties of Prime Minister'.[46]

Churchill immediately set about forming his War Cabinet and went to bed at 3 am 'with a profound sense of relief'. At last he had 'the authority to give directions over the whole scene. I felt as if I were walking with destiny . . . and I was sure I should not fail.'[47]

The king, as ever cautious, experienced no such relief. The next day the decision still preyed on his mind. 'I cannot yet think of Winston as PM,' he wrote. 'I met Halifax in the garden & I told him I was sorry not to have him as PM.'[48] Gloucester was sympathetic in his letters from France, recognising that his brother must be having 'an awful time with forming a new Government with such little good material to choose from'.[49] The matter was still troubling the king when he wrote to Churchill to express concerns about his wish to appoint his old friend Lord Beaverbrook to run aircraft production. Doubtless the king had heard reports of Windsor's treasonable conversation with Beaverbrook earlier in the year. But Churchill had his way. As for Beaverbrook, he was so pleased to be part of it all that 'he was like the town tart who has married the Mayor', observed Chips Channon gloomily.[50]

The unrelenting catastrophe unleashed across the English Channel unfolded with such extraordinary speed that in London it was almost impossible for officials in the Cabinet War Rooms to gain a clear view of the battle. The king and queen, like everyone else, waited for news reports on the wireless which built up a frightening picture of war raging across the Continent. On 11 and 12 May the battle intensified in the Netherlands and Belgium. French reinforcements trying to move forward to help the Dutch struggled because they found the Germans already controlled key bridges. When the small, poorly equipped Dutch army was forced to retreat, it found German troops already established behind on the coast. In Belgium, the defenders had counted on the fortified Albert Canal, 80 miles of waterway which stretched across the country through the capital, Brussels. Yet again German paratroopers took the defenders by surprise, landing on the roof of Fort Eben-Emael, which guarded the main bridge, enabling enemy troops to breach the all-critical Albert Canal.

European monarchs were in fear of their lives. During the night of 13 May, King George was summoned to the telephone to answer a long-distance call from the Netherlands. To his astonishment it was Queen Wilhelmina of the Netherlands. George VI had never met her before, but there was no mistaking the note of desperation in her voice as she begged for his help. He knew that the Dutch held an instinctive unease about the British nurtured since the Boer War, fought on southern African territory originally settled by the Dutch. Yet here was the Queen of the Netherlands on the telephone at five in the morning pleading directly with the King of England for British aircraft to defend her country. George VI, unaccustomed as he was to taking calls out of the blue from a foreign queen, was keen to help, and alerted the appropriate officials. He soon found there was little that could be done that was not being done already.[51]

Later that morning Queen Wilhelmina's only daughter, Princess Juliana, and her husband, Prince Bernhard, and their two daughters arrived at Buckingham Palace. Their shocking account pressed home the frightening reality of the catastrophe that had overtaken the Netherlands. They had woken in the early hours to loud and continuous gunfire nearby from a German attack. It sounded as though they were too late to escape, that capture was inevitable and they would fall into Nazi hands. In spite of Dutch neutrality the Germans had attacked once again, *Blitzkrieg* fashion, on a country unprepared. Queen Wilhelmina had called a Cabinet meeting for 4.30 am but the news was that the Netherlands was all but taken and all around them the sounds of war were terrible. It was difficult to retaliate, such was the scale of Hitler's all-out attack. Queen Wilhelmina needed help fast. Above all, Prince Bernhard's account impressed on George VI the shock of the efficiency of the German parachute troops, 'who were arriving in Holland by hundreds, in various disguises'.[52]

Their worrying conversation was put to a stop by yet another important telephone call, now from the port of Harwich, in Essex. Queen Wilhelmina had landed in England. The German parachute commando teams had gained control so fast in The Hague that she had fled to Rotterdam and boarded the British destroyer, *Hereward*. Her hopes of rejoining her forces were soon crushed by the scale of the German assault. The crisis was so grave that the Admiralty recalled the *Hereward* to Harwich, and the queen had to abandon all hopes of returning to the Netherlands that day. Her dramatic escape was so close-run that she evaded capture by the Nazi paratroopers by just thirty minutes.

The king was waiting at Liverpool Street that afternoon to greet her as her steam train pulled into the platform. The train door opened to reveal a 59-year-old woman in a mackintosh, with no luggage save her jewels and tin hat. She had the air of a person who commanded respect and talked only of returning to the Netherlands as soon as possible. In spite of her indomitable spirit, the calamity of her country and her life, now in ruins, was underlined by the fact that her only luggage was not enough to keep out the cold or cover modesty. Beneath the mackintosh she was wearing only her nightdress and had no change of clothes. As she was rather large nothing could be readily found at the palace that would remotely fit her.[53] But agonising defeat and domestic trials could not subdue this queen with the Boadicea-like spirit who, George VI noted, although under great strain, was determined to get help for her country.[54]

Meanwhile, in France, the Duke of Gloucester wanted to speak to the King of Belgium in person to do anything he could to strengthen his resolve and offer support. He and William Scott set out on 13 May, but were unable to reach the Belgian border and returned to the Hotel Univers in Arras. The next day they set out again, this time transferring north to Lille. This move quite possibly saved Gloucester's life, because that night the Hotel Univers was bombed causing several deaths, including the occupants of the rooms adjacent to those held by Gloucester and Scott.[55]

In London on 14 May 'the bad news began to come in', wrote Churchill, with typical understatement.[56] It was a confusing picture and it concerned not Belgium or the Netherlands—but France. As the French and British armies moved north into Belgium they had created a gap between them and the French forces guarding the border through the Ardennes. It was widely believed that this densely forested area was impassable for a modern army. But now the impossible was happening. There were reports that armoured divisions were roaring through the Ardennes into France with a speed and fury and on a scale that was inconceivable for Allied leaders.

Three German panzer divisions broke through at Sedan in France near the Belgian border, 150 miles north-east of Paris. French defenders, lulled by nine months of inactivity in a peaceful landscape, were flung into the deadly fire of blazing tanks and dive-bombing. Anthony Eden, the new Secretary of State for War, brought the latest update to the king that afternoon. The Germans were 'making headway in their attack' on the weakest section of the French line and had seized crucial bridgeheads over the River Meuse. Eden, concerned at the effectiveness of German paratroopers in the Netherlands, was hurriedly organising a new volunteer Defence Corps to prepare Britain for enemy parachutists.[57]

Further north that day events in the Netherlands were at a critical stage. Queen Wilhelmina used the king's broadcasting room at Buckingham Palace to speak to the people of the Netherlands in an attempt to raise morale. By mid-morning Dutch commanders received a German ultimatum: surrender or the port of Rotterdam, the Netherlands' largest industrial target, would be bombed. Even though negotiations resulted in a ceasefire, by late afternoon ninety German bombers were in the sky above the city so unprepared for enemy treachery. The *Luftwaffe* failed to abort their mission. Nothing could save the docks which exploded into a firestorm as vegetable oil tanks caught fire. Anyone in the area was doomed. Those who tried to escape were sucked into the fireball. Some 900 people lost their lives; 80,000 lost their homes. By dawn one square mile in the centre of the city had been flattened. If this pitiless obliteration was the price of any hesitancy on the part of the Dutch government to recognise the absolute power of the Reich, it was a message all Europe noted.

Churchill was not five days into his leadership and there was an even bigger shock in store. His famous account outlines what happened next.

May 15 1940. 7.30 am. The telephone next to Churchill's bed rang.

The voice spoke in English. But it was Monsieur Reynaud, the French premier, from Paris.

'We have been defeated,' he said.

Churchill could not quite gather himself. The voice continued with some urgency.

'We are beaten. We have lost the battle.'[58]

The French premier explained the scale of the German breakthrough into France through the Ardennes. Churchill tried to reassure him that the offensive must end and there would be a chance to counter-attack. But nothing could calm the French leader in his conviction that defeat for France was imminent. 'The idea of the line being broken, even on a broad front, did not convey to my mind the appalling consequences that now flowed from it,' Churchill wrote later. Despite Poland and Norway, 'I did not comprehend the violence of the revolution effected since the last war by the incursion of a mass of fast moving armour.'[59] Churchill agreed to go to France in person to understand the situation.

The crisis deepened rapidly that morning. Rotterdam was still blazing. The Dutch commanders were informed that the same fate awaited the Dutch cities of Amsterdam and Utrecht. Within hours came the news that the Netherlands had surrendered. At 11 am the Dutch laid down their arms. It had taken just five days for the Germans to overrun the country.

The Duke of Gloucester and Lord William Scott were driving into Belgium when they learned the disastrous news from the Netherlands. They were determined to reach King Leopold and headed towards the front in Belgium with an escort of military police. As yet unaware of the catastrophe unfolding behind them in France, they continued deeper into the country, reaching a secret destination near Tournai in east Belgium.

Gloucester was taken to the King of the Belgians who was shattered and disheartened. They had a long talk in which Gloucester did his best to strengthen the Belgian monarch's resolve. Gloucester knew full well how stretched the Allied defences were in Belgium. He had visited the RAF squadrons only a few days earlier and seen that the pilots doing sorties day and night were exhausted.

Leopold of Belgium was 'very depressed', Gloucester observed. His army was unable to hold its position. Young men of Belgium were being sacrificed in vain in the face of a merciless German advance. He was convinced that German spies and infiltrators were so pervasive it was like an entire '5th column' of troops operating within the country. The Belgian plan of slowing the enemy by blowing up the bridges was failing because wires were sabotaged or brave defenders were shot in the back as they tried to light the fuse. The Dutch surrender and the desolation of his country had a devastating effect on his morale. Gloucester and Scott found themselves wondering how long Belgium could stand firm.[60]

The Duke of Gloucester hoped to return to Belgian GHQ but there was no chance. As they were driving back they were caught up in the retreat. The Allies were withdrawing east behind Brussels. At Tournai, Gloucester was suddenly in the thick of it all. With no warning they were being strafed by enemy bombers that were directly overhead. All around them bombs were falling. Buildings

15.5.40

GENERAL HEADQUARTERS,
BRITISH EXPEDITIONARY FORCE.

My dear Bertie,

I saw Leopold this morning. He seemed very depressed about the way his army did not stay on their positions long enough. It was due to the "5th column" as is usual nowadays. Some of the bridges were not blown, either because the wires were cut or the man who was going to fire the fuze was shot in the back. With the Dutch army or at least some of it laying down their

The Duke of Gloucester wrote to George VI on 15 May 1940. He found his distant cousin, King Leopold of Belgium, 'very depressed'. German infiltrators were acting as a '5th column' within Belgium, disrupting planned defences, such as blowing up the bridges. (THE ROYAL ARCHIVES ©HER MAJESTY QUEEN ELIZABETH II)

along the road exploded into flame. Above them planes dived low, dropping their deadly load. Suddenly their car was on fire. Somehow Gloucester and his escort managed to get out of the vehicle. They dived into a narrow alleyway, dodging falling debris and tiles, unable to see what was happening because of clouds of dust. From their position they could feel the earth vibrate from the bombing. On the main road the dark outline of their car was engulfed in flames.[61]

While the Duke of Gloucester was under attack, the former King of England was not at his post in the Paris Mission. He was neither with the British troops nor the French. Nor was he on his way back to Britain to see what he could do. No— the former king and his would-be queen had decided that war-torn countries had little to offer; better to sit in the sun and wait it out. Fashionable Biarritz in south-west France was their destination, well away from the noise of battle.

People were fleeing from Paris. The roads were jammed with cars and carts brimming over with household goods. Many vehicles had broken down and were blocking the road. Most people, young, old, infants in arms, were on foot, car-rying the most meagre of essentials. They trudged patiently on the long straight roads, driven by the fear of what might come, always on the look-out for the enemy. But the journey for the duke and duchess on 16 May proceeded smoothly. In the Hotel du Palais in Biarritz the duke knew he and Wallis could count on a little light relief. There was a wonderful promenade along a great sweep of sandy beach, distant views of surfers bracing themselves against the Atlantic, beach-front casinos and glamorous night life; altogether a much more suitable setting for his bejewelled wife complete with her stunning flamingo brooch.

6

THE DECISIVE STRUGGLE

··

'The decisive struggle is now upon us . . .'

—George VI on Empire Day, 24 May 1940

There was little at the start of the king's relationship with his new prime minister to dispel his initial concerns. Neville Chamberlain, gentleman to the last, had the courtesy to arrive on time for meetings at the palace and took pains with his briefing, even if the king found him, occasionally, somewhat 'long winded'.[1] Churchill was a man larger than life; his presence a force hardly containable in mere flesh and blood, sturdy though his figure was. At this stage of the war, he was a man on a mission, with much to do and much to put right. Invariably he was delayed for meetings at the palace and, when he did appear, the two did not immediately find common ground on which to communicate. Sometimes Churchill only had a few minutes to spare and the king felt he was treated in a casual manner. Even the good-natured queen was perturbed. Bertie's forthcoming traditional Empire Day speech was never far from his mind and she knew he was keen to be fully informed. Apart from the crisis in the Low Countries, the king realised Italy was 'boiling up for entering the war against us'. He expected to see his prime minister on 16 May 1940, only to learn he had gone to Paris to 'hold' the hand of the French premier, Reynaud.[2] Was there yet another German offensive? Were the Allied generals discussing a counter-attack? It was impossible to know, but equally impossible to relax not knowing, allowing thoughts usually ignored to formulate. Hitler was turning Europe into a maelstrom and it seemed that nothing and no one could prevent it.

Six days into his leadership, the man who felt very certain of his appointment with destiny was facing a crisis arguably unprecedented by any prime minister before or since. At 3 pm on 16 May Churchill flew under heavy skies to

Paris. His own unforgettable description best conveys the scene in French HQ. 'From the moment we got out of the "Flamingo"' it was obvious that the situation was incomparably worse than we had imagined,' he wrote. 'The Germans were expected in Paris in a few days at most.'[3]

Churchill found the French military leaders waiting in an imposing room in the Quai d'Orsay in Paris, the grandeur of their surroundings a stark contrast to the general air of hopelessness. 'Utter dejection was written on every face,' he observed. Outside smoke lingered at the windows from bonfires in the garden. He realised the French were already burning their State archives. It was as though they were defeated already.

The French commander in chief explained the position with the help of an easel on which was pinned a map of France, a black line showing the ominous German bulge at Sedan. The German *Blitzkrieg* had opened up a gap of more than 50 miles of front around Sedan, he said. The vast force of German armoured vehicles and panzers roaring through the Ardennes 'was advancing with unheard-of speed'. Hitler appeared to have saved his best troops for this secret advance. Had the Allies fallen into a trap by moving forward into Belgium? The French did not yet know whether this massive German incursion was heading for the coast to encircle Allied troops and attack them from behind or was making straight for Paris.

There was silence.

Churchill spoke. Where was the strategic reserve?

What happened next was 'one of the greatest surprises of my life', he wrote. '*Aucune!*' came the reply. 'None.'

'I was dumbfounded . . . NO STRATEGIC RESERVE . . . What were we to think of the great French army and its highest chiefs?'

The French, attempting to defend hundreds of miles of front, had not had the foresight to keep a mobile reserve on hand to move to attack where the need was greatest. In the room with the smoke curling at the window, Churchill could feel his anger rise. 'We had a right to know,' he wrote. 'Both armies were fighting in line together.' Looking out below, he saw the officials were still 'bringing up their wheel barrows and industriously casting their contents into the flames'.[4]

An old man now by military standards at sixty-five, the 'bulldog' reaction was automatic. His instinctive response to the French defeatism was defiance. He was convinced there must be a way to seize the advantage. He would not accept defeat.

The French wanted ten more squadrons from the Royal Air Force. Churchill knew that Britain's survival depended on keeping twenty-five squadrons in Britain. Below this number, Britain could not defend itself. So far the majority of British air squadrons blazing into 'the hell along the Meuse' had paid with their lives. The Germans had been waiting with anti-aircraft fire. He telegrammed the War Cabinet: 'Situation grave in the last degree,' he warned. Four extra squadrons had already been approved. Now he asked for the outstanding six squadrons.[5]

Anxiously awaiting the outcome of the French talks, the king learned at 12.30 am what had happened and that the War Cabinet had approved the final six squadrons requested by the French. It confirmed his worst fears, in spite of Churchill's refusal to look defeat in the eye. The situation was grave in the extreme.[6] He realised that the public were not yet aware of the danger. German propaganda had emphasised their victories in the Netherlands and Belgium. It was not widely known that the Germans had thrust through the Ardennes and that France could fall. Even Lord Halifax, the Foreign Secretary, invariably the voice of calming reason, had been unable to provide the king with his customary reassurance. They discussed the danger of German parachutists 'and what they could do'. A recent meeting with Sir Archibald Sinclair, the new Secretary of State for Air, heightened the sense of alarm. Sinclair warned that the surprise British bombing of German industrial targets could bring immediate reprisals. He asked the king where he would go in this event. George VI replied 'that I would naturally remain in London as long as the Government remained here'.[7] He would stand or fall with his ministers.

The king was still waiting at the palace, desperate for news, when suddenly the familiar figure of Gloucester entered the room, still looking 'the country squire', confident and in good health. Somehow in the thick of it all, bombs falling about him, his younger brother had magically missed the worst that Hitler could do, bringing a smile to the king's face.

Gloucester and his team had waited until the noise from the Stukas ceased before they emerged from their hiding place in Tournai. As soon as they could they had fled the town on foot. The duke had been bleeding badly, according to Lord Scott, who felt deeply responsible for the second adult in line to the throne.[8] Gloucester was ordered to rear HQ for medical treatment and then sent back to England. He was not injured, he explained, but had caused 'embarrassment' to the British Command, since somehow bombs had landed wherever he was staying. Gloucester had retreated through the French port of Boulogne, apparently tempting fate once more, since the very hotel where he was sleeping was bombed that night.[9] Once again it was feared that Gloucester was dead. But when the raid was over the duke emerged from the hotel's underground shelter, unharmed and unaware of the furore. Their mother had been 'simply <u>horrified</u>' at Gloucester's news.[10] But the king found his brother his usual unflappable self, unscathed and with 'no ill effects to his nerves'.

As the two men talked in Buckingham Palace on 20 May, Gloucester, full of bravado, was doubtless putting everything in the most optimistic light to help fortify his brother. The king, much encouraged, told his mother later, 'this [German] advance is only being done by tanks and they have been careering round the countryside, through towns and back again.' The main German army was following behind slowly and had yet to meet the French. Whilst he understood that the French generals 'appear to be hopeless', the Belgians were fighting well and Lord Gort, commanding the British troops, 'is in good heart'. The situation, he reassured Queen Mary, could yet be reversed.[11]

Across the Channel, as events raced far ahead of the reports to London, Lord Gort was reaching a very different view. He had little confidence in a long-promised French counter-attack and alerted the War Cabinet to the possibility that his men might be forced into a fighting retreat towards the coastal French port of Dunkirk. Churchill believed in counter-attack. But as a precaution, at Cabinet on 20 May he gave orders for the Admiralty to 'assemble a large number of small vessels in readiness to proceed to ports and inlets on the French coast'.[12]

Deep inside the famous white cliffs of Dover, Vice Admiral Bertram Ramsay, who was responsible for safeguarding the Straits of Dover, was charged with masterminding a potential secret evacuation of the British Army. At first sight, it was not clear that such a request was even possible. The ancient tunnels underneath Dover Castle were his headquarters. On inspection just before the war, this warren of white chalk passageways were musty and cold, looking as though they were last used in the Napoleonic Wars. There were few tables or chairs, no staff or typewriters and 'maddening communications', he had told his wife. Nine months on and the underground labyrinth was still barely equipped for such an ambitious operation.

That very afternoon he summoned officials from the Admiralty and the Shipping Ministry to a conference in the power-generation room in the tunnels—which gave the secret plan its name: Operation Dynamo. It soon became obvious that in addition to the modestly equipped headquarters, Operation Dynamo was also lacking a fleet of vessels with which to conduct a naval rescue. Apart from personnel vessels 'of various sorts' at Dover Command, there were just thirty passenger ferries, twelve naval drifters and six small coasters available.[13] Afterwards in the streets of Dover, where the sound of guns in the battle raging across the Channel could be heard, he could only wonder how many men could be saved against impossible odds.

'What days we are living in and what changes . . . ' the Duke of Kent wrote to a friend.[14] The king had agreed to his transfer from the Admiralty to the Royal Air Force and on 20 May he took up his appointment as a staff officer in RAF Training Command.[15] The glamorous Duke of Kent, now attired in the dashing uniform of a group captain in the RAF, did not have a combat role. None the less he could see at last what was going on at close hand and try to make a difference to morale. *The Times* commented on Kent's 'close interest in welfare' and noted the isolated position of many RAF stations and the extreme pressures facing the staff.[16] The duke's post was an entirely new departure; there was no organisation dealing with the welfare of men serving in Training Command. It was up to Kent to start the section and he threw himself into the new role.[17]

His first few days were spent at the Staff College at Andover and soon his engagement diary was filled with planned visits to RAF stations across the country. It was a critical time to be reviewing all the airfields involved in training. Losses in the French campaign were high and the RAF was recruiting rapidly. The man who knew a great deal about fine art, antiques and exquisite porcelain now found equal interest in such practicalities as the state of the latrines, the mess room, and the facilities for feeding the pilots. Nothing was too much trouble.

When the king met Kent at Buckingham Palace for lunch at the end of his first week it was clear that his youngest brother had at last found a field in which he felt he could play a useful part.[18] The king had sufficient confidence that he asked Kent to represent him in the forthcoming independence celebrations in neutral Portugal. He had seen the Portuguese ambassador that week who told him 'Portugal was alive to the Fifth Columnists'. Enemy aliens, foreign refugees, potential 'Quislings': men and women suspects could be equally dangerous.[19] The king had learned from Queen Wilhelmina many stories of treachery in the Netherlands. He wanted Kent to reassure the Portuguese that Britain would fight to protect neutral countries and to urge them to take precautions against enemy suspects and spies.

That week in Britain a new bill extended the scope of the Emergency Powers Act. Anyone with pro-German sympathies could now be interned without trial. Oswald Mosley was one of the first to be incarcerated; his wife, Diana Mitford, a few days later despite having only recently given birth. Other prominent Fascists and German sympathisers followed. The king himself was taking no chances even with members of the Royal Household. He had already taken steps to deal with his pro-German Lord Steward, Walter Buccleuch, making discreet arrangements for him to 'resign' from his post. He wanted a new Lord Steward of impeccable credentials. 'These powers are so wide and sweeping that the Government have the power to control every person . . . in this country,' the king observed.[20]

There was one person—not so easily controlled—who was in danger of behaving as though he was beyond the scope of the Emergency Powers Act. Something of a loose cannon, his loyalty in question, the Duke of Windsor returned to his post in Paris leaving Wallis in Biarritz, only to find he was pining for her. Those who witnessed the duke's behaviour on his short return to the Military Mission do not seem to have formed a favourable impression. The Germans were closing in with deadly efficiency on the Allied troops and yet the duke appeared strangely detached, as if he had all the time in the world although the Netherlands had fallen. The uncomfortable possibility that he was still preoccupied with his own agenda at a time when the whole country was fighting could not be discounted. The Duke of Windsor knew that the Duke of Gloucester had been safely removed from the advancing German army and made welcome at Buckingham Palace. But there was no such family invitation extended to him and his wife. His loyal friend Fruity Metcalfe told his wife he felt very uneasy about the duke: 'He might do *anything* . . . ' he said.[21]

In London, barely forty-eight hours after writing in optimistic terms to his mother, the king found pressing anxieties about the fate of the British Army in France overtook all other concerns. He was determined to get a clear understanding of the situation in France in readiness for his Empire Day speech on 24 May. Now of all times, as he vacillated between hope and despair with each conflicting report, he wanted to deliver a speech that could do justice to the efforts of the British people. Men and women were fighting 'for King and Country'. Posters proclaimed this across the land. In the embattled Britain of May 1940 he had to live up to their expectations and earn the great title that had been bestowed on him. There was no way of knowing in advance whether he could keep the stammer in check but he did all he could to manage his fears by rehearsing his speech with Logue at the palace in the days before.[22] Their work together was important to the king, their privacy absolutely sacrosanct. Interruption was forbidden unless the emergency was extreme. But the military situation was changing so swiftly that the king dreaded the need for last-minute alterations.[23]

The very evening before his speech, the Chief of the Air Staff, Sir Cyril Newell, revealed that the situation in France was indeed 'critical'. After the breakthrough at Sedan, the Germans swiftly made an arc around Allied troops. Their panzers reached the French coast at Abbeville some 100 miles south of Dunkirk on 20 May. Abbeville fell the next day and now enemy tanks were at the port of Boulogne—just 50 miles from Dunkirk. The Air Chief Marshal built up a picture for the king of the speed of German panzer divisions, French Command which had 'gone to seed' and the perilous position of the BEF who were in grave danger now of being trapped in France. The king found the news 'so worrying' that he asked Churchill to come to the palace after dinner.[24]

Churchill arrived at 10.30 that night. The king knew he could be prone to emotion, full of rhetorical flourish, possibly even the worse for drink, but that night the prime minister had a grave message. German tanks were indeed at the gates of Boulogne and shelling the harbour. All would depend on the French counter-attack but, if this failed, Churchill had no choice other than to order the BEF back to England. There was still a chance to save the troops through the French ports of Calais and Dunkirk but it was a race to reach these ports before the Germans. Distance was critical. Calais was a mere 20 miles north of the Germans at Boulogne and Dunkirk a similar distance north again. The longer the Belgian army held the German line to the north the better. The evacuation would mean the loss of all guns, tanks, ammunition and stores in France. But this was the least of it. 'The very thought of having to order this movement is appalling, as the loss of life will probably be immense,' the king wrote on 23 May.[25]

Although he lived in a beautiful palace, it was also his home, imbued with a feeling of security as long as he could remember. Now his home, like every other home in the country, was under threat. Even with the windows protected and the treasures gone, around him here and there, touches of gold and silk proclaimed a place of beauty and peace. It was hard to believe that a battle of life and death was being played out just across the Channel. Churchill understood the awful proximity of the enemy, the BEF remorselessly attacked: the very survival of the British Army at stake. This was the last ditch. He himself was ready for the fight, whatever the personal cost. 'We are determined to persevere to the very end whatever the fate of the great battle raging in France may be,' he had told Roosevelt. He considered it likely that Britain would be attacked 'on the Dutch model', with paratroopers descending in their thousands over London before long. 'Our intention is, whatever happens, to fight on to the end in this Island. Members of the present Administration would likely go down during this process should it result adversely, but in no conceivable circumstances will we consent to surrender.'[26]

It is not surprising that when Logue saw the king on 24 May, he looked grey and tired; worn beyond his years.[27] The future was unknowable. German commandos descending on Buckingham Palace as they had in the Netherlands? A government fighting to the end? A Rotterdam-style bombing on British cities? Glimpses through the palace windows of the streets beyond brought home the looming threat: barbed-wire entanglements, soldiers in uniform and, hanging in a blue sky, the grey barrage balloons. The arrival of his therapist and friend brought some relief. Elizabeth was there, giving encouragement. Then Logue and the king went together to the broadcasting room where George VI took up his position and waited for the red light.

'The decisive struggle is now upon us,' the king began. He explained that he would 'speak plainly' in this hour of trial. 'It is no mere territorial conquest that our enemies are seeking; it is the overthrow, complete and final, of this Empire and of everything for which it stands and, after that, the conquest of the world.' With well-chosen words, he set out the forces ranged against them. 'Against our honesty is set dishonour, against our faithfulness is set treachery, against our justice, brute force.' He called for courage and resolution and self-sacrifice. 'Let us go forward to that task as one man . . . and with God's help we shall not fail.'[28]

The moment seemed so immense that afterwards Logue took the king's hand and the two men sat in the enveloping silence of the broadcasting room. There was no need to speak. Both recognised the simple words had lost none of their power in the king's delivery. For the king it was a tangible relief. He confided to his diary, 'easily my best effort'. He could not resist adding, 'How I hate broadcasting.'[29]

The next day the king received a despairing letter from King Leopold. '*Mon cher* Bertie,' he began. 'We were very moved by your impressive speech yesterday evening.'[30] Leopold warned George VI that his shattered Belgian troops were struggling to hold their line. He was doubtful how much longer they could continue. As commander in chief of the Belgian army he felt responsible for the continuing onslaught on Belgian youth when the case was looking hopeless.

George VI feared that if the Belgians laid down their arms the BEF was in danger of being surrounded on three sides by Germans. Every day the Belgians held their position made a difference. Lord Gort had ordered a counter-attack to try to break the German line and stop British troops from being overrun. Fighting was intense but the British were beaten back.[31] By 24 May the last of the British troops at Boulogne were evacuated. The fall of Boulogne put yet more pressure on troops at Calais: the next key port to the north.

The garrison defending Calais under Brigadier Nicholson were trying to stop enemy forces from reaching the beaches at Dunkirk. At first they understood that they too would be evacuated when it was no longer possible to hold the town. Churchill was opposed. 'This is not the way to encourage men to fight to the end,' he wrote full of fire to the Secretary of State for War on 25 May. He ordered a telegram to be sent to Brigadier Nicholson stressing the importance of the port's defence. 'The eyes of the Empire are upon the defence of Calais, and His Majesty's government is confident that you and your gallant regiment will perform an exploit worthy of the British name.'[32]

Destroyers were still kept in readiness to relieve the men when it was no longer possible to protect Calais. All day on 26 May the Calais regiment bravely held out. At nine in the evening their dire position was spelled out in another telegram. 'Every hour that you continue to exist is of the greatest help to the BEF. Government has decided you must continue to fight . . . Evacuation will not (*repeat* not) take place . . .'[33]

Churchill felt physically sick after sending this telegram. He was asking the garrison there to face capture or almost certain death. But their sacrifice would not be wasted. It could buy two or three days for the BEF, a magnificent gift for their luckier comrades making their way to Dunkirk. The garrison's brave stand made it possible to exploit the Gravelines waterline between Calais and Dunkirk. Sluices were opened and water spread across the low-lying land giving welcome protection to the men now making their way to Dunkirk.

The king spent the day visiting RAF stations to decorate pilots who had been bombing Germany. He felt deeply depressed. Before him stood young men who had seen the battle; men of few words whose heroism and self-sacrifice was beyond question. He knew that more than a quarter of a million more men were still in France awaiting an unknown fate; young men who had not sought war, but none the less were being asked to be prepared to lay down their lives. What chances of survival did they have? The odds did not look good. The burden was almost overwhelming: 'The thought of losing Gort & his band, all the flower and youth of our country, the Army's backbone in officers and men is truly tragic.'[34]

But that evening, at 6.57 pm, the Admiralty gave the signal to commence Operation Dynamo. Vice Admiral Ramsay now had forty Dutch *schuits* in addition to the passenger vessels commandeered at Dover and Southampton. Sea-transport officers were in the process of carrying out a survey across Britain's southern harbours from Harwich to Weymouth to find yet more suitable ships: drifters, fishing boats, tugs and barges, anything that could be enlisted to the cause. From the depths of Dover Castle, his team now worked through the night in an atmosphere of determination to succeed against the odds.

The operation began in a modest way as the first boats slipped into the darkness across the Channel to the sound of anti-aircraft fire. The Admiralty believed they had just two days before enemy fire would bring a halt to the rescue. With so little time and under impossible harrying from the enemy, at most they hoped to save 45,000 men.[35] Prayers were said in a short service at Westminster Abbey, and to Churchill, seated in the choir stalls, it felt as though 'the pent up, passionate emotion' of the congregation filled the soaring spaces of the abbey along with a primeval fear of 'the final ruin of Britain'.[36]

As Nicholson's gallant men held the line in Calais, at the Military Mission in Paris the next morning the spotlight was on the Duke of Windsor. Fruity Metcalfe was astonished when he telephoned his home at 8.30 am to find the duke had left Paris two hours earlier, his convoy of cars loaded with possessions. Fruity was incensed. 'My *late* Master,' he told his wife, 'has run like two rabbits!' To make matters worse the duke's exit at 6.30 am appeared to have been carefully planned, although he had not so much as hinted of his intentions to his most faithful friend. The Metcalfes had stood by the Windsors through all their troubles. They had exposed themselves to criticism for supporting the Windsors' wedding and opened their doors to them when the royal family shut theirs. But the years of loyalty appeared to count for nothing. Fruity was abandoned with not even a car to make his own escape. There was no shortage of italics in his letter to his wife. '—*Utterly* I despise him . . . He deserted his job . . . he's deserted his country now, at a time when every office boy and cripple is trying to do *what he can*. It is the *end*.'[37]

Although Fruity portrayed his former friend's departure as desertion, Windsor's biographer, Philip Ziegler, has argued that the duke did have the sanction of his commanding officer, Howard-Vyse, when he left Paris, although he also points out that Churchill drafted—but did not send—a telegram to him referring to 'a great deal of doubt as to the circumstances in which Your Royal Highness left Paris'.[38] But whatever doubts were in the minds of those at home, it was soon clear that the duke was striking out on his own path. While the British troops he had been so keen to see earlier in the year were fighting for their lives on their way back to Blighty, the duke embarked on a different course, heading first to the south of France. The fact that he did not join the British exodus from France is perhaps indicative of the lack of threat he felt from the Nazis. Both he and Wallis believed that what they called 'the little island' might be forced to sue for peace. Was it possible that Churchill and his 'glamour boys'—as they nicknamed his supporters—could survive for long?

That very day Lord Halifax did indeed launch an attack on Churchill. As the storm clouds gathered over Dunkirk, differences brewing between Halifax and Churchill over the wisest course of action erupted in three stormy meetings in the War Cabinet on 27 May 1940 that risked dividing the leadership and playing into Hitler's hands. Halifax believed that Britain should approach the Italians to open negotiations with Hitler.[39] His ideas gained momentum when Churchill told his War Cabinet that the French premier was under pressure to seek terms with the Führer. Churchill was keen for Britain to distance herself from any ally seeking to negotiate, but Halifax pressed his case. The best hope of saving Britain and Empire lay in negotiation, not war. There were plenty of good arguments to back up his view: America remained aloof, Italy was about to enter the war, Belgium and France were close to collapse, and the British Army *en masse* could be taken prisoner. In Halifax's eyes, Churchill's ill-judged heroics were more reminiscent of 'Toad of Toad Hall', according to his biographer, Andrew Roberts.[40] 'I thought Winston talked the most frightful rot,' Halifax wrote furiously in his diary, adding that he told the PM exactly what he thought of him.

Churchill would not countenance opening negotiations at that juncture. It would sap morale at a critical moment and, if negotiations were needed, better terms could be won later. But he had to play for time. His position was not yet secure and Halifax enjoyed considerable support. That evening Halifax threatened to resign if there was no negotiation.[41]

Churchill had already asked his Chiefs of Staff for a report about Britain's ability to continue alone. How long could Britain hold out? The answer was grim: the slender thread of hope lay with the RAF. The navy and the air force together could prevent a seaborne invasion of Britain. If the RAF took a knockout blow, the navy could not hold out indefinitely. To win this battle, Germany had to destroy Britain's key aircraft industries, based at Coventry and Birmingham. Churchill found the report, which he read 'at the darkest hour' before Dunkirk, 'grave and grim'.[42] For him, Dunkirk was critical. Was Britain about to lose her finest fighting men?

Halifax's case was strengthened by the news the next morning. Just thirteen days after the Dutch surrender, King Leopold ordered the Belgian army to lay

down their arms. The news was 'great shock', George VI wrote in his diary on
28 May. 'The evacuation of the BEF will be almost impossible with the Germans on three sides of us.'[43]

He feared that the left flank of the retreating Allied troops would now face
the full might of German armour. He was in no doubt about the gravity of this
new situation. There was every chance the Germans would reach the beaches
first, forming a circle around the exhausted Allied troops and cutting off escape.
Even if the Allies got to the beaches, the *Luftwaffe* could concentrate their fire
power into annihilating them. The evacuation of Dunkirk surely now required
a miracle? There was a nagging doubt that could not be dismissed. Churchill
was so sure he was right. But was he right or was he gambling with people's
lives? Beyond question he was brave and a man to inspire, but was his generous
spirit compromising his ability for cool judgement?

Despite the critical debate running in the War Cabinet, Churchill did find
time for the king that day. George VI asked after the troops in Calais. It was
grave news. There was no movement inside the town, Churchill explained. He
feared that the British battalions holding the port 'had all been shot down.
It will have to be confirmed. No quarter had been given.' The town was in
German hands. On top of the loss of Calais, the Belgian capitulation put the
BEF 'in an even more desperate position'. None the less, Churchill 'hoped very
much' to evacuate as many troops as possible.[44] Unbowed by the pressures upon
him, the prime minister used his stirring rhetorical gifts to the full that day and
won heart-felt backing for his views from the full Cabinet, outmanoeuvring
Halifax. Negotiation and compromise at this point, he insisted, would reduce
Great Britain to the status of 'a slave state'.[45]

Across France the billboards proclaimed the defeat of Belgium as the Duke
of Windsor travelled south once again to reunite with his wife in Biarritz. From
there they continued east, driving across southern France together to their home
at Château de la Croë on the Riviera not far from the Italian border.[46] Their
efforts were hampered by the thousands of refugees, carts and cases crammed
with possessions, heading the other way. An Italian invasion of southern France
was threatened. Benito Mussolini wanted his share of the spoils and was casting
a greedy eye on the alpine regions. Windsor continued driving towards the Italian border, apparently untroubled by the danger. 'Europe is lost,' said the duke.
'This is the finish.'[47]

The Windsors reached their Riviera sanctuary on 29 May. With its grounds
stretching to a shimmering Mediterranean, La Croë was a little oasis of peace far
removed from the horror unfolding on the beaches of Dunkirk; a gleaming white

palace with a small army of staff where the Windsors could hold court of their own. 'The sky is blue, the sea smooth,' Wallis wrote to her Aunt Bessie. 'Everyone is calm and the gardeners (all Italians) are planting flowers for the summer.'[48]

How was it conceivable that the woman who had shown demonstrable fear at the hostility of press and public at the time of the abdication could remain so composed in the face of an advancing German *Blitzkrieg*, a possible invasion by the Italian army and the imminent risk of the surrender of France?

One answer to this is contained in a memo drafted a few weeks later by Edward Tamm of the FBI for J. Edgar Hoover, the director. Tamm told Hoover his information came directly from the British Secret Service. According to Tamm's source, when the Windsors had checked into their Biarritz hotel, news of their arrival was immediately broadcast on a German commercial station. Even the rooms they occupied were correctly revealed: Suite 104E. The announcement in Berlin was made in 'a matter of minutes' of their checking in. The British Secret Service, reported Tamm, believed that Wallis herself had found some way to keep the Germans, perhaps even Ribbentrop himself, informed of their itinerary and schedule.[49]

Across northern France, the remains of the BEF were converging on Dunkirk. England was the destination. At first it had been a rumour; then an order. They came in their thousands, some following the main roads, many along lanes and paths in smaller groups to avoid bombing. Some troops still kept formation; marching briskly, taking orders. Others merged with the disorderly rabble of refugees fleeing the advancing German line. The wounded, who could continue no longer, waited hopelessly on the roadsides. Around the retreating army were flashes of fire and the ominous rumble of bombing from the diminishing front line. The terrible need to keep going against hunger and thirst and exhaustion was overwhelming against the possibility that they might be cut off. How to get back to Britain was the compelling thought in all men's minds. For mile after mile, the long straight French roads, blocked with humanity struggling to escape, seemed to fill the world. There was little warning of air attack; eyes were fixed on the skies. German Stukas seen as mere black dots on the horizon could be above them in seconds, lunging over the scattering line, releasing bombs indiscriminately.

Nearer Dunkirk fires blazed as the retreating army destroyed anything of use to the enemy: horses were shot, records burned, guns smashed and transport of all sorts disabled. The harbour had been bombed and was blocked by the half-sunk wrecks of ships. The vast beach of golden sand was backed by holiday homes now blackened and charred. Groups of men, some injured, their dark shapes thick on the beach, waited for their turn to join the long queues stretching far out to sea. Those nearest to boarding a vessel stood up to their necks in water. Would they make it on to a boat before the Stukas returned? The smoke from fires hung over the beach. A smell of putrefaction and the acrid stench of burning fuel hung in the air. To the unending supply of new arrivals it looked like a very contemporary hell.

From deep within the white cliffs of Dover, Operation Dynamo was still struggling to gain momentum. Some 7,669 men came back on Monday 27 May but there were not enough ships. Many more were needed. The Admiralty was taking emergency measures. Suitable craft were commandeered from southern harbours and boatyards. Word of the impending catastrophe unfolding on the French beaches was beginning to spread along the coast, making its way across every sleepy inlet and harbour, every estuary and landing stage. And every able man and boy wanted to be part of it, to bring a soldier back to England. Information started to flood into the Shipping Ministry. Once the mission was understood, everyone with some sort of craft wanted to be part of this great venture. Anything that could float across the Channel would do. It was something they could do to pit their small might against the immense forces of aggression that were ranged against their island. They had no doubt. They would bring their boys back home.[50]

The king kept a record in his diary. By Wednesday 29 May he was told that 30,000 men had been safely evacuated. He agonised over the fate of the quarter of a million men still in France. 'I am so dreadfully sorry for these men as I do not see how any but a small percentage can get out.'[51]

But the little ships of England were ready and waiting. By the end of May crafts of all kinds began to descend on the British channel ports ready to help the navy and make the great journey. Yachts, fishing boats, lighters, tugs, liners, sloops, corvettes, gunboats, motorboats, barges, trawlers and even dinghies; volunteer seamen ready to brave German fire came forward in large numbers to do all they could to support the efforts of the Royal Navy. Anything that would float was hauled into the water by men too old to face such hazards but who had no intention of missing it. Hundreds of craft crossed the Channel under a waning moon, like a furtive migration, homing in on the essential ports intent on bringing the fighting men back. For Churchill, it was as though there 'was a white glow, overpowering, sublime, which ran through our island from end to end'.[52]

On Thursday the king learned the number had risen to 80,000 men, more than they had ever thought they could get off the beaches. By Friday the extraordinary spirit that had taken a grip of the whole country was uplifting. Volunteers were coming forward in their hundreds to help with local defences. A flotilla of small craft had joined the great tide of vessels to bring the army back. Despite heavy beach surf that day, there was little enemy bombing. 'We have now evacuated 133,000 men of the B.E.F and 11,000 Frenchmen,' he recorded on 31 May. It was beginning to seem like salvation.[53]

Yet still in France the unending line of men continued to converge on the beach, drawn in the right direction by the scent of the sea and the disconcerting column of grey smoke, rising above the town with increasing intensity, speaking of heavy German bombing. They emerged from the dunes, blistered feet, boots heavy with sand, to an unbelievable panorama. As far as the eye could see, played out on a summer scene, was a private war with all its attendant misery. When the tide was low the beach stretched for a mile to the water; its surface covered with men; tens of thousands reaching to the shoreline and beyond. And in those watery queues where men stood, it seemed for ever, exhausted, cold to the bone, eyes achingly trained on the horizon, the sighting of a boat brought exquisite anxiety: how big was the vessel; how long before it reached the shore; would it be bombed before that? Those in command created orderly defences; the badly wounded were to be left behind. Those men who were still able to fight turned around to hold the line; fighting along the diminishing front was heavy.

Largely out of view, a great air battle was underway as the RAF fought to keep the beaches clear of German bomber squadrons, sent sometimes in waves of forty to fifty aircraft. But British fighter pilots were making as many as four or five sorties a day in their efforts to stop the German fighters getting through. On the beaches there was some anger towards the RAF as periodically, with little warning, German Stukas dived among them, dispensing death or injury at will. The waiting men fled for their lives, desperate to keep their place in the queue afterwards. In Buckingham Palace, one lady-in-waiting dared to hint at the rumours she had heard referring to 'panic on the beaches'. Queen Elizabeth flashed her disapproval. 'I don't believe it . . . Never say that of the great British people.'[54]

On the morning of Saturday 1 June 1940 Lord Gort himself arrived at Buckingham Palace. Churchill had ordered him to evacuate to avoid a 'needless triumph' to the enemy should he be captured, and and he reached London at 9.30 am.[55] 'He is a most extraordinary man not to show any signs of fatigue or worry after all he has been through in the last three weeks,' observed the king.[56] Gort had left Major-General Alexander in charge of a small force holding the perimeter. There were fears the eastern perimeter would not hold much longer. Evacuation efforts were intensified. The king learned that 175,000 British and 34,000 Frenchmen had been rescued.[57] But that morning, from first dawn, German bombers bore down with deadly accuracy. Thirty-one ships sank that day, many laden with troops who after enduring impossible odds had finally thought escape and survival was in their sights.

The next day, 4,000 valiant British troops were still holding the line on the outskirts of Dunkirk, with artillery fire menacing the main route and the enemy close to the bridgehead. Another heroic push was planned for that night, with ships from British, French and Belgian ports descending on Dunkirk in the darkness. By Sunday the total of those saved had swollen to 215,000 British and 60,000 Frenchmen. On 3 June, the day Paris was bombed, the king was recording ever-increasing numbers: 224,000 from the BEF and 85,000 Frenchmen.[58] And more men were still coming over. By this time, the RAF had lost 177 aircraft including more than a hundred fighters over the previous nine days. On 4 June, the king was relieved to hear that 327,000 Allied troops were now safely landed in England. The Dunkirk 'victory' was intoxicating.[59]

At last it was possible to hope again. The people of Britain appeared to have done the impossible. What other nation would send out every kind of boat and bathtub that would float to fetch its army back? It inspired Winston Churchill to address Parliament with a rousing speech. 'Even though large tracts of Europe and many old and famous states have fallen or may fall into the grip of the Gestapo and all the odious apparatus of Nazi rule, we shall not flag or fail. We shall go on to the end. We shall fight in France, we shall fight in the seas and oceans, we shall fight with growing confidence and growing strength in the air; we shall defend our Island, whatever the cost may be. We shall fight on the beaches, we shall fight on the landing-grounds, we shall fight in the fields and in the streets, we shall fight in the hills; we shall never surrender . . . '[60] His oratory, full of fire, moved many MPs to tears. The king, deeply affected as he heard about the speech, made a note of his prime minister's stirring lines in his diary: 'We shall go on fighting to the end, even after this country has been laid waste, we shall fight from the New World to redeem the Old.'[61]

On Wednesday 5 June, the final tally rose to 335,000 men. No one had dared to hope for such success. To the people of Britain it was something of a miracle, something to feel good about at last. To celebrate the return of the backbone of the British Army, the next day George VI paid an unexpected visit to Aldershot Command. He was among the men who had risked all for their country and wanted to show his respect. They cheered their king, these men who had endured so much, all carrying the mark of heroes. George VI went to several barracks with the same response.[62] But despite the elation of Dunkirk and the fighting talk of deliverance, the overall situation was deteriorating fast across Europe.

The victorious German armies were just 21 miles across the Channel, holding the coastline and poised to strike at any time. In Norway, Allied forces defending the north were needed for the expected battle for Britain's survival and rapidly withdrawn. On 7 June, Haakon VII and his son, Crown Prince Olav, escaped from their defeated country on HMS *Devonshire* and were escorted back to London. The king was pleased to see his Uncle Charles and Cousin Olav when they finally arrived both 'in good form' after their long ordeal.[63] Norway finally surrendered on 10 June. After two months' hard fighting, Norway had withstood the German invasion for longer than any other country.

Poland, Finland, Denmark, the Netherlands, Luxembourg, Belgium, Norway—and now, on the threshold of surrender, France too.

Britain stood alone.

Yet still the map of Europe was being redrawn at giddying speed.

Mussolini in Italy declared war on Britain and France on 10 June 1940. 'May he rue the day when he gave the order,' wrote the king.[64] Swastikas hung from the Arc de Triomphe on 14 June. Later that week, the Soviet Union annexed the three Baltic states, Estonia, Latvia and Lithuania. Pressure was building on the Balkans. If the French surrendered, Churchill feared that the new French government might be forced to declare war on Britain. The king was in no doubt of the German programme: 'the invasion of this country comes next.'[65]

Many believed the country would fall as quickly as the others. The question for so many was should Britain surrender too? Was there indeed a choice? 'Are we witnessing . . . the decline, the decay and perhaps the extinction of this great island people?' Chips Channon entered in his diary.[66] Many wealthy families hurried to send their children to safety in Canada or America, the destination of choice for those who could afford it rather than the English shires, such was the fear that the country was about to be overrun. But the king and queen wanted their daughters to stay. The king talked it over with his prime minister. Would Princess Elizabeth and Princess Margaret be a liability? Churchill, full of fight, 'said "No."'[67] The king took his prime minister's advice. They would be together:

a man, his wife, their two children, just like every other family. It sounded so ordinary and so natural. No one could guess how much it meant to him.

Hitler was certain that Britain would have to seek peace. He still wanted an 'Anglo-German understanding'. Loose talk between the Under-Secretary of State at the Foreign Office, Richard 'Rab' Butler, and a Swedish diplomat in London, Bjorn Prytz, in which Butler cited Halifax as saying 'common sense and not bravado' would dictate British policy, was widely reported, creating the impression that there was still room for negotiation.[68] The octogenarian Marshal Pétain in France summed up the views of many when he said, 'It is easy but also stupid to think of fighting to the last man. It is also criminal . . . ' For others, such as Weygand, who had taken over as supreme commander of the French Army, Britain stood no chance. 'England will have her neck wrung like a chicken,' he said.

The British prime minister took a different view. Churchill had been at the helm barely six weeks. The king, despite his initial reservations, was beginning to recognise his strengths as his powerful oratory became the rallying cry across the empire.

On 18 June, Churchill rose to address the House. Despite all the demands on his time, he had toiled over the speech, crafting the emotional phrases, the pages annotated in his red or blue ink. He was acutely aware of the national crisis and the importance of the speech. And now at 3.49 pm the House fell silent as he stood. The final version was set out before him in blank-verse form to help him meet the occasion with the right emphasis.

'The whole fury and might of the enemy must very soon be turned on us,' Churchill warned. 'Upon this battle depends the survival of Christian civilisation. Upon it depends our own British life and the long continuity of our institutions and our empire . . . ' Failure would draw the whole world, including the United States, 'into the abyss of a new Dark Age . . . Let us therefore brace ourselves to our duties, and so bear ourselves, that if the British Empire and its Commonwealth last for a thousand years, men will still say: "This was their finest hour."'[69]

Everyone knew what was coming. It had been well rehearsed on cinema screens as the famously obliterating *Blitzkrieg* had toppled the capitals of Europe. Now it was the turn of Britain. Time was running out and, in spite of Churchill's brave words, the end was too terrible to contemplate.

George VI and Queen Elizabeth stood firm by Churchill and his ministers in London, waiting for the onslaught. The Duke of Gloucester in the army and the Duke of Kent in the RAF were ready to do all they could.

But no one in Britain knew the precise whereabouts of the ex-king.

On 19 June, as bombs were falling on the east coast of England, and France was on the point of surrender, Lord Halifax sent telegrams to the British Consulates at Nice, Marseilles and Bordeaux. 'Please send me any information you have or can get from consular offices under your supervision regarding the Duke of Windsor's whereabouts and do anything you can to facilitate his return to this country.'[70]

The ex-king of England had disappeared.

7

TREACHERY

....

'Against our honesty is set dishonour, against our faithfulness is set treachery . . . '

—George VI, 24 May 1940

The case of the vanishing duke was pursued with great vigour but scant regard for the truth by certain sections of the press. The duke and duchess were not at their château near Antibes by the sea or in Biarritz. In Italy there were reports on 20 June 1940 that 'Winston Churchill has ordered his arrest on grounds that he "showed a hostile attitude"'.[1] *Il Messaggero* in Rome raised the prospect that 'the duke might again become King under an Italo-German conquest of Great Britain'.[2] Later reports claimed the British Army had already 'risen against King George and was demanding the return of the Duke of Windsor to the throne'. The *New York Times* soberly brought an end to the conjecture on 21 June with the news that '24 hours of speculation as to their whereabouts' had closed that morning when the duke and duchess surfaced in Barcelona.[3]

The duke took the trouble on 21 June to telegraph news of his safe arrival to Churchill. 'Having received no instructions have arrived in Spain to avoid capture. Proceeding to Madrid. Edward.' Helpfully his telegram stated: 'His Royal Highness is at the Ritz Hotel.'[4] Churchill's swift reply was unambiguous. 'We should like Your Royal Highness to come home as soon as possible.'[5] But the former king was in no hurry to return home. The fate of Britain was unknown, and if it did fall, there might, at last, be a role for Wallis and himself. On 23 June, he and his wife stepped through the polished doors of the stunning baroque palace of the Ritz in Madrid. The capital had suffered heavy bombing in the Spanish Civil War but in the fashionable heart of the city the Ritz had been renovated and was ready to welcome any visiting aristocracy.

Joachim von Ribbentrop knew exactly where the Windsors were staying and began to glimpse an exciting way to enhance his position with Hitler still further.[6] The German Foreign Minister was heady with the victories of the last few days. Waiting at Hitler's side in the bright sunlight outside the French Armistice wagon had been a moment to savour. Hitler had chosen the exact site for the Armistice ceremony in the Compiègne Forest north of Paris where Germany's humiliating defeat had been signed in 1918. But this time roles were reversed. The French arrived, their faces like stone. Inside the wagon Hitler, Ribbentrop, Goering and Hess could scarcely suppress their excitement as the terms were read out. A vast swathe of north and west France, including Paris and all Channel and Atlantic ports, would be occupied by the Germans. The 84-year-old French Marshall Henri-Philippe Pétain would run the remaining two-fifths of unoccupied France. Almost two million French men became prisoners of war.[7] Ribbentrop basked in the glory of the German victory parade in Paris as an unending train of armed Aryan youth marched down the Champs-Elysées against a backdrop of a giant swastika unfurled from the Arc de Triomphe. Now, away from public view in his army headquarters, Ribbentrop could see a route to even greater personal triumph through an intriguing telegram marked 'Strictly Confidential'. It was from yet another resourceful German ambassador—this time in Madrid. Dr Eberhard von Stohrer's missive concerned the Duke of Windsor. Should we 'detain' the duke in Spain, Stohrer enquired?[8]

Ribbentrop knew how keenly Hitler wanted to settle 'the British question' so that he was free to pursue his interests in the east. He believed that Britain must want peace and could see that the pro-German, pro-peace, ex-king could be a trump card—one that he was uniquely placed to play from his earlier acquaintance with the duke and duchess. Knowing the duke's ardent desire to re-establish a role for himself, he might be a pliable collaborator. Would he collude with the Germans in the same way that Major Quisling had in Norway? The duke had once enjoyed a tremendous following. It was probable the British would take their former much-loved Prince of Wales back to their hearts. The duke's appearance in Spain was extremely convenient. Although Spain was neutral, under the right-wing dictatorship of General Franco it was ideologically aligned to Nazi Germany and harboured many Nazi supporters—the perfect milieu to establish contact.

'Is it possible in the first place to detain the Duke and Duchess of Windsor for a couple of weeks in Spain?' Ribbentrop replied to Stohrer. A little trouble with their exit visas could perhaps be discreetly arranged with the Spanish authorities, he suggested. He was anxious to ensure that no suggestion appeared to come from Germany.[9]

Ribbentrop need not have worried. The duke himself was in no rush to return home despite Churchill's order. Now of all times, with Britain on the point of invasion, he decided to make a stand with the palace. For all his grand pronouncements about world peace, he felt himself unable to make peace with his family, unless his conditions were met. Status and prestige was high on his list of requirements. For himself, the duke wanted a suitable appointment. And for Wallis, exactly the same treatment by the palace as the Duchesses of Gloucester and Kent. 'My wife and myself must not risk finding ourselves once more regarded by the British public as in a different status to other members of my family,' he insisted to Churchill on 27 June.[10] Money once more loomed large in his thoughts. Any increase in taxation because he was no longer living overseas must be compensated with additional income from public funds.[11] Telegrams flew back and forth between London and Madrid, with both sides uncompromising.

The British ambassador in Spain, Sir Samuel Hoare, found he had his work cut out keeping the Duke of Windsor on message. It was widely rumoured that he was in Spain to facilitate peace moves and the duke's indiscretions soon reached not just the British, but the Americans as well. The American ambassador in Spain, Alexander Weddell, was sufficiently shaken by the Windsors' forthright views expressed to a member of the embassy staff that he alerted the US Secretary of State, Cordell Hull: 'The most important thing now to be done was to end the war before thousands more were killed or maimed to save the faces of a few politicians,' the duke had declared. The duke believed that countries that had not prepared for war should not embark on 'dangerous adventures'. His wife went even further. In Wallis's opinion, 'France had lost because it was internally diseased.' She believed that a country that was not in a position to fight 'should not have declared war'. Weddell shrewdly pointed out to the Secretary of State that these views reflected an 'element in England, possibly a growing one' who support Windsor and 'who hope to come into their own in event of peace'.[12]

The Germans, too, were not long in getting the complete measure of the situation. Stohrer, working with supreme efficiency through Spanish intermediaries, reported accurately to Ribbentrop on 2 July that Windsor would not return to England unless 'his wife was recognised as a member of the royal family and if he was appointed to a military or civilian position of influence . . . Windsor has expressed himself . . . in strong terms against Churchill and this war . . . ' he explained.[13]

It had taken barely a week for the duke's ill-judged stance, aired liberally in Madrid, to reach London, Washington and now Berlin—where Ribbentrop saw a great scheme to bend the duke's grievances to his own advantage.

'We are now alone in the world waiting,' the king confided to his diary. It was pouring with rain in London when he learned of the French capitulation. 'The news from France could not be more depressing.'[14] The world was waiting to see if Britain would make peace with Germany. Churchill did not waver. He ordered the Foreign Secretary to ensure that all public officials were 'strictly forbidden' to talk of peace.[15] The public were behind him. 'After eight months of wondering what the war was about, the people suddenly knew what to do,' observed one journalist, George Orwell. 'It was like the awakening of a giant.'[16] Resilience—even humour in adversity—was characteristic of the time. 'French sign peace treaty. We're in the finals!' proclaimed one newspaper on 18 June. 'And it's to be played on the Home Ground,' quipped a commissionaire in one of London's smart clubs.[17]

But the people of Britain knew they were vulnerable. *Blitzkrieg* was another name for obliteration. They were ill-equipped and ill-prepared: a nation of shopkeepers Napoleon had called them, but it had fallen to this generation to be tested in this new and terrible way and somehow win. With the country facing a very determined aggressor, renewed effort was put into defence. The king began by parting company with his Lord Steward, the brother of the Duchess of Gloucester. 'Walter Buccleuch came to say good bye,' the king entered in his diary on 26 June. 'It was a rather painful interview as he has been "dubbed" as being pro-German in his attitude towards the War & has said stupid things, but we parted amicably.'[18] The king's new Lord Steward was a man of impeccable reputation: the 14th Duke of Hamilton, formerly the Marquis of Clydesdale. The dashing Hamilton, known to the public for his daring flying exploit over Everest, had also become the youngest squadron leader of his day in 1927, taking on the City of Glasgow Squadron. His three brothers commanded squadrons and Hamilton was now in command of air defence in Scotland and the Air Training Corps. A man of such apparently loyal fighting pedigree appeared much more suitable to represent the Royal Household.

Buckingham Palace's gracious spaces were being transformed as it became a stronghold for royal resistance. Judging by the accounts of Uncle Charles and 'Cousin Wilhelmina'—as she now was known—the monarch was a likely target in the early hours of any invasion.[19] The king, however, was determined to remain in London with his ministers and Elizabeth would not leave him. The maids' quarters in the basement were adapted into a more permanent shelter, with steel supports to give a measure of protection against a direct hit and wooden partitions to create small chambers for staff. The furniture did little to add to the comfort. It was an incongruous mixture of objects deemed to be essential, including, oddly, axes fixed to the wall, and items judged too precious to leave in the rooms above, such as a collection of antique clocks whose ticking did nothing to ease the nerves in long hours spent underground.[20] There was barbed wire thick as hedges in the palace grounds and a shooting range where the king and his staff practised daily. Elizabeth too, abandoning her usual soft pinks and lilacs for shooting gear, took lessons at the range in firing a pistol. 'I shall not go down like the others,' she said valiantly.[21] A feeling of security was finally established with armoured cars on standby at the palace and an escort selected from the Brigade of Guards and the Household Cavalry.

Still doubtful about the royal defences, Uncle Charles suggested that the king should test the procedure in the event that German commandos parachuted over Buckingham Palace. Full of assurance, George VI sounded the alarm and the two kings retired to the palace gardens to watch acclaimed British security in action.

There was silence. To George VI's embarrassment, no guards appeared. Nobody was interested in the alarm. He sent for an equerry who returned apologetically to explain that there was no response since the police officer on duty 'had heard nothing' of any attack. Once the police realised the king wished to test the procedure, guardsmen duly obliged and began to search the palace gardens for parachutists. But they did not look quite ready to take on crack enemy commando teams. They were more reminiscent of a hunting party in the country approaching the herbaceous borders 'like beaters at a shoot'. Suitably warned, the king made arrangements to strengthen safety measures.[22]

There were moments of relief from the unremitting bad news from the Continent. The king was pleased to congratulate three officers who, by some miracle, had escaped from Calais, slipping across to Dover in a motorboat: Captain Williams, Captain Talbot and Lieutenant Millett. They described the scene as Calais fell. The Rifle Brigade had sustained the most casualties. Those who survived were taken prisoner. Brigadier Nicholson, who Churchill had instructed to hold the line, was still alive. He was last seen being whisked away by the Germans in a car.[23]

The queen, determined to play her part, visited hospitals treating the wounded from Dunkirk. 'Sometimes one's heart seems near breaking under the stress of so much sorrow and anxiety,' she confided to Eleanor Roosevelt. It was unbearable to 'think of our gallant young men being sacrificed to the terrible machine that Germany has created'. It made her angry, she admitted, but also 'when we think of their valour, their determination and their great grand spirit, pride and joy are uppermost'.[24]

Keen to understand how ready the army was to face combat with the enemy and knowing it had been forced to abandon most of its equipment in France, the king discussed the military situation with Gloucester. George VI already knew from his daily briefing papers some 90,000 rifles, 1,000 guns, 2,000 tractors, 8,000 Bren guns, and 400 anti-tank weapons had been left behind on the Continent. 'No wonder there is a difficulty in re-equipping the BEF,' he thought.[25] Churchill estimated across the whole country there were no more than 200 medium or heavy tanks. More worrying still, it was known that the British Army lacked heavy weapons.[26]

Gloucester toured British bases, welcomed Canadian and Australian divisions and endeavoured to do his best to create that indefinable morale-boosting quality that a royal visit could inspire. He was soon able to report back to the king on the resourcefulness with which defences were being formed. Miles of coastline were eerily transformed with coils of barbed wire, mines and improvised barriers such as layers of scaffolding to protect against an amphibious assault. Thousands of concrete pillboxes were hurriedly built in June. Like toy bricks dropped randomly by giants, anti-tank obstacles and concrete bollards were placed on roads and railway lines. Ingenious schemes such as oil defence were proposed to compensate for the shortage of weapons. If the German troops tried to land, oil could be pumped through fuel pipes installed on target beaches and set alight. The king knew that everything his practical brother described would be accurate, but barbed wire, pillboxes and scaffolding on the beach did not seem enough.

Neither did the tens of thousands of men aged between seventeen and sixty-five not already in military service who hurried to sign up to the Local Defence Volunteers. This 'Dad's Army', initially equipped with a generous provision of wartime spirit but not much else, rehearsed sometimes bloodthirsty solutions to help them obstruct the enemy: pitch forks, golf clubs, homemade Molotov cocktails and even potatoes studded with razor blades. Roadblocks were set up and eagerly manned. In the open countryside, enemy aircraft attempting to land would encounter further snags in the form of sharp stakes and awkwardly placed farm machinery.[27]

The Duchesses of Gloucester and Kent joined in the vast effort, visiting first-aid posts, hospitals, the Women's Auxiliary Air Force (WAAF) and the Women's Royal Naval Service (WRNS) whose numbers were growing fast as women

hurried to help their men. Women assisted with everything from parachute
packing and manning of barrage balloons in the WAAF to driving, signalling
and loading torpedoes into submarines in the WRNS. Despite the fear of parachutists aiming to seize the royal family, the only change that Alice noticed to
her security procedure was the addition of a detective, who moved into Barnwell with his family. He was at her side for every official visit and she soon had
a nickname for her loyal escort: 'the faithful Corgi'.[28]

As a welfare officer in the RAF, the Duke of Kent gained a bird's-eye view of
Britain's air defences during June of 1940. The airfields were camouflaged and
difficult to find. In the maze of English country lanes it was easy to be lost or
late and such was the terror of Germans emerging from nowhere in disguise
that if he stopped to ask for directions, villagers would invariably plead igno-
rance at the sight of a stranger. 'Careless talk costs lives,' declared the posters.
The press was prohibited from revealing the movements of the royal family, but
none the less he was recognised and this, too, could cause delays. One ardent
royal enthusiast was determined to show him he had no fewer than three photographs of the Duke of Kent in his front room. When he finally reached his
destination, sentries with fixed bayonets at RAF station entrances ordered him
to halt and could take precious minutes to satisfy themselves that he really was
the Duke of Kent.[29]

With a full engagement diary he soon understood the intimidating odds
for the RAF. The *Luftwaffe*, heady with victories in France, had almost double
the number of aircraft. German airfields were now established within striking
distance of Britain in a sweep of conquered lands from Norway to Brittany in
France. The French campaign had taken a devastating toll. There was a desperate shortage of pilots; Fighter Command had lost sixty pilots during the
Dunkirk campaign alone.[30] Britain was down to 700 fighters, although they
were being made at the formidable rate of 470 a month.[31] There were grave fears
the Germans could win this battle simply by wiping out Britain's radar stations,
airfields and aircraft factories. Britain's famous Royal Navy surely would not
hold out indefinitely if the *Luftwaffe* won victory in the skies?

Kent began to familiarise himself with the different divisions: Fighter Command, Bomber Command, Coastal Command, Flying Training Command,
Maintenance Command and even Balloon Command. Defending Britain
required a herculean feat of organisation. Once enemy aircraft were detected,
30,000 observers, many of them women, would track them, estimate their
numbers, height and position and pass the information to Fighter Command.
With intense practice, it took just six minutes from the initial radar detection

to getting British fighters in the air heading for the target. The Duke of Kent, once a party man, was now totally immersed in war work; his diary no longer filled with social engagements but tours of duty. He had been dismayed at the conditions existing for the air crews at the start of the war and did all in his power to make life easier for them. His work, quite often hazardous, had taken over his life. He even offered to open his home just outside London to pilots and crews hoping that Coppins would be a refuge where they could at least enjoy a meal, play the gramophone and have some sort of rest. The only drawback, he thought, was that Coppins was close to RAF Northolt and RAF Uxbridge and could be rather noisy.[32]

Churchill's words captured the spirit of the times. Britain would fight, 'if necessary for years, *if necessary alone*' (his italics).[33] Indefatigable, the prime minister appeared on Pathé newsreels to be everywhere, always at the centre of a crowd, his sturdy frame walking faster than his years would suggest, his smile reassuring, his bowler hat sometimes raised on a stick, a token of the man, as his short stocky figure was swallowed up by the press of people. He did appear to stand alone, as though holding some private imaginary flag erect, never wavering, carrying the country. He was the figure of certainty: we would win. But to remain optimistic at such a time of dire uncertainty would make costly demands on a man no longer young.

While to the outside world Churchill the leader was beginning to assume iconic status, Churchill the man was feeling the pressure. Behind the scenes, the king was not the only one who 'did not find him very easy to talk to', as he confided to his friend Halifax.[34] All was not well in Churchill's 'private paradise', Chips Channon deduced after learning of the squabbles between ministers.[35] Churchill's wife, Clementine, went even further. She tore up the first draft of her message to her husband but then had a change of heart and felt she must send it: 'My darling, I hope you will forgive me if I tell you something that I feel you ought to know,' she wrote on 27 June. An unnamed colleague in his entourage had been to see her, she explained. She understood 'there is a danger of you being generally disliked by your colleagues and subordinates because of your rough, sarcastic and overbearing manner'. She warned him that people were finding his 'irascibility and rudeness' hard to bear and that she herself had 'noticed a deterioration in your manner and you are not so kind as you used to be'. She knew this was out of character. Previously his staff had always reported 'loving you'. But now she warned him of creating 'a slave mentality' in his subordinates. If orders were bungled, 'except for the king, the Archbishop of Canterbury and the Speaker, you can sack anyone and everyone. Therefore with this terrific power you must combine urbanity, kindness and if possible, Olympic calm.'[36]

Churchill took his wife's criticism generously but the pressures were immense. How was Britain going to win and with what? The Americans would not join the fight and requests for American destroyers were refused, but they were prepared to help with ammunition, rifles and field guns.[37] Churchill requested that a chart was made up of the thirty army divisions to follow their progress to complete equipment. Each division was represented by a square, subdivided to represent rifles, guns, gun carriers, anti-tank rifles, anti-tank guns, field artillery, and transport. Only when certain targets were reached could each square of the chart be painted red.[38]

The prime minister wanted not just America, but the whole world, to see that Britain would fight on. Even small neutral states within Europe were courted in an effort to stop them aligning with the Axis powers. The Duke of Kent played a part in this initiative, leading the British delegation to neutral Portugal in late June. The official reason for his visit was to celebrate the 800th anniversary of the foundation of the Portuguese State and the duke arrived on 26 June to find the whole country in a carnival atmosphere. Church bells rang out, bullfights were staged, a medieval pageant of Portugal's seafaring history was re-enacted through Lisbon by torchlight. Publicly out came the old familiar charm as he entertained ministers, viewed exhibitions and attended a banquet as a guest of the President of Portugal.[39] Privately, he did his best to reassure the Portuguese prime minister that the English cause was not lost. Britain would do all in its power to support the neutral countries of Europe.

One of the most testing decisions of British resolve was how to deal with the French navy. If this fell into German hands, it would erode Britain's margin of safety at sea. The dangers would increase dramatically for merchant ships and convoys in the Atlantic; the Admiralty were arranging crucial American rifle convoys. If the French would not bring their ships to British ports, the War Cabinet concluded the French fleet had to be seized, disabled or destroyed. For Churchill, it was 'a hateful decision'.[40]

The largest concentration of French vessels was in the Mediterranean at the port of Mers-el-Kebir on the coast of French Algeria. Negotiations were protracted. The French would not agree to British terms. By late afternoon on 3 July the atmosphere in the Admiralty and the War Cabinet was tense, Churchill following proceedings closely. At 5.54 pm the British opened fire on the French. The battleship *Bretagne* was soon ablaze, and five other ships were damaged. Some 1,297 French sailors lost their lives that day. For Churchill, this grim strike at Britain's 'dearest friends' was essential. 'It was made plain the British War Cabinet feared nothing and would stop at nothing.'[41]

Queen Elizabeth, feeling rather braver than could be discerned from her charmingly draped and befurred image, summed up the mood in a letter to Mrs Roosevelt. 'We are all prepared to sacrifice <u>everything</u> in the fight to save freedom.'[42]

The Duke of Windsor was finding much to enjoy about life at the Ritz in Madrid. Inexplicably he found himself the sudden centre of interest, with Spanish leaders and nobility keen to pay court. He renewed his acquaintance with his cousin, Prince Alfonso, 6th Duke of Galliera, a great-grandson of Queen Victoria who also shared his passion for flying.[43] Oblivious to the insensitivity, he also spent time with the Civil Governor of Madrid, Don Miguel Primo de Rivera, leader of the local Falangists—the official Spanish Fascist party—who was eager to escort the Windsors—a liaison duly noted by the *New York Times* as 'Windsors Dine with Fascist'.[44]

Almost farcically, while the Germans were using the Spanish to establish contact with the Duke of Windsor, he, in turn, was trying to establish a link with the Germans and the Italians. The Windsors' two homes in France, each a little shrine to the exquisitely civilised, were causing concern to Wallis. Would their lavish collections of fine art, silver, and other treasures be safe from looters? Apparently oblivious to the fact that he was seeking favours from his country's enemies, through an intermediary the duke asked officials at the German embassy in Madrid to protect his house in the Boulevard Suchet in occupied Paris. Ribbentrop was delighted to oblige. A teletype survives from Ribbentrop's office giving orders on 30 June to undertake 'unofficially and confidentially an unobtrusive observation on the duke's residence' and instructing the German ambassador in Madrid, von Stohrer, 'to inform the duke confidentially through a Spanish intermediary that the Foreign Minister [Ribbentrop] is looking out for its protection'.[45] The Windsors sent a similar request through the Italian embassy in Madrid to the Italian government to protect their Château de la Croë at Cap d'Antibes, should the Italians occupy the Riviera.[46] It is perhaps a measure of the duke's detachment from reality that he was prepared to attempt to ask such a favour from the enemies of his country who were busily engaged in all-out war and issuing invasion dates. It was beginning to look as though the duke had other plans.

Meanwhile, the Duke of Windsor's ill-timed haggling with British officials intensified. Churchill urged him to resolve his problems with his family once he was home, but the duke refused to return unless 'I know the result'.[47] For the duke it was a matter of honour. He could not see that he was indulging in a form of emotional blackmail; all he could see was the humiliation for Wallis if no one from the royal family acknowledged her. After arguing with the Windsors 'for hours on end', by the end of June the British ambassador, Samuel Hoare, told Churchill there was only one outstanding issue on which the couple would not back down. They wanted assurances that on their return their place within the royal family should be confirmed, even if it was just a token gesture: to be received by the king and queen at the palace and to have this announced in the court circular. Just fifteen minutes of the king and queen's time could resolve this dangerous rift, Hoare reasoned.[48]

It was too late. The harm had been done. The Duke of Windsor's negotiations at this most difficult of times had undermined the king. George VI did not feel equal to the task of managing his wilful older brother if he returned to England. What sort of king would he be with the Windsors forever at his heels with veiled threats and impossible requests? Having talked it over with both his mother and his wife, the king was resolved and would not compromise. When he met the prime minister on 3 July he spoke frankly: 'I did not see what job he could have in this country & that "she" would not be safe here.'[49] George VI was so convinced that Wallis lay behind his brother's bad behaviour that he could not bring himself to use her name in his diary, referring to her simply as 'she'. Winston had always been Windsor's friend, but now the king was on first name terms with him. George VI sensed that even Winston's unending patience with his brother was beginning to wear a little thin.

While negotiations continued over the duke's future, British officials hoped, at the very least, to move the duke and duchess out of Spain—with its many German agents and sympathisers—to neutral Portugal. They had to wait while the Duke of Kent was in Lisbon; the prime minister of Portugal did not wish to have both dukes in the country at the same time. But on 3 July the Windsors finally arrived in Lisbon where arrangements had been made for them to stay in a villa owned by a wealthy Portuguese banker, Ricardo Espirito Santo Silva. It was a stunning setting, with distant views over the Atlantic, the ceaseless sound of the crashing of waves on rocks down below. But the duke did not have time to take in the beauty of the surroundings. Officials handed him a telegram he would never forget. It was from Winston Churchill.

'Your Royal Highness has taken active military rank and refusal to obey direct orders of competent military authority would create a serious situation. I hope it will not be necessary for such orders to be sent. I most strongly urge immediate compliance with the wishes of the Government.'[50]

The duke read the telegram visibly shaken. It was tantamount to a threat of court martial. The marked change in tone from his most loyal ally, Churchill, was a shock. Since the abdication he had counted on Churchill seeing his point of view.

The prime minister's first telegram was followed swiftly by a second bombshell. There was no longer a demand for him to come home. Instead, he was offered a post as the Governor of the Bahamas.

The duke was stunned. It was a bolt from the blue. In his eyes the Bahamas was one of the least significant spots anywhere in the empire, a coral archipelago in the Atlantic some 150 miles off the coast of Florida. As he read and re-read the telegram he knew at once this was a personal banishment.

'I have done my best,' Churchill told the duke, in a 'grievous situation'.[51] For officials in London, there was one overriding question. Would the duke accept?

Shaken by the indignities piled upon him from London, the duke began to see advantages in the position in the Caribbean. He could avoid the shame of returning to Britain a lesser man, his wife's exclusion from court plain for all the world to see. In the Bahamas, he could keep his pride intact. He could be his own man in Wallis's eyes, and maintain his distance from George VI and British policy. With great reluctance, he accepted. The Duke of Kent privately expressed the family relief in a letter to Prince Paul of Yugoslavia: 'to accept to be Governor in a small place like that is fantastic!'[52]

But it was not long before a disturbing new report reached officials in London, damning Windsor still further. This time, it was not troublesome telegrams from Windsor himself, but British intelligence from a source close to Konstantin von Neurath, a former Foreign Minister of Germany and now Reich Protector of occupied Czechoslovakia. On 7 July Sir Alexander Cadogan, under-secretary at the Foreign Office, received a report of sufficient concern that he passed it up the line and it reached the palace that same day. A handwritten note on the letter also confirms 'PM to see'.

> My dear Cadogan. A new source, on trial, whom we know to be in close
> touch with Neurath's entourage in Prague, has reported as follows:
> 'Germans expect assistance from Duke and Duchess of Windsor, latter

MOST SECRET   F. I/9.

                                    C/4653.

                                    LONDON.

                                    7th July, 1940.

My dear Cadogan,

        A new source, on trial, whom we know to be in close touch

with Neurath's entourage in Prague, has reported as follows:-

            Germans expect assistance from Duke and Duchess
            of Windsor, latter desiring at any price to become
            Queen. Germans have been negotiating with her since
            June 27th. Status quo in England except undertaking
            to form anti-Russian alliance. Germans propose to
            form Opposition Government under Duke of Windsor
            having first changed public opinion by propaganda.
            Germans think King George will abdicate during attack
            on London.

                        Yours sincerely,

The Hon. Sir Alexander Cadogan, G.C.M.G., C.B.

A British intelligence report of 7 July 1940 which was escalated rapidly to the
prime minister claimed the Germans had been 'negotiating' with the Duchess
of Windsor (THE NATIONAL ARCHIVES)

desiring at any price to become Queen. Germans have been negotiating
with her since June 27th. Status quo in England except undertaking to form
anti-Russian alliance. Germans propose to form Opposition Government
under Duke of Windsor having first changed public opinion by propaganda.
Germans think King George will abdicate during attack on London.'[53]

George VI was confronted with evidence that showed the Germans proposed to replace him with his brother. Reading the letter in the palace there
were so many questions. How much 'assistance' had his brother led them to

expect? Was it possible that Windsor would betray his own brother? George VI's view that '*she*' lay behind the trouble appeared vindicated by the source. The Germans seemed to recognise what he had long suspected—that Wallis desired 'at any price to become Queen'. He could only speculate on how the information was reaching sources close to von Neurath. Who was his brother mixed up with in Portugal?

When the prime minister next came to Buckingham Palace, on 10 July, the king found, with some relief, that he and Winston could at last begin to see eye to eye on the issue of his brother. Winston, who had always extended the hand of friendship and loyalty to the ex-king, appeared to be changing his view and agreed with the War Cabinet 'that it was better that D [David] should not come here'. The king, in turn, was able to open up a little to his prime minister on this most painful family issue. Instead of being made to feel at fault for what appeared to be an unbrotherly stance, he felt he could explain his position and be understood. 'D had always tried to make out to Winston that I was working against him. This was most unfair as I had done my best to make him real-ise . . . what I had done, had had to be done for the country's sake.'[54] Now there was intelligence to support his point of view.

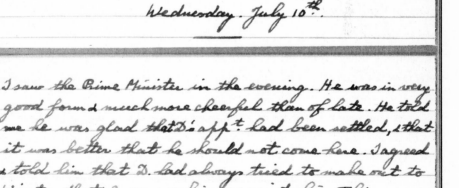

Extract from George VI's war diary on 10 July 1940 (THE ROYAL ARCHIVES © HER MAJESTY QUEEN ELIZABETH II)

There was a heavy blanket of cloud over the east coast of England at 7.30 am on 10 July 1940 as pilots from RAF Coltishall, near Norwich, scrambled to intercept a lone German reconnaissance plane. This proved to be the opening salvo on a day that would mark the start of the Battle of Britain as Goering's *Luftwaffe* intensified the bombing of convoys in the Channel. At 1.50 pm the ominous sound of German bombers filled the air off the Kent coast. With a deafening crescendo suddenly more than sixty enemy aircraft were directly above the biggest convoy sailing that day, codenamed 'Bread'. It was the biggest formation yet crossing the Channel, the ships below desperately dispersing as bombs fell. British fighters roared into attack against German bombers. A maze of vapour trails circled high above the ships as planes soared and plunged above them.[55] Although success that day went to the RAF, it was a menacing foretaste of what the *Luftwaffe* had in store for Britain's Channel convoys, the lifeblood of the country.

While the *Luftwaffe* gave Britain a warning of Hitler's intent, Ribbentrop hoped he might have a rather more brilliant solution to 'the British problem' which would upstage his rival, Goering, and place him firmly within Hitler's charmed circle—and Windsor seemed to be playing into his hands. Unchastened by Churchill's evident displeasure, the duke continued to air his pro-peace, anti-British government views liberally in Portugal, duly logged by staff in the American, British—and German—embassies. Stohrer's counterpart in Portugal, the German ambassador, Oswald von Hoyningen Huene, sent a confidential memo to Ribbentrop on 11 July explaining that, most conveniently, the duke wished to stay in Europe and delay his travel to the Bahamas 'as long as possible'. Was the duke buying time while the Germans brought the British to the negotiating table? The German ambassador built a portrait of an ex-king who was now ready to betray his country and who was being sent away deliberately so that he could not provide leadership to the peace movement in Britain. The duke 'is convinced that if he had remained on the throne war could have been avoided, and characterises himself as a firm supporter of a peaceful arrangement with Germany', concluded Huene. 'The duke definitely believes that continued severe bombing would make England ready for peace.'[56] For Ribbentrop, here at last was 'the king across the water', apparently willing to negotiate as soon as the threat of heavy bombing brought the proud British nation to the table.

Ribbentrop sent an immediate reply to Stohrer in Spain marked 'Special Confidential Handling. Top Secret'. The German Foreign Minister had a cunning plan to exploit Windsor's grievances still further. The first step was for Stohrer to find a way to bring the duke back to Spain where the Germans had more influence. Ribbentrop advised Stohrer that the invitation was best handled by the Spanish: perhaps friends of the duke could find a reason to ask him to return? Once safely in Spain, the duke would be told: 'Germany wants peace with the English people, the Churchill clique stands in the way of that peace, and that it would be a good thing if the Duke would hold himself in readiness for further developments.' To achieve peace, Germany 'would be prepared to accommodate any desire expressed by the Duke, particularly with a view to the assumption of the English throne by the Duke and Duchess.' Windsor was to be left in no doubt that if he co-operated with Germany, Ribbentrop in turn would help him and the duchess lead 'a life suitable to a king'.[57]

Knowingly or otherwise, the duke's actions continued to support the German plot. He found fresh grounds to pick a quarrel with British officials. Although arrangements were made for him to sail to the Bahamas on 1 August, he threatened not to leave unless his new—and increasingly petty—requests were met. For two weeks angry telegrams were exchanged with London and, once again, Churchill was drawn in. At issue: the duke wanted his personal valet and chauffeur exempted from military service to join him in the Bahamas, an unfortunate precedent to which officials could not agree. The duke had also booked his passage to the Bahamas via New York in order to take his wife shopping and to see her doctor. Churchill would not permit this. There was a risk the duke would rally the cause of peace during the critical build-up to the American elections in November. When the Foreign Office went to the lengths of arranging for his ship, the *Excalibur*, to be diverted to Bermuda rather than stop in New York, the duke was incensed and wrote to Churchill in strong language, threatening resignation.

The duke was keen to please Wallis, and Wallis, faced with the prospect of travel to some far-flung island, was keen to be reunited with her worldly wealth. Her possessions loomed large in her mind, perhaps all the more important to her while her royal position was so visibly denied. Oblivious to the dangers, it was not sufficient for the Germans to keep watch over her treasures in France, she now wanted her maid, Jeanne-Marguerite Moulichon, to go into enemy territory to collect them. She persuaded the duke to make arrangements for the intrepid Mademoiselle Moulichon to return to occupied Paris to pick up 'all the Windsor linen', and other essentials. Her best chef from La Croë should also come with them to the Bahamas. Once again, the duke obliged, despite the fact that this required further co-operation with his country's enemies.[58]

Just how was this German co-operation secured? British intelligence had now woken up to the case. Cadogan soon received a report from his source in Lisbon who made contact with a 'Mr Gray', described as a tall Englishman

with white hair, who was working as a private secretary to Windsor. 'Mr Gray',
who was in fact 'Major Gray Phillips', was indeed assigned the onerous task
of overseeing the transport of all the Windsors' private possessions. Perhaps
uncomfortable with the position in which he had been placed, Gray Phillips
appears to have confided to Cadogan's informant the great care with which the
Germans honoured the duke's requests.

'Special camions were sent to and fro and a detailed inventory list was made
of all the furniture and personal property of the Duke and Duchess of Windsor
which was shown to the Duchess for approval, to give her the opportunity to
say if there was anything missing. Some of the more valuable belongings were
transported in limousines and special instructions were given for everything to
be in perfect order. The desire of the Germans to please the Duke and Duchess
of Windsor was absolutely marked and evident . . . '[59]

Cadogan still did not know just *how* Windsor's staff were liaising with the
Germans. On 19 July this changed, with new intelligence revealing at least one
point of direct contact: through the owner of the very house where the duke
and duchess were staying. Windsor was seeing a great deal of Ricardo Espirito
Santo Silva. 'We have now learned from a reliable and well-placed source in
Lisbon that Silva and his wife are in close touch with the German embassy and
that Silva had a three hour interview with the German Minister on the 15 July.'[60]

This British intelligence once again was duly passed on to the prime minister. Signor Santo had been trusted. He had been permitted to host the Duke of
Kent when he had stayed in Portugal. His integrity was accepted in the city and
he traded with British banks. But was this the whole story?

Lord Halifax himself took the next intelligence report directly to the prime
minister. It presented a very different view of the charming and wealthy Signor
Santo: 'Politically he is a crook. He is handling very large sums in bank notes
and dollar securities from Germany via Switzerland to the Americas. These
monies are almost certainly German loot from the captive countries . . . '[61]

The Holy Fox and Britain's Bulldog took in the report together. Somehow,
under their watch, the ex-king of England appeared to have fallen into the hands
of a criminal financier who was reporting his every word directly to the Germans.

I n July 1940 Hitler himself had still not given up on the idea of negotiating
terms with England. Churchill and his Cabinet supporters' desire to fight
on in the face of glaring military defeat was an anathema. Many in the Nazi

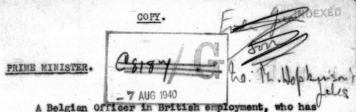

COPY.

PRIME MINISTER.

— 7 AUG 1940

A Belgian Officer in British employment, who has just returned from Madrid and Lisbon, came to see me yesterday and told me that

1) Senhor Esperito Santo, head of the Bank of that name in Lisbon, is very pro-German and a centre of peace propaganda. H.R.H. the Duke of Windsor visited him in Lisbon and according to Senhor Esperito Santo, manifested extreme defeatist and pacifist sympathies.

I find that Mr.Jebb, Foreign Office, has heard similar reports about H.R.H.

Senhor Esperito Santo is regarded as financially sound by British banks, with whom he has many dealings. Politically he is a crook. He is handling very large sums in bank notes and dollar securities from Germany via Switzerland to the Americas. These monies are almost certainly German loot from the captive countries.

(2).....

Lord Halifax took the intelligence on Ricardo Esperito Santo Silva directly to the Prime Minister. The British now believed the owner of the house where the Windsors were staying was a German informant who was 'almost certainly' involved in laundering 'German loot from the captive countries.' (THE NATIONAL ARCHIVES)

leadership still believed in a powerful pro-peace movement in Britain. Goebbels wrote of two parties in Britain: 'one thoroughgoing war party and one peace party'. Opinion, he believed, 'was completely divided'.[62] Hitler's defiant address in the *Reichstag* on 19 July claimed he too wanted peace. 'Mr Churchill . . . no doubt will already be in Canada,' he goaded. 'For millions of other people, however, great suffering will begin.' He appealed 'once more to reason and common sense in Great Britain . . . I see no reason why this war should go on'.[63]

Suddenly from New York to Rome a spate of press reports appeared alleging that a new British government was forming around the Duke of Windsor and that George VI might be forced into abdication. 'The Duke of Windsor has telegraphed King George,' reported *Gazetta del Popolo* on 22 July, urging him to form an extraordinary Cabinet 'to include former Prime Minister Neville Chamberlain and David Lloyd George as well as Viscount Halifax'.[64] 'Plenipotentiary Cabinet for Britain Urged on King by Windsor' headlined the *New York Times* on 23 July, adding helpfully that 'plenipotentiary' means the 'power to negotiate treaties'.[65] The Finnish and Danish press also carried reports that the Duke of Windsor and the former Liberal leader, Lloyd George, were working towards a peaceful settlement with Germany.[66]

Foreign Office officials, eager to damp down reports, concluded it was fraudulent enemy propaganda deliberately exploiting the Duke of Windsor's stand in Lisbon to try to precipitate a crisis in Britain. The reports were so sensationalist it was decided not to grace them with a denial.[67]

Lord Halifax, one of Britain's former top appeasers, was chosen by the Cabinet to give the reply to Hitler's speech. If he spoke out it would help to dispel enemy propaganda claiming that he still sought to be part of a new 'peace cabinet'. 'Peace should be based on justice,' Halifax declared in a broadcast on 22 July. Hitler's appeal 'was to the base instinct of fear, and his only arguments, threats . . . We shall not stop fighting until Freedom is secure.'[68]

Despite such fighting talk from Britain's former appeaser, behind the scenes Hitler would not give up his efforts to make contact with those who favoured peace. In late July he made his wishes plain not just to Ribbentrop, but also to Rudolf Hess. In a lengthy discussion which would inspire his slavishly loyal deputy for months to come, he impressed on Hess his keen desire for peace with Britain if he could only find a way to reach the eminent aristocrats and other leaders in British society who had expressed pro-peace views.[69] Intriguingly at this time, and almost certainly in a desire not to antagonise Britain's ruling classes whose support might soon be needed, certain prisoners of war found themselves singled out for favoured treatment. Among the chosen *prominente* was the queen's own nephew, John Elphinstone, who had been serving in the Black Watch when he was captured at Abbeville before he could be evacuated.[70]

But for Ribbentrop, in the high-stakes game of negotiating peace, Britain's ex-king was the greatest trophy of all. Stohrer, the German ambassador in Spain, chose the duke's trusted friend, Don Miguel Primo de Rivera, the Civil Governor of Madrid, for the delicate mission of luring the Windsors back to Spain. Stohrer updated Ribbentrop with their plan on 23 July. De Rivera was making arrangements for the duke and duchess to leave Lisbon for a long excursion in the country where they would cross the border at a prearranged location with the help of the Spanish secret police. The duke and duchess 'very much desired to return to Spain', Stohrer told Ribbentrop. 'The Duke was considering making a public statement disavowing present English policy and breaking with his brother.'[71]

Ribbentrop briefed Hitler on his progress later that evening. Together the leader of the German Reich and his Foreign Minister devised Operation Willi—their codename for the British duke. A young and ambitious SS *Brigadeführer*, Walter Schellenberg, chief of counter-intelligence for Himmler, was selected to run the operation and found himself summoned urgently to meet Ribbentrop.

According to Schellenberg's memoirs, the Führer himself gave approval for the Germans to place fifty million Swiss francs at the Duke of Windsor's disposal, if 'he was ready to make some official gesture dissociating himself from the manoeuvres of the British royal family'. The Führer—evidently sympathetic to the duke's little weakness—was quite prepared to go to a higher figure if necessary. The duke was to be set up in readiness as a compliant 'king across the water' should his brother prove less than amenable when Britain was brought to its knees. 'Hitler attaches the greatest importance to this operation,' Ribbentrop told Schellenberg. 'He has come to the conclusion that if the Duke should prove hesitant, he himself would have no objection to your helping the duke to reach the right decision by coercion . . . ' Schellenberg was ordered to outwit the British Secret Service 'even at risk of his own life'.[72]

Schellenberg flew on a private plane to Madrid the next day and conferred with the German ambassador, Stohrer, whose plot to lure the duke back to Spain was shaping up well. Stohrer's confidential emissary had gone so far as to raise the prospect of a return to the British throne by the duke and duchess. 'Both the Duke and Duchess gave evidence of astonishment' and told Stohrer's emissary that this was not possible after the abdication. When the emissary 'expressed his expectation that the course of the war might bring about changes even in the English constitution the Duchess especially became very pensive . . . '[73]

Just how complicit were the duke and duchess in the plot to return to Spain? The duke was an intelligent man. He had had meetings with known Fascists, such as Don Miguel, and had liaised with the Germans successfully through intermediaries over his possessions. He did not co-operate with official British wishes at a time when the country was in dire crisis. Nor did many of his views aired at the time express British policy. And Stohrer, at least, understood that it was the duke and duchess's 'firm intention' to return to Spain.[74] It stretches credibility that the Windsors did not know something of what was going on. Even the British ambassador to Spain, Hoare, heard that the Duke was intending to return. According to Stohrer, the Windsors went so far as to secure the necessary travel permits. He informed Ribbentrop that the duke, 'after energetic pressure, had now obtained through the English Embassy in Lisbon a visa for Spain'.[75]

To ensure the duke's continued co-operation, Stohrer sent a skilfully drafted letter to make him fearful of British intelligence while also offering assurance he would be a free political agent in Spain. The letter to the duke included 'the very precisely prepared plan for carrying out the crossing of the frontier'. Schellenberg meanwhile had arrived in Lisbon to fine-tune the German plan with the Portuguese. Just in case anything should go wrong, a fall-back plan was set in place to enable the Windsors to fly to Spain. Finally, added Stohrer, 'Schellenberg requests that the Chief of the Security Police be informed of the planning'. Reinhard Heydrich himself, the sinister head of the Gestapo, was to be in on the plot.[76]

In London in late July, Churchill was preoccupied with the urgent business of bringing an American rifle convoy safely into port. With 200,000 rifles on board, it was the largest consignment of weapons yet. Their loss 'would be a disaster of the first order', Churchill warned the First Lord of the Admiralty on 27 July.[77] In the midst of preparations, Churchill was alerted to troubling new intelligence concerning the Duke of Windsor. Just how much he knew of the plot brewing in Lisbon is unclear but he did realise that suddenly the duke was unwilling to sail to the Bahamas on 1 August as agreed, and summoned the cavalry in the most unlikely form of Sir Walter Monckton. Churchill judged that the respected lawyer who had navigated the duke through the quicksands of the abdication would be the ideal man to steer him on to the right path once again. Seated in Number 10 before the prime minister, Sir Walter was soon made aware of the gravity of his mission, although this particular brief he would later ponder with some amusement was one of the oddest of the 'Odd Jobs I have Done'.[78] His task: to outwit the enemy and make sure that the duke and duchess sailed on the *Excalibur* to the Bahamas on 1 August, without fail.

The challenge ahead for Monckton was being made harder by the day as Schellenberg's team worked tirelessly to convince the duke that his greatest threat came from British intelligence. In Portugal, within the walled gardens of their exquisite seaside villa, Boca do Inferno, the duke and duchess suddenly found they were not enjoying their holiday. Thanks to Schellenberg, the atmosphere was increasingly frightening. One of their Portuguese guards warned the duke of a plot by British intelligence to assassinate him. The duchess received a similar threat hidden in a bouquet of flowers delivered to their residence. Portuguese intelligence suspected a bomb would be planted on board their ship, the *Excalibur*. The Windsors were left in no doubt their lives would be in danger if they complied with British demands to sail for the Bahamas on 1 August. A stone shattered a window at their villa one night, as though the would-be assassin was trying to break in. A thorough search of the house in the small hours added to the growing unease. When the frightened Windsors suggested transferring to a hotel in central Lisbon, the Portuguese expressed worries about 'intelligence reports from various countries concerning the hostile intentions of the Churchill regime towards both Windsors'. The duke found himself in the position where he did not know who to trust. There were rather too many suave and well-groomed men for comfort, offering to open doors that promised everything. And the more they pursued their themes, the more his anxiety grew. He began to consider it possible that his once loyal friend, Churchill, did now want him out of the way. Thanks to Schellenberg's network of spies, there was no shortage of advisers on hand ready to convince the duke that he would be much safer in Spain.[79]

Sir Walter Monckton was not the usual action hero as his flying boat sped into the bay near Cascais near Lisbon on 28 July. He was in a totally different category to the likes of his adversaries: Reinhard Heydrich, Walter Schellenberg and Joachim von Ribbentrop. These were men whose allegiance could turn on a sixpence, always listening for undercurrents threading through the various plots. The serious, well-meaning Monckton, safe as houses, unlikely to run off with a chorus girl, was a mystery to them. He exuded an air of Britishness; the bowler hat, briefcase and quality overcoat marked him out at a distance as an English gentleman. At close hand, the dark round-rimmed spectacles and neatly combed receding hairline imparted the slightly studious air of an academic. Was he a civil servant? Was he a powerbroker in some subtle form of British disguise? Was he open to offers? He did not look like serious opposition. The 49-year-old lawyer from Kent was not trained in espionage and did not carry a gun. It is perhaps not surprising that his presence soon had Schellenberg foxed.

The head of counter-espionage for the Gestapo could not believe that the man 'who calls himself Sir Walter Turner Monckstone' was really a lawyer from Kent. Schellenberg was convinced this was cover and his real identity was more likely to be 'a member of the personal police of the reigning King by the name of Cameron', he reported to Berlin on 30 July 1940.[80]

But whatever his reason for being there, the Germans were soon aware that in the presence of Monckton, the duke's wavering upper lip had stiffened. He appeared less sure of the future. With just two days to go before the duke's ship was due to sail from Lisbon, the Germans decided to raise the stakes. It was time to play some key cards: first, the duchess's hapless maid, Jeanne-Marguerite Moulichon.

Mademoiselle Moulichon had at last reached the Windsors' house in Boulevard Suchet in occupied Paris where she packed several trunks with the Windsor treasures, including their very costly and luxurious linen. But her plan to take the express train to the south of France in time to reach Lisbon for the departure of the *Excalibur* was soon in tatters. When the car arrived to take her to the station, the door opened to reveal—not the friendly Spanish officials that she expected, but a German escort. The terrified maid was informed she was detained in France.[81] If the duchess wanted to travel with her favourite Windsor linen she would have to wait in Europe for it.

The next card to be played was the duke's Spanish friend, Don Miguel Primo de Rivera, who was flown to Lisbon at the eleventh hour to try to persuade Windsor to delay leaving Europe. Rivera swayed the duke, using his charm and influence to convince him that the attack on Britain would soon force both the British government and George VI from the country. It would be much better if the duke remained in Europe to act as mediator. Further claims were made about British intelligence plots against the duke. The duke wavered. Don Miguel Primo de Rivera was so convincing that the duke begged Monckton for a few weeks' delay to gather more intelligence on the alleged British plot against him. It took all Monckton's persuasive powers to induce the duke and duchess to set sail the next day.[82]

Ribbentrop schemed to the last. He contemplated abduction, but decided against it, as he needed the duke compliant. Shortly before midnight on 31 July, the night before departure, he was ready to play his ace: the duke's own host, Ricardo do Espirito Santo Silva. Santo Silva was enjoying a drink at the duke's farewell party at a local hotel, but was summoned to Huene's home on Ribbentrop's orders in the small hours. Huene asked him to reveal to the duke that Germany was determined to 'force England to make peace'. The Germans wished the duke to keep himself prepared for such an eventuality. 'Germany would be willing to cooperate most closely with the Duke and to clear the way for any desire expressed by the Duke and Duchess.'[83]

On 1 August, the morning of the duke's departure, Santo Silva, duly briefed, had one last exchange with his royal guest. Their conversation was reported back to Berlin by Huene. 'The duke paid tribute to the Fuhrer's desire for peace,' wrote Huene, 'which was completely in agreement with his own point of view.' To Santo Silva's appeal that the duke 'cooperate at a suitable time to establish peace, he agreed gladly'. But Windsor had decided to wait for the opportune moment and, until then, to follow orders from the British government. To do anything too early 'might bring about a scandal, and deprive him of his prestige in England'. He was fully prepared 'for any personal sacrifice' when the time was right 'and would remain in continuing communication with his previous host and had agreed with him a code word upon receiving which he would immediately come back over'.[84] From the evidence of this telegram, it would appear the duke was fully prepared to facilitate a peaceful settlement once bombing brought the British into talks with the Nazis but until then he would go along with commands from Westminster.

It was 1 August 1940. A large crowd gathered to watch the Windsors' departure for the Caribbean. They were obliged to wait because Schellenberg plotted to the end to convince the Windsors it was not safe to sail. The duchess was much exercised about her mislaid household goods. Quite apart from the troublesome absence of her maid from Paris, she was divested of other treasures owing to an inexplicable breakdown in one of the cars in their luggage convoy. It took time to make alternative arrangements and then further delays arose as a staged arrest was organised on the ship, with a witness claiming he had seen suspicious evidence of sabotage.[85]

The Windsors remained fearful, uncertain whether there was a British plot to assassinate them or a German plot to murder them and blame the British. Like canaries in a mine, their staff were required to board first. Monckton escorted the duke and duchess up the gangway. Further reassurance was provided by the Portuguese police who made a full search of the entire ship. There was even an armed officer from Special Branch summoned by Monckton. At last the *Excalibur* cast off, its dark hull easing down the mouth of the River Tagus towards the open Atlantic.[86] Schellenberg watched at a discreet distance as his complex plans dissolved in the mist gathering over the estuary, finally defeated.

With any lingering hope for a negotiated peace through the duke that summer now gone, Hitler instigated Directive 17. The raids on the Channel were just the opening. The *Luftwaffe* was instructed to crush the RAF with 'all means at its disposal'. The Battle of Britain could commence. The delay, however, had worked in Churchill's favour. In just a few weeks, his chart showing his weapons target for the army divisions showed progress in bright columns of red.

But in Germany the idea of an Anglo-German peace agreement was not completely dead. Ribbentrop's botched effort created an opportunity for the deputy Führer himself. Rudolf Hess thought he might be able to succeed where Ribbentrop had failed. The peace party in Britain could not just vanish. There must be another way of making contact.[87]

On 8 September, Rudolf Hess's mentor and personal adviser, Dr Albrecht Haushofer, was summoned to a strictly confidential meeting. He kept a secret record of his discussion with Hess entitled 'ARE THERE STILL POSSIBIL-ITIES OF A GERMAN ENGLISH PEACE?'. Haushofer spoke his mind, explaining that the British leadership had no confidence in any treaty with Hitler. 'In the Anglo-Saxon world,' he told Hess, 'the Fuhrer was regarded as Satan's representative on earth and had to be fought.' Hess would not give up. There had to be another way. He pushed Haushofer for the names of any highly placed individuals that he knew of in Britain. 'Was there not somebody in England who was ready for peace?'[88]

Under pressure, Haushofer did come up with a name. Over the following days he worked out a route whereby they might be contacted. On 23 September 1940 his curious handwritten letter was posted to an intermediary in Wembley, a 'Mrs V Roberts at 6 Hill Croft Crescent'.

My dear Douglo

Even if there is only a slight chance that this letter should reach you in good time, there is a chance, and I am determined to make use of it . . . If you remember some of my last communications in July 1939 you—and your friends in high places—may find some significance in the fact that I am able to ask you whether you could find time to have a talk with me somewhere on the outskirts of Europe, perhaps Portugal. I could reach Lisbon any time . . . within a few days after receiving news from you . . . Letters will reach me in the following way. Double closed envelope. Inside address: Dr A.H. Nothing more! Outside address:

Minero Silricola Ltd
Rua do Cais de Santarem 32/I
Lisbon, Portugal . . . Yours ever A.[89]

B., Sept 23rd

My dear Douglo —

Even if there is only a slight chance that this letter should reach you in good Time, there is a chance, and I am determined to make use of it.

First of all to give you a personal greeting I am sure you know that my attachment to you remains unaltered and unalterable, whatever the circumstances may be. I have heard of your father's death. I do hope. he did not suffer too much - after so long a life of permanent pain. I heard that your brother-in-law Northumberland lost his life near Dunkerque – even modern times must allow us to share grief across all boundaries.

On behalf of Rudolf Hess, Dr Albrecht Haushofer requested a meeting with his British contact, 'My dear Douglo', on 23 September 1940. (The National Archives)

The intended recipient invited for top-secret talks in Lisbon—'My dear Douglo'—was none other than the king's new Lord Steward of the Household: Air Commodore Douglas Douglas-Hamilton, 14th Duke of Hamilton.

PART THREE

AUGUST 1940–DECEMBER 1942

8

THERE WILL ALWAYS BE AN ENGLAND

'There will always be an England to stand before the world . . . as the citadel of hope and freedom . . .'

—George VI, creating the George Cross on 23 September 1940

The Duke of Kent witnessed at first hand each escalation in the Battle of Britain as the might of the *Luftwaffe* bore down across the country that summer. The Channel battles of July and early August 1940 were overtaken by a terrifying new phase where enemy pilots appeared to single out airfields and aircraft hangars, targeting the infrastructure of the RAF itself. It was Goering's 'Attack of the Eagle' which aimed to pulverise Britain's air defences. The skies darkened over England as the German bombers came over in waves. The *Luftwaffe* had the advantage of operating from new forward airfields from Norway to France. German confidence was also high; their airmen, in Churchill's words, the 'proud victors of Poland, Norway, the Low Countries and France'.[1]

Kent's brief to report on the welfare of pilots in Flying Training Command was soon expanded to include pilots throughout the RAF. He saw the devastation: RAF bases pockmarked with craters and wreckage strewn across southern England. Inexorably he was drawn into this new, intense world where warm friendships made in the morning were lost in the fury of an afternoon air raid. These were unbearable days; constant witness to the heart-stopping bravery of others. If he was present at a pilots' briefing before a sortie, all too often he could not bring himself to leave and would wait to welcome the bomber crews home after dawn. There was no time for boredom now as the RAF was caught in a battle for survival on which Britain's chances to fend off an invasion would also depend. For obvious reasons all Kent's movements were kept secret with no advance publicity but none the less Pathé newsreels survive showing him at the aerodromes inspecting aircraft, talking to the mechanics and posing with the heroic pilots themselves.[2]

Each day brought more alarming news. August 15 saw the largest air battle yet. A hundred German bombers targeted Tyneside, while 800 more aircraft headed for southern England.[3] Viewed from the coast the enemy aircraft advanced in such numbers they seemed 'to make an aluminium ceiling to the sky', observed one reporter.[4] Pilots were often raw recruits, hardly marked by life as they walked towards almost certain death with all the careless courage of seasoned fighters each time the sirens wailed. This was the time for heroes when flying aces took on legendary status; pilots such as 'Sailor' Malan, Douglas Bader, Brian Lane, George 'Grumpy' Unwin, Wallace Cunningham and many others.

On 16 August Churchill went to RAF Uxbridge, the headquarters of No. 11 Group Fighter Command. He descended to the Flight Operations Room of the underground bunker, 60 foot below ground. The air was stale and the atmosphere tense as staff plotted the battle in the skies by moving numbered blocks on the map table. On the wall the action of each squadron was shown by lights, 'Ordered to Raid', 'Enemy Sighted' and so on, the heroic efforts of each one translated into tangible results before them. For the prime minister it was all too immediate: life and death games played out in the skies, at once remote and horribly close: duelling with machineguns in an unfriendly element, death or wounding the outcome of the smallest misjudgement. Later that day, as he stepped into his car to leave, he turned to Major General Ismay, his chief military assistant, 'Don't speak to me, I have never been so moved.' He lapsed into silence. A few minutes later he added, never 'has so much been owed by so many to so few.' It was a powerful theme that he developed for a speech on 20 August. 'The gratitude of every home in our Island . . . goes out to the British airmen,' he told the House. 'Never in the field of human conflict was so much owed by so many to so few.'[5] The king visited the Uxbridge bunker a couple of weeks later, Churchill's words still resonating in his mind. 'No truer words have ever been used,' he wrote in his diary.[6]

On several occasions Kent's visit to an aerodrome coincided with the *Luftwaffe* and it was sometimes impossible to carry on the inspection with safety. Marina was worried as the duke had several narrow escapes. At one airbase, the house in which he slept was destroyed by fire within moments of him leaving; at another airfield in Kent he missed the bombs by just four minutes.[7] Those facing the enemy in the air were not so lucky. Churchill was informed that between 24 August and 6 September, 103 pilots died, 128 were seriously wounded and 466 Spitfires and Hurricanes were destroyed or put out of action. He estimated that a quarter of Britain's pilots had died in the Battle of Britain at this point. There were 260 keen new recruits ready to take on the challenge, but they were inexperienced and at greater risk. Fighter Command was in a perilous state. With exhausted pilots and damaged infrastructure, it was unclear how many more days of battering the RAF could sustain.

Just at this point, when it appeared that RAF stations and their crews could take no more, Goering changed tactics—unwittingly giving the RAF a breathing space. At 4.16 pm on 7 September 1940, a vast armada of aircraft approached the British coast. Goering had assembled the largest aerial formation ever seen, stretching a distance of 20 miles.[8] Engines throbbing, the heavy droning smothering all other sounds, on they came, homing in on the target. A sinister new phase of the Battle of Britain had begun. This time, civilians were in Goering's sights. The bombers were converging on the capital. It was the start of the London blitz.

Without warning, Londoners were suddenly visited by hell. The deafening noise of hundreds of aircraft overhead was paralysing for those below until the first bombs fell. Overcrowded slums were soon demolished. Within minutes the docks were ablaze, the East End transformed into fields of fire, the sky a lurid red. Nearly 400 bombers and 600 fighters pounded the docks in the East End of London that night. It was the first of twenty-three days and fifty-seven continuous nights of attack, which began with the familiar penetrating wail of sirens in the late afternoon. Hitler believed that this concentrated bombing might result in eight million Londoners going mad, a cowed population, weakened politicians and British submission to German will.[9]

George VI and Queen Elizabeth responded to the emergency in the capital with courage. His former reputation as a weak man whose ability was in doubt was misleading. It was a strong man who escorted the queen through the ruins of the East End as bombing escalated in September 1940. Almost every day they spent several hours talking to people in the affected areas of London. But the sight of royalty, apparently unsullied by war, clean and smartly dressed, sometimes provoked anger. On occasion they were even jeered and rubbish was thrown. But the hostility was soon to change.

On 9 September a bomb fell near the garden entrance of the palace, remarkably close to the king's study. Since it did not explode, George VI continued to use his room, only to understand the rashness of this course of action the following night when the bomb did detonate with such violence that 'all the windows on all the floors [were] broken by the upward blast'. The swimming pool was wrecked and the garden 'a fine mess'. It was only the wire netting on the windows to their private rooms that prevented further damage.[10]

As the king wrote to his mother, enclosing photographs of the damage, he could hear the sound of anti-aircraft guns nearby. The main structure of the palace was still sound, he reassured her, and the Office of Works were doing the best they could to fix all the broken windows 'with various forms of temporary stuff until they can get some more glass'; in the meanwhile he, Elizabeth and the princesses were sleeping at the bottom of Victoria Tower at Windsor having sandbagged the windows. Queen Wilhelmina had already taken alternative lodgings and they now moved Uncle Charles and Prince Olav out of the palace to the relative safety of Newbury, 60 miles away.[11]

If the king and queen were troubled they were keen not to show it. They came to London each day, transferring to rooms on the inner courtyard of the palace, and carried on with tours of the East End. But they were soon in no doubt that the palace was an official target. On 13 September it was cloudy and pouring with rain. The king had just arrived at Buckingham Palace and was upstairs with Elizabeth and Alexander Hardinge, his Private Secretary, in his sitting room overlooking the quadrangle. Even though bombing was to be expected, what happened next was so instantaneous, it was hard to take in.

'All of a sudden we heard an aircraft making a zooming noise above us, saw 2 bombs falling past the opposite side of the Palace and then heard 2 resounding crashes . . . ' There was just time to register that, despite the deafening noise, nothing moved in the sitting room, 'and then we went out into the passage as fast as we could get there. The whole thing happened in a matter of seconds. We all wondered why we weren't dead.'[12]

It became apparent that it had been a very near miss. The two bombs had fallen just yards from the king's study. The courtyard was transformed into two huge craters and the wreckage of bricks and glass. The chapel was destroyed. Water was gushing through a broken window downstairs. Shaken witnesses began to emerge who had seen the whole sequence unfold.

The German bomber had emerged very suddenly from the heavy cloud cover. The pilot flew in plain view down the Mall directly towards the target. With shocking inevitability, six bombs fell in quick succession directly over Buckingham Palace. Two of the bombs landed in the forecourt, two fell in the quadrangle, one in the chapel and another in the garden. Three men were injured who had been in the workshop under the chapel. All the other staff were stunned but unhurt, the king continued to his mother. 'They were all wonderful.' The children, too, Elizabeth and Margaret, were 'very calm over it all' when their parents returned to Windsor and explained what had happened.[13]

In public, the king and queen felt closer to British people as they toured the blitzed areas of London after this. Their home had been hit along with thousands of others. Behind the scenes, the king found it was not quite so easy to shake off the shock. 'It was a ghastly experience,' he confided to his diary on 19 September. 'I should not put it down in writing but I did feel the reaction after the bombing last Friday . . . I quite disliked sitting in my room at B.P. on Monday & Tuesday. I found myself unable to read, always in a hurry, & glancing out of the window . . . '[14]

The king was unnerved by another persistent thought that could not be readily dismissed. The attack on the palace was very accurate. Was it possible that a family member had passed specific information about its layout to the Nazis? Quite apart from his German cousins who George VI knew were involved in the Nazi cause—Philipp and Christophe of Hesse, the Duke of Saxe-Coburg and sons of Kaiser Wilhelm—Europe was scattered with royal relations who had an intimate knowledge of the English royal palaces and whose allegiances were, at best, uncertain. Only recently his older brother had seen his pro-German Spanish cousins.[15]

The Duke of Windsor's foolhardy behaviour in Spain and Portugal provided fertile ground for his sensitive younger brother's worst imaginings. George VI had seen the intelligence showing the Germans wanted to change the leadership in Britain and expected 'assistance' from the Duke and Duchess of Windsor. Now there was much to dwell on. 'D. was very loth at leaving Lisbon as some Spaniards had told him that if he went to the Bahamas there was a plot to kill him. And D believed this!!!!' George VI told his mother.[16] Had David done something that gave him cause to fear such retribution? Was it possible that the duke had acted in some way that was injurious to Britain? Did he think he had been discovered and that was why he was so full of fear?

If the Germans hoped the bombing would help to drive the king from his palace they were to be disappointed. Although George VI could be reduced to a nervous wreck at the very thought of making a speech, when it came to personal safety, the same did not apply. Lack of courage was not an issue. Rules about air-raid warnings were for others. Palace staff had seen him sometimes leave the shelter before the all-clear as though disdaining of his own mortality.[17]

When the king saw the prime minister that week Churchill was worried that the full-scale invasion of Britain was imminent. In the battered and draughty palace, against a backdrop sound of the Office of Works in the midst of temporary repairs, the two men discussed the impending danger. The RAF was bombing ports on the French coast every day to disrupt German preparations and carry out reconnaissance. The king asked about Britain's coastal defences. 'Our preparations are all ready for any eventuality,' Churchill told the king defiantly.[18]

Knowing that worse was in store, the king and queen continued their tours, deeply moved by the fortitude of people they met, usually left unmarked and soon forgotten. At last the queen felt 'she could look the East End in the face' with some understanding of what ordinary people were going through.[19] They became a reassuring symbol for millions: the queen a motherly figure wearing muted dove greys and lilacs, evidently much moved by the suffering she saw; beside her the king, defiant and undefeated amidst the growing wasteland of devastation. The king was keen to acknowledge the strong, selfless bravery of men and women he was seeing each day, who risked their own lives to help others, often acts of supreme courage, unseen and with little recognition. It occurred to him there should be a civilian award for outstanding heroism.

'I have decided to create at once a new mark of honour for men and women in all walks of civilian life,' he announced in a broadcast on 23 September 1940. He felt so passionately about the need to acknowledge the courage of others that he proposed to give his own name to the new distinction, 'the George Cross'. It would rank next to the Victoria Cross and took the form of a plain silver cross with a circular medallion inscribed with St George and the Dragon and bearing the words 'for Gallantry'. 'The walls of London may be battered,' he said, 'but the spirit of the Londoner stands resolute and undismayed . . . There will always be an England to stand before the world . . . '[20]

The Windsors appeared oblivious of the high level of official interest that sailed with them across the Atlantic Ocean to their distant exile. The plots and counterplots of recent weeks were all too fresh in the memory in spite of calming blue seas empty of threatening vessels or would-be assassins from either side. They were of course aware of the private security man there to protect them, but not that he was carrying a gun, with—it is alleged in some sources—instructions to use it in any emergency involving the Windsors, who were not to leave the ship in Nazi hands alive. Luckily there was no 'B' movie scene and the *Excalibur* sailed serenely into New Providence Island, the largest island of the Bahamas, on 17 August.

Such was the excitement of the Bahamians at the prospect of greeting the brother of His Majesty the King that almost the entire population turned out to welcome the Windsors in what the *New York Times* judged to be 'the most enthusiastic demonstration in the colony's history'. The mood was jubilant. Bands played, flower girls strewed roses on the path before them, and British flags were waved with gay abandon.[21]

The Bahamian reception committee had put considerable thought into how to make the Windsors feel at ease. This was no simple task since a telegram from the Colonial Office in Whitehall had preceded their arrival setting out the rules. While the duke should be addressed as 'His Royal Highness' and receive a half curtsey, 'Wallis was not entitled to this'. Knowing from press reports the sensitivity of this issue for their new governor and his lady, local officials alighted upon a unique solution to honour the duchess. The governor's wife usually sat with officials for the reception ceremony. But as a 'special mark of distinction for the rank of Duchess', they had arranged for a singular dais 'half way between the general floor level and the throne level', reported the *New York Times*, and royally decorated with a heavy red cloth. Wallis had her throne.[22]

From her elevated position, the duchess could take in the scene. Before her were thousands of brightly dressed men and women in their Sunday best, cheering happily and determined to greet her and her husband with all the warmth the sun-drenched islands could offer. Tropical blooms and decorative bunting dotted the spectacle with more splashes of vivid colour. There were welcoming speeches and a local military band was summoned to play, the whole scene set against a distant view of scorched white beaches fringed with palms and the remarkable green of the bay contrasting with the royal blue of the Atlantic, stretching as far as the eye could see.

Unfortunately Wallis found herself suffering from the heat and was struck with the feeling of being 'buried alive' and 'so absolutely far away'.[23] She confided her 'despair' to Betty Lawson-Johnston, adding rebelliously, 'of course one must obey the dictate of this Churchill or be beheaded.'[24] But there was nothing to ease her disappointment when she and the duke went around their new residence, Government House. The Windsors walked from room to room, taking in an impression of heavy Victorian furniture and shiny blue paint, the irritating whirring of electric fans somehow failing to reduce the overwhelming heat. 'And also not being able to have any of our silver, linen, etc' she continued to Betty, 'you can imagine how unattractive living is—'[25] Surely this was no residence for the governor? Her dismay at the lack of elegance and wanton neglect of their proposed new home was total. The Windsors decided to seek a large sum to renovate it from the local House of Assembly. Surely £5,000, at the very least, was essential?

Even though they had travelled 4,000 miles, the duke soon found past difficulties were lying in wait to bait him. It did not take long to find out about the secret telegram that had been sent before their arrival instructing local officials not to curtsey to his wife. The duke was certain that such small-mindedness from the Colonial Office must have been directed from the palace. The well-worn groove of anger flared up once more as he pondered what he saw as the 'mean and petty humiliations' which he thought his own family promulgated relentlessly.[26]

But the Windsors discovered there was one unexpected consolation in their 'Elba of 1940'. The Bahamas turned out to be a playground for the super-rich of the western world. Although the vast majority of the population was poor and black, these islands of striking contrasts were also a magnet for some of the world's wealthiest people, and the Windsors were keen to make their acquaintance.

Sir Harry Oakes, who ran a British-Canadian gold mine, owned almost a third of New Providence Island and was quick to offer help with the new governor's concerns over his accommodation. Oakes had moved to the islands in the 1930s, drawn by the tax-free economy, and was involved in major developments to modernise the only airport and construct a golf course to attract tourists. An even more imposing figure was Axel Wenner-Gren, a Swedish entrepreneur who had started out in life as a door-to-door salesman and had risen through his own enterprise to become one of Europe's wealthiest men as the creator and owner of the Electrolux Company. He had come to the Bahamas to see the world's largest yacht, the 360-foot *Southern Cross*, whose beautiful streamlined shape glistened white against the still green waters of the bay. Wenner-Gren, a man ruled by the balance sheet rather than emotion when making investments, found good reason to be enchanted and bought not only the yacht, but also a private island just off the shore of the city of Nassau, complete with a mansion which enjoyed spectacular views across Cabbage Beach over the Caribbean. It wasn't long before his new acquisitions had new names to capture their special charm: Hog Island became 'Paradise Island' and the mansion became Shangri-La.[27]

The Windsors were ready to savour a taste of the generous hospitality at Shangri-La, the only problem being that it was deemed desirable by British officials that they should not make contact with Wenner-Gren—a fact that was not lost on the FBI. FBI files show that on 13 September—coincidentally the day that Buckingham Palace was bombed in London—the director of the FBI in Washington, J. Edgar Hoover, received a lengthy confidential briefing about the duke and duchess which he duly passed directly on to General Watson, the secretary to the president in the White House. The report was from the deputy director of the FBI, Edward Allen Tamm, who had in turn been briefed by what he described as an 'exceptionally reliable' source.[28]

Tamm's source was, in fact, the British Secret Service and his account gives insights into the official view in London at the time. Tamm highlighted the pervasive influence that the duchess held over her husband and described her as 'exceedingly pro German in her sympathies'. There is 'strong reason to believe that this is the real reason why she was considered so obnoxious to the British government that they refused to permit Edward to marry her and maintain the throne,' wrote Tamm. Despite having been 'repeatedly warned' by British officials to be 'exceedingly circumspect' in his dealings with the German government, the duke 'is in such a state of intoxication most of the time that he is virtually *non compos mentis*. The Duchess has repeatedly ignored these warnings.'[29]

In the hands of the FBI, the Windsors' activities in Spain and Portugal came close to treason. Tamm claimed 'the British Secret Service established conclusively that the Duchess of Windsor had recently been in direct contact with Joachim von Ribbentrop and was maintaining constant contact and communication with him'. In order to prevent this, the British government selected the Bahamas as the best location to ensure the Windsors would be 'virtually isolated' from anyone in official circles—a decision that was reached without consultation with the king. Whilst it was thought this should stop 'any channel of communication with von Ribbentrop' there was, however, a new concern: that Wallis might 'align herself' with Axel Wenner-Gren.[30] It is not clear from the FBI report who briefed Tamm from the British Intelligence Service but it does appear that Wallis was blamed more than her husband in the summer of 1940. At this point, the British intelligence received happened to be more damning for Wallis. This included details of the Germans' painstaking consultation over the Windsors' possessions to her specification, and the report showing that the Germans understood the duchess 'wished at any price to become Queen'.

As for Wenner-Gren himself, he was deemed an unsuitable contact because of his ill-judged efforts to play the role of international peacekeeper in which he promoted himself to both British and German authorities as an adviser on the international situation. He had held meetings with Hermann Goering four times, most recently in March 1940, in the hopes of facilitating peace—and protecting his business interests.[31] He had business connections to Germany for over thirty years and one of his plants in Sweden was once involved in munitions manufacture.[32]

According to Tamm, the British government had taken the unusual step of assigning the aristocrat Lady Jane Williams Taylor to try to keep the Windsors and Wenner-Gren apart.[33] Lady Jane was a 'distinguished social leader', reported the *Palm Beach Daily News*, and 'a popular matriarch of the international set in Nassau'. Her home was a showpiece, and her granddaughter, Brenda Diana Frazier, 'the most beautiful debutante of the 1938 social season'.[34] Such companions were seen as well placed to divert the Windsors from the more dubious Axel Wenner-Gren.

Unknown to the duke and duchess as they settled into their duties on the island, their circle in the Bahamas was of keen interest to the Espionage Department of the FBI. Tamm's staff soon found they had their hands full as a succession of witnesses came forward that autumn to pass on their fears about the duke and duchess. One concerned member of the public told the FBI about Wallis's 'long association with Herr von Ribbentrop while he was in this country as a whisky salesman' and considered it likely that the Windsors were still operating as Hitler's 'Flying Column'.[35] This view was backed up by a second informant who claimed an autographed photograph of von Ribbentrop hung over Wallis's dressing table in Nassau—hardly a very secret place if she was playing 'the spy'. In another FBI memorandum, Wenner-Gren was the obvious weak link. He had 'excellent connections with Germany' and his munitions plant in Sweden 'at one time was partly owned by Krupp'.[36] Yet another witness, who seemed to be exceptionally well informed, stated 'that she knew definitely that the English government had instructed the Windsors . . . to stay off the boat of Axel Wenner-Gren, but they had disregarded these instructions completely'.[37] Perhaps the most original idea came from a conscientious classifier at the FBI who was sufficiently concerned to write to Hoover's office on 19 October 1940. She noticed that Mrs Simpson used a particular dry cleaner in New York. 'The possibility arises that the transferring of messages through the clothes might be taking place.'[38]

The duke's behaviour in the summer of 1940 in Spain and Portugal had opened a Pandora's box and a world of suspicion was unleashed. Quite how he planned to communicate with the enemy remained a mystery for the FBI espionage chiefs, but improbable rumours wove themselves into the very air like background music wherever the tanned, white-uniformed duke appeared.

The conflagration in Western Europe spread east during the autumn of 1940. Smaller countries became caught in the titanic clash between German and Soviet interests, the first sparks throwing the spotlight on yet another great-grandson of Queen Victoria. George VI did not know his distant cousin well and was powerless to help King Carol II of Romania as the Nazi leadership piled pressure on his government. The grave news from Eastern Europe came at a time when the London docks were ablaze, London was lit up like a beacon for German bombers, and the anti-aircraft fire could be heard from Windsor where the king and queen spent many nights underground.[39] The Romanian king left his son, nineteen-year-old Prince Michael, on a precarious throne and fled, eventually reaching exile in Mexico.[40]

'Something I am sure is brewing up for the near future,' the king wrote in his diary in early October. There was a sense of imminent threat. Telegrams poured into the Foreign Office 'in an unending stream'.[41] The Germans helped themselves to Romania and took over its rich oil fields. Bulgaria—bordering Romania, Yugoslavia and Greece—was next in the line of fire. George VI wrote to King Boris of Bulgaria on 12 October urging him to maintain Bulgarian neutrality, but once again Nazi pressure was overwhelming. There were countless further reports that set nerves jangling: the king tried to follow the fearsome reckoning. 'Italy will also probably attack Greece. Germany may advance through Spain to Gibraltar . . . the invasion of Britain may come now or next spring . . . Greece is crying for help.'[42]

In London there were so many 'Red Warnings' with enemy aircraft overhead each night that it was hard to sleep and keep a clear perspective. German bombers were venturing further west. Bombs missed the castle but dropped frequently in Windsor Great Park. Whitehall, the West End, the Treasury and Number 10: all suffered damage.[43] When Churchill came to lunch at the palace he admitted to the king that the War Cabinet finally 'had "kicked" him out of No 10—but only for sleeping purposes!!' Churchill did not like sleeping underground in the room specially prepared for him in the War Cabinet rooms.[44] The Archbishop of Canterbury too was disturbed. The king learned he was bombed out of Lambeth Palace and noted he was 'looking much older'.[45]

Suddenly, on 28 October 1940, the whole Mediterranean region lit up like a tinderbox as Italian troops poured over the Albanian border into Greece. The Italian dictator Benito Mussolini had felt his dignity to be greatly ruffled with each new German advance. He, the great *Il Duce*—attired in full military gear and lots of medals as he set out to revive Italy's magnificent Roman past—felt upstaged. Italy was losing out in the new world order as Germany seized control of Europe. He saw only the glory as he escalated his very own Italian 'parallel war'. For him there was good reason for optimism. Italian forces were already fulfilling what he saw as their destiny as they won victories against the British in Africa. Mussolini had ordered troops in the Italian colony of Libya to cross the border into Egypt, where British troops were protecting British interests at Suez. Italian troops had advanced 60 miles into Egypt, occupying the key Egyptian port of Sidi Barrani. Now Mussolini envisaged a speedy victory against the Greeks as his troops stormed the mountainous terrain on the border.

For the Duke and Duchess of Kent the developments around the Mediterranean directly threatened their own family. Marina's relatives were becoming marooned as the flames of war fanned across south-east Europe. Her mother, the elegant Princess Nicholas, a Russian grand-duchess known for her serious outlook and charity work, would not leave the home she had once shared with her husband in the suburbs of Athens, and nor would the king of Greece, George II, Marina's cousin.[46] The Axis threat was also edging ever closer to Marina's sister and brother-in-law, Olga and Paul, in neighbouring Yugoslavia. As Regent, Prince Paul was anxious to hand over a free country to his nephew, Prince Peter, and found the strain immense as he struggled publicly to maintain Yugoslav neutrality, believing this to be the best policy in spite of the fate of other neutral countries. Privately Prince Paul appealed to George VI for help, but there was little that either the king or Churchill could do. George VI acknowledged the Yugoslav urgent need of weapons in a letter to Prince Paul on 15 November. 'I only wish that it was possible for us to supply you with them at once,' he wrote. But all British industry was needed for 'making up fast our losses'.[47]

In November, as London burned, Chamberlain died. Fighting a battle of his own against cancer, his reputation was also under attack for pursuing the policy of appeasement. The famous picture of him, a lone figure waving a slip of paper, his guarantee of 'peace in our time' from Hitler, seemed irrelevant in such tumultuous days. But George VI felt he had lost a valued friend. He knew Chamberlain felt his spectacular fall from grace acutely in the final months of his life and had written to comfort him, acknowledging the significance of his efforts to preserve peace, since 'they established in the eyes of the civilised

King George V (*right*) believed that when he died, his oldest son, Prince Edward (*left*), 'will ruin himself within twelve months'.

King Edward VIII's desire to marry the divorced American, Wallis Simpson, would lead to an irreconcilable schism within the royal family. This photograph was taken in 1931 when she was presented at court.

HANDS OFF OUR KING ABDICATION MEANS REVOLUTION

King Edward VIII's abdication in 1936, one of the greatest threats to the survival of the monarchy in the modern era, caused public outrage.

The royal family were noticeably absent from the wedding of Edward and Wallis, the Duke and Duchess of Windsor, in France, June 1937.

Edward's younger brother, Prince Albert, the Duke of York, 'broke down & sobbed like a child' the day before he became the new king, George VI, in December 1936.

His wife, the Duchess of York, became Queen Elizabeth.

King George VI was in constant dread of public speaking, fearing his disabling stammer would prove the rumour that he was 'unfit to rule'.

To stabilise the monarchy King George VI (*second from right*) hoped to bring his brothers into line. *From left to right*: the Duke of Kent, the Duke of Windsor and (*far right*) the Duke of Gloucester.

Edward, the Duke of Windsor, had made a promise on his abdication to retire from public life. But he secretly arranged a tour of Nazi Germany in 1937 during which he and Wallis were fêted.

King George VI's youngest brother, the playboy Duke of Kent, also provoked controversy. Society hostess Betty Lawson-Johnston was one of his intimate confidants.

The Duke of Kent's name was linked to many other society beauties including Edythe Baker (*left*), the acclaimed jazz pianist, and Paula Gellibrand (*right*), dubbed 'Britain's most painted woman'.

The Duke of Kent's life changed in November 1934 when he married the beautiful
Princess Marina of Greece and Denmark.

The Duke and Duchess of Kent became known as 'that dazzling pair'.

King George VI had concerns about his other younger brother, the Duke of Gloucester, whose drinking exploits with his army friends were rumoured to be excessive.

In November 1935 the Duke of Gloucester married Lady Alice Montagu-Douglas-Scott, the outdoor girl here transformed in her wedding dress designed by Norman Hartnell.

Ecstatic crowds gathered outside Buckingham Palace
when Prime Minister Neville Chamberlain returned from
negotiations with Hitler in Munich on 30 September 1938,
promising 'peace for our time'.

George VI with President Roosevelt, June 1939. Europe was catapulted to the
brink of war, and there were moments when the strain showed.

When Winston Churchill became Prime minister in May 1940, King George VI found him difficult to talk to at first.

As the British army retreated to Dunkirk in May 1940, the Windsors set out on their own path with seemingly traitorous intent. British intelligence revealed that the Germans expected help from the Windsors and believed the king would abdicate once bombing began in earnest.

Waves of German bombers formed 'an aluminium ceiling to the sky', according to one reporter, during the London Blitz of 1940.

When King George VI and Queen Elizabeth began their visits to the bombed East End of London, the reception was not always friendly.

After the bombing of Buckingham Palace on 13 September 1940, the king and queen inspect the damage with Winston Churchill.

The Windsors' glamorous
tours on the *Southern
Cross*, the world's largest
yacht, owned by the
Swedish entrepreneur Axel
Wenner-Gren, provoked
the interest of 'C', Britain's
Chief of MI6, as well
as President Roosevelt.
Wenner-Gren was believed
to be 'friendly to Nazis'.

The last photograph of the Duke of Kent with his wife, Marina, before his fateful mission, August 1941.

King George VI was determined to honour the bravery of the people of Malta. Here he stands in salute on the bridge of HMS *Aurora*, June 1943.

Omaha Beach, Normandy, on D-Day, 6 June 1944. King George VI persuaded Churchill not to join the D-Day armada.

VE Day, 8 May 1945. *From left to right:* Princess Elizabeth, Queen Elizabeth, Winston Churchill, King George VI and Princess Margaret at the victory celebrations.

George VI with his daughters, the princesses, and his mother, Queen Mary, talking to a young officer in 1946.

world, our entire innocence of the crime which Hitler was determined to commit'.[48] The Duke of Gloucester represented the king at his funeral on 14 November. The former prime minister, who had come to embody Britain's vain struggle for peace, found peace at last in Westminster Abbey, in a London now tangled with barbed wire and pitted with trenches and the burned-out shells of buildings.

Within a few hours of the service in Westminster of Britain's most famous peacemaker, the watchmen on the battlements at Windsor Castle heard an ominous roar, not easily identifiable but obviously threatening. It grew nearer and nearer. Was Windsor Castle about to be obliterated? The brilliant bombers on the still moonlit night could identify every turret and tower. But unbelievably, as though by ghostly command, the dark shapes of the enemy planes were set unwaveringly on a northern course.

The skies were clear above Coventry that night. A distant noise could be heard shortly after 7 pm, a faint droning at first, which grew into a deafening crescendo as suddenly a fleet of enemy aircraft were directly above. Goering had a new tactic to test. The first 'pathfinder' planes with improved navigational tools dropped their incendiaries and lit up key sites—aircraft factories, power supplies, communications. Then came wave after wave of bombers releasing high-explosive and incendiary bombs. The people of Coventry had little time to react. By eight that evening Coventry Cathedral was a furnace, the tracery of its Gothic windows black against the leaping flames, witness to the city's terrible devastation as more than 200 fires broke out in the narrow streets of the medieval and Tudor city. By midnight for petrified citizens trying to shelter underground it was as though the entire world above them was burning. The fire could be seen 100 miles away, the city a blazing torch under the full moon.

When news reached the palace of the scale of the destruction, George VI was determined to visit the stricken city. Early in the morning on 16 November he arrived to find himself in the smoking remains of a scene that was hard to take in. It was 'just like Ypres after the last war', the king told his mother.[49] The local mayor came to greet him, still unshaven but wearing his bowler hat, and guided the king through the smouldering debris to what was once the town hall. A reception committee had gathered to welcome him, waiting in pools of light thrown up by candles in beer bottles, and tried to find the words to convey to the king the bewildering tragedy that had overtaken them.

The town centre had disappeared. Here and there were gaunt, blackened chimneys and tottering walls. Someone had placed a makeshift cross on the ruined cathedral from charred beams. The search was ongoing for bodies caught under the rubble. More than 500 people had lost their lives; 1,000 more suffered injuries. A third of the city's factories were obliterated and thousands of homes crumbled as though they were mere doll's houses. The people of Coventry had endured 500 tons of high-explosives in one night. For Joseph Goebbels, Operation Moonlight Sonata was such a success he added a new verb to his lexicon of horror: 'to coventrate'.

The king was guided for several hours through piles of debris that were once streets. 'I was horrified,' he wrote. Many of those he met were still 'quite dazed after what they had been through . . . The shock to them was very great . . . The people in the streets wondered where they were, nothing could be recognized . . . '⁵⁰

But they could recognise their king. The unexpected arrival of his familiar face in this scene of unearthly inhumanity had a significant impact on broken morale. 'England was behind us,' said one. 'We no longer felt that we were alone.'

The week Coventry was bombed, telegrams were flying across the Atlantic about the Duke and Duchess of Windsor. There was an emergency concerning the duchess's teeth. Wallis needed medical treatment in America that was not available in the Bahamas, prompting much official concern. There were fears the ex-king might exploit the intense press interest surrounding his first visit to America with Wallis. The last thing the British wanted was for the duke to have an opportunity to air his pacifist views at a time when America was not yet in the war and help was desperately needed. None the less, not liking to thwart a medical emergency, the Colonial Office did grant the Windsors a week's leave to go to Miami.

Alarm bells soon began to ring. The Windsors planned to cruise to Miami on Wenner-Gren's magnificent yacht, the *Southern Cross*—a fact that was not lost on the media. The Colonial Office sent a cypher telegram on 11 December 1940 warning the duke of unfavourable publicity with his name linked to Wenner-Gren, 'who is referred to as "Goering's Pal"'.⁵¹ None the less, it was Wenner-Gren's luxurious white yacht that eased smoothly into Miami harbour, the Windsors on board, waving to the crowds below and flagrantly ignoring Colonial Office sensitivities. The duke and duchess proved to be a magnet for publicity, and in a matter of days concerns about Wenner-Gren's presence in Miami reached 'C', the head of MI6, himself.

INDEXED

MOST SECRET

C/5496.

LONDON,

14th December, 1940.

My dear Henry,

     My representative in New York has wired
that Wenner Gren, who is now in Miami with the Duke
and Duchess of Windsor, is the subject of attack in
the American Press and Radio, as being friendly to
Nazis, and associated with the appeasement circles
there.

          Yours ever,

C

H. L. d'A. Hopkinson, Esq.

Letter from 'C' to the Foreign Office on 14 December 1940 to warn of intelligence about Wenner-Gren (THE NATIONAL ARCHIVES)

Sir Stewart Menzies, or 'C', wrote to Henry Hopkinson at the Foreign Office on 14 December to express his concern about the trip. Wenner-Gren was regarded as 'friendly to Nazis, and associated with the appeasement circles . . . '[52]

Despite repeated warnings to distance himself from Wenner-Gren, the duke waited until he returned to the Bahamas before replying to the Colonial Office. The Swedish entrepreneur 'is a very prominent and important resident of the Bahamas', Windsor insisted, involved in development schemes that provide 'vast amounts of employment'.[53] His stoic defence appears to have raised a few eyebrows and copies of the correspondence between the governor and the Colonial Office about Wenner-Gren were sent to both the Foreign Office and

Guy Liddell, the counter-espionage chief at MI5.[54] While British officials were unforthcoming about just what was held against Wenner-Gren, they none the less expected the governor to take account of guidance from London.

Encouraged by the welcome he had received in Miami, it was not long before the duke wrote to the British Colonial Office requesting leave in America once again. He wanted to 'visit Wallis's family in Baltimore', he explained and 'to communicate with the White House and the British embassy in Washington'.[55] But the Foreign Office learned that the duke had recently given a controversial interview to a popular American magazine, *Liberty*, which was just about to be published. Harried officials raced to get hold of the article and find out just what the duke had said.

'C' himself passed on a summary from America to Henry Hopkinson at the Foreign Office. 'Next issue *Liberty* Magazine will contain interview with Duke of Windsor which infuriates heads of news services who have seen advance copy . . . Article contains useful ammunition for appeasement group/ condemns Lend Lease/ suggests "Giving" is questionable/ . . . agrees that German people want Hitler and therefore there can be no revolt/ there will be a new order in Europe . . . '[56]

Churchill fumed. 'There is a vein of innuendo running through the whole article which is hard to interpret in any other sense than as defeatist and pro German,' Halifax told the prime minister.[57] Both men were keen to provide Roosevelt with support against strong isolationist views in America and were concerned that American goodwill could be so effortlessly squandered with a few foolish words from the duke. Since the fall of France the Germans held a key advantage in the Atlantic war. From their new forward ports in France, German U-boats could prey on Allied vessels some 400 miles further west and were hunting so successfully in 'wolf packs' along the Atlantic convoy routes that hundreds of Allied ships were sunk. Windsor's untimely words could cost the British precious support. The prime minister wrote angrily to Windsor. The article ' . . . can indeed only bear the interpretation of contemplating a negotiated peace with Hitler. That is not the policy of His Majesty's Government.'[58]

Despite the frustration in London over the duke's public remarks and his association with Wenner-Gren, the Windsors were given permission for a second trip to America. As Halifax pointed out, if they were stopped, it would encourage the small section of the US press who treated 'the Duke and Duchess as martyrs'.[59] Wallis herself appeared unaware of the alarm in Whitehall over their travel arrangements when she wrote to her American friend, Betty

Lawson-Johnson, on 2 April 1941. Intriguingly her correspondence shows she had found another millionaire whose exquisitely appointed yacht was to her liking: Alfred Sloan, the chairman of General Motors.

Wallis gaily informed Betty that they were on a tour that April of the islands of the Bahamas on his yacht, *Rene*. Sloan had lent it to them for a week 'and we are taking advantage of it to visit the other Islands of the Bahamas which it is the Duke's duty to see'. Wallis confided to her friend that she would 'never become enamoured' of the Bahamas and the weather was not good; 'however the boat is such a beautiful one that one doesn't mind so much'.[60]

The choice of Alfred Sloan's yacht was unfortunate since he, too, was attracting the interest of the authorities. Under his leadership, General Motors had made a major investment in 1929 in the German car manufacturer, Adam Opel. As a General Motors German subsidiary during the 1930s, Opel grew to become Europe's largest vehicle manufacturer. By the late 1930s, much of the machinery of the *Blitzkrieg* was being manufactured at the plant: armoured cars and trucks, components for German aircraft, detonators for torpedoes.[61] Sloan's colleague, the charismatic James Mooney, who ran General Motors' overseas operations, came under FBI scrutiny for his efforts to act as a mediator of a negotiated peace. Mooney had met Goering several times in 1939 and there were continuing fears that he was acting on his own initiative to take steps for peace and bring about 'a New Order'.[62] In February 1941, the US consul in Zurich, James Stewart, warned the State Department that he believed some General Motors staff in Paris were acting as intermediaries with senior Nazi figures in Paris.[63] Although Sloan argued that the German subsidiary, Opel, operated independently of General Motors, there were concerns that he, Mooney and other executives believed that businessmen could play a role in making the peace and that international finance came before politics.

As luck would have it, while sailing on Alfred Sloan's yacht around the Bahamas the Windsors suffered an accident and the story was picked up by the *New York Times*. In rough seas, Sloan's 234-foot vessel was beached in shallow waters 3 miles off one of the outer islands. *Rene* sent out a distress call.[64] In the event, the incident passed without mishap; however, the publicity highlighted the Windsors' connection to the chairman of General Motors. In addition to the duke's links to Wenner-Gren, this appears to have proved the last straw for rattled State Department officials. FBI records show the British Embassy in Washington informed the US State Department on 16 April 1941 that the Windsors would round off their tour of the islands of the Bahamas by returning to America to spend a few days with friends at Palm Beach, Florida.[65] This prospect caused such concern in Washington that President Roosevelt himself ordered an extraordinary covert exercise.

That very day the Assistant Secretary of State, Adolf Berle, asked the FBI 'to assign someone in an undercover position to watch the Duke and Duchess during their visit'.[66] His request reached Hoover and immediately rang alarm bells. As he notified the US attorney general on 17 April, a US Secret Service agent was already attached to the duke and duchess for the visit, and he 'would undoubtedly immediately detect the presence of any undercover agents'.[67]

Hoover, however, soon learned that the president himself had requested the secret FBI operation and pressed ahead with the cover. Meanwhile Berle, equally anxious to carry out his orders, informed the attorney general on 18 April that he had also arranged for 'a Special Agent attached to the Department of State' to act as a personal guard.[68]

The Duke and Duchess of Windsor, oozing glamour and looking improbably regal, appeared oblivious to the intricate network of agents adopting discreet undercover positions within earshot as they swept into Palm Beach. They aimed to relax in the Everglades Club, play golf and dine with some of their millionaire friends. By 9 am on 19 April, Tamm had the whole set-up covered, as he informed Hoover at the FBI. Agent Tyson of the Secret Service, and—to the American's surprise—a British man as well, Sergeant Holder of Scotland Yard was at the ready. 'This makes it impossible to get within 100 yards of the Duke for surveillance purposes,' Tamm warned Hoover. The Special Agent in Charge, Peter Wyly from the Miami police, was intending to inform Secret Service agent Tyson of the presence of the FBI, continued Tamm, but under no circumstances would he 'notify the Scotland Yard man of our activities . . . '[69] Meanwhile Special Agent W.H. Osborne was introduced as a member of the Palm Beach police department. And so it went on . . . [70]

Overkill? Almost certainly. The agents enjoyed five days of spectacular entertainment with some of America's wealthiest individuals—now possibly under suspicion as peace-seeking financiers involved in creating a 'New Order' with the Germans. At a cocktail party on 18 April, the guests included the social-climbing Jessie Woolworth Donahue, daughter of Frank Woolworth, the founder of the Woolworth chain; her son, the notorious gay playboy and Woolworth heir, Jimmie Donahue; Mr and Mrs William Vanderbilt; Mr and Mrs Harold Vanderbilt; and a spattering of film stars and local celebrities such as Captain Alistair Mackintosh, who according to *Life* magazine 'spins through Palm Beach social season like a whirling top'.[71] Over the following days cocktails were liberally consumed, along with lavish luncheons, dinners and other amusements. Agents had their work cut out identifying all the guests at every occasion, including one attended by some 300 people. The world's most glamorous addresses, yachts, sports clubs and myriad other points of interest were carefully researched. Doubtless, it was a huge relief for all agents concerned— undercover or otherwise—when the Windsors finally departed for Nassau on 23 April, not in a yacht this time, but a plane belonging to William Vanderbilt.[72]

While the farce was unfolding in Miami as intelligence officers tried hard not to trip over each other as they identified a growing list of Everglades millionaires, the FBI received instructions from the US State Department to take action over Axel Wenner-Gren. Rumours had been circulating for months about his alleged activities. To complete his transformation of Hog Island into his own personal Paradise Island, he and his wife had decided their view would be greatly enhanced with the addition of a large lake, drained by two wide canals to the sea. Suspicions began to grow about the purpose of the canals. Were they large enough to hide German U-boats? To what end was he photographing the land on an island in south-east Bahama? Who did he meet when he set sail in his yacht, the *Southern Cross*?[73]

On 18 April 1941, Hoover sent a memo to Tamm stating that the president himself desired an FBI investigation into 'certain activities' of Axel Wenner-Gren.[74] Within a few weeks 'C' in London briefed officials in the Foreign Office about the latest American thinking: 'We have been informed on good authority that the President has recently expressed some anxiety about the Bahamas entourage, and to have remarked that he has been given to understand that HRH was to have been discouraged by His Majesty's Government from visiting the United States . . . '[75] It would appear that the president was not satisfied that the British were keeping Windsor under control.

Apart from concerns about the 'Bahamas entourage' the report from 'C' also made clear what was held against Wenner-Gren: ' . . . he [Wenner-Gren] is concerned with the preservation of a Capitalist form of society in the Western Hemisphere and is therefore aligned to the well-to-do classes here in the United States who oppose American entry into the war on the grounds that it might hasten the breakdown of the Capitalist system. There is no positive pro-Nazi tendency but a definite appeasement line of thought based on the hypothesis that a prolonged war will wreck civilisation and destroy established values . . . '[76]

Finally 'C' also enclosed a copy of an intercepted communication from Norman Whitehouse, a diplomat's brother who had recently dined on Wenner-Gren's yacht with the Windsors and then wrote about it to a friend. His account provides a vivid snapshot of the conversation on board in the spring of 1941.

Wenner-Gren himself talked of the 'tragedy of the whole war' and argued
that 'it would be possible to arrange peace'. The duke agreed with his friend.
'It would be very ill advised of America to enter the war against Germany as
Europe was finished anyway . . . ' As for the duchess, she expressed her view
most succinctly of all. 'If the US entered the war, this country [America] would
go down in history as the greatest sucker of all times.'[77]

While the American president, the British prime minister, J. Edgar Hoover,
'C' and a host of agents kept tabs on the indiscretions of the Duke of
Windsor, the double-cross section of British intelligence was discreetly taking
an interest in George VI's new Lord Steward.

The letter sent by Rudolf Hess from a 'Dr A.H.' in Germany in September
1940 did not have a chance to reach its intended recipient, the Duke of Hamilton. It was intercepted by the British censor and passed straight on to the
intelligence service. It did not take long before it made its way up to the head
of MI5's double-cross section, Major 'Tar' Robertson, an intelligence officer of
such repute he was known in the service just by his initials: T.A.R., short for
Tommy Argyll Robertson.[78]

Tar Robertson was building a name for running some of British intelligence's
most sensitive and elaborate espionage cases, recruiting and running double
agents, exploiting any situation that arose to try to gain a British advantage.
At first sight, the intercepted letter to the Duke of Hamilton threw up more
questions than answers in his mind. What was the king's Lord Steward up to?

Agent W.G. White reported to Tar Robertson that there was evidence before
the war that Hamilton was 'an advanced appeaser' who 'may now be a peace
mover'.[79] A quick search of the news cuttings files revealed that *after* the German invasion of Poland, Hamilton had written publicly to *The Times* in October 1939 referring to the 'injustices' done to the German people in the past and
pointing out that once the threat of aggression from Germany was removed,
war was 'wrong and meaningless'.[80] His mysterious German correspondent, 'Dr
A.H.', was swiftly identified as Dr Albrecht Haushofer, Rudolf Hess's advisor,
a man understood to be the Nazis' greatest expert on the British Empire. As
for the intermediary, Mrs Violet Roberts, the apparently innocent housewife
from 6 Hill Croft Crescent, Wembley—was she, too, a spy? Why was she corre-
sponding with influential Germans?[81]

At a meeting at MI5 on 20 January 1941, Tar Robertson decided that more information was needed before he could work out how to exploit the case to British advantage. Most crucial of all, where did the Duke of Hamilton's loyalties lie? Could he be trusted? Later that morning Tar Robertson went to see Air Commodore Archibald R. Boyle in the Intelligence Section of the Air Ministry and it was agreed that Hamilton must be questioned about the letter. If Hamilton was trustworthy, Tar wanted to know whether the duke was prepared to reply to Haushofer—in which case the double-cross section might be able to run the case.[82]

It is likely that Mrs Roberts and the Duke of Hamilton were both placed under surveillance because some weeks elapsed before the case was taken forward. The Duke of Hamilton was summoned for an interview at the Air Ministry on 11 March and was surprised to find himself suddenly in an uncomfortable situation. He was shown the letter addressed to him from Dr Haushofer and questioned as though under suspicion.

Hamilton admitted that he did indeed know Albrecht Haushofer. He had met the German professor during the 1936 Berlin Olympic Games where he had been introduced to Goering and other senior Nazis.[83] Subsequently Haushofer stayed with Hamilton when he came to England 'on frequent occasions'. Their liaison was sufficiently close that in July 1939 Haushofer took it upon himself to warn the Scottish duke of imminent war—a letter which Hamilton still had stored in his bank.[84] Hamilton said he knew nothing of Mrs Roberts, the address in Lisbon, or the letter itself, but he was ready to go to Lisbon 'if it would be of any service to the country'.[85]

Tar Robertson had decided that the Duke of Hamilton should be sent to Lisbon to rendezvous with Dr A.H. It seems likely that MI5 was satisfied that Hamilton was in the clear at this point, although there was continuing uncertainty about Mrs Roberts. Robertson concluded that whether Mrs Roberts was a spy or not did not affect the decision regarding the duke.[86]

Tar was extremely keen to see Hamilton before his departure to Lisbon to prime him carefully on the story he should tell Haushofer. The duke needed a very good explanation as to why he had not answered Haushofer's original letter. Tar suggested that Hamilton should tell the professor he had replied at once but his reply must have got lost in transit. Boyle agreed with Tar's plan but was anxious 'to get the story absolutely tidied up and clean' before sending the duke out to Lisbon.[87] But finally the Duke of Hamilton, the complete Scottish gentleman unused to the wiles of the double-cross section, was briefed and ready for his improbable mission.

The king had no idea his Lord Steward had attracted the interest of the intelligence services. His all-consuming focus was the state of war. The magnificent dome of St Paul's Cathedral was photographed in December 1940 framed by flames climbing hundreds of feet around it and clouds of smoke blotting out the sky.

It became a potent symbol, sacred, an icon of London's suffering in the blitz. In January there were reports 'we are to be invaded', wrote the king, '& Hitler will use gas'.[88] He became ill in February and confided to his mother the constant stress of living 'so much on a mental plane' as he conscientiously read all the papers and telegrams 'which give one all the nasty ideas of what might happen . . . '[89] It was hard to shake off a constant feeling of agitation mentally preparing for the very worst. Further convincing intelligence came from the Foreign Office of specific invasion dates between 14 and 28 March 1941. The main attack was thought to be in the north, advancing west to Leeds and Liverpool, with strategic hits elsewhere. 'A million invaders, a quarter of whom parachutists. 3 days of intense air bombing etc. prior to invasion. Gas not to be used,' the king wrote. 'This is all very worrying as anything may happen suddenly.'[90]

St Paul's surrounded by flames, December 1940 (Keystone/Getty Images)

The king briefed his mother on what to do when the invasion came. He urged her not to rush back to Windsor. The castle would not be safe, with air attacks expected given the factories in the nearby towns of Slough and Langley. A few days later he wrote again. 'Winston tells me he is going to remain in London as long as possible before moving,' he told her, 'and I shall have to be with the government of course.' He had hand-picked the bodyguards who would serve as a mobile unit ready to escort Queen Elizabeth and the princesses to one of four or five different sites, depending on where the invasion force landed. 'The latter is very hush hush and only six people know . . . besides E and I.'[91] In subsequent letters he discussed the best homes for his mother as a refuge.[92]

George VI's attitude to Winston Churchill had changed significantly. Listening to him broadcast to the Americans on 9 February, his spirit still unconquerable, his efforts indefatigable, the king wrote out Churchill's words in his diary. 'We shall not fail or falter, we shall not weaken or tire. Neither the sudden shock of battle nor the long drawn trials of vigilance and exertion will wear us down. Give us the tools and we will finish the job . . . ' The king was totally won over. 'I could not have a better prime minister,' he concluded that night.[93] Even on the question of David, Churchill's 'silly attitude' of 1936 had quite gone, he told his mother.[94] At last Winston understood 'what harm he can do'.[95]

But over their weekly lunches there was little news to bring any comfort. During the winter the heroism of the Greeks had stood out like a beacon, showing the world that the Axis was not invincible as they drove the Italians out of their country and back into Albania. 'Hence we will not say that Greeks fight like heroes, but that heroes fight like Greeks,' Churchill declared, as ever finding the right words. Over tea at Coppins, the Kents' friend Chips Channon was touched at Marina's 'pride and pleasure' in the Greek advance.[96] Churchill was keen to support the Greeks and wanted neighbouring Yugoslavia to join the fight. But in the spring of 1941, as King Boris and his ministers caved in to Nazi pressure and German troops moved into Bulgaria up to the borders of Yugoslavia, Marina watched anxiously as the fate of her relatives in Greece and Yugoslavia seemed precariously entwined.

Prince Paul was trapped between the British request that he join them in the fight to save Greece and Hitler's threatening stance against his own country. He set out in secret to Berchtesgaden in early March. Hitler was persuasive, he cajoled; he made his position seem reasonable. Ribbentrop said little, cold eyes watching his prey, waiting for another leader to crumble. Hitler offered to respect the sovereignty and territorial integrity of Yugoslavia. The Regent wavered, tormented by the decision.[97]

Olga's Greek relatives telephoned most nights pressing him to join their cause. George VI knew that the Regent was listening to Hitler's 'honeyed words', and wrote a personal appeal, pointing out that the Germans' word 'is never, and least of all now, to be trusted. We count on you.'[98] It was no use. Prince Paul was a nervous wreck. Chips Channon at the Foreign Office was the first in Kent's circle to learn on 24 March that Prince Paul was signing with the Axis. 'My heart bled only for my poor distracted Regent,' he wrote in his diary.[99] 'I cannot believe that the Regent, whom I love more than anyone else on earth, could do anything dishonourable or against the interests of England which he loves as I do.'[100]

Protests swept across Belgrade at the prospect of a secret pact with Germany. There was a *coup d'état*. The military seized control. Yugoslav tanks took positions outside the palace. In London Chips rang Marina distraught. Prince Paul was branded a traitor in Yugoslavia and London, he explained. His actions were seen as worse than King Boris of Bulgaria, Carol of Romania or even Leopold of Belgium: 'he sold out England.' Chips joined the Kents at their home waiting anxiously. 'I dread every wireless bulletin,' he wrote, 'lest it tell us that Paul has been butchered in the traditional Balkan manner.'[101]

The same thought had evidently occurred to Prince Paul who visibly paled when the military escort came for him. 'The Prince saw us not only as revolutionaries, but as his executioners,' observed one army officer, 'and probably believed that I was taking him to the gallows.'[102] Paul fled Yugoslavia with Olga, leaving his cousin's son, seventeen-year-old King Peter, frightened and tearful on the throne.

The Kents set out apprehensively to Chequers to lunch with the prime minister on 30 March aiming to plead on behalf of their relatives. Marina hoped her sister and brother-in-law could join them in England. The war had trapped more of her family on the opposing side arguably than any other member of the royal family. Only her cousin, the dashing Prince Philip of Greece, was serving in the Royal Navy, now part of the Mediterranean Fleet. She sat next to Winston Churchill and put the case for her beleaguered brother-in-law and sister. 'Of course, Prince Paul could not possibly come here,' Churchill replied at once. His actions had turned him into an outcast. Officials were seeking out a location where Paul could be held safely, he explained, as a 'sort of semi-prisoner-of-state'.[103] Both Marina's sisters now were enemies of the Allied cause.

Far from saving Yugoslavia, the constant vacillation and the final *coup d'état* had provoked Hitler's anger. The end, when it came, was swift and terrible. Belgrade suffered concentrated bombing from the *Luftwaffe* in Operation

Punishment. The might of the German army bore down on Greece and Yugo-slavia as the Nazis showed their Italian ally how a *Blitzkrieg* was done.

There was trouble too for the British in the scorching heat of the Western Desert where gains made by their Commonwealth forces were lost as fast as they were won. The British Army had been weakened by Churchill's decision to send divisions to Greece while Hitler had dispatched the brilliant General Rommel to Libya to strengthen the Italians. Rommel wasted no time in seizing the initiative and the British had to abandon their advance more than 300 miles into Libya as far west as Benghazi. By 11 April the situation was reversed as the British Commonwealth forces were driven back into Egypt, apart from hold-ing on to the Libyan port of Tobruk, with its all-important deep harbour, the troops there under siege from the Germans.

Events came to a swift conclusion in Yugoslavia and Greece. Yugoslavia fell first, and it was the turn of King Peter to flee the country to Cairo.[104] By the end of April in Greece, too, the ancient ruins of the Acropolis in Athens, a potent symbol of the birthplace of democracy, looked out over a Nazi-occupied city. For one man the revulsion he felt that Greece had come to this, led him to the ultimate sacrifice. According to local legend, Konstantinos Koukidis, the guard on flag duty at the Acropolis on the fateful morning of 27 April, was ordered to run up a swastika banner. For him this was impossible. He lowered his country's blue and white flag. Then, without warning, he quickly wrapped himself in the precious Greek flag and, before he could be stopped, plunged 200 feet over the Acropolis rock to his death, his yell of defiance echoing in the still morning air. The red and black Nazi colours of a giant swastika were raised over the ancient Acropolis, dominating the Athens landscape below.

That same spirit of unyielding defiance remained in Marina's mother, Prin-cess Nicholas, who refused to leave Athens when her family went into exile. The German commanding officer who came to requisition her home found an old woman sitting bolt upright in her chair who greeted him without a smile. She did not seem a threat in her constricted little world: indeed all her thoughts were for others. Calmly she asked if she could continue with her charitable work. In the turmoil of the city under fire she was a figure to respect and the Germans treated her so. They left her alone, even granting her the freedom to tend her husband's grave at Tatoi.[105]

In Britain, for George VI, in a battered palace, surrounded by a bombed city, the outcome looked bleak. It was as though courage alone was not enough. The bravery of the Allied troops and the people caught in the front line at home was beyond question. Each week brought news of some great act of heroism.

Even with this sacrifice, Allied victory began to seem unobtainable. The enemy appeared unbeatable. Any advance proved unsustainable. The war was uncontainable, escalating across the white-hot deserts of Africa, the timeless villages of Europe, the distant tropics of the Far East and even plumbing the secret depths of the oceans. Britain and Empire was threatened to the core.

The empire had taken on an air of permanence under his indefatigable great-grandmother, Queen Victoria. It was sustained through the reign of his grandfather, Edward VII, and reached its greatest extent under his father, George V. It had fallen to him to preside over such a spectacular downfall, with no end in sight. The Axis countries, engorged with power and swollen with victory, appeared like an indescribable evil force, whose ugly reach had perhaps even ensnared his own brother.

9

EVER WIDENING CONFLICT

....

'The Range of the tremendous conflict is ever widening . . . '

—George VI, Christmas 1941

A drama which cast a suspicious light on the king's Lord Steward, and even members of the royal family, began to unfold on 10 May 1941.

Once again, London was under attack. All night long, wave after wave of German bombers transformed the sleeping city into great walls of fire, burning air and black toxic smoke. Many Londoners lost their lives as Goering's bombing campaign reached an appalling crescendo. Some 400 miles to the north, the relative peace of Scotland was fractured by a single German Messerschmitt Bf 110 flying low over moorland at around 10 pm as night set in. The solitary plane was detected by radar approaching the coast of Northumberland, heading west across southern Scotland. The Duke of Hamilton, on duty that night as commanding officer at RAF Turnhouse near Edinburgh saw 'that normal action had been taken . . . to shoot down the enemy aircraft'.[1]

A local farmer, David McLean, on Bonnyton Moor, 10 miles south of Glasgow, saw what happened next. 'I heard the plane roaring overhead,' he told the *Daily Record*. He ran to the back of his farmhouse. In the darkness, he heard a crash about 200 yards away and then, almost instantaneously, 'saw the plane burst into flames'. He felt stunned and 'a bit frightened' when he suddenly realised a parachute was falling to the earth. 'Peering into the darkness, I could see a man hanging from the harness.'[2] A German was landing in the middle of the moor.

The German arrival was greeted with a certain amateurishness as the farmer ventured into the blackness armed with a hayfork since no other weapon was to hand. He brought the lone pilot into his farmhouse where his mother offered him a cup of tea and the enemy airman revealed he was on a goodwill 'Special

Mission'. This stunning news from the night visitor from Germany was hard to swallow and in no time the Renfrewshire Home Guard was on the scene. The prisoner was detained in little more than a Scout hut for a few hours, before being taken to Maryhill Barracks in Glasgow. He gave his name as 'Captain Alfred Horn' and insisted with some urgency that he must see the Scottish aristocrat, the Duke of Hamilton. Only the Duke of Hamilton would do.[3]

The requisite blue blood duly arrived in the imposing form of Douglas Douglas-Hamilton, 14th Duke of Hamilton, Keeper of Holyrood House and the king's Lord Steward. To Hamilton's amazement the mysterious parachutist now chose to reveal that he was none other than Hitler's deputy: Rudolf Hess. The German airman with his swarthy features, close-knit eyebrows and heavy build did indeed look the part. None the less, it took some time before the wing commander was convinced that the dark-eyed foreigner with the injured foot really was the Deputy Führer. It became apparent that the enemy intruder was on a peace mission. Unnervingly for the duke, it was a peace mission in which it was presumed by the German before him that he himself would be an eager participant.[4]

This was all the more puzzling because he had not met Hess before, although Hess seemed to know a great deal about the duke. Hess had specifically targeted his family seat at Dungavel House as his destination. This was not because the large rambling castle in the centre of a grouse moor with turrets and a small airstrip was easy to spot from the air; rather it was the end of a longer-term plan. Hess appeared to have made a concentrated effort that took many months of preparation to reach him. He said that he had tried to reach the Duke of Windsor in Lisbon the previous year. That plan had failed, but now, claimed the Deputy Führer intently, 'he was on a mission of humanity'. He believed that there was a significant following in favour of peace in Britain and that the British aristocracy were in a position to oust Churchill and facilitate a negotiated settlement. 'The Führer did not want to defeat England,' Hess claimed, 'and wished to stop the fighting.'[5]

The Duke of Hamilton found himself once again in a most delicate position. Hess's actions appeared to imply he was a co-conspirator in a peace mission of breathtaking audacity. Furthermore, Hess's story created the impression they had some kind of prior understanding. Hamilton, Hess believed, was an 'Englishman' who 'would understand his point of view', contact his family to say he was safe, and 'ask the king to give him parole'.[6] Hamilton did not hesitate. He escalated the matter not to the king, but directly to Churchill.

The prime minister, however, had found temporary relief from the horrors of war in a Marx Brothers film and refused to contemplate plots involving the Duke of Hamilton and a lone German parachutist of swarthy appearance intent on saving the world. All evening distressing news broke about the impact of the previous night's raid on London. 'There was nothing I could do about it,' Churchill wrote later, 'and I was glad of the diversion.' But the duke would not be put off and his news soon provided an even better diversion. 'Hess in Scotland!' wrote Churchill. 'I thought this was fantastic.'[7]

The story of Hess's flight was first announced in Germany on Munich Radio on 12 May. A few hours later, the British issued a brief press release from Downing Street.[8] The news was greeted with incredulity and nowhere more so than at the palace. The king was amazed to hear on the radio at midnight that 'Hitler's dearest friend' had landed near Glasgow, his astonishment increasing in the morning when his private secretary, Alexander Hardinge, revealed that the Duke of Hamilton appeared to be involved.

Like everyone else, his first thought was that his Lord Steward must be in some way implicated. 'Perhaps the post of Lord Steward is bewitched or is it Germanised?' he wrote in his diary on 13 May. 'My Lord Steward . . . has only been appointed for a year.' The king trusted Hamilton and found it hard to believe he was guilty of anything. There were so many possibilities. He had asked Walter Buccleuch, his predecessor, to leave 'owing to his sympathy with the Nazis'. Could it be that Buccleuch, rather than Hamilton, was Hess's real target? 'Hess might have landed two miles from Drumlanrig [Buccleuch's castle] instead,' the king wrote in his diary.[9] This ambiguous entry could mean

Extract from the king's war diary, Tuesday 13 May 1941: George VI thought the post of Lord Steward was 'bewitched' (THE ROYAL ARCHIVES © HER MAJESTY QUEEN ELIZABETH II)

that the king thought the Deputy Führer's mission would make more sense if he had been trying to reach his former Lord Steward. Had Hess identified the wrong family seat? Alternatively the king may have thought it would have been better had Hess landed a couple of miles from Buccleuch's residence since then only his previous Lord Steward would have been implicated.

George VI was still puzzling over the matter when the prime minister came to lunch. It had been a difficult week. The bombing on Saturday had dealt London a hammering. The capital's most iconic buildings had been hit. 'The House of Commons is a shambles,' wrote the king. Big Ben had escaped unscathed but 'Westminster Hall suffered . . . and Westminster Abbey, the shrine of this country, was hit.'[10] Now, as the two men helped themselves from the silver tureens on the sideboard, the unexpected flight of the Deputy Führer brought a welcome air of relief from the strain.

Hess's landing 'would do us good', Churchill said. The Germans had declared that Hess was mad, but who would believe that? Both men could imagine how angry they would be if Beaverbrook or Eden suddenly took off and flew to Germany without warning. The prime minister explained that Hess had been interviewed by Sir Ivone Kirkpatrick from the Foreign Office. Hess had given Kirkpatrick 'unofficially' what amounted to the same old peace offer. Hitler was prepared to agree to peace terms that left the British Empire intact—if he could have a free hand in Europe. But, said Churchill, according to Hess, Hitler refused to negotiate with the present British government. Evidently the prime minister was in a playful mood. The king noted, 'Winston was sure I did not want him to resign!! Just when things looked brighter for us.'[11]

Churchill believed Hess was effectively undertaking a 'deed of superb devotion' to his hero, the Führer, who he worshipped, by sacrificing himself in his efforts to bring back for his leader peace with Britain.[12] While he was in favour of revealing the truth to the press, others in the Cabinet believed there was more to be gained by a certain amount of discretion or even deliberate disinformation. If speculation that Hitler himself had authorised the mission or that there was a serious rift in Nazi high command was not dismissed, this could damage Nazi morale.[13] Churchill took some persuading but eventually agreed. On 17 May 1941 he notified President Roosevelt of the true situation, adding that this was for his own information. 'We think it best to let the press have a good run for a bit and keep the Germans guessing,' he wrote. 'I cannot doubt there will be deep misgivings in the German armed forces about what he may say.'[14]

Taking such a line proved a brilliant strategy and so began a conspiracy that has run and run to this day. There were so many possibilities. Hamilton found it hard to clear his name. He went to see the king on 16 May to explain in person how he had become entangled in the extraordinary affair. 'As my Lord Steward he felt it was right to come & see me,' noted the king. The duke tried hard to give a good account of himself and showed the king summaries of his interview with the Deputy Führer as well as two that Kirkpatrick had done. He wanted the king to see the far-fetched thinking behind Hess's mission. Hess did appear to believe that he could fly into enemy territory, deliver a message to those he thought still favoured peace and then somehow fly back to Germany. 'Hamilton also told me that Hess had asked him to ask me to give him his "Parole" while he was here!!' wrote the king incredulously. 'All the leading Nazis think they are gods everywhere, as well as in Germany . . . a time of detention here may sober him down & teach him to look at things from a more rational angle.'[15]

The Duke of Hamilton found himself viewed as a possible suspect despite the fact that on 22 May the Secretary of State for Air, Sir Archibald Sinclair, exonerated him in the House. 'The conduct of the Duke of Hamilton has been in every respect honourable and proper.'[16] But the denial only served to feed the suspicions.

And nowhere were the suspicions growing faster than in Moscow. Stalin's labyrinthine mind was in overdrive imagining plots within plots masterminded by his deadly adversaries, real or imagined. Trickery was afoot: of that he was sure. Hess's flight was of supreme importance. The timing was key. German troops were massing ominously on the Soviet border. Fear of invasion was imminent. If Hitler's deputy negotiated with Britain's 'peace party' to secure a settlement in the west between the British Empire and the German Reich, the Germans could unleash their full might on a new Eastern front. It was hard to make sense of the prolonged British silence on Hess's flight. Stalin became obsessed by the mission and he was remarkably well briefed.

Soviet intelligence learned of the mission almost immediately through 'Sonnchen', otherwise known as Kim Philby, who worked for the Secret Intelligence Service or MI6. On 14 May Philby informed the Soviets that Hess had arrived in Britain with a peace plan, which he hoped to communicate through the Duke of Hamilton. Soviet intelligence came to the view that the mission must be undertaken *with* Hitler's approval and this posed a real threat. It was puzzling for the Soviets when a peace deal was not announced, but Philby had an answer for that too. Hess was being kept in reserve to conclude the peace deal when it most suited the British: 'a trump card in waiting'.[17]

Soon all manner of theories emerged to support this interpretation. The Duke of Windsor had made no secret of his pro-peace, pro-German stance, and the Duke of Kent was known to have been close to him in the past. Rumours began to spread pointing out the fact that Kent had been in the area on the fateful night and Hamilton's diary showed he had met Kent several times that spring. Some believed that the Duke of Kent had been waiting for Rudolf Hess at Dungavel House, along with other plotters who were committed to facilitating peace, perhaps even bringing back the Duke of Windsor. The fact that Hess appeared to believe he could land in Britain, deliver his message and then return safely to Germany to continue the negotiations lent weight to the idea of an on-going peace process. Alternatively, had Hess been lured to Britain by some kind of elaborate intelligence sting in which Hamilton and Kent were involved, albeit perhaps unknowingly? Cunning plans involving MI5, MI6 or the Special Operations Executive—and even a Hess double—multiplied.[18] In these schemes, Kent was a decoy used by British intelligence to fool senior Nazis into thinking that rebel British MPs were ready to negotiate peace or even reinstate the Duke of Windsor.

None of these theories have been proved, but, intriguingly, the Duke of Windsor's reckless behaviour in the summer of 1940 might well have been the catalyst that prompted the chain of events that led to Hess's blind gamble. The duke's actions had helped to foster the belief in Nazi high command that the peace party was still strong in Britain and it might be possible to organise a coup in Britain. Disappointed by Ribbentrop's failure to enlist the Duke of Windsor as the next 'Quisling', Hitler turned to his trusted deputy, Hess, to see if he could have greater success in reaching those in the 'peace party' who were believed to be prepared to support the king to get rid of Churchill or organise a palace coup.[19] The archives demonstrate that Hess in turn consulted his long-standing friend and mentor, Karl Haushofer, and his son, Albrecht, over the summer of 1940.[20] Albrecht convinced Hess that there were many in Britain who favoured an Anglo-German agreement and their correspondence in September 1940 shows that he had identified the 14th Duke of Hamilton as the best point of contact, a man 'who has access at all times to all important persons in London even to Churchill and the king'.[21]

The next stage was to organise a means of communicating with the unwitting duke. By chance, Karl Haushofer had recently heard from an English acquaintance, Mrs Violet Roberts, the widow of a Cambridge academic. Somewhat conveniently she had identified a means for Haushofer to reply to her via a PO Box in (still neutral) Lisbon. Here was the perfect intermediary in the form of an apparently innocent housewife living in Wembley. Albrecht Haushofer

carefully drafted the letter to the Duke of Hamilton. The message was despatched with high hopes. But weeks turned to months and there was no reply.

Hess did not know that the letter was intercepted by MI5 and withheld from
the Duke of Hamilton, who did not see it himself until March 1941.[22] In Berlin,
with the long months of waiting for a British reply to the letter from 'A' to the
duke, Hess became desperate. He, too, was in danger of failing Hitler as Ribbentrop had failed before him. He, too, longed for Hitler's approval. Hess knew that
the German invasion of the Soviet Union was imminent and the Anglo-German
question had to be resolved urgently. The Deputy Führer could see the disaster
for Germany if an Eastern front in opened up while still at war with the British.
Hess did not lose faith in his plan, only in his means of communication, which
had faltered.[23] Consequently he decided to fly directly to Britain and contact the
'peace party' himself. The stakes were undoubtedly high. But with war imminent with the Soviets, the stakes were even higher if he failed in his purpose.

Hess had plenty of time to ponder the leaps of faith guiding his own actions
as he languished in the Tower of London. He had fallen into the hands of the
very Churchill 'clique' that he had sought to depose. An unknown future at the
hands of his country's enemies lay ahead. In London, officials were still trying
to make sense of his mission in early June. It fell to John 'the Snake' Simon, the
former Home Secretary—a man whose own brand of icy cool had enabled him
to take on the bugging of the King of England without hesitation—to interview Rudolf Hess. Perhaps he could make more sense of Hess's mission where
others had failed.

But the man whose brilliant powers of deductive reasoning had led him to
the peak of the British establishment found himself face to face with something
entirely different. Lord Simon was polite but searching, shining the spotlight
on dark and murky corners of Hess's mind that did not stand up to scrutiny
well. There were contradictions, heated assertions, false beliefs and a curious
reluctance to state with any real clarity the purpose of his mission. Patiently,
over a three-hour interview, Simon kept leading him to the brink with such
phrases as 'I think now we are coming to the real purpose of our interview'
and 'I think now we come to the point', only to find Hess diving into irrelevant
cul-de-sacs. But finally Hess repeated the grounds of the peace terms. 'And do
you come here with the Führer's knowledge or consent?' Simon asked. This did
provoke a direct response. 'Without his knowledge. *Absolut*,' and he laughed.[24]

Could he be believed? His interviewers were not sure. It was not long before
the team responsible for his care thought he *was* suffering some form of mental

illness. 'Hess's mental condition, which was somewhat masked before, has now declared itself as a true psychosis,' wrote the army psychiatrist, Colonel Rees, on 19 June. Amongst his delusions was a conviction that there was a plot to poison him and an irrational overestimation of the importance of the Duke of Hamilton, a man who his 'prophet friend', Professor Haushofer, had marked out as a person 'appointed by destiny' to help his quest for peace. He 'refused to be enlightened' on his mistake and insisted 'the king of England would never let these things happen' if he was informed. While Hess had prolonged episodes in which he appeared normal, the delusions were key to his thinking. 'We may have a mental patient on our hands permanently,' warned Rees.[25]

As for his 'prophet friend', Albrecht Haushofer quickly found his life was in the balance as the finger of accusation pointed at him. His fate in the immediate aftermath of the flight suggests that Hitler had no idea his deputy was about to take off and was trying to make sense of what had happened. German records found after the war showed that Haushofer was summoned to Berchtesgaden on 12 May where he wrote a detailed report for Hitler on his English contacts and in particular what he knew of the Duke of Hamilton.[26] He was then despatched to a Berlin prison to be interrogated by the Gestapo. Such steps would not make sense if Hitler was aware of his deputy's plans and had authorised the peace initiative.

Thousands of miles away in the Bahamas, the Duke of Windsor also saw reasons to be fearful. He had toyed with the Nazi leadership in the summer of 1940. He had sought favours for his possessions and entered into discussions about being a king in waiting ready to serve a large peace party in Britain: a winning German card to play when the time was right.

But Windsor had slipped from their grasp and now the positions were reversed. Hess, the prisoner, was a British trump card in waiting. This made the duke uneasy. What would it take for a U-boat to emerge from the distant blue horizon with German troops ready to storm Government House? The prospect seemed all too real to the duke and did not necessarily have a convincingly satisfactory conclusion.

The duke's new fear was duly recorded by the FBI. Edgar Hoover wrote to inform Assistant Secretary of State Adolf Berle and the matter was escalated to the president himself. 'Information has been received from a confidential source close to the Duke of Windsor at Nassau that the Duke is very much worried for fear of being kidnapped by the Germans and being traded for the release of Rudolf Hess.'[27]

A t 4 am on 22 June 1941, there was no Anglo-German agreement as Hitler launched the biggest invasion in history. Three and a half million Axis soldiers were allocated to the fight against the Soviet Union. Leading the way were crack troops, efficient, undefeated, expecting to win. Some 600,000 vehicles went with them; apparently unstoppable, roaring across the undefended land. Behind the panzers came the standard divisions with horse drawn transport. Above, the *Luftwaffe* annihilated carefully worked-out targets with deadly precision: airfields, aircrafts, communications disappeared; over 1,200 Soviet aircraft demolished on the first day. A mechanical wave of destruction that surged into the Soviet Union like a tide, rooting out hidden pockets of resistance, killing with practised efficiency, leaving death and burning villages under smoking skies. Stretching across a front of 1,200 miles, the scale of the horror made earlier *Blitzkriegs* seem like a dress rehearsal.

George VI and Queen Elizabeth heard the shocking news before church that Sunday on the wireless at 9 am. No warning or ultimatum given, the king noted in his diary, 'just the usual indictment against another power by Goebbels and Ribbentrop'.[28] They were at Windsor Castle, the ancient walls towering around them imparting a sense of security from the horrors of war where just a few miles away one-third of all London's streets were impassable, the ghostly outlines of former buildings rising from the rubble. The king had seen Liverpool, Birmingham, Bristol, Plymouth, Portsmouth, so many great cities wrecked, entire districts flattened. Belfast, too, with its huge shipyards, had been blitzed for the first time. The Gloucesters arrived by chance just after the raid, the duchess deeply distressed by the casualties. 'I was almost overcome with emotion myself when a young man, who had just lost his sight, would not let go when I took his hand,' she wrote afterwards.[29] How would this arresting news of a whole new Eastern front affect the course of the war?

Churchill, 'the arch anti-Communist' according to his Private Secretary Colville, was very clear over what had to be done. 'If Hitler invaded Hell I would at least make a favourable reference to the Devil in the House of Commons,' he declared. Although Churchill had opposed communism for twenty-five years, he now devoted the day to preparing his broadcast offering help to the Soviet Union. 'We have but one aim and one single, irrevocable purpose,' Churchill announced on BBC radio. 'We are resolved to destroy Hitler and every vestige of the Nazi regime . . . ' The king remarked on Churchill's clarity of purpose when he met him for lunch on 24 June. 'When Winston has made up his mind about somebody and something nothing will change his opinion. Personal feelings are as nothing to him, though he has a very sentimental side to his nature. He looks to one goal and one goal only: winning this war. No half measures.'[30]

Over the following weeks the king found his prime minister intent on going west, to America. He had long believed that the New World was the best hope of saving the Old; of shifting the balance in this ever-accelerating, all-consuming conflagration in a way which brought real hope of an end. But Roosevelt's hands were tied. The Lend-Lease Act had been passed and he had extended US patrols protecting merchant shipping in the Atlantic. It was not enough. In the Atlantic, losses were so serious critical supplies could run out. British morale was at a new low, bringing fresh criticisms of Churchill.

The king remembered his visit with the queen to meet Roosevelt before the war fondly. He trusted the older man and felt they shared an important friendship; in turn Roosevelt showed a paternalistic concern for the younger man. 'May I add that I really hope you are taking care of your own health because your continued fitness is of real moment to the world,' the president had written affectionately on 1 May 1940.[31] Perhaps he recognised the burden of public office for George VI. The king wrote again on 3 June 1941, gently reminding the American president that the 'spirit of the people here under the strain of the terrible and indiscriminate bombing is truly remarkable'.[32] Roosevelt, however, was slow to respond. The king decided he would send out his youngest brother. He had sufficient confidence in the Duke of Kent, now promoted to air commodore, to entrust him with an extensive tour of North America later in the summer.

During July German troops swept across the Soviet Union with such speed it was feared that the Soviets might succumb to the German *Blitzkrieg* as quickly as countries in Western Europe. The great Russian bear appeared mortally wounded. The Germans were soon halfway to Moscow, blasting a path with mechanical precision through wide Russian landscapes, confident of victory. Behind them was a trail of destruction; a level of brutality inflicted on civilians that no one would forget. German bombers launched their first air raid on Moscow on 21 July. The Russian psyche reeled. The forces ranged against them seemed incomprehensibly evil. The Soviets counter-attacked with ferocity, but hundreds of thousands of prisoners were taken. In the west it began to seem possible that the swollen German army, heady with victory in the east, would be back to launch the final strike against Britain before too long.

It was against this worrying backdrop that the Duke of Kent left Marina and their two children, Edward and Alexandra, at the end of July to become the first member of the royal family to fly the Atlantic. It took almost sixteen hours in a bomber to make the journey. 'Very uncomfortable,' he told the king. 'Impossible to sleep. Very cold and altogether unpleasant. But I am very glad I did it.' The press were waiting for him on arrival in Ottawa in Canada, delighted to welcome a member of the British royal family.[33] All went smoothly and it was a promising start to the Canadian leg of his tour which encompassed visits to aircraft factories and schools of the Canadian Air Training Scheme. 'It is fantastic—like another world to arrive here and find normal life—sprinklers on the lawns—cars everywhere—every kind of food—& everyone talking of holidays,' Kent confided to his brother. Canada was so far removed from the war that he found 'it's difficult for them to realise what it means'. But he was overwhelmed with the enthusiasm and all that was being done for the war effort. 'Canada has done a great work and they are 20% ahead of schedule.'[34]

Kent travelled from coast to coast across Canada by flying boat: Ottawa, Winnipeg, Regina, Calgary, Edmonton, Victoria and Vancouver. 'I've flown and flown,' he told the king. He had changed his view of flying. 'I now hate it as I always get a headache but it is the only way to do a tour of this sort . . . '[35] There were various mishaps as Kent tried to stay on schedule despite bad weather. He arrived in a powerful storm in Quebec province and had no sooner left the sea plane before it was turned over by gale-force winds and sank. More bad weather forced his plane down near Montreal but his team improvised with local transport to get to their appointment on time. Kent invariably won over the crowds as he expressed Britain's gratitude for all that Canada was doing.[36] Indeed, throughout this rather taxing tour the duke was reassuringly unflappable, always giving the impression that there was nowhere he would rather be so much as in this chilly windblown corner of the world inspecting yet another factory.

While Kent was in Canada he was watching closely for any developments in America's involvement in the war. The queen did her best to capture the hearts of American women in a radio broadcast on 10 August. She wanted to thank them and acknowledge the many different ways in which help had been given. Elizabeth highlighted their shared ideals. 'To *you* tyranny is as hateful as it is to us; to *you*, the things for which we fight to the death are no less sacred . . . We fight to save a cause that is yours no less than it is ours,' she said. 'However great the cost and however long the struggle, justice and freedom, human dignity and kindness, shall not perish from the earth.' It was a well-judged speech which she concluded by talking of building 'a kinder, and a happier world for our children'.[37]

Four days later a statement was released which revealed that the British prime minister and the American president had met in person for the first time during the war. Churchill worked hard at fostering Britain's relationship with America. He arrived for the secret conference in Placentia Bay, Newfoundland, on the *Prince of Wales*, equipped with a personal letter of introduction from the king and his own profound desire to further collaboration between the two countries. The old mesmerising Churchill charm was used in generous measure to win the president over, Churchill's view being that the two nations were as one: sprung from the same soil, blood cousins, their language, their ideals, that intrinsic need for freedom, all held in common; and now England needed real help or it would perish. The service on the quarterdeck by the big guns Churchill saw 'as a deeply moving expression of the unity of faith of our two peoples' and he chose the hymns himself for the solemn moment, including 'For Those in Peril on the Sea' and 'O God Our Help in Ages Past'. 'Every word seemed to stir the heart,' he wrote.[38] Over three intense days of talks, in private Churchill spoke frankly of his worst fears. In public, their discussions became crystallised in the Atlantic Charter, a joint statement published on 14 August expressing the common ground between the two countries in the form of eight shared principles. Reading details of the historic conference in Canada, Kent could see that although there was no commitment to America joining the war, the charter set out shared ideals, including that all people had a right to self-determination and both countries were working for a world free from want and fear.[39]

'The meeting of Winston and FDR I hope was successful,' Kent wrote to the king from Toronto. 'I am sure it is very important that they should have met and got to know each other.' After six weeks in Canada, Kent was now ready to go to America.[40] It was his turn to remind Americans of the many irresistible bonds to England, that far-off place fighting for its very life. News had spread of his Canadian tour and by the time he reached New York in late August there was such a press of enthusiastic crowds that the police had to hold them back. They cheered wildly as the duke emerged from a Lockheed bomber at La Guardia Airport; a slim figure in a dark suit, standing alone, with little trace now of the flamboyance of earlier years. The crowd was delighted with this royal ambassador.[41] Although tired, his wide smile and friendly wave were winning hearts. The flash of cameras held the spell. In the newsreels all America would see the British spirit.

Kent's American tour was a personal triumph. He toured shipyards in Norfolk, met operational squadrons at Langley Airport and went on to Baltimore—'city of renown!' he teased the king, where the mayor 'kept on making allusions to "our Wallie"'.[42] But Kent discreetly avoided any faux pas and remained focused on his mission. At the Glenn Martin aircraft factory in Baltimore, Kent charmed his audience of 13,000 men and women. 'Every hour that you work, saves the lives of women and children . . . ' he told them.[43] The undisputed highlight of his tour was to meet President Roosevelt, who he found 'charming', and his wife Eleanor, who 'really is pleasant'. Kent had 'endless conversations' with Roosevelt at the president's house in Hyde Park, covering many aspects of the war.[44]

It was only when he reached Quebec in Canada on his return journey that Kent found time to write to his old friend, Betty Lawson-Johnson. Any hopes he had once entertained of having a chance to see her while in America had been quickly dispelled. Now he had stopped to rest he realised he was exhausted, but his letter to Betty reveals the stresses of the tour and how totally the former playboy was swept up in the Allied cause:

> I am so sorry not to see you but I think that you were right—it would have been impossible in Washington—as I only had a very few minutes to myself and in the evening I sat up with the President . . . What a hectic time I had in the US—and I was confused and rushed about. I wish I could have stayed longer and seen more places—I talked to the workers at Glenn Martin's Plant which really did good I think and then I addressed the Press Club—You've never seen such a terrible collection of people. Naturally they don't know there is a war on & want to keep out of it and not give up their comfortable lives but they <u>must</u> do more . . . there is too much talk and they don't listen and they don't listen enough to us as to what they should make and how they should make it after we have had the fighting experience . . . I am feeling rather exhausted as I really have worked hard and I hope done some good over here. The Air Training Scheme is doing wonderfully well and is most impressive. Naturally I want to get home but even this tiring visit has done me good and made a break from the strain of England—but it's a <u>gloomy</u> thought to go back to the long blacked out bombing winter. Pray god it will be the last.[45]

George VI saw his youngest brother on his return and was pleased to find him looking well despite the long hours of flying. Kent had much to report to the king about the details of his trip. He had particularly enjoyed his time with the president. Amongst other things they had discussed the importance of Iceland. This large island on the border between the Arctic and Atlantic Oceans was strategically sited for North Atlantic shipping lanes. America was taking on more of a role in the Atlantic war by despatching US Marines to take over the defence of

Iceland from the British. The king found the American presence reassuring, as though 'only 500 miles separate us now [from America] instead of 3,000'.[46] Kent explained that the president 'seemed very anxious I should go to Iceland on my return', a simple request that the brothers felt they should honour.[47]

Finally, it was the turn of the Duke and Duchess of Windsor to woo the Americans in their own inimitable style. They had at last received permission for an extended tour once the duke had assured Churchill that he would not say a word out of line with British policy. Wallis was very clear about priorities. 'It will be divine to see you both again,' she wrote excitedly to Betty, although she was worried that she might not have the right look. 'Just think I haven't been in a shop for over a year and a half, we will make a strange looking couple . . . It will be lovely to see the world again.'[48]

Embassy staff, however, were most keen to manage what the world would see of the Windsors. When the duke and duchess arrived in Washington on 25 September they were accompanied by an embassy official, Rene MacColl, and under strict instructions to avoid talking to reporters. But the enduring fascination of the Windsors ensured that the cameras were never very far away. Even without an interview, the press could deduce a considerable amount from observation alone as the Windsors appeared visibly overburdened with life's little luxuries for a wartime visit. Column inches reported in full on the couple's seventy or eighty pieces of luggage which required a lorry to transport from the station. Their choice of hotel also prompted comment: the Waldorf Towers in New York, a luxurious sanctuary for millionaires.

The duke was received at the White House where he met the president at a luncheon although, noted the *New York Times*, Mrs Roosevelt '"deeply regretted" that she could not possibly be present' owing to a prior engagement.[49] But others were at home for the duke, including Alfred Sloan, who entertained him in the General Motors Building on 27 October, as well as old friends, Katherine and Herman Rogers and the Lawson-Johnstons.[50] The duchess's shopping expeditions were followed with keen interest, but when one tabloid paper reported that she had bought more than fifteen hats and had the tills ringing merrily in expensive couturiers including Mainbocher, Rene MacColl swung into action to dismiss the alleged excess of accessories. 'I think it is quite ridiculous and not a little unfair particularly in such times, for such fantastic statements to be made regarding purchases of clothing.'[51]

While the Windsors were in America, behind the scenes intelligence gathering on the 'Bahamas entourage' was gaining momentum. Wenner-Gren's business interests came under the spotlight on both sides of the Atlantic when he sought to develop a large tract of land on the Grand Bahama Island. Declassified telegrams show that the authorities were much exercised. The United States government considered that his connections in Germany 'were sufficiently close' to make them reluctant to approve a scheme that would give him 'considerable control in areas that might either now or hereafter be of some strategic importance', concluded Viscount Halifax, now the British ambassador in Washington. Wenner-Gren's grand development plans were rejected.[52]

Another millionaire who once counted the Windsors as friends was also under growing scrutiny, with members of the duke's circle now declaiming each other. 'C's people' notified the Foreign Office of an intriguing interview in September 1941 with Herman and Katherine Rogers. The Rogers had left Europe that summer, returning to America via Bermuda. According to the intelligence report, Mr Rogers 'was put through a (friendly) interrogation by the Bermuda Censorship Authorities'.[53] During the conversation Charles Bedaux's name was raised. Rogers had paused. He 'felt rather conscience stricken', he said, 'at denouncing someone who in the past had helped him, but felt obliged to do so'.[54]

In the intimacy of the interview room, faced with the seriousness of the issues that lay behind the questions, Mr Rogers began to reveal his worries. The 'speed-up king', he believed, had found a new and altogether more disturbing outlet for his talents. It had begun gradually. During the battle for France, Bedaux had befriended the Germans and welcomed them to his château—the very château where the duke and duchess had been married. Bedaux now drove a German car and controlled 'a large German staff' in the centre of Paris, said Rogers. His task: to organise 'Jewish industries taken over by the Germans in France', and to ensure 'the maximum production was achieved'. Rogers pointed out that his information was not obtained at first hand, but 'he was convinced of its authenticity'. He strongly disapproved of Bedaux and was sure he 'was doing the Allied cause in France more harm than any other American'.[55]

The interviewer in Bermuda scribbled on the typed record that Herman Rogers was 'an extremely nice straight type of American' who was 'extremely anxious to help in any way possible'. But just how straight was he? Rogers informed the authorities that when Mrs Simpson had accepted the offer of hospitality at the Château de Cande in 1936, Bedaux 'at that time was unknown to the Duke of Windsor, Mrs Simpson or Mr and Mrs Rogers themselves'.[56] But there is evidence that Rogers *did* know Bedaux well before this and had accompanied him on an expedition across British Columbia earlier in the 1930s.[57] Rogers appeared to be economical with the truth as he ran down Bedaux. Such was the atmosphere of mistrust, those who were once friends in Windsor's circle now turned on each other in their efforts to distance themselves from the all-enveloping cloud of suspicion.

Queen Elizabeth was preparing for her usual Sunday routine on 7 December at Windsor. The wireless was on in her room and suddenly claimed her full attention. The reporter was talking of Japanese bombing of Americans. It did not make sense. She went straight to the king. Could it be true? It seemed unbelievable. They listened together to the BBC news.[58]

At 9 am came the familiar sound of the beeps counting down and then the 'bombshell'. Thousands of miles away in the Pacific, the American fleet at Pearl Harbor in Hawaii had woken up to the unmistakeable sounds of war. There had been no warning. The unimpassioned voice of the newsreader calmly listed the devastation, conjuring up a vision of unimaginable horror.[59]

The raid alarm had only just sounded on the USS *Arizona* in Pearl Harbor when the first bomb hit. Within minutes another bomb was thought to have struck an ammunition store, triggering a massive explosion. More than 1,000 sailors were feared dead as the battleship sank. Across the US fleet anchored at Pearl Harbor it was a scene of carnage. Torpedoes tore through metal as hulls and bows shuddered. Bombs exploded through decking. Fire and smoke blotted out the familiar world of the ships and water gushed down corridors and burst into cabins where men were still sleeping. Sailors tried to dress and reach the guns but it was already too late. Several US battleships, cruisers and destroyers were hit and damaged. Scores of planes were smashed. The death toll was not yet known.

The king and queen waited anxiously for further news. The scale of Japanese duplicity was immediately apparent to the king. Such an attack must have taken 'weeks, probably months to prepare'. It looked as though the Japanese had deliberately prolonged US-Japanese negotiations to lull the 'USA into a feeling of security' as they prepared their lightning strike on Pearl Harbor.[60] Over the following twenty-four hours the king and queen learned of Japanese assaults on Shanghai, Hong Kong, Singapore and Malaya as well as US territory at Guam, Midway Island and Wake Island. The Japanese had aimed for a pre-emptive strike against the US navy as a prelude to expanding the war in the Far East around the limitless blue horizon of the Pacific.

Events moved swiftly that week. Each day brought more nerve-wracking news. On Monday 8 December, Britain and America declared war on Japan.

On Tuesday 9 December, at the prime minister's weekly lunch, the king learned more of the appalling Pacific news. Churchill told him it was thought that three US battleships were sunk and three seriously damaged. In fact the figure was higher. But the king was under no illusion what this meant: 'the USA has already lost command of the sea in the Pacific. A very serious situation for our ships the *P of W* & *Repulse* who are out there . . .'[61]

On Wednesday 10 December, the king and queen were touring factories in south Wales. They were in the quiet Welsh town of Bargoed when Sir Alan Lascelles, Assistant Private Secretary to George VI, returned from the telephone 'with a face of doom', observed the queen. She thought, 'Oh, what's happened now?'[62] It was another 'very real shock'. The great battleship *Prince of Wales*, and the battle cruiser *Repulse*, had been sunk by the Japanese, said Lascelles.[63] The Royal Navy would no longer be able to provide support to troops fighting in the Malayan Peninsula.

Surrounded by a scene unchanged for centuries and as yet untouched by war, the horror of the latest news intruded sharply. The sleepy Welsh town, with its steep slate roofs, the view of distant blue hills beyond scattered with sheep, brought no peace. The king hated to think of the men going down with their ships. He could see the decks and the quarterdecks, crammed with life. 'I thought I was getting immune to hearing bad news,' he confided to Churchill that day, 'but this has affected me deeply as I am sure it has you. There is something particularly "alive" about a big ship, which gives one a sense of personal loss apart from considerations of lack of power.'[64] More than 800 sailors lost their lives.

The king and queen continued their tour of the industrial towns of the Welsh valleys. Whatever happened, they wanted to maintain an assured performance. They learned on 11 December that Germany and Italy had declared war on America. The king telegraphed Roosevelt. 'We are proud indeed to be fighting at your side against the common enemy. We share your inflexible determination and your confidence that with God's help the powers of darkness will be overcome.'[65]

But 'the powers of darkness' were winning. In the Western Desert, after General Rommel's first offensive driving British and Commonwealth forces back across Libya to the Egpytian frontier, Churchill had pushed for a counterattack which also failed. In the Far East, both the American and British navies were no longer able to support Allied troops as they faced up to Japanese troops marching through the Malayan Peninsula to Singapore. The Soviet Union was doing her best 'against the most fearful, organised Army which has ever been seen or heard of in the world', the king wrote to his mother.[66] But the

Germans had swept more than 700 miles into the USSR, captured the Ukraine with its industrial wealth, and reached the outskirts of Moscow. Lost in an immense white landscape, they battled on through smothering drifts of snow. The Germans had fought and won 500,000 square miles of Soviet land and many believed it was only a matter of time before the Soviet Union succumbed.

The great relief that America had joined the war seemed to be outweighed by an unceasing stream of difficulties. There were those who thought that continued war was the wrong policy. At Westminster, MP Chips Channon was one of many who were uncertain how much longer the government would survive. The sinking of the *Prince of Wales* and the *Repulse* proved to be the catalyst for a wave of profound despair. The prime minister appeared exhausted, barely up to the task. The outlook was 'bewildering'. The government was intently disliked and Chips considered it 'is doomed: I give it a few months. No government could survive such unpopularity for long . . . '[67]

And Churchill did indeed look worn as he stood next to Roosevelt on the steps of the White House that Christmas Eve. His figure was a little stooped, it seemed, from the endless weight of bad news and the burden of his legendary—but, as he would have seen it, glorious self-inflicted—task as guardian of the western world. As he got into his stride, however, his words to the assembled crowd conveyed the hugeness of the emotion as the two nations stood side by side at last 'in the midst of war, raging and roaring over all the lands and seas, creeping nearer to our hearts and homes'. He talked of casting aside the 'cares and dangers' to make 'an evening of happiness in a world of storm' for the children, before returning 'to the stern task and formidable years that lie before us, resolved that by our sacrifice and daring these same children shall not be robbed of their inheritance or denied their right to live in a free and decent world.'[68]

Britain had been at war for almost two and a half years. With the fate of his empire, his country and quite possibly his government in doubt, the king, too, prepared his Christmas speech. He was ill that December, and felt 'very cheap'.[69] Elizabeth thought he had been overdoing things. There had been no moment to rest. She suggested they stay at Windsor rather than attempt to make the journey to Sandringham. As ever Logue was at his side as he delivered his message on Christmas Day. 'The range of the tremendous conflict is ever widening,' said the king. 'It now extends to the Pacific Ocean. Truly it is a stern and solemn time . . . ' The king's faith in their purpose did not waver, even if it required the greatest sacrifice. 'As the war widens, so surely our conviction deepens of the greatness of our cause . . . '[70]

He may have been overshadowed by Churchill, his delivery may have been flat, but his constancy, loyalty and presence was now an intimate part of everyone's lives and a heartening symbol of resilience. He was there, and that mattered. The glass in the windows of the palace may have been broken, the rooms cold and draughty, the bombs close at hand: but the king did not desert his post. He stood there for everyone. In the words of one of the most popular songs of 1941, he was one of us: '*The king is still in London, in London, in London,/ Like Mr Jones and Mr Brown,/ The king is still in London town.*' The musical accompaniment was jaunty and the tone light-hearted but the lasting message of resistance echoed around the country through the dance halls and jazz clubs across the land.

A sentry stands at the palace gates
Though he's not dressed in red
His eyes are looking everywhere
But he never turns his head.

The royal standard waves above
For everyone to see
The king is with his people
Cos that's where he wants to be.

The king is still in London, in London, in London
And he would be in London town
If London Bridge was burning down.

He's got a house in London, in London, in London
And there within the palace yard
The soldiers of the king, stand guard.

Strike up the music, roll out the drums and let all the trumpets play
Tell all the world we're facing the music
Here we all are. And here we'll all stay.

The king is still in London, in London, in London
Like Mr Jones and Mr Brown
The king is still in London town.[71]

10

IT'S MY BROTHER

....

'It's not a burden. It's my brother . . . '

—George VI's Christmas speech, 1942

The opening weeks of 1942 were marked by one crippling blow after another. Singapore, that exotic lynchpin of the Empire's defences in the Far East, was under attack. From the chill of Norfolk at Appleton House on the Sandringham Estate, a white landscape of snow visible through the windows, there was nothing the king could do about events unfolding in the tropical jungle on the other side of the world. The Japanese were 100 miles away from Singapore in mid-January, he noted. Two weeks later that gap narrowed to just 20 miles. 'I don't think [Singapore] can be held for very long,' the king wrote anxiously.[1]

He found the prime minister in a fractious mood when they met at the beginning of February. The king did not know that Churchill had suffered a mild heart attack on Boxing Day while in America, but he could see that 'the PM is angry and worried' over events in the Far East. The troops should have built tank traps and pillboxes in the jungle, Churchill fumed. This had not been done.

He told the king when the Japanese come 'we must kill them in the swamps and in the jungle'. While the Soviets were fighting to the last man, it would be unconscionable for the British to surrender.[2] Churchill sent a message to that effect to the commander in S.E. Asia. 'The battle must be fought to the bitter end,' he wrote. 'Commanders and senior officers must die with their troops.'[3] This uncompromising order appeared to recognise defeat already.

For all the fighting talk, the king felt 'very depressed about everything', he confided to his diary on 13 February. There seemed to be no grounds for hope; nothing to relieve the never-ending, oppressive anxiety. 'Spent a very depressing weekend and felt nothing was right,' he wrote two days later.[4]

On 15 February the very worst was confirmed.

Some 80,000 British, Indian and Australian troops surrendered to a smaller Japanese force. It was the largest British-led wartime surrender in history. Britain and empire reeled from the critical blow. The great waterways of the Pacific were now vulnerable, the *Daily Mirror* told its readers. Australia could be invaded. 'India is threatened. The Middle East may follow.'[5] The bell began to toll for the British Empire and its Bulldog champion.

Studying the papers at Windsor Castle, the king saw there was an avalanche of criticism against Churchill and his government. *'It is a fact that we can lose the war. It is a fact that today we are losing it.'* The public had been told to prepare for worse news 'but it is the *Government* that needs warning', stated the *Daily Mirror* editorial. 'So long as the same over-confident, old-fashioned minds muddle on, under the same delusions!'[6] The *Daily Mail* was even more vitriolic. 'There are two Mr Churchills,' it declared. No one could complain at the first Mr Churchill, the man who 'inspired the nation' at Dunkirk. 'With the second Mr Churchill the nation is perplexed.' He had too much control. All the reverses of 1940 and 1941—Dunkirk, Greece, Crete and Libya—were 'accepted as the legacy of the shortsightedness and incompetence of previous governments . . . But we are now in 1942. The disaster of Singapore cannot be placed on any other shoulders than those of Mr Churchill . . . '[7]

The endless failures seemed to have seeped into the national consciousness. Gloom and doom were in the very air. In public at the palace, the famous British stiff upper lip was much in evidence, but in private, one of the few people with whom the king could unburden himself of his worst fears was his mother. He deplored the loss of Singapore and confided his worries to her about the condemnation in the press. 'It will take all our energies to stop more adverse comment & criticism from the press and others,' he told her.[8] Elizabeth admitted to her mother-in-law she and Bertie 'have been very tired and troubled of late . . . '[9]

The king asked Alexander Hardinge to gauge opinion and find out how much support there was for Winston Churchill. He had complete faith in his prime minister, but was this hard-won trust misplaced? He knew a government reshuffle would be wanted and 'told Alec to find out what is in people's minds over all this'. Quite suddenly an alternative figure had emerged, thrown up by the quicksands of British politics: the left-wing politician, Sir Stafford Cripps, who had just returned from his post as Ambassador to Moscow and appeared to be a key link between East and West. However, when Hardinge consulted Anthony Eden and others he found complete agreement: 'Winston is the right,

& indeed the only person to lead the country through the war.' But there was a general concern that he was doing too much and that aspects of defence should be delegated.[10]

Churchill was in a difficult mood next time he met the king for lunch on 17 February. George VI found him 'very angry over all this, and compares it with his hunting the tiger with angry wasps around him . . . '[11] Churchill reorganised the War Cabinet, finding a role for Cripps as minister without Portfolio. He faced the Commons with a 'scowl', according to Chips Channon, and seemed to have 'lost the House'. Even when the government won a vote of confidence on 25 February, there were those like Chips, who still thought it 'doomed'.[12]

Churchill knew there was worse to come. For all the fine rhetoric, victory could not be won by valour alone. Tanks could not be destroyed by courage. Armies could not hold out and battleships command the seas without adequate support. Where were the resources to come from? 'Burma, Ceylon, Calcutta & Madras in India and part of Australia may fall into enemy hands,' he advised the king solemnly.[13] For Churchill, the great imperialist, who in his youth had fought colonial battles in the Sudan, India and South Africa, a man for whom the British Empire was in his DNA, it was a grievous prospect. But for a growing few the very idea of empire was in question. They were fighting for freedom yet how did this sit with 400 million people subject to British imperial rule? While many in the colonies were proud to be part of it, independence movements were gaining ground. The empire was under assault from all directions. When the king was alone he despaired. 'I cannot help feeling depressed at the future outlook. Anything can happen . . . ' he confided to his diary.[14]

Was their cause just? The feeling that right was on their side and victory would come was no longer so assured. The queen gained comfort from her religious beliefs which she shared with the king. Their almost daily visits to sites of severe bomb damage had brought them face to face with the heart-rending suffering of others. To see these decent people emerging from those ashes, cheerful and unbeaten, greeting the royal couple with welcoming smiles and, above all, trust, raised questions for the king and queen. How much more would the ravenous evil of the war demand? It was not easy to understand it all and to make sense of God's purpose. According to his biographer, John Wheeler-Bennett, the king was 'a man of simple faith' but this faith was 'sincere and profound . . . and uncomplicated'. It took the form of outward ceremony rather than constant spiritual seeking. The BBC Home Service introduced a short morning programme of daily prayers in December 1939, *Lift Up Your Hearts*, and the king was a keen listener. This unquestioning faith sustained him in the worst moments of the war.[15] Whatever the future held for the empire, he was absolutely clear that Britain was locked in a conflict with Hitler with whom there was no possibility of compromise.

The king formed an ambitious plan for the Duke of Gloucester to visit the war zones across the British Empire. As his representative Gloucester could pay tribute to the efforts of Allied troops around the world and try to enhance British relations with countries that were edging ever closer to the ever-expanding war zones. The four-month tour would give him a bird's-eye view of the vast conflagration across the empire at a time when the Axis powers were winning across the world.[16]

There was just one problem. His brother had become a father for the first time. The Duke and Duchess of Gloucester had tried for years to start a family. When Alice became pregnant the previous summer they were overjoyed and, on Queen Mary's advice, kept the news secret until there could be no doubt.[17] Finally, just before Christmas, the Gloucesters had a son of their own. The army man with a passion for sport suddenly found their home seemed deserted when his wife and son were in hospital. The baby's weight, clothes, even the order of his names was the subject of much excited discussion: Prince William Henry Andrew Frederick finally agreed upon. Now the king was asking him to say goodbye to his young family and travel to some of the world's worst trouble spots.[18] Bertie was contrite but none the less keen for his brother to go. 'I hope it will fit in with your plans,' he urged.[19] Not mentioned in the letters, but understood by both brothers, was the danger of such a tour. The king promised his sister-in-law he would act as guardian in the event 'anything should happen'.[20]

Gloucester's first stop was Gibraltar, where he visited the light cruiser, HMS *Penelope*, which had just returned from the embattled island of Malta. The duke knew the king was deeply moved by the plight of Malta. The island was becoming a byword for valour and endurance. In a commanding position in the middle of the Mediterranean, its 100 square miles provided the Allies with key airfields and harbours for the defence of North Africa. As a result it had become one of the most bombed places on earth. That April alone the bombing was so intense, it exceeded by thirty-six times the bomb tonnage released on Coventry. Air Commodore Hugh Lloyd, in charge of Malta's aerial defences since 1941, had placed a sign on his door bearing his signature attitude: 'Less depends on the size of the dog in the fight, than on the size of the fight in the dog.'[21]

But the little dog with the big fight was often flattened. Malta was crushed—all but that unconquered invisible spirit. Its sun-baked, whitewashed buildings were reduced to glistening piles of rubble, and its quarter of a million people desperately hungry. As Gloucester toured HMS *Penelope*—now nicknamed HMS *Pepperpot* on account of its hull riddled with holes from shells and shrapnel—he could see the scars of battle. He did his best to represent the king as he acknowledged the courage of the crew and met the wounded in hospital.

Gloucester went on to Egypt, once again threatened by Rommel's troops who had chased the Allies back across Libya towards the all-important port of Tobruk, 100 miles from the Egyptian border. In soaring temperatures over a banquet in Cairo, Gloucester endeavoured to build amicable relations with King Farouk I, no easy task since the Egyptian king was rumoured to be courting the Germans and Italians and his country was still neutral despite British occupation.[22] The next stop was Libya to meet the front-line troops. His tour coincided with a massive dust storm. Visibility was almost instantly reduced as an apparently solid wall of dust rising several hundred feet engulfed them. The Allied troops had endured many such sand storms and Gloucester had a chance to experience the conditions for himself: skin, like sandpaper; eyes, red and itchy; throat, hoarse and dry; breathing, difficult. *The Times* correspondent interviewed him on a windswept plain to find him intent on building morale and 'most impressed by what I have seen of the Eighth Army'.[23]

From here, the Duke set out to the heart of the Middle East, a region that was imperilled by the ever-expanding Third Reich. To the north, the Germans had reached the Black Sea in the southern Soviet Union, while to the south, Rommel's troops in Northern Africa were menacing Egypt. There were fears these two German armies would link up through the Middle East, allowing this crucial region to fall to the Axis. In Tehran the duke greeted the Shah of Persia in the fairy-tale surroundings of the white Marble Palace, with its fabled dome and brilliant mosaics. Gloucester, who was more comfortable in plus fours shooting on the moors, valiantly adapted to the *Arabian Nights* setting—with some success. The duke 'has done much to cement the friendship' between Persia and Great Britain, enthused *The Times*.[24] Onwards in the heat he went, his stamina never letting him down as he brought his own brand of diplomacy to the threatened Middle East, taking in Jerusalem, Haifa, Damascus, Cyprus and Amman before returning to Cairo. Determined to send reassuring news to his anxious older brother, he wrote to the king: 'Everywhere I have found the troops well and cheery.'[25]

But there was no good news for the king in the spring of 1942. The Axis countries were gaining ground everywhere. Churchill appeared reduced, his performance at the reopening of Parliament on 13 April described by Chips Channon as 'uneasy, halting, almost inarticulate'.[26] Morale plummeted further as the

Germans began a series of raids on British towns noted for their beauty. 'We shall bomb every building in Britain marked with three stars in the Baedeker guide,' a Nazi spokesman, Baron Gustav Braun von Sturm, is said to have boasted. He was referring to the Baedeker Tourist Guide to Britain and, sure enough, there were attacks on the historic West Country city of Exeter followed by the famous Georgian town of Bath. The king felt outraged as he and Elizabeth wandered among the wreckage of the famous Bath Assembly Rooms. But with sickening inevitability further Baedeker raids followed on Norwich, York and Canterbury.

Reports from the Pacific that spring underlined the oppressive air of imminent disaster. One territory after another fell to the Japanese. The defeat at Singapore was followed by the Dutch East Indies, the British Christmas Island—a landing post for a north-west approach to Australia—and then, in April, the Philippines. The British colony of Burma—along with its rich resources of oil and minerals—fell into Japanese hands in May and brought the Japanese to the very gates of the jewel in the crown: India. The king's empire was being battered from within and without and nowhere more so than in India. Indian leaders, like Mahatma Gandhi, demanded a commitment from the British for independence, something which the British government was unwilling to concede. The king felt 'very worried over the question of India'. The proximity of the Japanese made it all the more important in his eyes 'to get all Indian opinion together in a combined war effort at this perilous moment'.[27]

Gloucester was willing to undertake the hazardous journey from Africa to India that June as the king's representative, although he confided to his mother he would be delayed for another month and 'I want to see Alice and William so much'.[28] He wrote reassuringly to his brother, at the very least his visit 'might do more good than harm'.[29] But approaching the west coast of India in heavy monsoon turbulence, even Gloucester found it hard not to feel apprehensive about just what might lie ahead as his plane juddered and dived.

To his relief his Indian hosts in Karachi provided a welcoming reception with more than 100 guests eager to shake the hand of the king's brother. The Indians had already provided a large fighting force, an unprecedented two and a half million men and there was much to thank them for. After a packed schedule seeing Indian warships and civil defences in Karachi and Delhi, the duke travelled further east to meet men who had survived the horrors of the campaign in Burma.[30] In searing temperatures and heavy monsoon rains, he visited hospitals where young men counted themselves lucky to be alive after the traumas of battling the Japanese across Burma as well as the equally deadly jungle and tropical disease. The unending misery of global war was plain as he made his way around overflowing hospitals in Ranchi and Calcutta and met troops and inspected civil defences in cities across India.[31]

Gloucester had reached Ceylon before bad news from the Western Desert caught up with him. Rommel had routed the Eighth Army in Libya. The important Libyan port of Tobruk finally fell on 21 June. Rommel's men captured 33,000 British and South African troops who had surrendered to a much smaller German force. It was a great propaganda coup for the Axis. The Germans entered Egypt and Rommel grandly pronounced to Hitler, 'I am going on to Suez . . . ' For Churchill, who was with Roosevelt in America, planning the North African campaign, it was one of the 'heaviest blows' of the war. 'Defeat is one thing. Disgrace is another,' he commented to Roosevelt.[32]

The future was unfathomable; the army apparently losing the resolve to fight. Bad news was the daily diet. How long before this island race, dogged and enduring, gave up? In the last week of June opposition to Churchill mounted. The atmosphere in the House was edgy and explosive. Speakers tested opinion; questions were increasingly hostile to the government. All week the intrigue continued; the anxiety spreading to the public.[33] Churchill hurriedly returned from America.

The British position in Egypt was critical. Rommel pressed his advantage, his men heady with victory and reinforced with captured vehicles and supplies. The British were beaten back, and back . . . Fires were burning at the British Embassy in Cairo as confidential documents were destroyed. Water shimmered across the Nile delta as flood defences were hurriedly prepared to stop the Germans. Mussolini flew to Libya in anticipation of making a grand entry into Cairo and claiming victory. By the end of June, Rommel's army reached as far as El Alamein near the Egyptian coast, an insignificant railway station, just 250 miles from the Suez Canal.

On 1 July 1942, John Wardlaw-Milne moved a vote of censure in the House of Commons. Winston Churchill looked put out, listening with undisguised annoyance to the endless criticism. Wardlaw-Milne's speech was gathering momentum until, quite suddenly, he made an unexpected suggestion: that the Duke of Gloucester became commander in chief of the army. His intention was serious: to find a way to end inter-service rivalry. But the ripple of amusement that rolled across the House grew into a roar of 'disrespectful laughter', observed Chips Channon. The tension was broken and Winston's face brightened 'as if a lamp had been lit within him . . . '[34]

The press had a field day. The duke's great-great-great-uncle, the Duke of York, infamous for marching his troops up the hill and down again—with no notable gain, was mentioned. Perhaps fortunately for the Duke of Gloucester, he missed the vicious headlines. But he heard of them and tactfully declined to comment as he continued his onerous tour. Meanwhile Churchill seemed shorn of his magic touch as blistering criticism from the opposition was aired.

The debate 'was not edifying', the king confided to his mother, 'and does such a lot of harm abroad'. The government did win by 475 votes to 25 but he told Queen Mary, 'the people who are really to blame for our state of unpreparedness is the present House of Commons.'[35] From the gates of India, the deserts of Africa and the depths of the Atlantic, the relentless tide of war brought no relief to the Allies. And in the Soviet Union Hitler's invasion force was cutting a great swathe across the Steppes into the oil-rich Caucasus, while his Sixth and Fourth Armies pushed on to Stalingrad. There were many who believed that it was only a matter of time before Hitler won the war.

Wreath for Whitehall, *Daily Mirror,* 17 February 1942 (© MIRRORPIX)

While the future looked bleak that summer, the conviction that a betrayal must lie at the heart of the repeated British failures reached its height. 'Churchill is being double crossed,' one unnamed informant expressed the views of many in a letter to J. Edgar Hoover, 'and this is the reason why the British have withdrawn so easily from everywhere: Hong Kong, Singapore, Malaya, Burma, Libya and Tobruk . . . '[36] The informant was reflecting a widely held belief that the Duke of Windsor was doing 'everything he can' to inspire the troops not to fight, but withdraw, and ensure German victory.

Such allegations were being taken seriously by US intelligence. In the wake of Pearl Harbor, Roosevelt was keen to improve information gathering by co-ordinating the efforts of different departments and also working with Canadian and Mexican intelligence services.[37] Commander C.A. Perkins, of US Navy Special Intelligence, was put in charge of West Coast operations and Mexican intelligence. He was sufficiently worried about Windsor that he informed the Office of Naval Intelligence in Washington of his concerns. 'While it seems utterly fantastic,' he wrote on 11 February 1942, none the less, his officials were hearing reports that the Duke of Windsor 'may be one of the most important Nazi agents based in the Western Hemisphere'.[38]

Commander Perkins felt he had grounds for his suspicions. Windsor had been close friends with Axel Wenner-Gren and the Swedish businessman was placed on the US blacklist in January 1942. Concerns about Wenner-Gren had persisted for months but in the end it was the remarkable scale of Wenner-Gren's business interests in Latin America—and the opportunities this afforded for benefiting the enemy—that prompted the US State Department to act. The Americans intercepted a letter to Wenner-Gren from the President of Peru, Manuel Prado, which revealed that the Swedish magnate was intending to construct a harbour at Chimbote Bay and to industrialise the Santa Valley.[39] He was equally busy in Mexico, with planned investments of more than $100,000,000.[40] Collaborating with the alleged pro-Nazi Maximino Avila Camacho, a brother of the President of Mexico, he was involved in a vast enterprise to build highways in Mexico and was trying to create an 'Export Control Board'.[41] His grandiose schemes would give him enormous economic power in the region; the State Department had had enough.

Commander Perkins understood that the decision to put Wenner-Gren on the blacklist involved President Roosevelt himself. There is reason to believe, Perkins wrote, 'considerable Nazi funds have, during the past year, been cleared through the Bahamas to Mexico'.[42] But who was controlling these funds and why? There was not much to go on. Press reports revealed that the Duke and Duchess of Windsor planned to visit Wenner-Gren, who had settled in Mexico while his assets were frozen in the Royal Bank of Canada.[43] Was some kind of financial transaction involved? Just to further complicate matters, Perkins was aware that Windsor's cousin, Carol of Romania, had also settled in Mexico. 'Windsor planned a visit, incognito, to Carol of Romania at Acapulco, Mexico,' he informed his superiors in Washington. 'Carol's consort, as well as the society group at this resort, constantly have been reported pro-Nazi.' A series of coincidences? Or was it more than that? 'Such associations indicate that there may be something to the reports received by this office that the subject [Duke of Windsor] is pro-Nazi,' Perkins concluded.[44]

Wallace B. Phillips at the Washington Office of Naval Intelligence replied to Perkins, anxious to damp down his concerns. His reply is perhaps illustrative of official thinking at the time. Although the duchess is 'bitterly anti-British', Phillips wrote on 18 February 1942, he personally believed the duke would not knowingly betray his country, although 'he might do it unwittingly'. He did accept it was likely that Wenner-Gren 'was up to no good in Mexico' and confirmed that the former Romanian king, Carol II, was not permitted to visit the USA and was unwelcome in Britain. He also agreed with Perkins's suggestion that the duke's former equerry, Frank Budd, who was now living in Mexico, needed further investigation. 'We shall have to take some steps to determine his relationships both to the duke as well as to the Nazis.'[45]

With the Axis countries reaching ever further round the globe, both British and American intelligence services stepped up operations in South America. Correspondence between 'C' and the Foreign Office shows a succession of suspected German agents were tracked leaving Lisbon and other European ports for South American destinations. British intelligence was also liaising with the FBI's Special Intelligence Service formed in 1940 to investigate enemy interests in South America. It was led by the highly respected Percy 'Sam' Foxworth, who hid his secret operations under the respectable cover of a firm of lawyers on the 44th floor of the Rockefeller Building in New York. But with one and a half million Germans settled in South America, despite several hundred undercover agents carrying out surveillance and watching South American ports, it was no easy task to pinpoint German spy rings—let alone any possible connections to Windsor or Wenner-Gren.

As South American intelligence operations were underway, agents and businessmen in Europe who might be helping the enemy were also under scrutiny.

Charles Bedaux was on the list of suspects. Since Herman Rogers's interrogation, the case against him had been mounting. In the eyes of the US authorities
he appeared to be gambling openly on a German future as he worked with the
Nazis on his visionary scheme to tame the Sahara and bring the desert to life.
He proposed new pipelines that would move first water, and later oil and gas,
across the region. Somerville Pinkney Tuck, American chargé d'affaires who
met him in Vichy France, described him as 'mentally unmoral'. Bedaux did
not see 'anything wrong, as an American citizen, in his open association with
our declared enemies', he reported.[46] While Bedaux believed his magnificent
engineering projects would be for the benefit of humanity, for the investigators
his schemes looked like trading with the enemy for self-advancement as he prepared for a 'New Order' under the Germans.

British intelligence demonstrated the Germans had a continuing interest
in the Duke of Windsor and tried to use Bedaux to gauge the duke's views.
One British intelligence report reveals the Germans asked Bedaux to confirm
whether the Duke of Windsor would be prepared to accept the British throne
in the event of a German victory. According to the intelligence, 'Monsieur
Bedaux declined to do so, as he was no longer friendly with the Duke of Windsor.'[47] However, Bedaux told Robert Murphy, US chargé d'affaires to the Vichy
government in France, that the Germans did 'plan the restoration of the Duke
of Windsor as King of England'.[48]

And while the intelligence gathering on both sides of the Atlantic was gaining momentum, the public remained ever vigilant, the number of Windsor
watchers growing steadily. As the daily news confirmed Allied losses, to the
man in the street anything seemed possible. One observer told the FBI that
Churchill was being double-crossed because the duke had bribed British government officials with large estates and titles once he regained the throne under
the Germans.[49] Many believed Wallis was the weak link, still capable of passing
secrets on to the Germans. Most intriguing of all was correspondence from a
worried informant from Minnesota. He wrote to Hoover on 1 March 1942 to
explain that the duke had already been kidnapped in readiness for taking the
British throne under German occupation and it was a substitute now living in
Government House in the Bahamas. Working from a picture in the *Minneapo-
lis Tribune*, he told Hoover, 'The Windsor look is not there at all—the Hohenzollern look is very definitely there.' Had Windsor been replaced by a German
relative? If the duke in the Bahamas was a double, where in the world was a
possibly 'kidnapped' duke, with or without the Hohenzollern look, and how
was he to be returned unscathed?[50]

Improbable though it was, the conditions for the return of the Windsors to the English throne began to look possible as the Axis continued to make gains around the globe in the spring and summer of 1942. In a climate of fear, nothing could be ruled out. On 1 July 1942 German panzers under Rommel launched an attack on Allied troops holding the line in Egypt at El Alamein. This godforsaken patch of white-hot desert, too close for comfort to Alexandria and Cairo, became the focus of desperate fighting. If Cairo, that exotic jewel set in a sea of sand, fell to the Germans, everything that Britain and her empire stood for was in question. Allied defeat would almost certainly mean the loss of Egypt and Suez, the vital silver thread between east and west at the heart of the empire. How long before the Middle East fell to the all-powerful Third Reich? The British had been fighting for almost three years and the enemy still appeared invincible.

On 4 July 1942, two days after the vote of censure in the House, the Duke and Duchess of Kent had a third child, Prince Michael, completing their family circle at Coppins. Since the new baby was born on Independence Day the Kents hit upon the idea of asking Roosevelt to be a godparent. 'I am much thrilled and very proud to be Godfather,' Roosevelt replied warmly. He was unable to attend the christening at Windsor Castle but King George agreed to stand proxy for him. 'Tell the king that I will hold him to strict accountability,' Roosevelt responded playfully, 'until I am able to take over the responsibility of god father myself.'[51]

In the event, George VI was absent, owing to pressure of work. Nor was there anyone from Marina's side of the family; her mother still confined to Nazi-occupied Greece, her sisters in Germany and Kenya. But the family christening brought together members of the wider royal family, including Uncle Charles of Norway and George of Greece.[52] Cecil Beaton took a series of photographs at Coppins to mark the occasion. The family portraits that idyllic summer day spoke of a private world where, it seemed, nothing could go wrong. The new prince, his eyes fixed intently on his mother, the duke protectively leaning towards them both; the duke with his eldest son in the garden by a wall of roses almost smothering them; the duchess in the drawing room, the duke sharing her chair as he sat on the armrest: husband and wife in a relaxed moment together captured for all time.

The celebrations complete, the Duke of Kent was soon on the road again with a gruelling schedule of wartime visits across southern England and the

Isle of Wight. Ironically Kent's hard work had earned him a reprimand from the king the year before. On several occasions 'provincial districts selected by his Majesty for a visit happened to have received visits from the Duke of Kent only a short time before', Alexander Hardinge had protested to Kent's private secretary, John Lowther. Kent was only supposed to carry out tours connected to his appointment in the RAF but Hardinge complained 'frequent visits are made to industrial centres, dockyards, etc which appear to have the most meagre connection with . . . the RAF'. Perhaps feeling vulnerable that his own visits did not compare favourably with those of his charming youngest brother, the king was said to be 'far from satisfied'.[53] Was Kent's conscientiousness entirely innocent; the reformed playboy eager to help all he could? Or was he still a law unto himself, unable to play for the team? The king insisted that the two private secretaries liaise over royal schedules to avoid duplication.

Lowther's diligent letters of thanks after each tour show there had been no let-up in Kent's tough schedule in the summer of 1942. 'HRH trusts that nobody was the worse for standing about in the pouring rain,' he wrote after a visit to Civil Defence teams in Cowes on 19 August.[54] That same day he was in Newport meeting Civil Defence workers and 'was most impressed by their fine turnout and their excellent bearing'.[55] And so it continued across southern England during August; days passed, shaking hands, encouraging, smiling, listening to speeches.

While the duke was in the south, Lowther was busy setting up his next foreign trip. He wrote to the Foreign Office on 31 July explaining that arrangements had been made for the Duke of Kent to go to Iceland the previous year but the trip had been cancelled 'owing to some difference of opinion in the cabinet'. This trip was now rearranged for the end of August and approved by both the prime minister and the king.[56] Because the duke would visit US forces in Iceland, Lowther took the trouble to ensure that the Foreign Secretary and the US ambassador were consulted.[57] Lowther also informed the War Office, the Ministry of War Transport and the Passport Office.[58] His final letter was to Commander Harold Campbell at Balmoral setting up the travel arrangements for the duke's return on 31 August. 'I shall be going to Iceland with HRH,' he added helpfully, 'but shall be in the office on Monday until 6.00.'[59]

Mindful of the previous clash with the palace over the duke's tours of duty, Lowther left no stone unturned to ensure that every relevant department was informed of the forthcoming trip to Iceland.

21st August, 1942.

Dear Mr. Stafford,

      I enclose the passports of the party going to Iceland.   I should be most grateful if you would have these put in order, and the necessary visas arranged for Iceland.

      His Royal Highness will be travelling as an Air Commodore in the R.A.F.;   I shall be going as a Lieutenant in the R.N.V.R.;   Mr. Strutt as a Pilot Officer in the R.A.F.;   and the valet, Hales, is now a Leading Aircraftsman.

      We shall be leaving on Monday evening. Would it be possible, therefore, for you to return the passports to me some time on Monday?

      Yours sincerely,

J. W. Stafford, Esq., O.B.E.,
Passport Office,
Queen Anne's Gate, S.W.1.

One of many letters sent by John Lowther, Kent's private secretary, showing Iceland was the destination (THE ROYAL ARCHIVES © HER MAJESTY QUEEN ELIZABETH II)

The Duke of Gloucester was absent for the family gathering for the christening of his new nephew since he was still overseas. When he returned to Cairo in mid-July after a month in India he found a very different atmosphere from that of earlier in the year.[60] Some 160 miles away the battle raged around the railway station of El Alamein. The Allies put up tenacious resistance. Rommel had dug in. General Auchinleck, now in command of the desert army, told Gloucester that he had checked Rommel's advance but it was clear that Allied desert offensives were proving hard to sustain.

After a worldwide tour of 42,500 miles the indefatigable duke finally took off for England, landing at a new American base just a couple of miles from home at Barnwell Manor. Alice was delighted at his sudden appearance.[61] 'It really seems incredible,' she wrote to Queen Mary, marvelling at modern air travel. 'He left Khartoum, five o'clock Tuesday evening & was in this house about eight o'clock the following evening!'[62] The duke was reunited with his family at last and they set out to Scotland. Gloucester planned to tell the king in person the astonishing bird's-eye view he had gained of the world at war. He knew the king would be anxious to hear his news. He had encountered optimism and camaraderie from decent, determined men engaged in a struggle that looked unwinnable. The theatre of war was now vast, too vast. The truth must be voiced.

The Gloucesters joined the king and queen at Balmoral on 25 August. They were dining together that evening, appreciating the family reunion away from London, when the king was summoned to the telephone. It was an urgent call from Sir Archibald Sinclair, the Secretary of State for Air.

The king returned, white-faced, quite unable to speak. Alice was sitting next to him and realised he was 'in deep distress'. She saw him write a note to Elizabeth which was duly passed down the table.

The queen caught her eye and Alice understood that they were to lead the ladies from the room. In the drawing room everyone was apprehensive. 'We all assumed that the news must be Queen Mary's death,' Alice wrote later, 'not imagining anything else more awful that could have happened.'[63] Elizabeth went back to Bertie and soon returned with the shocking announcement.

The Duke of Kent was dead.

The details were sketchy. Kent had left his young family at Coppins on 24 August. He took the night train to Scotland. After lunch the next day he had boarded a Sunderland flying boat with Lowther and two other members of his staff. Flight number W4026 DQ-M took off from the bay at Cromarty Firth, near Invergordon, at around 1.10 pm. The flying boat had crashed overland and exploded into a giant fireball. It was thought there were no survivors.

It fell to the king to tell his mother. The stoic and undemonstrative Queen Mary was demolished by the death of her youngest son. It was a 'catastrophic' blow, her lady-in-waiting Cynthia Colville observed later. Kent was her favourite; the emotional heart of the family. 'I felt so stunned by the shock I could not believe it,' Queen Mary wrote in her diary.[64]

At Coppins it was Marina's former nurse, Miss Fox, who took the call. She was staying to help with the new baby but when Marina heard her footsteps up the stairs and the knock on the door, she sensed at once that something was wrong.[65] Falteringly, news of the fatal accident was broken to her. Then came shock. Unknowingly she and her husband had said their last goodbyes the day before. The rhythm, the life in the household was unchanged: the children slept, flowers from the garden scented the night air, his empty chair was waiting; but her husband was not coming back.

The next day brought a flicker of hope. A survivor was found; a tail gunner, Andy Jack. Dazed and confused he had wandered the local area until he was discovered, still unable to shed any further light on what had gone so catastrophically wrong. But then the duke's body was identified. He wore an identity bracelet and also a wristwatch; his name inscribed on both. There was no room for doubt. Even his cigarette case bore his name.[66] His staff, including his private secretary, John Lowther, were also confirmed among the dead.

The king wanted a simple, dignified ceremony for his brother. So many British families had suffered terrible losses from death in active service; the royal family could not call attention to their bereavement. None the less, in the gothic surroundings of St George's Chapel at Windsor, the scene of so many family occasions, the modest service on 29 August for friends and family to mark the violent early death of the Duke of Kent was one of the more intensely emotional.

All week, the king had worked to hide his pain, formally acknowledging 'it is a tragedy that [George] of all people, just when he was coming into his own, should have been taken from us . . . '[67] His brother's final letter had arrived, inconsequential in its content and yet so powerfully moving as he turned it over in his hand, the envelope bearing George's trademark signature—a 'G' written with theatrical flourish.

The envelope bore George's trademark signature 'G' (THE ROYAL ARCHIVES ©
HER MAJESTY QUEEN ELIZABETH II)

My Dear Bertie

I am so glad that I can come to you on Sept[ember] 1—& am much
looking forward to it . . . I will let you know when I'll be arriving—naturally if the weather is bad in **I** _ I may be delayed a day but I pray not. The
children are enjoying Appleton so much & it is <u>very</u> kind of you letting
them go there & it does them so much good . . . with best love to you both
& looking forward to seeing you—Yours George.[68]

In the confined dark space of the medieval chapel, sitting in the carved
wooden pews as his brother's funeral began on 29 August, George VI, a man of
such unyielding restraint, found that, for once, he was unable to hold back his
feelings.

Noël Coward described the scene. 'I tried hard not to cry, but it was useless,'
he confided to his diary. 'When the Duchess came in with the Queen and
Queen Mary I broke down a bit, and when the coffin passed with flowers from
the garden at Coppins and Prince George's cap on it I was finished. I then gave
up all pretence and just stood with the tears splashing down my face. I was
relieved and heartened to see that both Dickie [Mountbatten] and the King
were doing the same thing . . . '[69]

Marina, heavily veiled, looked a fragile figure in black. She was escorted by the queen and Queen Mary to a seat at the high altar. The coffin was close by; his cap a powerful symbol of his presence; the flowers she had chosen from Coppins a vibrant mass of colour. In reply to her friends such as Betty Lawson-Johnston who sent messages of condolence, she had just two words: 'Am heartbroken.'[70]

As the days passed, Marina found it hard to recover from the pain. 'I can scarcely realise all that has happened I feel so stunned', she wrote to Betty. 'The emptiness all round & the ache in one's heart and mind make one feel so unreal,' she wrote on 12 September. ' . . . He is very near to me too—helping me to go on living from day to day & helping me to carry on. There will be much to do on the lonely road that lies ahead—but I pray God for courage and strength to do the things that my husband would have wished for—for his sake and for our children's. How utterly life can change from one moment to the next . . . & yet for him it is only a glorious continuation. Our baby made him so happy—he is such a little angel—and such a constant living part of him & those last happy weeks . . . '[71]

Queen Mary would not allow her daughter-in-law to become lost in grief. There were stern admonitions that she must bear her loss like any other war widow. Queen Mary had lived her life by duty and her daughter-in-law must do the same. Marina struggled; alone in a foreign country, her emotions at sea, never quite belonging to the inner circle of the royal family, her mother-in-law's request was one she could not meet. The king, recognising her difficulties, decided she needed her own family. Her mother could not escape from Greece, but he convinced Churchill, who still saw Paul and Olga as traitors, that an exception must be made for Marina's sister. On receiving the king's telegram, Olga left Kenya at once. The sisters separated by war and invasion were reunited at last.[72]

Thousands of miles away, absent from the funeral and its aftermath, the Duke of Windsor also grieved. Kent was the brother with whom he had always shared an understanding, whose youthful waywardness had united them both. His death underlined his severance from his family. At a memorial service in Nassau, he broke down and wept inconsolably.

At first Windsor thought there might be a thaw in his relationship with his family. He wrote to his mother and the letter she sent in reply was the most tender he had received from her. The king, too, wrote optimistically to his mother: 'perhaps as you say his grief may now pave the way for a better understanding in the future.'[73] But any slight softening in family relations was not to last. It became clear that the duke wrongly blamed the king for not permitting him to see Kent in America the previous year. He felt he had missed his last chance to see his beloved youngest brother. He pushed once again 'that the title HRH should be "restored" to his wife', the king observed to his mother and complained of 'what he calls my "attitude" towards him'.[74] The royal family closed ranks once more. The brief correspondence gave the increasingly rancorous Windsor more fuel to fan the flames: proving to him at least that his family were against him.

There was no reconciliation between the brothers.

Of George V's five sons, only two remained to serve the Crown.

As the days passed, rumours began to spread about the doomed flight. That summer a Court of Inquiry was established to investigate the causes of the crash. There were so many unanswered questions.

Firstly the route: why was the Sunderland flying overland in the first place? The usual route to Iceland was to fly over the North Sea, hugging the Scottish coastline for some 85 miles before turning north. The crew appeared to have changed direction, taking a shortcut over land far too early. Was this an error or did the pilot change the flight plan for some unknown reason?[75]

The plane's altitude was also a mystery. It was hard to understand why an experienced pilot was flying at only 650 feet in a region known for its higher hills and crags. The pilot, Flight Lieutenant Frank Goyen, was chosen because he had more than 1,000 hours of flying time in a Sunderland.[76] Why would such a competent pilot take a grave risk near Eagle's Rock? At this point in the journey the flying boat should have been over the sea and at an altitude of 4,000 feet.

Then there were questions about the timing of the crash. Flight W4026 was reported to have left Invergordon at 13.10 pm.[77] The farmers nearby claimed the accident occurred at 14.30 pm. Since Eagle's Rock was only around twenty minutes' flying time from the take-off point at Invergordon, there appeared to be a period of time unaccounted for. Was it possible that the plane flew inland for some other reason or even to pick up an extra passenger?[78]

Such uncertainties fuelled speculation that the Duke of Kent was not going to Iceland at all but was on some other secret assignment. The flight plan submitted by the pilot before departure was never revealed, prompting fears of a cover-up. This would have answered questions about the pilot's intended route, destination and the number of passengers.

The Court of Inquiry in 1942 was held in secret and its findings, too, have disappeared. However, Sir Archibald Sinclair, Secretary of State for Air, presented a summary in the House of Commons on 7 October. Investigators found no fault with the aircraft itself, he explained. There was nothing wrong with the four engines or with the navigational equipment that was recovered from the site. Sinclair put the blame firmly on the pilot: 'The responsibility for this serious mistake in airmanship lies with the captain of the aircraft,' he told the House. The captain had 'changed flight-plan for reasons unknown and descended through cloud without making sure he was over water and crashed'.[79] In his defence, the weather conditions were so bad that Dr John Kennedy, one of the first on the crash scene, considered visibility was no more than 30 yards, the cloud and rain was so heavy.[80] For Sir Archibald Sinclair there was no conspiracy. It was human error.

This definitive statement did not bring an end to the rumour. The unexpected death of the king's charismatic youngest brother appeared to signify something more sinister, and foreign intelligence services were keen to get to the bottom of it. It seemed entirely plausible that the duke could have been involved in a secret peace initiative. That summer, Hitler was at the height of his powers. Europe was crushed and the armies of the Third Reich were laying waste to the USSR, attacking the oil-rich Caucasus region and even threatening the Middle East. If ever there was a time for Britain to make peace, it was now.

Speculation grew that Kent was not on an authorised RAF tour to Iceland at all, but a secret peace mission, perhaps to Sweden or elsewhere. A personal incentive was found for Kent to seek peace, unofficial but none the less fuelling the rumours. The British had encouraged talk between the Poles and the Czechs to make plans for after the war and the far-reaching discussions had raised the possibility of a Polish monarchy being created. One Foreign Office despatch, reporting on the possible peacetime Polish-Czechoslovak Federation, reveals 'non-official Poles discuss rather hopefully the possibility of persuading the Duke of Kent to accept the Polish throne after the war'.[81] Even if Kent was not acting for himself, was he perhaps on a 'special mission' to Stockholm to win the peace? And if Churchill was being double-crossed by a pro-peace party, perhaps he knew about it and authorised the intelligence services to sabotage the Duke of Kent's mission?

Preposterous as these claims seem, they were taken seriously by German spies, notably by the German ambassador to Portugal, Baron Oswald von Hoyningen-Huene. Huene had proved his worth to Ribbentrop reporting on Windsor during the summer of 1940, and now was equally diligent in gathering information on Kent. His source, he told Ribbentrop, was 'the innermost circles of the British Club here' in Portugal where suspicion was growing 'that an act of sabotage' was involved. According to members of the British Club, 'the Duke of Kent, like the Duke of Windsor, was sympathetic towards an understanding with Germany and so gradually had become a problem for the government clique'.[82] No evidence has emerged to back up Huene's view.

However, for Stalin, embattled in Moscow—his soldiers bearing the brunt of the war, the Allies unwilling to open a second front in Europe that year—there was a very real fear of being double-crossed. Rudolf Hess's flight had never been satisfactorily explained and the continued British silence on the matter was confusing. It did not seem beyond the bounds of possibility that a 'peace party' was gathering momentum once more and that Hess was some way involved. Could Kent's 'special mission' somehow be linked? Stalin's agents demanded information about Hess.[83]

The previous closeness of Kent with his oldest brother also resurfaced as grist for the rumour mill. There seemed no limit to the possibilities. Perhaps the Duke of Windsor had enlisted the help of his youngest brother in a new peace initiative with a view to reclaiming the throne? Kent and his German cousin, Philipp of Hesse, had had talks before the war. Philipp of Hesse remained a close friend of Hitler during 1942 and his younger brother, SS officer Christoph of Hesse, rose to become head of Goering's signals intelligence agency.[84] Were these German cousins involved in a plot to advance Nazi interests in Britain? Philipp of Hesse's twin brother, Prince Wolfgang, would later claim that Hesse and Kent had both served as intermediaries for Windsor and Hitler, although evidence to support his claim and shed light on the timing of any meetings has never surfaced.[85] Despite Sinclair's account of the air crash to the House as pilot error, there was no shortage of colourful theories offering ever more remarkable claims.

But for George VI, the matter was closed. He did accept the official verdict. He arranged to meet the air chief marshal in charge of Coastal Command, Sir Philip Joubert de la Ferté, on 30 August. The air chief marshal, no doubt feeling uncomfortable that this tragedy had occurred under his command, explained how even an experienced pilot might have been confused about his location.

'The Langwell Woods & the bend in the road were very similar to those two features in Dunbeath and in bad weather could very easily be mistaken . . . ' he began.[86]

But the King had asked to see Sir Philip 'on purpose' and went out of his way to reassure him that he attached no blame. 'I realised George's death was an accident,' he said.[87]

T he king and queen went in person to meet Eleanor Roosevelt at Paddington Station on 23 October. The queen had given up her own rooms at Buckingham Palace for her distinguished American visitor, but the wartime austerity still proved to be a culture shock. 'Buckingham Palace is an enormous place, and without heat,' observed Eleanor Roosevelt. There was little to take the chill off her palatial room except a small electric fire, the thin orange glow having no impact against the bracing chill. The glass had been blown out of the windows, to be replaced incongruously with a cheap substitute called isinglass. Any hope of sinking back into a hot bath to relax after her journey for a few minutes was quickly dispelled. A black line along the side of the tub indicated the modest water limit. The dining room, too, posed strange contradictions. It held out great promise—the table elegantly laid with gold and silver—but at dinner that first evening the quality of the food and the meagre portions, made a disappointing contrast. Mrs Roosevelt was seated between the king and Churchill. She had met Churchill before and had not found him an easy dinner companion; his imperial stance made her feel uncomfortable. Tonight she was suspicious that he had been drinking and he seemed preoccupied.[88]

There was a very good reason for the British prime minister to have his thoughts elsewhere. After the devastating failure at Tobruk, Churchill had flown out to the desert and appointed a new field commander: Lieutenant-General Bernard Montgomery. That very night as they sat in Buckingham Palace came the crucial test as the British were ready to launch their own attack against Rommel in Egypt. The second battle of El Alamein had been weeks in planning. 'Monty' and the Eighth Army had trained intensively for the coming conflict. The British and empire troops, at 200,000 strong, significantly outnumbered Rommel's army and had the benefit of new Sherman tanks from America as well as the advantage in the air.[89] But Rommel had laid half a million mines across the desert to a depth of 5 miles. Churchill knew that while they were relaxing at the palace, heroic sappers and infantry were struggling through the minefield—named the 'Devil's Gardens' by the men—trying to clear a path for the tanks to follow. The prime minister was fretful, restless, 'a cat on hot bricks', observed one courtier. Unable to contain his agitation, eventually he left the table to speak to Downing Street.

The change in atmosphere after this call was heralded before the prime minister re-entered the room by the sound of his voice. He appeared to be singing and indeed, as his voice grew louder and closer, he *was* singing, rather badly, and a somewhat unexpected choice: *'Roll out the barrel, we'll have a barrel of fun, roll out the barrel, we've got the blues on the run . . .* '[90] A footman opened the door and Churchill reappeared, evidently pleased with what he had heard. The valiant sappers and infantry were making faster progress through the minefield than had been achieved before, around 220 yards per hour. A single file of tanks was slowly beginning to wend its way through the Devil's Gardens, throwing up a trail of dust and sand. The fightback had begun.

As the king and queen escorted Mrs Roosevelt around London's wartime icons—St Paul's, the blitzed areas of the East End, the Tilbury shelter that housed 3,000—their tour was punctuated with heart-stopping news from the desert. The Allies had the upper hand but Rommel's troops were fighting hard and the battle became a fearsome war of attrition. Montgomery lost nearly a third of his tanks but German losses were equally high and there was a breakdown in their supplies. Although the Axis position was logistically unsustainable Hitler ordered Rommel 'not to take even one step back'.[91] Some of his men fought to their last round of ammunition.

Like the first pale crack at dawn, the long-awaited turning point in North Africa appeared initially like a chimera. 'I bring you victory,' said Churchill, ever optimistic, when he came to lunch at the palace on 3 November. Intercepted German telegrams revealed that Rommel 'did not see how he could hold out as his troops were all very exhausted'. Was it good news at last? There had been too much anguish over past defeats to believe that the indomitable Rommel could be vanquished. Like some mythic figure, his face appearing anywhere was synonymous with victory. The uncertainty was hard to bear. Could they really win? 'What rejoicing there shall be,' the king wrote in his diary that night.[92]

The next day the king was planning his speech for the opening of Parliament when he and Logue were interrupted by the telephone. It was rare for them to be disturbed. The two men exchanged glances. What kind of emergency could this be?

Logue sensed at once the change in tone in the king's voice as he heard him say eagerly: 'Well read it out, read it out . . . ' At the other end of the line a telegram was being read.

The effect on the king was immediate. 'Good news, thanks,' he said simply, almost as though he still dare not respond with more enthusiasm in case the spell was broken and the story changed to the familiar words of defeat. But Logue saw his excitement. The British Eighth Army had broken through Rommel's line and his troops were retreating under heavy fire from the RAF, he explained.[93] The tables appeared to be turning. British armoured formations were attacking the Germans from behind. It sounded like a triumph. It *must* be a triumph. He trusted in the words enough to enter them in his diary: 'A victory at last, how good it is for the nerves.'[94] He attached a copy of the memorable telegram, it's message now indelible in his mind.

'I was overjoyed when I received the news . . . ' the king wrote formally to Churchill the next day, keen to pass on his 'warmest congratulations on the great victory'. Churchill was equally heartfelt in his reply: 'No Minister in modern times . . . has received more help and comfort from the king.' Churchill spoke of his 'devotion to Yourself . . . and to our ancient and cherished Monarchy—the true bulwark of British freedom against tyrannies of every kind . . . '[95]

Day by day at last, the good news started to come in. Thirty thousand Axis troops surrendered to the British Eighth Army and 350 enemy tanks were captured. By 7 November, further west along the African coast, Operation Torch was underway, the largest amphibious operation yet mounted. After months of planning, American and British troops invaded Morocco and Algeria, part of French North Africa. The Allied aim was to create a pincer movement behind Rommel's troops, who were retreating towards them from Montgomery's men in Egypt. Meanwhile to the east, by 13 November, Monty's men had fought their way back into Libya and reclaimed the all-important port of Tobruk.

On hearing of this important victory, Churchill wanted it shouted from the rooftops. Everyone should feel the momentous significance of this event and take heart. He ordered the church bells to ring out. Silenced since Dunkirk, the sound echoed across England, reverberating around ravaged cities and ringing out from every town and village. It was the start of a new hope that perhaps the worst was over. 'Now this is not the end,' Churchill told an appreciative audience in Mansion House. 'It is not even the beginning of the end. But it is, perhaps, the end of the beginning.' As usual, Churchill had the words that rang true: he was not going to give false hope, but the feel of some solid victory at last after all the dismal defeats washed through the country in winter like a warm summer wind.

An even more decisive watershed was reached in the Soviet Union that month. The long and bitter struggle for Stalingrad was over. Those caught in the siege were transformed by the brutality of war beyond recognition, compelled to fight to the death. But on 19 November the Red Army broke through the German line. Within a few days they had encircled the German 6th Army, trapping 300,000 Axis troops in the frozen city.

That Christmas the king was torn between the impatience of new hope and the exhausting prospect that lay ahead. Christmas once again brought little relaxation, filled as it was with the dread of the live broadcast. He had practised with Logue as usual, and once again counted on the loyal support of his therapist for the broadcast on Christmas Day. The two men went together to the broadcasting room and waited for the red light. The king began slowly, speaking of the 'eternal and unchanged' Christmas message of 'thankfulness and hope . . . hope for the return to this earth of peace and good will . . . ' Across the world millions were listening, from the hospitals of Calcutta and the streets of Cairo to the flattened ruins of Malta.

As the speech progressed, Logue found he was no longer following the words on the page. He was listening to the king, who was now mastering the words, the microphone, all his fears, as though the speech problems had never been.[96] The speech had its own momentum, and all too soon the twelve minutes were drawing to an end. George VI's closing thoughts drew on a story once told by Abraham Lincoln. A boy was struggling up a hill, carrying a smaller child. 'Asked whether the heavy burden was not too much for him, the boy answered, "It's not a burden. It's my brother." So let us welcome the future in a spirit of brotherhood, and thus make a world in which, please God, all may dwell together in justice and peace.'

It was clear from the warm response in the broadcasting room that this was the king's best delivery yet. Elizabeth, as always, was quick to congratulate him. 'That was splendid, Bertie,' she said. The king thanked Logue for all his help. He felt 'altogether different', he told his therapist. For the first time, 'I had no fear of the microphone.'[97]

PART FOUR
....
JANUARY 1943–JANUARY 1952

11

TESTED AS NEVER BEFORE
IN OUR HISTORY

....

'Our nation and Empire stood alone against an overwhelming
enemy . . . tested as never before in our history . . . '

—George VI, 6 June 1944

In the New Year, the breakthrough in North Africa of the closing weeks of
1942 was swiftly followed by a long-awaited turning point in the Soviet Union.
Pathé newsreels played in the cinema in Buckingham Palace in February 1943
caught the final moments as the tide turned decisively at Stalingrad. The king
felt deep admiration for the 'unyielding resistance' of the Soviet people, and
the 'heroic qualities' of the Red Army.[1] To stirring strains of music, Soviet guns
closed in on what was once a city. 'The history of warfare has never known
such a large encirclement and annihilation,' announced the deep voice of the
Pathé narrator. 'Hundreds of thousands of bodies lie frozen in and around the
city . . . They rot in the land which they wanted to enslave.' Inside the city,
'the twisted disordered relics of an army committed to destruction by Adolf
Hitler' fought on in temperatures of -30 degrees centigrade, near starvation,
taking refuge in the ruins, the cellars, sometimes even the sewers. For these
'wrecks of men' there was none of the glory that Hitler had predicted. The original 330,000 soldiers of the German 6th Army trapped in the derelict city were
reduced to two pockets of starving men. Pathé provided a powerful image of
German surrender: a line of dark figures set against wide grey skies and a smoking city. As the camera panned, a never-ending line was revealed, stretching on
until the dark shapes were mere dots lost in a vast white landscape.[2]

The sheer scale of the Soviet sacrifice to win this decisive victory was painfully shown by the numbers. Stalingrad had cost the Red Army the lives of half
a million men; half a million Axis troops also died. By contrast at El Alamein,
2,300 British and empire forces died and 2,100 Germans and Italians. Stalin felt
his country was bearing the load and pushed for Britain and America to open
up a second front in France. Roosevelt was keen to support the Soviets when
he met Churchill in Casablanca in Morocco. The prime minister argued this
was still far too dangerous and urged Roosevelt to delay the final assault on
Germany while they launched an attack on Italy, which he described persua-
sively as 'Hitler's soft underbelly'. Reading the daily reports, the king knew of
the political and military conflicts between the world leaders and worried that
the stupendous British effort made in the first three years of war was now being
eclipsed by much greater powers.

George VI heard the prime minister became unwell when he returned from
the conference in Casablanca. The rumour mill began around Whitehall. Had
the change in climate affected him? Churchill appeared in Cabinet on one occasion feverish, wrapped in a shawl. Word spread that he was an obstinate patient;
headstrong, fond of drink, yet essentially unfit.[3] The endless pressure was taking
its toll, and now the man whose passion for the empire was in his very blood
and bones was dependent on those for whom this had no significance. George
VI had come to rely on the closeness of his friendship with Churchill. 'Ever
since he became my Prime Minister I have studied the way in which his brain
works,' the king told his mother. 'He tells me, more than people imagine, of his
future plans & ideas & only airs them when the time is ripe to his colleagues
& the Chiefs of Staff . . . '[4] But by mid-February pneumonia was diagnosed.
The king could not see his prime minister and his worries about the situation in
North Africa began to escalate.

The Americans were expedient, prepared to compromise and work with the
Vichy French leaders who had collaborated with the Germans. The king was
troubled. For him there was a principle at stake. 'We must be firm,' he wrote in
his diary, and not make deals with 'any kind of quisling'.[5] Plans were not falling
into place and the king felt the strain of 'being in the know'. Britain was reliant
on her allies to win the war, but, he told his mother, the USA and the USSR
'are both thorns in the flesh'. The Americans were failing to deliver on their
promises, while the Russians put 'every obstacle in our way when we try & help
them'.[6] Even though Churchill was recovering from a serious bout of pneumonia, the king went to Chequers on 8 March to discuss what he saw as the 'deteriorating' situation. But when he entered the room he was evidently shocked

to see his friend much reduced. 'I implored him not to overwork himself as he must get really well again,' the king confided later to his mother.[7] None the less, waiting outside the meeting room, Churchill's secretary, Elizabeth Layton, soon heard a forceful exchange of views from inside, 'the two tongues wagging like mad! But I fear my boss still holds the floor!' The two men parted on the best of terms; Churchill, instructed to stay in the warm, '*would* go to the door', observed Elizabeth.[8]

The closeness between the two men did not mean they shared the same opinion, and differences also surfaced on personal matters. Prince Paul was condemned as a quisling in the British press, but the king knew through Marina's sister, Olga, that this was not just and also that Paul was close to a nervous breakdown in his British imprisonment in Kenya.[9] Churchill maintained his tough stance. He saw no reason to worry over a man 'who did so much to harm his country' and failed to work with the Allies to strike 'a united blow for its liberties'.[10] But the king understood the complexities of the Yugoslav situation that led to Prince Paul's decision. He was not alone in his support for Prince Paul; ministers also appealed on his behalf. Churchill was overruled and in April the British government agreed to move Paul and Olga to less restrictive detention in South Africa.

Over the course of spring 1943 the massive Allied North African offensive culminated in victory on 13 May. The prolonged battle under hot African skies was at an end. The Allies could at last savour their rich prize, fought over so many times and so hard won. Some Americans proudly referred to it as their 'Tunisgrad'. In England a service was planned to mark the victory at St Paul's Cathedral. At the last minute, however, this was hastily rearranged when it was feared that the time of the service had been leaked. The information that Britain's leadership as well as the royal family were all to be gathered together in one very identifiable spot in the centre of London might prove irresistible to German bombers.[11] Considerable anxiety, never shown, affected the calmest spirits. But all went well. The king appeared majestic, the queen radiant, Churchill shining with exuberance, St Paul's still in place.

The king understood just what this victory meant to Churchill and wanted people to realise, as Lascelles put it, that Winston was the real 'father of the North African baby' although publicly he gave the credit to Roosevelt.[12] The king's telegram of congratulations to his prime minister was published in *The Times*. 'I wish to tell you how profoundly I appreciate the fact that its initial conception and successful prosecution are largely due to your vision and to your unflinching determination,' wrote the king. The campaign 'has immeasurably increased the debt' that the country owed him.[13] The prime minister was equally unstinting in his reply. 'No Minister of the Crown has ever received more kindness and confidence from his Sovereign,' Churchill responded. 'This has been a precious aid and comfort to me.'

The Times on 18 May followed up Lascelles's suggestion that the exchange of telegrams demonstrated the role of the British king within a modern democracy. The heads of the government are 'His Majesty's Ministers' who 'bear absolute responsibility', wrote *The Times*. George VI's telegram did indeed demonstrate his 'whole-hearted attribution of credit' to his prime minister for his vision and direction. It was for the sovereign to provide helpful counsel and Churchill acknowledged how well George VI had fulfilled that role. *The Times* considered that this was a 'discharge of a duty that only the Sovereign can perform and that only the few can see him performing'. Unlike ministers, the monarch provides continuity and his knowledge 'comes to transcend that of any individual statesman'. The editorial paid tribute to George VI as 'an unfailing public example of courage, confidence and devoted energy'.[14]

Just how much George VI's conscientious style of monarchy meant to people became even more apparent in the trip he made to North Africa in June 1943. The king, who was a little 'tired and feverish' on arrival in Algiers according to Harold Macmillan, Minister Resident to the Allied Force Headquarters, was none the less elated. To escape Northern Europe and its dark saga of war, transferred in a matter of hours to the brilliant light of North Africa in an atmosphere charged with success, was the stuff of dreams. In that sun-soaked world of action he dined with General Dwight Eisenhower, met the two feuding French generals, Henri Giraud and Charles de Gaulle, rode in an open car along the North African coast and received an ovation from more than 500 men on a beach in Algiers who were delighted by his impromptu visit. By 19 June he was in Tripoli with the Eighth Army and took the opportunity to knight Montgomery. The British general was concerned about the risks the king was taking in North Africa. There remained the threat of German paratroopers and shipping routes across the Mediterranean were far from safe. Whatever the dangers, the king was insistent that his tour must include Malta. The defeat of the Germans in North Africa was bringing an end to their misery.

The king sailed by night on HMS *Aurora* from Tripoli across the Mediterranean. The sun rose to reveal a perfect morning, the calm sea glistening in the early light as the island came into view. The enemy was just 60 miles away in Sicily, enemy aircraft within reach; but the horizon was still clear. The king was on deck, his eyes taking in the view of the harbour. George VI was much touched by the suffering of Malta. To be here was a moment he had awaited for a long time. 'I had set my heart on it,' he told his mother.[15]

Even at a distance, it was evident that word had spread. The king's visit had only been announced a few hours before; but that was enough. In the rush to celebrate the Maltese had made decorations out of anything they could find; bunting, flags, even curtains were flung out of windows making gay splashes of colour. People thronged from their bombed-out houses and cellars to see his ship arrive. The quayside was crammed; a solid mass of people.

The people of Malta had endured persistent heavy bombing, almost to the point of annihilation. Their valour was beyond question. And now here was their king coming to acknowledge their bravery. As the ship drew closer, George VI stood out on the bridge, a single figure, absolutely still in the dazzling sunlight, taking the salute.

It was a moment to be encapsulated in memory forever. The crowd went wild, their ecstatic welcome drowning out all other sounds as the *Aurora* manoeuvred into the harbour. 'A wonderful sight,' George VI wrote in his diary. 'Every bastion and every viewpoint lined with people who cheered as we entered.' And as the king finally stepped on land, now one with the crowd, the bells in the churches still standing began to ring out. He was intensely moved.[16] 'I shall never forget the sight of entering the Grand Harbour at 8.30 a.m. on a lovely sunny day, & seeing the people cheering from every vantage view point, while we were still some way off,' he told his mother. 'Then later, when we anchored inside, hearing the cheers of the people which brought a lump into my throat, knowing what they had suffered from six months constant bombing . . . '[17]

The king who shook Field Marshal Gort's hand on the jetty and then drove to Valetta Palace was very different to the broken man who had taken over the throne seven years before. His conscientious approach, the quality of the people around him, his willingness to take ministers' advice and above all his own determination to play his part well had transformed him into the monarch that people wanted to see. The square in front of the palace was crammed with more than 100,000 people, waiting for a glimpse of the slight figure in the white uniform. He stepped out on to the balcony beside Gort and waved. There was still one giveaway about his intrinsic personality: there was no speech.[18] The king who felt so strongly for the people of this island did not attempt to express in words what the day meant. It did not matter. Everyone knew what had brought their king to this bombed-out spot.

His tour was a triumph. Pathé reported on 'scenes of unparalleled enthusiasm'. Unstinting in their welcome, 'the George Cross islanders thronged the streets cheering and clapping through the seven hours the tour lasted'.[19] George VI stood resolute for long hours in the growing heat, keeping a promise he had made to himself many months ago in the darkest days of the war, when an event such as this seemed nigh on impossible. 'You have made the people of Malta very happy today, Sir,' commented David Campbell, the lieutenant governor as he prepared to set sail at the end of a very busy tour. 'But I have been the happiest man in Malta today,' he replied.[20]

The exuberant welcome of the Maltese people was like reaching an oasis in the barren landscape of war. At last the struggle against what the king saw as 'the forces of evil' was halted and it felt good. But there was a price to pay for his North African tour. The unaccustomed heat, the debilitating stomach upsets and the strain of the venture had taken its toll. When he returned to London on 25 June, the queen was shocked to find her husband had lost a stone in weight.

Two weeks later, on 8 July 1943, war was wiped from the front pages with news of the brutal murder of the wealthiest man in the Bahamas: the British baronet, Sir Harry Oakes. The reports were distressing for the duke and duchess who counted Sir Harry as one of their friends. His corpse was found in the very bed where the Duke of Windsor had slept as a guest when Government House was refurbished. The crime scene was particularly horrific. The baronet appeared to have been bludgeoned to death and doused in petrol. Feathers from a pillow were scattered over his body. His pyjamas and mosquito net had burned, but the fire had failed to take and the bloodied corpse lay on the bed, face and chest scorched.

Rashly, the duke tried to control the press response, only to become mired in the shocking headlines himself. For reasons that have never been clear, he attempted to stop news of the murder leaking out by closing the cable office. But his efforts at press censorship were about as futile as trying to control the tide; reporters streamed on to the island.[21] Worse, convinced the Nassau police would have no detectives of the right calibre, the duke took it upon himself to bring in a detective of his own choice: Captain Edward Melchen of the Miami Homicide Bureau. Windsor met him in person at Oakes's mansion and discussed the case for twenty minutes.

After this, with apparently breathtaking efficiency, Melchen and his deputy, Captain James Barker, arrested Sir Harry Oakes's son-in-law, the colourful playboy Count Alfred de Marigny. De Marigny was deemed to have a motive, since he had never won Oakes's approval for marrying his daughter, Nancy, and there was no love lost between father and son-in-law. In less than two days the detectives produced fingerprint evidence to damn him; evidence that could condemn de Marigny to death. Nancy duly arrived on the scene, as glamorous as a Hollywood film star, and determined to clear her husband's name. The press was captivated. A count, a baronet, an ex-king, a beautiful woman and a murder: sensational headlines were guaranteed for weeks.

That July the Allies launched the first stage in their offensive against Italy with the invasion of Sicily. Rome was bombed for the first time on 19 July and Mussolini himself overthrown in a coup and arrested on 25 July on the orders of the King of Italy. In London everyone was 'stunned and excited. Dazed and jubilant . . . ' wrote Chips Channon, capturing the mood that week in his diary.[22] But even with the prospect of the fall of Fascism in Italy, each new twist in the bizarre saga of the 'Murder in Paradise' was rarely far from the front pages.

Once the case reached court shocking evidence emerged that the very detectives that Windsor had chosen had fabricated the fingerprint evidence against Alfred de Marigny. A murder mystery of Agatha Christie proportions began to unfold. Who did kill Sir Harry Oakes? Why did the detectives try to frame Count Alfred de Marigny? The case collapsed and remains unsolved to this day. But the duke's clumsy involvement linked his name to the sleazy headlines and tarnished him with the detectives' dishonesty.

No matter how hard the duke and duchess attempted to atone for their mistakes, events conspired to add momentum to their downward spiral. There was much speculation about the cover-up, with irregular financial dealings on the island high on the list of concerns. Some thought the duke brought in private detectives and failed to summon the FBI because he had borrowed substantial sums from Sir Harry himself and feared exposure.[23] For others it was possible that the duke was involved in illegal currency speculation and wanted to avoid close scrutiny by settling the case. Believers in this theory alleged that Wenner-Gren used his yacht to transport large amounts of cash to Mexico on behalf of both the duke and Oakes.[24] Suspicions about money-laundering and links to a criminal underworld continued to weave themselves into the narrative of the unsolved case. For others still, the duke was innocent but Oakes was mixed up with the Chicago mafia who wanted to invest in a casino on the islands. The truth has never been established, but in the absence of evidence to clarify the duke's suspicious role in the bungled investigation, the case has never helped his cause.

The violent murder of Sir Harry Oakes was just one striking episode in a succession of troubles that engulfed members of the duke's circle during 1943. His friend Wenner-Gren, 'last reported somewhere in Mexico', according to the *New York Times*, continued to protest his innocence as his plans for a powerful Mexican cartel collapsed and his American assets were seized.[25] As governor, Windsor was obliged to condone his friend's downfall, signing the Blacklist Order in which Wenner-Gren's companies in the Bahamas came under government supervision. Axel Wenner-Gren 'will not be permitted to return to Nassau', the duke announced in response to a question at a press conference.[26] His property developments, his fleet of dredgers and his fish-canning plant on Grand Bahama Island were confiscated.[27] Windsor was obliged to give quotes to the press as though he had no objections to the State Department's actions, telling the *New York Times* he was 'intensely interested' in the continued running of Wenner-Gren's canning plant by US General Foods.[28] Even Wenner-Gren's magnificent yacht, the *Southern Cross*, the subject of intense media scrutiny while at the disposal of the Windsors, was seized by the Mexican government for naval purposes.[29]

A greater downfall lay in store for the first millionaire who had come to the Windsors' assistance after the abdication, Charles Bedaux. The Americans had him in their sights as he worked on his pipelines in North Africa even before the Allied desert victory. He was arrested by the French on behalf of the Americans in December 1942 but released on health grounds. His freedom did not last long. A few days before Roosevelt arrived in Casablanca to meet Churchill, Bedaux was re-arrested in Algiers and held by the US Military Police in North Africa.[30] General Eisenhower sent the Chief of the FBI's Special Intelligence Service, Percy Foxworth, to interview Bedaux in North Africa but the plane crashed over dense jungle, killing everyone on board. The 'Speed-up King' became caught up in tortuous delays as the wheels of bureaucracy turned slowly and almost a year elapsed before he was extradited to Miami. He was under suspicion for trading with the enemy, possibly even treason, and FBI files show Hoover himself kept a close eye on the case.[31]

Bedaux's former association with the Windsors worked against him as he became a high-profile suspect. Before the war his connections to the Nazi leadership had received publicity when he set up Windsor's German trip. It was considered possible that he was still in contact with such high-ranking Nazis as Robert Ley, Fritz Wiedemann and Ribbentrop through Nazi officials in Paris.[32] His company, Bedaux International, had been affiliated to Deutsche Bedaux in Berlin, Italian Bedaux and Bedaux Cie in Paris before the war and Bedaux's continuing connection as an industrial agent for the Germans was suspected.[33] His ambitious engineering schemes such as the pipeline across the Sahara lent weight to this view. His friends in America came under intense surveillance, including the Austrian, Friedrich von Ledebur, whose brother, Joseph, was pro-Nazi and had arranged business affairs for Bedaux. The FBI was keen to reach Ledebur before Bedaux's own lawyer and he was interviewed under some pressure, eventually conceding only 'that he hated his brother bitterly' and that 'in the event Bedaux is a Nazi collaborator, he wants nothing whatsoever to do with him'.[34] The case against Bedaux mounted as his 'Censorship Report' concluded that he was *persona grata* to German military authorities in France and has acquired large properties near Paris for the Germans and himself'.[35] Most damning of all was a document found amongst Bedaux's papers which appeared to show he was spying on the Allies, supplying information on shipping and other transport. Bedaux denied any knowledge of the document and insisted it had been planted in his papers.[36]

When he was permitted to write a letter, Bedaux appealed for legal help from Albert Raymond, the very man who had taken over the running of US Bedaux Company and benefited so spectacularly from Bedaux's difficulties in 1937 while arranging the Windsors' proposed tour. But Raymond, reeling under the bad publicity for the company, declined to help. Ledebur, no doubt feeling the close scrutiny of the FBI, also declined. On 14 February, alone in the Miami courtroom, Bedaux learned he was to be charged with treason.

Bedaux was not a man to be caught without a plan. The following day he was discovered unconscious. It emerged that he had regularly requested sleeping pills from the guard which he had secretly saved. It was a large enough dose to kill him, although it took three days. 'Bedaux, Mystery Man, Facing Treason Charges, Kills Himself Here,' announced the *Miami Daily News*.[37] To his family his suicide was seen as a sign of his decency; he wished to spare others coming under scrutiny on his behalf. But to the authorities and in the press his action was seen as an admission of guilt and he was portrayed as a traitor, his name invariably linked to the Windsors in the papers.

Even the man who married the duke and duchess, the Reverend Robert Anderson Jardine, managed to attract the interest of the American authorities. 'Windsor's Cleric and Wife held for Deportation Trial,' announced the *Washington Post* in May 1943. The reverend and his wife were arrested in Los Angeles on a deportation warrant and charged with overstaying their time in the country.[38] It began to seem as though any acquaintance of the Windsors, from super-wealthy yacht owners to the English clergy, was viewed as a possible threat.

With the duke's former connections under such scrutiny, the State Department was not prepared to grant immunity from censorship to the duchess. The Duke of Windsor was concerned that her mail continued to be intercepted and raised the matter with Lord Halifax in the British Embassy. The reply from Adolf Berle, Assistant Secretary of State, on 18 June 1943, was unequivocal. 'I believe the Duchess of Windsor should emphatically be denied exemption from censorship. Quite aside from the more shadowy reports of the activities of this family, it is to be recalled that both the Duke and Duchess were in touch with Mr James Mooney of General Motors, who attempted to act as a mediator of a negotiated peace in the early winter of 1940; they have maintained correspondence with Bedaux,' continued Berle, and 'they have been in constant contact with Axel Wenner-Gren, presently on our Blacklist for suspicious activity . . . '[39]

The duke felt the slights and humiliations deeply. While his brother appeared to have grown in stature, the papers regularly proclaiming this fact, he appeared visibly diminished, his allies apparently in disgrace. Since the abdication he had let himself be led by Wallis, who was drawn like a magnet to the super-rich regardless of their ethics and now these associations seemed ill-advised. The duke felt cut off from his old life, and did not know how to make his way back into it. Even long-standing friends were no longer keen to see him. When Beaverbrook was in New York in May 1943 and learned his visit to the city coincided with Windsor's, he would not take the duke's calls. The once 'devoted tiger' left instructions for his assistant to say he was out. It was only when the ploy was in danger of becoming obvious that he felt obliged to meet, but the old camaraderie was missing.[40]

There was one person still looking out for the duke in spite of everything that had happened: Winston Churchill. A committed monarchist, Churchill, who had taken such a hard line on Prince Paul and the King of Belgium, was reluctant to give up on his old friend in spite of knowledge of his disloyalty. Churchill wanted to help with the painful separation between the brothers. During his trip to Washington in May 1943 he did make time for Windsor in his packed schedule and spoke to him frankly. The king was 'unhappy over this family estrangement', he said, and wanted to improve relations. Was there anything the duke could do?[41]

But the duke's conviction that he had been wronged was now so ingrained he could not see the olive branch that was being offered. Unable to acknowledge the part he or his wife had played in maintaining the rift, he lashed out with further damning accusations against his brother. 'I have taken more than my fair share of the cracks and insults at your hands,' he wrote, and referred angrily to what he called the king's 'belligerence' and 'studied insults'. The king's first year or two was not easy, he acknowledged, but 'ever since I returned to England in 1939 to offer my services and you continued to persecute me and then frustrate my modest efforts to serve you and my country in war, I must admit that I have become very bitter indeed . . . '⁴²

While Windsor hoped to recover from the humiliations that he suffered, another great-grandson of Queen Victoria, Philipp of Hesse, suffered a precipitous downfall from which there appeared to be no return. His prospects were inextricably linked with the fate of Mussolini. Philipp of Hesse still trusted in Hitler when he was summoned to his headquarters at the Berghof in the Bavarian Alps in late April 1943. He was told he was needed by the Führer for 'special tasks' but just what these involved was never fully clarified. From his luxurious hotel, the Berchtesgadener Hof, he enjoyed spectacular views across the mountains, yet with each passing day it became clear he was a prisoner unable to leave without permission from Hitler. He felt threatened, although no threats were issued and whenever the two men met there was nothing to indicate he was out of favour. To those around them, they appeared close, the Führer frequently summoning the prince in the evenings to discuss the fast-changing situation in Italy.⁴³

It was Philipp's father-in-law, the King of Italy, Victor Emanuel III, who ordered the arrest of Mussolini on 25 July. Mussolini was hidden from the Germans, whisked from one location to another before being held in the mountains in central Italy at Gran Sasso. The new leadership were negotiating with the Allies, and announced the Italian surrender on 8 September 1943.⁴⁴ That same day Philipp of Hesse and Hitler had an amicable conversation over dinner and well into the small hours. There was no warning of the horror ahead. Hesse was making his way back to his hotel when two SS men emerged from the blackness and told him he was under arrest. He had only just left Hitler's company and yet the arrest was on the Führer's orders.

Hesse was 'interviewed' by the Gestapo in Berlin and stripped of his identity. His Nazi rank, his title as a Prince of Hesse, even his papers were removed. It was prisoner 'Herr Wildhof' who was escorted by criminal police to Flossenburg concentration camp in Bavaria. By a cruel calculation, there was a small gallows placed not far from the window of his cell. 'Herr Wildhof' was obliged to see what he had failed to see before: in plain view, the barbarity of the regime he had supported. Death was meted out without dignity or humanity on emaciated men and women. Carts were piled high with corpses, their bodies intimately mingled in death, more bone than flesh visible, their faces with sunken eyes, prominent cheekbones and the tight yellowing skin of starvation diets. As well as the frequent hangings a few yards from his cell, he could hear the soft crack of gunfire executions in the distance. His own death seemed imminent each time the door to his cell opened. For Philipp his dizzying fall into this frightening hell was undeserved and he protested frequently to Hitler and Himmler.[45] They were not listening.

He was unable to get word to his family but the guards did take the trouble to inform him of the death of his brother, Prince Christoph. Prince Christoph had been serving in the Luftwaffe seeing action in France, the Soviet Union, North Africa and Sicily, fighting to the last for the German cause. On 7 October 1943 he was recalled to Germany and took a flight from Rome. The plane never arrived. No obvious reason for the crash of the twin-engined light aircraft into the Apennines near Ravenna was ever found.[46] For Philipp, mourning his brother's fate from the confines of his cell, it was impossible to rule out sabotage.

The most shocking treatment was reserved for Philipp's beloved wife, Princess Mafalda, a daughter of the King of Italy. Hitler blamed the Italian royal family for the coup against Mussolini and in his eyes she became 'a bitch' and 'a traitor'.[47] Having fled for refuge to the Vatican in Rome, she was lured out again into Nazi captivity on the promise of receiving a message from her husband. It was a cruel trick. She was flown back to Germany, her royal status far from being an asset, now a death sentence. In Buchenwald concentration camp she was kept in the Isolation Barracks along with other high-ranking prisoners. Her cell was located in the most dangerous part of the camp, close to an armaments factory that was an Allied target, the fear of bombing adding to the inmates' torment.

During 1943 there was a new hit by Ambrose and his Orchestra that caught the public mood. Seventeen-year-old Princess Elizabeth and thirteen-year-old Princess Margaret played it on the gramophone in Balmoral, provoked to tears by the poignant words despite the jaunty strains of the dance music echoing down long corridors once graced by Queen Victoria.[48]

One of our planes was missing
Two hours overdue
One of our planes was missing
With all its gallant crew.

The radio sets were humming
They waited for the word
Then a voice broke through the humming
And this is what they heard.

Coming in on a wing and a prayer
Coming in on a wing and a prayer
Tho' there's one engine gone and the other won't be long
We're coming in on a wing and a prayer . . . [49]

The song captured the growing feeling of optimism. The skill and daring of RAF pilots and their crews fired popular imagination. Spectacular images of the breathtaking dambusters raid on the Ruhr had been printed worldwide and fired popular imagination. Less eye-catching but equally dangerous were the targeted Allied assaults against the German armaments industries: the I.G. Farben chemical works in the Ruhr, the ball-bearing plants at Schweinfurt and others. The bombing of German cities continued. The Allied bombing on Hamburg and the resulting firestorm killed an estimated 45,000, exceeding the toll of the London blitz. From the air the terrible storms of fire below confirmed that reprisals were at last being dealt to an enemy that had seemed indomitable. The Allies were winning the war in the Atlantic too and were able to step up the transport of US troops and supplies to Europe. The US Army Air Force worked alongside the RAF in England, adding to the momentum of the assault against the Axis.

At Barnwell in Northamptonshire the Duke and Duchess of Gloucester were increasingly aware of the presence of American airmen in the neighbourhood. The gardens of Barnwell were overgrown, the lawns 'shaggy' wrote the duchess, the yew hedges 'with long whiskers!' There was no one with time to take them in hand. For the Americans the rambling grounds had all the old-world charm and romance of an English manor house. 'I have just looked out the window and seen about 50 or more Americans having their photograph taken against the old castle. Quite uninvited!' the duchess observed on one occasion.[50] The

Gloucesters decided to open the gates so that anyone could visit the gardens. Alice noted from the windows of Barnwell there was one particular young airman who haunted the gardens after each sortie, as though drawing strength for his daily ordeal from their peace and beauty. One day she realised he had failed to return. She was distressed to find he had been killed over Germany.

The constant air traffic had a marked effect on her household, disturbing its orderly routines. Once she was in the sitting room when she became aware of a terrible loud noise, the sound deafening as it approached ever nearer. There was scarcely time to register that the plane was very low, black smoke and flame billowing in its wake. 'It'll be down in a minute,' someone yelled. Alice was already running. Two-year-old William was asleep in his pram outside. She reached the pram 'which leapt out of my hands' as the crash occurred close by. To her relief, William was safe.

The duchess found the animals on the estate came to distinguish the different sounds. 'German engines made a different sound—anumb, anumb, anumb— and the ponies recognised this and associated it with danger,' she wrote, 'and began to tremble and get fidgety.' The bull mastiff showed the greatest terror, 'wriggling under the bed or sofa as soon as he heard them coming'. The pheasants were the most alert. The shock waves alone from heavy bombing raids on the Midlands and Coventry would set them off. She and the duke heard 'the pheasants crowing before we heard the bombs explode'.[51]

The Gloucesters joined the king and queen at the family retreat at Balmoral in early autumn and found the king in an optimistic mood. The tide was still moving in the Allies' favour. Allied troops had liberated Sicily and landed in Italy. 'My darling Mama, you will have heard the announcement of Italy's unconditional surrender on the wireless,' the king wrote on 8 September. At last Rome appeared to be in their sights.[52] In the Scottish Highlands, tramping across grouse moors in the rain away from the pressures of their London life, it seemed possible to start talking about the future. Princess Elizabeth would reach the age of eighteen on 21 April 1944. The law was being changed to enable her to become a Councillor of State in her own right, one of five members of the royal family appointed to take on certain responsibilities for the monarch. The Duke of Gloucester would no longer be needed as Regent in the event of the king's death.

George VI was keen to find a new position for his brother. Gloucester had been taking on some of Kent's portfolio but the duke felt that he was not doing enough. The king discussed the matter with Churchill and soon found a solution. He asked Gloucester to take over the role planned for Kent before the war as Governor-General of Australia.[53] The king explained the decision to his mother, fearing she would worry about another family separation. 'With Harry out there as my personal representative, he can be given a roving commission as well, even to cover India. It would . . . give him a real, live interest in Empire affairs.'[54] Gloucester himself was delighted at the prospect, feeling at last he had a new challenge, and Alice, who was still hoping for another baby, supported him.[55]

Despite the high hopes in the summer, it was the Soviets, not the British and Americans, who stole the headlines with a succession of victories. After Stalingrad, the Red Army had fought its way west across the vast Russian steppes locked in a battle of attrition with the armies of the Third Reich. Following the great Soviet tank victory at Kursk in the summer of 1943, the Soviets continued west on a wide front, reaching Kiev in November, some 800 miles from Berlin, closer than the Allies. Meanwhile in Italy the British and Americans found Churchill's 'soft underbelly' proved to contain all the muscle and gristle of the German military machine. German panzers and infantry bore on Allied liberators and blocked the path to Rome, 950 miles from Berlin. German commandos rescued Mussolini in a daring raid from his imprisonment in a ski resort high in the Apennines on 12 September. The king was worried about the impasse. 'Fighting in the mountains is hopeless,' he wrote in his diary. 'The men are in good heart but the conditions are dreadful. Mud, rain, and cold for weeks now.'[56] The Allied assault ground to a halt in central Italy along a series of German defences running coast to coast some 80 miles south of Rome known as the Winter Line. The key point in this line, poised on a rocky outcrop that rose sharply 1,700 feet above the small town of Cassino, was a fifteen-centuries-old monastery, the headquarters of the Benedictine Order and an 'all-seeing eye' across the surrounding land held by the Germans.

The strain seemed never-ending. Churchill spoke of his worries about Hitler's new secret weapon to the king. There were rumours of German rockets that could annihilate London but Churchill was more measured. He had discussed the matter with scientists, he said. The rockets were reputed to have a range of up to 300 miles. Fired from France they could reach London and could cause 'terrific damage and loss of life'. It sounded like something out of science fiction, but the scientists could not rule it out; 'it was possible, but not probable', he explained.[57] Was Hitler about to seize the upper hand again? How was this new fear to be met? Churchill was soon out of the country for conferences in the Middle East: in Cairo in Egypt with Chiang Kai-Shek of China and President Roosevelt; in Teheran in Iran with Stalin and Roosevelt; and then back to Cairo. Just before Christmas the king learned his prime minister was ill for a second time that year with pneumonia, which had affected his heart. 'This is an added worry for me,' he confided to his diary.[58]

Queen Elizabeth hoped the Christmas break would provide some respite. She joined the king in Buckingham Palace on 23 December 1943 for the usual tradition of giving the servants their presents. Then it was back to Windsor where this year the family was joined by Prince Philip, a lieutenant in the Royal Navy. Princess Elizabeth was excited to see him and in very high spirits. They had first met when Elizabeth was thirteen and since then both Marina and Lord Louis Mountbatten had created opportunities for the young couple to see each other. Philip was already closely connected to the family. Through his father, Prince Andrew of Greece, he was a cousin of Marina and a great-nephew of Princess Alexandra, the king's grandmother. Through his German mother, Princess Alice of Battenberg, Philip was also a descendant of Queen Victoria and a nephew of Louis Mountbatten.[59] 'We had a very gay time,' Princess Elizabeth revealed to her governess, Marion Crawford, that Christmas, 'with a film, dinner parties and dancing to the gramophone.'[60] The king could not fail to miss the effect of Prince Philip on his serious older daughter. 'She had a sparkle about her that none of us had ever seen before,' noted her governess. He and the queen wanted their seventeen-year-old daughter to take her time before making any choice.

In the New Year the king's private hope that the war might be over by the end of 1944 was soon crushed. When Winston returned to London it was clear that he had felt the pressure of dealing with the conflicting needs of their allies. Stalin could be difficult and rude, making costly demands, while Roosevelt appeared careless, caving in to the Soviets without prior agreement. Churchill tried to make light of it all to the king. 'With a Bear drunken with victory on the East and an Elephant lurching about on the West, we the UK were like a Donkey in between them which was the only one who knew the way home.'[61] The king saw that Churchill himself appeared rather weak and 'seemed to have lost some of the fire in his eyes'.[62]

The battle at Monte Cassino came to symbolise the titanic struggle ahead for the Allies. In January, the Allies launched their first assault on this key route into Rome. The conditions were appalling. Water sluiced down the mountains; gun areas were invariably knee-deep in mud; greatcoats frozen with ice; the assault failed. After much deliberation, the Allies agreed to destroy the iconic Benedictine monastery where they believed German troops were hiding.

On 15 February, 1,400 tons of bombs from US planes wiped 1,500 years of history from the face of the map. For the Allied troops on the ground it was unearthly, as though the Benedictine monastery above them suddenly exploded under the shattering air and artillery barrage, while behind them Vesuvius was smoking ominously 40 miles away. After the bombardment, a terrifying silence fell over the Italian landscape. Had the German defenders withdrawn?

All too soon German troops dug into the hillside took advantage of the ruins to strengthen their defences. The sacrilege had brought no advantage. The second assault had failed. Morale for British troops fighting in Italy was so low it was estimated that 30,000 of them fled their posts or were absent without leave.[63] A third assault was launched in March. Once again, success eluded the Allies. The few Germans who abandoned their billets left behind the strange smell of Dutch gin, Balkan tobacco and sweaty leather.[64] But the site remained in German hands.

12
SOMETHING MORE THAN COURAGE

....

'Once more the supreme test has to be faced . . . What is
demanded from us is something more than courage, more than
endurance . . . '

—George VI, D-Day, 6 June 1944

I n the spring of 1944 the king was preoccupied with the preparations for Operation Overlord, the invasion of Normandy in northern France. He met General Eisenhower, the Supreme Allied Commander, and was briefed by General
Montgomery, in charge of Allied ground forces for the operation and Admiral
Sir Bertram Ramsay, the mastermind behind Dunkirk, now Naval Commander
of Overlord. Their daring ambition to launch an army across the Channel into
the heart of enemy territory appeared fraught with danger. This was a feat that
had been beyond the Spanish Armada, Napoleon, and Hitler himself, and yet
now his War Cabinet proposed to do it. The history of warfare had no parallel.
The largest amphibious assault of all time was to involve 5,000 vessels in the
sea and an army of men to move into enemy territory: 160,000 soldiers on the
first day alone. To land Allied troops on five different beaches across a 50-mile
stretch of Normandy involved Channel-crossing plans, transportation plans,
air-force plans, deception plans, contingency plans . . . and formed such a complex web of detail the king found the more he learned 'the more alarming it
becomes in its vastness'. The odds could tip towards disaster on something as
chance-laden as the wind direction.[1]

Some 150 of the Allies' most senior commanders gathered on 15 May in St
Paul's School in West London to discuss final preparations. The school had
been evacuated at the start of the war, but the incongruous air of the class-
room remained; the pervasive scent of chalk and ink and well-thumbed books

lingering obstinately among the plain wooden surroundings, notices about scholarships still pinned to the walls. Standing before an enormous plaster model of the French beaches, the military leaders each in turn unfolded the part their men would play in this great armada. Churchill and the king listened—the only persons present permitted the comfort of armchairs as the vast conception took shape. 'And what a plan!' Churchill wrote later. 'It involves tides, winds, waves, visibility, both from the air and the sea standpoint, and the combined employment of land, air, and sea forces in the highest degree of intimacy and . . . in conditions which . . . cannot be fully foreseen.'[2] When the American and British military leaders finished, the king was much moved to have witnessed two nations working together so closely in such an inspiring way. He found himself stepping forward to the dais to make an impromptu speech. 'This is the biggest Combined Operation ever thought out in the world,' he said. 'I wish you all success & with God's help you will succeed.'[3] As he left General Eisenhower spoke to him with confidence. With 11,000 planes in the air, and the largest armada in history, he said, Operation Overlord 'will not fail'.[4]

In the countdown to D-Day the king was preoccupied with visiting the troops, determined to see all those involved in Overlord. Southern England had turned into an immense military camp. Training was also intense in coastal waters. Driving to each port taking part in the operation, the countryside seemed at its most poignantly beautiful in the warm weather of late May. He knew high casualty rates were expected on the beaches: one estimate as high as 20,000 deaths on the first day alone. Meeting the young men who were being placed in such grave danger for their country was not easy. Exchanges focused on practicalities, but the stirring nature of their self-sacrifice was understood. Churchill was equally moved. He was 'even more energetic' than usual, observed his bodyguard, Walter Thompson. At the ports he was greeted by smiling faces and cheering men and Churchill, sometimes too full of emotion to give a speech, would say simply, 'Good luck, boys!'[5]

The prime minister felt strongly that he should be there, part of the historic moment, leading his men into battle like times of old. He had made arrangements in mid-May to view the initial attack from one of the bombarding ships in the Channel, *Belfast*.[6] If possible he wanted to land on the beaches on the first day. When the king found out about Churchill's plan at their weekly lunch at the palace just a few days before D-Day he was alarmed, but knew his prime minister too well to directly contradict him. Instead he told Churchill that he, too, would join him. They could be in the thick of battle together. Both men agreed to raise their plan with Ramsay, the naval commander.[7]

The king's private secretary, Alan Lascelles, who had taken over from Hardinge, knew that military leaders opposed Churchill's plan and brought a note of reality to the proceedings. Who was going to help the eighteen-year-old Princess Elizabeth if both her father and prime minister lay 'at the bottom of the English Channel'? he demanded. And what captain could endure 'the paralysing effect' of trying to fight his ship in the inferno of battle with his king and his prime minister on board? Lascelles was quite clear. Winston was behaving 'just like a naughty child . . . his naughtiness is sheer selfishness, plus vanity. Just to satisfy his love of theatre and adventure . . . '[8] He persuaded the king to write to the prime minister on 31 May, advising him that neither of them should go. 'We should both, I know, love to be there,' the king wrote to Churchill. But he pointed out what a great setback it would be, not just to him personally, but 'to the whole Allied cause, if at this juncture a chance bomb, torpedo or even a mine, should remove you from the scene'. Churchill was not listening. He would be with his men.[9]

The king and the prime minister had a meeting with Admiral Bertram Ramsay the next day in the map room. The mastermind of Dunkirk's evacuation found himself confronted by an obstacle of an altogether different kind. As Churchill reiterated his inflexible determination to be in the thick of the coming battle, every line, every inch of those comfortable curves stiffened and took on that pugnacious 'bulldog' stance: jaw set, lips compressed, eyes on fire. No argument held sway with him. The high risk of mines, torpedoes, shells and air attack meant nothing. When the king revealed that he might be on the same ship beside him, Admiral Ramsay was appalled. Churchill pointed out that the Cabinet would need to approve the king's decision and they were unlikely to consent, but failed to apply the same reasoning to his own plan. Even the constitutional issue—that the prime minister could not leave the country without permission from the king—he brushed aside on the grounds that he would still be in a British ship and therefore in British territory. 'When I left I could see Ramsay was a bit shaken,' the king noted in his diary.

For the king the prospect of losing his prime minister at this most critical of times was all too real. Churchill's selfish insistence upon what was no more than 'a joy-ride' added considerably to the strain in the run-up to D-Day.[10] On the evening of 2 June, the king was ready to travel in person to Portsmouth to stop Churchill boarding *Belfast*. He tried one last personal appeal, expressing his concern for Churchill's safety. Finally, on 3 June, the king learned that Churchill, begrudgingly, had agreed to his wishes, 'only because I have asked him not to go'.[11]

The king found the waiting to the countdown for that dreaded, longed-for moment unendurable. Hoping to relieve the tension, he went riding with his daughters in Windsor Great Park. It was the first time in four years that he had ridden his black pony through the peaceful countryside.[12] Churchill meanwhile lingered at the ports. He was at Southampton with Ernest Bevin, the minister for labour and national service, as the Northumbrian 50th Division embarked. Some of the troops touched his coat as they passed, as though some part of that Bulldog courage would brush off on them. According to his bodyguard, one of the men called out, 'Have you got a ticket, Sir?' He held up his pass. 'It entitles me to a free trip to France.'

'I wish I had,' Thompson heard Churchill reply. 'If only I were a few years younger, nothing would keep me away.' The generous spirit of the troops as they prepared to fight for their country and his profound exhaustion combined to heighten Churchill's emotions. The future of England hung on what these men could endure. According to Thompson, both the prime minister and Bevin were at times unable to hold back their tears.[13] In a private conversation with the government chief whip, James Stuart, a few days later, Lascelles discovered that Churchill had been making personal preparations for his trip to France in the run-up to D-Day, talking on one occasion 'as if he were about to die' and arranging his private papers.[14]

Any sense of relief the king felt that he had stopped some private folly of his prime minister was short-lived. News came the next day that the Allies had finally liberated Rome, but at Windsor Castle there was no chance to celebrate. The king was telephoned with the message that the entire D-Day plan for 5 June was in doubt. Just as had been feared: an uncontrollable element had infiltrated the exacting and complex D-Day plan. A storm was blowing in from the Atlantic. Strong westerly gales were whipping the English Channel into a frenzy of wind and wave. High seas would make it almost impossible for the landing craft to convey the troops from the ships to the beaches safely. Great banks of thick low cloud would jeopardise the bombing missions of Allied aircraft. Operation Overlord had to be postponed. For hours the king waited for more news, looking out from Windsor Castle at unending grey skies and heavy cloud across the rolling Berkshire landscape. He knew how confined the men would be; waiting in the crowded quarters of their ships in English ports, tension rising with the delay.[15]

Finally there was news of a short clearing in the weather on Tuesday 6 June. General Eisenhower gave the order. As dusk was gathering on Monday evening the vast operation thundered into life. The Airborne Divisions went out first into the night. Paratroopers and glider-borne troops were to land in Nazi occupied France and target bridges and enemy communications. Minesweepers worked their way towards Normandy in choppy seas through the small hours, while aircraft hunted down U-boats. Behind them, from the ports of England into the Channel, emerged the great armada into the night. 'As dawn came,' wrote Churchill, 'the ships, great and small, began to file into their prearranged positions for the assault.'[16] Soldiers stared in wonder at the sight of their great numbers; everywhere, and from many different countries, vessels proceeded forwards to the great plan. It was without precedent, almost unbelievable, and gave the waiting men who would soon be on the beaches a precious jewel of hope. At Buckingham Palace from 5 am the noise of overhead aircraft streaming across the Channel was deafening.[17] Off the coast of France gun and rocket batteries pounded the coastal defences. Soon the first landing craft were in the fury of battle; tossed in heavy surf as men struggled to land regardless of the hazards of mines, barbed wire and enemy fire.

The king was due to broadcast to the nation later that day and planned to try to unite the empire in prayer. 'I have wanted to do it for a long time,' he told his mother.[18] Logue arrived at the palace at around 6 pm to help rehearse the speech. He found the events leading up to D-Day were taking their toll of George VI.[19] Some 170 miles away the decisive ordeal for the Allied troops was unfolding. George VI, so familiar with every detail of the D-Day plan and the great cloud of boundless hope it carried with it, could only wait and pace the floor and smoke and ache for news.

'Four years ago, our Nation and Empire stood alone against an overwhelming enemy, with our backs to the wall,' the king began. 'Tested as never before in history, in God's providence we survived the test; the spirit of the people, resolute, dedicated, burned like a bright flame, lit surely from those Unseen Fires which nothing can quench. Now once more a supreme test has to be faced. This time, the challenge is not to fight to survive, but to fight to win the final victory for the good cause . . . We and our Allies are sure that our fight is against evil and for a world in which goodness and honour may be the foundation of the life of men in every land.' He closed with the words of Psalm 29 to call the empire to prayer: 'The Lord will give strength unto this people; the Lord will give this people the blessing of peace.'[20]

While the Allies were engaged in one of the most decisive battles of the war, the Duke of Windsor was fighting a little operation of his own. Increasingly he found his wife was no longer cut out for a life of public service in the Bahamas. 'Some days I feel I can't resist slapping everyone in the face,' she confided to her aunt that spring. 'I use up a lot of energy hating the place,' she wrote two months later. 'Being shut up here is like being a prisoner of war only worse.'[21] He was captive to her moods and felt responsible for their 'Elba'. But what really rubbed salt into their wounds that June was an article that appeared in the *American Mercury* which was painfully unflattering to them both. Spelled out in black and white for the public, the duchess was scorned and their relationship trivialised. Poring over the article in Nassau, the duke did not recognise even a grain of truth; rather he became convinced there was a plot to discredit them in the American press.[22]

'In the ninth year of her reign over David,' wrote reporter Helen Worden, the duchess's 'face has taken on harsher lines . . . Her jaw, if anything, is squarer because of decisions which have been hers, not David's . . .' For the *Mercury*, Wallis was shallow: her clothes were the key to her personality and she was nothing more than 'a clothes horse'. Since she moved to Nassau she had 'averaged a hundred dresses a year. Most of them cost about $250 apiece, though many ran much higher . . . She also has complete sets of rubies, emeralds, diamonds, topaz, onyx and turquoise, one for each day of the week.' Her collection of jewels could be sold for more than a million dollars and her furs were of equal value. 'Much of the self-confidence and poise she displays stem from her perfection of grooming.' When she was asked to travel lightly the duchess 'turned on the man who dared to suggest this with supreme scorn in her voice. "You are out of your mind," she stormed. "Don't you think I know my people?"' She insisted on at least thirty-one trunks for one weekend. 'She still thinks her public wants display.' Her lavish spending on herself was contrasted with her thriftiness towards her staff. Detectives who had worked long hours on one trip were thanked—with great largesse—merely with hotel postcards autographed by her and the duke.[23]

In the eyes of the *Mercury*, Wallis, 'the woman I love', that matchless paragon for whom the duke had given up the greatest position that there is, was reduced to something cheap, vain and tawdry whose lack of love for her husband was exposed. The duke looked a fool in front of the American public. If the duchess had led 'the simple life for love of him' after the abdication, declared Worden, people would have said: 'Three cheers! This is the real thing . . .' But

The Duchess of Windsor portrayed by the *American Mercury*

her self-indulgence had made the public 'indignant'. According to one English-man interviewed by Worden, 'the stoning of her house on Regent's Park at the time of the king's abdication would be as nothing to the reception she would get today'.[24]

The duke had a blind spot. Far from recognising any defect in his wife, all he could see was a conspiracy. Although he felt bruised by the close attentions of the intelligence services, such was the seriousness he attached to the matter, he turned to the FBI to investigate this damning calumny. FBI files show the duke discussed the article 'at great length' with J. Edgar Hoover, who in turn approached Jerome Doyle, the new Chief of the US Special Intelligence Service (SIS). His unusual brief was to undertake 'a discreet survey of SIS contacts in

New York city to ascertain if there were any concerted efforts being made in literary circles in New York to injure the character of the Duchess of Windsor'.[25] To the duke's enduring discredit he appeared to suspect there might be a Jewish intrigue against his wife and told the FBI 'that he believed that Miss Helen Worden, author of the article, was Jewish'.[26]

SIS agents were duly diverted from their wartime work to undertake a survey of the American press, including the editors of *Cosmopolitan*, *The Woman* and other influential media figures. The SIS report concluded that 'there was no concerted effort by anyone at this time to injure her [the duchess's] reputation in the eyes of the American public'. Furthermore the sources contacted 'did not believe that she [Helen Worden] is of the Jewish race'.[27]

The difficulties with the press on top of everything else brought fresh urgency to the duke's desire for a new position. Although he realised ministers in London were preoccupied with the battle raging in Normandy, he wished to resign his commission and seek a more prestigious role. The duke knew it was a critical time for the Allied leadership. By mid-July the Soviets had crossed the border into Poland some 450 miles from Berlin while the Allies were still more than 750 miles from Berlin battling through northern France. London was reeling from Hitler's new terror weapon, the pilotless flying bomb or V1. The fact that the duke raised the question of his employment now, of all times, highlights his increasing frustration.

In the papers he saw pictures of the king, apparently crowned in glory with the heroic troops in their moments of triumph: on the Normandy beaches in June, in Italy in July and August. Pathé showed George VI stepping down from a plane to a fanfare of trumpets, giving salutes to British and American troops in the brilliant sunshine, touring the bay of Naples, inspecting cruisers, congratulating the Eighth Army. 'Hardly a day passes by that British propaganda does not stuff us with the extent to which the King has established himself in the hearts of the people,' the duke commented to his solicitor, George Allen.[28] Why, he reasoned, was it not possible for an ex-king of England to have a role where he, too, could hold his head up high? Even their younger brother, Gloucester, was trusted as Governor of Australia, representing the king in a loyal Dominion. Surely some sort of roving diplomatic post, perhaps in America, was not asking too much? A diplomatic post had the added advantage of conferring tax immunity. As a private individual he would pay tax in America, and there was a risk that Wallis was liable for a substantial back payment.[29]

The duke was delighted when he was in America in September to be invited to meet Churchill in Washington. Churchill praised the duke's work in the

Bahamas and acknowledged that of course he should feel free to resign. But when it came to a question of what future role the duke could have, the prime minister proved hard to pin down. The issue continued to be discussed during the autumn but the duke found a curious inaction when it came to finding him a job. The idea of his taking on a role within the British Embassy in Washington was discreetly dropped. The Canadians too had no diplomatic role for Windsor. Churchill mooted the idea of appointing him Governor of Ceylon, until it became apparent that a governor with imminently suitable credentials had only just settled in. Another idea was to send the duke to India as Governor of Madras until some bright spark pointed out that this put the British establishment in a tricky position since several Indian princes had been deemed unsuitable for the post on account of their marriage arrangements. The king was in favour of Latin America, but Halifax expressed his doubts. For British officialdom there was the sticky question of whether, by virtue of royal birth, he had an unalienable right to a privileged position as a diplomat? The answer was emerging as a resounding 'no'.

Equally troublesome was where the ex-king should live. Beautiful Paris, hardly touched by bombing, was liberated on 25 August 1944. The German general, Dietrich von Choltitz, surrendered to the Allies in his Hôtel Le Meurice headquarters and Parisians lavished their Allied victors with unrestrained delight, stopping the solid flow of tanks and greeting solders like long-lost lovers. George VI reported to his mother that the Windsors' homes in Paris and Antibes were in perfect condition and he was liaising with the Foreign Office to return any belongings which had been stored for safekeeping.[30] But it was not clear to British officials that post-war France would welcome the Windsors. The duke's greatest hope was still pinned on a reunification with his family. He was unaware when he signed the abdication papers that he was effectively committing himself to permanent exile. In anticipation of coming back to society, through Churchill he requested yet again that Wallis be recognised as an HRH. Since the monarchy was no longer in jeopardy, the duke reasoned, surely 'family jealousy' would not prevent him returning to his home country with some measure of courtesy extended to his wife? The duke himself considered he had 'done everything in my power to heal the breach'.[31]

The palace took a different view. When the prime minister invited comments on the question of the ex-king's future the toughest line came from George VI's private secretary. 'There is in the British cosmos, no official place for an ex-King,' declared Alan Lascelles. It made no sense to him that a man who had publicly renounced the British Crown could take up a role representing either the monarch or the government. There was plenty of evidence of the duke's 'constitutional inability' to understand the difference between public and private interests, he reasoned. Invoking a story from the Old Testament of Rehoboam, son of Solomon, who fought his own brothers, Windsor, he thought, had a 'Rehoboam-like tendency to take up with undesirable and dangerous associates'. The 'scoundrel Bedaux' and 'the egregious Gren' were cited to make his point. Finally, for Lascelles, the Windsors' presence would be 'a constant agony to the present king'. As one of the richest men in the world, the duke could do almost anything, he concluded, 'but there is no room for two Kings of England'.[32]

Churchill did not agree. The duke had rights as both a British subject and a peer of the realm. 'Nothing that I am aware of,' declared the prime minister, 'can stop him returning to this country.'[33]

When Marina wrote to Betty Lawson-Johnson on 18 November 1944 she was just one of thousands of war widows still feeling the pain of the loss of her husband. '"His" dear memory is so alive and oh, how he is missed in many, many things . . . there is so much that no one but him could do,' she confided. There was always that sense of emptiness, perhaps a refrain from a song, an unintended glance at a photograph, or someone just like him approaching ensured that that dull ache was never far from the surface. She thanked Betty for her efforts in sending a Christmas parcel that had evidently failed to arrive. A newspaper clip that Betty had posted showing the Windsors 'high gambling' invoked a sharp response. 'Thank you for the interesting cutting—but how painful and cheap! Really "those two" are extraordinary people—what a strange life!' Marina's thoughts were firmly pinned on the end of the war. 'Oh how one longs for an end to the chaos and misery in the world.'[34]

Her relatives became caught in the fraught political and military complexities over Eastern Europe. Despite all the negotiations between the British, Americans and Soviets, it was becoming painfully evident that the fate of these countries would depend on the position of the armies when the war ended. The 'Old Bear', as Churchill referred to Stalin, adopted the viewpoint that whoever became the occupying force could determine the governance.[35] British efforts to challenge the strengthening hold of Soviet ideology in Europe deepened conflicts with the Americans who saw in Britain's manoeuvres an extension of her old imperialism. Marina understood the involved politics of her home country where Communist partisans were heralded as heroes for their role in the resistance. 'When the fighting ceases, *will* it be the end of the suffering?' Marina wrote to Betty. 'I am afraid the years to come will be hard.'[36]

The fearsome struggles in Romania presaged what might follow elsewhere in Eastern Europe. Ahead of the liberating Soviet army, a great-great-grandson of Queen Victoria, Prince Michael of Romania, carried out a coup in August to drive the Nazis from his country. But his bravery during the liberation did not bring the freedoms he hoped as Stalin tightened his grip. George VI raised the matter with Churchill, but the prime minister could do nothing. Romania had been an enemy before, he explained, and it had now fallen into the Soviet sphere of influence. Any moves by the British in Romania would only harm negotiations with the Soviets over Greece, Poland and Yugoslavia. The king confided in his mother. 'Poor Michael and his mother Zitta [Queen Helen] have been having a very worrying time from the Russians again,' he told her, 'and we can do nothing to help them for the moment.'[37]

As the Soviets advanced, Marina's middle sister, Elizabeth, Countess of Toerring-Jettenbach, trapped in Munich in south-eastern Germany, did not know whether British and American or Soviet forces would reach them first. Meanwhile, their oldest sister, Olga, was still detained in Johannesburg in South Africa with British public opinion firmly set against her husband, the alleged quisling, Prince Paul. He felt his disgrace deeply and found it difficult to recover without vindication of his actions. Soviet influence in both Romania and Bulgaria that autumn strengthened the hand of Yugoslav Communist partisans led by Marshal Tito, who invited the Soviets into Yugoslavia to help drive out the Germans. Prince Paul watched helplessly from a distance as he saw the alien landscape of Soviet ideology take root in his country and found himself sinking into a deep depression. As the Soviets gained the upper hand he began to feel vindicated by his earlier pro-Nazi stance and hoped he would no longer be regarded as a quisling in England.[38] But Marina could report no change in the public attitude towards her brother-in-law.

There was also little prospect of harmony in Greece where her mother was still in Athens. Churchill, apprehensive about the inexorable Soviet advance across south-east Europe and the possibility of Greek Communist partisans striking a coup against the Nazis, began to land troops in Greece in October. British soldiers entered Athens on 14 October cheered by ecstatic crowds. With the return of the exiled government a few days later, the Greek flag was carried to the Acropolis. To a fanfare of trumpets it was raised above the city, unfurling as it caught the wind above the birthplace of democracy. But factional fighting led by Communist partisans broke out and soon escalated into civil war.[39] With continuing uncertainty about the future role of the Greek monarchy, George II of Greece remained in exile. Two weeks after the liberation of Athens, 700 miles away the capital of Yugoslavia, Belgrade, was liberated by the Soviets.

The steady advances of Allied armies prompted speculation that winter that the conflict might soon be over. Cecil Beaton, on a visit to see the queen at Buckingham Palace, learned that the king and queen were already making preparations for the end of the war. Cement was ordered to carry out crucial repairs to the balcony at Buckingham Palace which had suffered from bomb damage and was no longer sound—a small acknowledgement towards the day that must soon dawn when victory would ignite nations and crowds would gather at the palace.[40] But until that day the king stood in the wet December weather, taking the salute at the Home Guard 'Stand Down' parade. Some 7,000 Home Guards, cheered by a huge crowd including their wives and children, passed before the king, queen and the two princesses.[41] Britain's 'cheap army', no longer needed, marched through streets in the pouring rain from Hyde Park down Piccadilly and Oxford Street to the accompaniment of eleven Home Guard bands, the large crowd encouraging them all the way. 'You have served your country with a steadfast devotion,' George VI broadcast later that day. 'I know that your country will not forget that service.'

The king and queen joined the Duchess of Kent at Euston Station on 16 December to say their goodbyes to the Duke and Duchess of Gloucester. Alice had recently given birth and now the young family, complete with the addition of three-month-old Richard, were embarking on a new life in Australia. Despite original doubts about Prince Henry, he had shown great loyalty and common sense and was about to take on his highest office yet. 'I hope they will be a success,' Queen Mary confided to her brother. 'It may give Harry a chance of showing what he is made of.'[42] The Gloucesters' journey was top secret and the small royal party at Euston, enveloped in London fog and the steam from the trains, did not attract attention. The day was grimly overshadowed by a dramatic German counter-offensive through the forests of the Ardennes. The Germans repeated their successful tactics against France in 1940 and Allied armies in Belgium and Luxemburg were taken by surprise.

The Gloucesters reached Liverpool and embarked on the New Zealand steamship, *Rimutaka*. The duchess was worried at the prospect of taking her two young boys through an Irish Sea still infested with German submarines. Rough seas, gale-force winds and a twisting route to avoid U-boats added to the tension. This increased still more on the second night when the duchess was hurriedly woken and instructed to dress and prepare for any eventuality. The captain of the ship had already advised her, with painful frankness, that if they had to take to the lifeboats, the new baby would stand little chance of survival from exposure. Dramatically, Richard's nanny had told Alice she was quite prepared to go down with the ship and the new prince. Now this prospect seemed suddenly real as the ship lurched with such violence that Alice herself almost passed out with a blow to the head when a trunk was flung across the cabin. Out of the darkness came a tiny voice of protest. 'I don't like it,' declared two-year-old Prince William.[43] He had been promised an adventure, but this was too much. Just as they turned to face the full blast of the Atlantic Ocean, the convoy almost passed directly over a waiting U-boat. *Rimutaka* had swiftly changed her direction as one of their convoy attacked and sank the German submarine. The princes heard the depth charges and waited, wide-eyed.

The first leg of their journey to the Mediterranean was not one conducive to settling young children. The ship's zig-zagging route in heavy seas made their sons so unwell that William had no interest in his third birthday when the crew wheeled in a magnificent birthday cake. Finally they reached the sanctuary of Malta. 'The harbour area is a very sorry sight,' Gloucester told his mother, but everyone's spirits rose at the warm welcome, with William happily waving to everyone.[44] All too soon it was time to continue their journey eastwards where they stopped in Colombo, Ceylon. Lord Mountbatten, now Supreme Allied Commander South-East Asia Command, took the royal party for an afternoon of swimming on a beautiful beach shaded with palms. Later over dinner, as the light faded, there was time to talk of the war in Asia. Maps were fetched and against the vivid backdrop of an ocean sunset, Mountbatten outlined to his cousins how the Allies repulsed the Japanese invasion of India, their offensives in Burma and the frustrations of the lack of resources as the military effort was focused on Europe.

It was dark when the Gloucesters embarked once more for the final stage of their journey. The portholes of *Rimutaka* were now blacked out, an ominous reminder of the proximity of the Japanese. On deck there was a constant watch in rough seas for enemy submarines. Unable to open the portholes, the Gloucesters found the heat in their cabins so stifling that they transferred to hammocks on deck. Here the strict rules of blackout still applied; not even a cigarette was permitted after dark. But the days of tension passed without incident, except for the scare when a guard tripped on the hammocks and frightened everyone, most of all himself. They were in sight of the sanctuary of Sydney harbour when news broke of a Japanese submarine close by and the *Rimutaka* docked hurriedly at Woolamaloo for the night. At last the next day the royal party disembarked in Australia where they were escorted along dusty roads to the capital and an ecstatic reception.[45]

There were some teething troubles on reaching Government House in Canberra. The residence had been renovated in anticipation of the arrival of the Duke of Kent, but little of the furniture that he had shipped over could be found. Somewhat disconcertingly the Gloucesters came across one of his sheets, a miracle as the house was bereft of furniture. Fortunately preparations for the royal family had extended to killing several snakes in the surrounding garden, but on the downside, the decorators appeared to have overlooked the need for an electric kettle, fridge or even light fittings. Even trickier the Gloucesters discovered they shared the house with rats, which the duchess, in her defence, tackled with a well-aimed book while waiting for help.[46] The duke, who readily admitted that he was not a man for office work, and had 'even laughed at it', now recognised he had to get to grips with official papers and requested a desk. He was glad to turn to the king for advice on all aspects of the role, although it was hard to maintain the formality and dignity of Buckingham Palace. 'Just as Harry was knighting some old gentleman a mouse dashed past with a tabby cat in hot pursuit,' Alice wrote to Queen Mary. 'It was . . . terribly difficult not to laugh.'[47]

On 23 December Logue was in the study at Windsor Castle absorbed in his customary annotations for the Christmas speech when the king made a surprising suggestion. He felt he was approaching a point where he could tackle the Christmas speech alone, without Logue by his side. For the first time since 1939 Logue could enjoy Christmas Day with his family at Beechgrove House in Sydenham. The two men pondered the idea; would it work? The queen came to join them, full of her customary reassurance. She promised Logue that she and Elizabeth and Margaret would help the king. For both men it was a critical transition. Logue felt 'like a father who is sending his boy to his first public school'.[48]

On Christmas Day 1944, shortly before 3 pm, Logue knew the king would be making his way to the broadcasting room. He, too, left his small family gathering to say a quiet prayer. Logue was waiting alone, full of apprehension as the moment came. Suddenly the king's voice filled the room; not hesitantly or awkwardly but full of assurance. 'As always I am greatly moved by the thought that so vast and friendly an audience can hear the words I speak . . . ' George VI began. He talked 'proudly and gratefully of our fighting men . . . ' He spoke of the wounded, those who were prisoners of war, and families torn apart by the calamities of war. But at last the lamps which the Germans had extinguished all over Europe 'were being re lit . . . The defeat of Germany and Japan is only the first half of our task. The second is to create a world of free men untouched by tyranny . . . ' For the king this was the great enterprise 'of the human spirit— man's unconquerable mind and freedom's holy flame. I believe most surely we shall reach that goal . . . '

The speech was a personal triumph. The king's disability appeared to be in check. Logue was elated and rang to congratulate him, his guests straining to hear the king's voice for themselves on another extension. 'My job is done, Sir,' Logue told the king.[49]

The new-found confidence of the king was perhaps reflected in the news from the front as the net was tightening around the remains of a crumbling Third Reich. The mighty Red Army attacked from the east while the Western Allies closed in from the west and south, against a diminishing German army. The tumultuous events were vividly relayed in cinema screens across the country. In January Soviet forces entered the obliterated city of Warsaw and swept westward almost 300 miles across Poland until they were just over 40 miles from Berlin. The Yalta conference in the Crimea on the Black Sea defined plans for Europe in February. Stalin held the upper hand and won concessions from Roosevelt, overruling Churchill in Poland and across Eastern Europe.

The Allied forces drew nearer to Berlin helped by concentrated bombing of German cities. In mid-February the historic city of Dresden was targeted; the tremendous firestorm sucking escaping citizens into its white-hot depths as though they were weightless. In March it was the turn of Cologne, still sitting serenely on the Rhine as it had for 1,000 years. When the terrible maelstrom was over, the ancient cathedral which had escaped the bombs presided over a wasteland. For mile after mile, rising through the clouds of dust, the once-handsome buildings had been transformed into steep cliffs and craggy heights no longer recognisable as the work of humanity.

But then came news from America. The unthinkable had happened. One of the triumvirate, President Roosevelt, was dead. The king knew that his health was delicate but his death from a stroke on 12 April was a shock. The great patrician was much mourned. 'We shall all feel his loss very much,' the king said to his mother.[50] He was convinced that the president's frailty was 'entirely through overwork due to the war'.[51] For the king and Churchill grief was entwined with concern. Who would replace him?

Central to the belief of King George and Queen Elizabeth that they were fighting a righteous war was the conviction that 'the Nazis are the forces of Evil'.[52] Soviet troops fighting their way across Poland did indeed come across something that broke all previous records of human bestiality: Auschwitz. The largest of the concentration camps was a well-guarded private world where life had no price at all. Its remaining citizens were little more than walking skeletons hardly able to express their joy at being free at last. They were surrounded by the dead; mountainous piles of naked bodies, in death so intimately placed, awaiting what appeared to be ovens. There were children, too, not rosy and plump-cheeked, but terrified, stripped of all humanity. Evidence of horrific experiments on children began to emerge. Living or dead, the same agonisingly tight skins and protruding bones marked them all. A pall hung over the place, and the overwhelming stench of illness and death. The precise organisation of this incomprehensible cruelty was also apparent to the Soviet soldiers. Some 348,000 men's suits and 836,000 women's dresses were neatly folded, along with piles of eye glasses, shoes, dentures and even seven tons of human hair near the gas chambers and crematoria which had been hastily dismantled by the departing Germans.[53]

The scale of the horror continued to unfold before a stunned world that spring: American troops entered Buchenwald, Dachau and Mauthausen, the British drove into Bergen-Belsen, the Soviets liberated Ravensbrück and Theresienstadt . . . and still there were more: Treblinka, Sobibór and Belzec. Labour camps with their cavernous underground chambers where prisoners never saw the light of day were discovered. Many of the liberators themselves were so overwhelmed they could not find the words to express what they saw. 'I have never felt able to describe my emotional reactions when I first came face to face with indisputable evidence of Nazi brutality and ruthless disregard of every shred of decency,' Dwight Eisenhower wrote later. 'I have never at any other time experienced an equal sense of shock.'[54] The king too was appalled. He was told of camps where the troops had 'found bodies littered about the camps & the ovens where they were cremated . . . & we found bodies already stacked in the ovens'. How could this 'bestial maltreatment' have happened? He gave vent to his feelings in his diary: 'the German people are all guilty in allowing these things to happen'.[55] But was this really true? The next day he wrote in more considered terms to his mother: 'The German people don't seem to know what they have allowed their leaders to do.'[56]

The king's cousin, Philipp of Hesse, became an unwitting witness to the Nazis' desperate efforts to disguise evidence of their crimes. At Flossenburg concentration camp during the last months of the war, there were many more hangings on the gallows outside his window. Stripped of their identity, even their clothes, Jews and other prisoners were taken naked from the guard room to the place of execution. In April, Philipp was herded on to a transport van with other notable prisoners and taken south to Dachau concentration camp.[57] But with the advance of the Americans at the end of the month he was ordered into a truck and driven around the Alps as the Nazis made a last frantic effort to evade the advancing enemy. In a particular refinement of cruelty he was finally informed of the fate of his wife, Mafalda, who had been imprisoned at Buchenwald. During an Allied bombing raid on the nearby armaments factory the previous summer her barracks had caught fire. She had been trapped under burning wreckage for some time before rescuers could reach her, still alive, but with her arm 'burned almost to the bone'.[58] An attempt was made to amputate her arm, but she died soon afterwards. Her horrific death took its toll of Hesse as he was shunted from place to place by the Germans. He and the other prisoners were told they would be killed before they could be captured. But he was caught by the Americans in the Italian Tyrol, and promptly arrested. George VI would learn of the fate of his cousin and other prominent German prisoners which was reported in the British papers in the closing days of the war.

Soviet soldiers shook hands with the Americans on the River Elbe on 25 April and the electrifying finale to the war was captured in newsreels for the world to see. On 28 April Mussolini and his mistress were shot by Italian partisans. Their battered bodies were hung upside down on meat hooks in a petrol station the following day before a vengeful crowd. The all-powerful would-be Caesar was strung up by his heels, his face beaten to a grotesque disfigurement.

In the depths of his safe and well-appointed underground bunker in the centre of Berlin, where the roar of the fast-approaching front line was dulled, Hitler was told of the vengeance wreaked on the body of his former ally. He had a plan to avoid the reckoning. The German people had fallen short of the task that was required of them. Himmler had betrayed him. The glorious Third Reich which he had created so brilliantly was crumbling all around. The Soviets were mere yards away, fighting to the death, revelling in laying Germany waste. It was time to leave the mess to those who had failed him. The mood in the bunker was calm but sombre as Hitler married his faithful mistress, Eva

Braun. She did her best, wore the dress that charmed him most and, smiling, pledged to share his fate. They both took cyanide, and to be sure, he shot himself and that was that. No self-doubt, no laments, no remorse for the 60 million sacrificed to his dreams. His secretary, Traudl Junge, later recalled his extraordinary dissociation from the almighty calamity of Europe that he had caused. 'His face was like a mask,' she said. He appeared to have a complete mental disconnection from the chaos, making his exit with the ease of putting on a new jacket and leaving the room.[59]

The world was waiting as the loathed Nazi leadership was hunted down. Joseph Goebbels and his wife poisoned their six young children and then killed themselves in the bunker shortly after Hitler's death. Heinrich Himmler attempted to flee but was eventually detained by the British and killed himself. Hermann Goering surrendered to the Americans on 6 May; Robert Ley was arrested in his pyjamas ten days later. Somehow, in the chaos, Joachim von Ribbentrop, a key architect of this immense catastrophe, slipped through the net of the foreign armies, still on the run in the crumbling ruins of his country.[60]

The Windsors, about to leave their safe wartime island, saw the fall of Germany, the flattened cities, the concentration camps with their ghostly skeletal inhabitants, and the architects of the Third Reich, caught on camera, desperate to escape. They could see for themselves the full horror of Hitler's Germany in the newsreels. The duke was in the wilderness, setting out with his wife on 3 May to Miami and an unknown future. Such was his fear of the Communists he was no longer sure if France was a safe refuge and his welcome in Britain was uncertain.

The end was near. Peace would soon be declared. So much hope was embodied in that word, yet it was hard to know what 'peace' would feel like after six years of war. The queen confided to a friend that she felt 'numbed' and 'stunned as well'.[61] Gradually the idea of peace, and all it meant, filtered through the collective psyche. The great triumphant finale was in sight. No detail was overlooked to prepare for the great day. In the royal stables the BBC *Forces Programme* was repeatedly played to the horses to acquaint them with unfamiliar sounds for state victory parades.[62] At the palace, the king had the repaired balcony tested for safety.[63] The Archbishop of Canterbury issued guidelines for appropriate forms of service to give thanks. Almost everyone in the country was planning a street party. There would be music and dancing and the lights would come on again. There was a last-minute rush for flags and bunting.[64] The king, who suddenly seemed very worn, prepared his victory speech.

And suddenly Britain woke up to the wonder of it all. The announcement of the unconditional surrender of the armed forces of Nazi Germany on 8 May was a day so long awaited, so well deserved, like no other. Victory Day had arrived. Tens of thousands descended on the capital. At 3 pm Big Ben struck and London fell silent. The prime minister broadcast to the nation from the War Cabinet Office, the very place where six years before Neville Chamberlain had announced the start of the Second World War. Churchill's voice was magnified to the waiting multitude through loudspeakers set up across central London. It was all over. The evil doers 'are now prostrate before us', he declared. 'Advance Britannia! Long live the cause of freedom. Long live the King.'

Bells rang out across London, tugs on the Thames sounded their horns, and the vast mass of people began to sing the National Anthem. When Churchill tried to make his way back from Downing Street to the House, he received such an ovation that his car was brought to a standstill, engulfed by a devoted crowd who pushed him all the way. People wanted to see their leader, to touch him, to let their babies see him, as though something of Churchill's spirit, embodied in that recognisable frame and broad smile, might be passed on. Eventually he arrived, responding to the elation in the House with his characteristic half bow. MPs cheered and waved handkerchiefs; some were moved to tears.[65] Later he appeared on the balcony at the Ministry of Health in Whitehall, puffing on a cigar, his hand raised in his VE sign. 'My dear friends, this is your victory . . .' he told the crowd. 'No, it is yours . . .' roared the reply.

The Mall was jammed with people drunk on victory, as though the high spirits were intoxicating. People were massing outside Buckingham Palace. They wanted to see their king, to share in that rich communion: six years of suffering, anguish and deprivation, and now hope, exploding at last into near hysteria. 'We want the King . . . We want the king,' they chanted. At last the feeling of peace was real. In memory this night could never fade.

Behind the scenes in Buckingham Palace, the two princesses, Elizabeth and Margaret, prepared to face the crowd with the king and queen. The king as usual looked smart in his naval uniform; Princess Elizabeth wore her ATS uniform: the formal dress perhaps a private bond between father and daughter. The queen and Princess Margaret were dressed in pale summer colours. Outside, beyond the doors, was the unmistakable sound of public clamour. As the balcony doors opened, a mighty roar came from the crowd, and as they stepped out on to the balcony, the ecstatic crowd roared louder still. This was the quintessential moment of victory.

Below was a sea of upturned faces, a throng that filled the streets down the Mall and beyond. The princesses hesitated slightly at the vast crowd, but these were the people of England, loyal and enraptured with their king and queen, and it was thrilling. People were in their best dresses and brightest clothes; babies had red, white and blue ribbons in their hair; even dogs had victory bows. Some people had climbed on lamp posts or statues for a better view; one man was scrambling up the palace gates. Down the Mall the press of people blurred into a mass of colour stretching into the distance. The cheering would not stop. The family came out again, and yet again, with Churchill beside them at 5.30. And still the crowds would not disperse. Eight times the royal family emerged on the balcony that day.

Lionel Logue at the palace witnessed their last appearance. Suddenly, and for the first time in years, the floodlights were switched on. Surrounded by the drabness of wartime London, the scene at the palace looked magical: like a 'fairyland', he thought. The clamour of the crowd intensified. The royal family stepped out once more, and Logue noted the queen's diamond tiara glittered in the lights as she turned to wave.[66]

Princess Elizabeth years later recalled that day. 'The excitement of the floodlights being switched on got through to us. My sister and I realised we couldn't see what the crowds were enjoying . . . so we asked my parents if we could go out and see for ourselves . . . After crossing Green Park we stood outside and shouted, "We want the King," and were successful in seeing my parents on the balcony, having cheated slightly because we sent a message into the house to say we were waiting outside. I think it was one of the most memorable nights of my life.'[67]

As night fell there was dancing in Piccadilly Circus, bonfires were lit, barrel organs played and the young princesses, escorted by officers, scarves on their heads, slipped unrecognised among the people. 'London was an amazing sight,' observed one nineteen year old in the crowd. 'Like an enormous Christmas party.'[68] The jubilant scenes in the capital were being repeated across the country. Even Queen Mary abandoned her dignified reserve and left Badminton House for the local club where the village was celebrating, she told Gloucester, 'and we sang songs with them while they drank beer and cyder, a most friendly affair'.[69]

Inside the palace, the king and Logue went to the broadcasting room, now elevated from the shelter to a room on the ground floor overlooking the garden. In the gathering dusk, the floodlights falling across the lawn gave the place an air of enchantment, Logue observed. The queen, looking radiant, came to wish the king well. Then came the cue light.

'Speaking from our Empire's oldest capital city, war-battered but never for one moment daunted or dismayed, speaking from London, I ask you to join with me in that act of thanksgiving . . . ' began the king.

To Logue, the strain on George VI was quite suddenly apparent. He had been beside the king for every wartime speech, but now found himself helpless as engrained fatigue appeared to overtake his former student. The king's monotone delivery lapsed into heart-stopping pauses and audible gulps, his efforts to control his speech showing visibly on his face. The words seemed to overwhelm him. 'Germany, the enemy who drove all Europe into war,' continued George VI, 'has been finally overcome . . . There is great comfort in the thought that the years together, that the years of darkness and danger in which the children of our country have grown up, are over, and please God, for ever. We shall have failed, and the blood of our dearest will have flowed in vain, if the victory which they died to win does not lead to a lasting peace, founded on justice and good-will . . . This is the task to which now honour binds us. In the hour of danger we humbly committed our cause into the hand of God and He has been our strength and shield. Let us thank Him for His mercies and in this hour of victory commit ourselves and our new task to the guidance of that same strong hand.'[70]

When he finished the crowd was still roaring its approval. Noël Coward summed up the mood of the day. 'We all roared ourselves hoarse . . . I suppose this is the greatest day in our history.'[71] On this triumphant day words hardly mattered. Elation filled the air. The island race had won and claimed 'this blessed plot, this earth, this realm, this England'.

13

FOR VALOUR

For Valour.

—Churchill to George VI on his death in 1952

Five years of war had served as a crucible that transformed the fortunes of each prince. The Duke of Kent was dead, in circumstances still mired in uncertainty. The Duke of Gloucester was lost to the European scene on the other side of the world in Australia. The former king was destroyed in all but name, bitter about his apparent continuing exile. But the fourth, George VI, appeared to have risen to new heights of achievement, redefining the monarchy for the modern age.

The king's meteoric rise came at a high price. Although his slim figure created an impression of youthfulness, it was no longer possible to disguise the toll that the stress of six years of war and heavy smoking had exacted. Both the king and his prime minister were utterly exhausted. Both men had pushed themselves beyond their limits to deal with each emergency, the urgent demands placed upon them invariably taking precedence over personal considerations. Churchill described himself as 'physically so feeble that I had to be carried upstairs in a chair by the Marines from the Cabinet meetings . . . '[1] The king feared he was burned out and told Gloucester, 'I shall be dead before getting north [to Balmoral].'[2]

The strain was apparent to those who knew King George well. The vitality was drained from his face, which looked worn and sometimes gaunt. The physical pressures of being poised to tackle each new crisis were so habitual that he could not adjust overnight. 'Feel rather jaded from it all,' he wrote in his diary shortly after VE day. 'I have found it difficult to rejoice or relax as there is still so much hard work ahead to deal with.'[3] For a man still young at forty-nine, who should have been in his prime, it was clear his slight frame had given more than he was able to give. He did allow himself one precious day's relaxation to take his older daughter to the races at Ascot. She had missed so much growing up in the war but nothing must spoil this, Elizabeth's first race meeting.[4]

The jubilation of VE day was tempered by the knowledge of the ongoing Japanese war. A generation of young men did not yet know whether it was their fate to join the continuing horror unfolding in the Far East. The king was one of the few in Britain who knew the world's first atom bomb was close to completion. On 12 July Churchill told him 'the Tube Alloy Experiment'—as they called it—was successful and would soon be dropped on Japan.[5] Stretching into the future, the king saw a troubled road ahead in a post-war nuclear world fraught with unknowns; a future which he viewed as neither 'very peaceful nor restful'.[6]

Looking back at the past, after the First World War his father was head of an empire not only still intact, but enlarged with a further 13 million new subjects. Now the Second World War was sweeping away Britain's supremacy. The country was close to bankruptcy, anti-colonial movements were gaining momentum and two new superpowers, America and the Soviet Union were fast emerging to confront each other. What good were smiles and handshakes on the Elbe as, in Churchill's words, 'the Russian bear sprawled over Europe' and America was poised to test a super-bomb that could wipe out an entire city in seconds? The king had confidence in Churchill to carry Britain's interests on a world stage, but elections were underway in Britain. The prime minister saw the king after one four-day tour in which he made fifty speeches to huge audiences through his loudspeaker. The king could see election worries were wearing Churchill down.[7]

There was another, deeply personal matter that intruded sharply on the king's peace of mind that spring. In the closing weeks of the war the American army in the Harz Mountains of Germany stumbled across a large hoard of German archives which were taken to Marburg Castle in the state of Hesse. The king was worried, but could not discuss his fear, that there might well be documents relating to his brother's dealings with the Nazis that could hurt the royal family. Then almost immediately came news of a hidden archive buried deep within the surrounding forest that the German leadership meant never to be discovered. Amongst the top-secret documents was indeed a file on the Duke and Duchess of Windsor. What would the Americans reveal to the world?

Since the summer of 1940, when the king was first alerted to intelligence linking his brother to the Nazi regime, he had known there could be further incriminating records in the vanquished country. Now these fears appeared to be confirmed. He could not see the duke's Marburg file immediately but had to wait for the official process. All captured German papers were being carefully logged and translated and shared between the Allies. The German archives were attracting serious interest. There were Nazi war criminals to be brought to justice at Nuremberg.

Without waiting to see the duke's Marburg file, the king authorised a highly sensitive mission into Germany of his own. He knew that several of his cousins, including Philipp and Christoph of Hesse and Charles Edward, Duke of Saxe-Coburg, had held prominent positions in the Nazi party. Even the ex-kaiser and his son Frederick Wilhelm had given their support to Hitler in the 1930s. Was there a risk that evidence might exist about these grandsons and great-grandsons of Queen Victoria in Germany that cast them in a bad light? More alarming still, would the records incriminate his own brothers, Windsor or even Kent, who had met his German cousins before the war?

Soon after the Americans liberated Kronberg near Frankfurt in West Germany, the royal librarian, Owen Morshead, together with a young intelligence officer, Anthony Blunt, set out on a delicate and risky assignment. Anthony Blunt, who was working for MI5, was also Surveyor of the King's Pictures and was useful because he had excellent German, Morshead noted.[8] Their destination was Schloss Friedrichshof, a magnificent castle in Kronberg once owned by the George VI's aunt, Princess Victoria, which had passed to the Hesse family, of which Prince Philipp was the oldest surviving son. The purpose of Morshead and Blunt's task has never been satisfactorily resolved.

Officially it has always been claimed that they were simply to retrieve family treasures, several thousand letters between Queen Victoria and her daughter, Princess Victoria, before looters helped themselves. But historians have long speculated that the search for family heirlooms was respectable cover for a much more sensitive search for any damaging Nazi records. Additional searches carried out by Morshead and Blunt do suggest that they were there to find any incriminating papers, hide them from prying eyes, and get them back to England.[9] Morshead and Blunt were later sent to the home of the ex-kaiser in the Netherlands and to Schloss Marienburg near Hanover, owned by Princes of Hanover who were loyal to the Nazis and related by marriage to the Danish, Greek and Spanish thrones.[10]

These troubling searches in Germany were taking place at a tumultuous time in British politics. The king was busy with appointments on the morning of 26 July while keeping an eye on the election results that were coming in. By lunchtime it was obvious there was a Labour landslide.[11] He felt sad when Churchill, for once on time, came to resign at 7 pm. The old Bulldog had been dealt a body blow and the king felt Churchill's pain. He struggled to find the right words and found himself talking about how 'ungrateful' the public seemed after the way Winston had led them.[12] 'My heart was too full to say much at our last meeting,' the king wrote to Churchill on 31 July. Still trying to do justice to all that had transpired, he wrote again that day. He felt his prime minister had shown 'supreme courage', and 'I shall miss your counsel to me more than I can say'.[13] The immediate severance of two great friends whose affection had been tested for many years under extreme circumstances was impossible to express with just words, except of course, unsaid, they both knew each other's true worth.

The king endeavoured to build a relationship with his new prime minister, Clement Attlee, although awkward pauses and long silences marked their first meetings. Lord Mountbatten tried to reassure Bertie that he was the 'old experienced campaigner' that people looked to in a world that was changing at a giddying speed.[14] But it was hard not to feel cut adrift as he said his goodbyes to the familiar faces of his outgoing ministers, Lord Simon, Lord Beaverbrook, Anthony Eden and others who had shared the journey with him since the abdication.[15] The king knew the Americans were about to use the largest bomb in the history of warfare. Nothing would be the same again. A few days later, the world reeled as the detonation of the nuclear bombs over Hiroshima and Nagasaki in Japan ushered in the atomic age.

Churchill may have been bruised by the election result, he may have been preoccupied by post-war Europe, the dawn of the nuclear age and the Japanese surrender—but he did not lose sight of the duke's Marburg file. Amidst the flattened cities and ruins of war, for him the British monarchy, that thousand-year pageant lit up with colour and history, stood out as a precious beacon of continuity and stability. The careless folly of one family member could not be allowed to damage its reputation. He found he was able to sideline his more democratic instincts. 'I earnestly trust it may be possible to destroy all traces of these German intrigues,' he wrote on 26 August to Clement Attlee.[16]

Declassified documents show Clement Attlee's government already had the matter in hand. Ernest Bevin, the former General Secretary of Britain's largest trade union, the Transport and General Workers' Union, was now Foreign Secretary and had written to Attlee on 13 August 1945 suggesting 'we should try to persuade the United States government to co-operate with us in suppressing the documents concerned'. Bevin believed it was not in the public interest to release the duke's Marburg file: 'The documents have no bearing on war crimes or the general history of the war' and yet, because of the individuals concerned, 'a disclosure would in my opinion do grave harm to the national interest'.[17]

Bevin helpfully set out for the prime minister just *how* the damaging evidence on the British monarchy should be suppressed. 'The only two copies which are known to exist are single microfilms sent to the Foreign Office and the [US] State Department respectively,' he wrote. He had already asked officials in Washington to place 'the maximum restriction' on their copy but there was still a crucial problem, he told the prime minister: 'There remains the question of the original in Marburg.' Bevin had established that access to the captured archives in Germany could be obtained quite easily and there was a real risk of 'irresponsible disclosure . . . We have therefore asked Sir William Strang in Germany to consider what steps can be taken . . . to suppress the file or keep it concealed.'[18]

The efficient Strang soon had the problem under control in Germany. A top-secret memo from the Earl of Halifax in Washington to the Foreign Office on 13 October reveals 'that the [US] State Department are still unaware that the original documents about the Duke are no longer at Marburg'.[19]

The British had whisked the duke's master file back to London—without the knowledge of their American allies—where it was safely stored in the vaults of the Foreign Office.[20] All that remained to be done was to persuade the Americans to destroy their copy and the duke's German file would never see the light of day.

For George VI the matter was not so readily disposed of. At some point that summer he, too, had access to details from the duke's Marburg file. He had already caught a glimpse of his brother's behaviour in Spain and Portugal after the fall of France through British intelligence at the time. But now, with Hitler's invasion threats and bombing still recent memories, he could reflect on the actual telegrams between Ribbentrop and his agents in the summer of 1940 and the harrowing prospect of what would have happened to his family under Hitler's regime. The entire German plot seemed to hinge on his brother's assumed treachery and betrayal. Churchill may have dismissed the telegrams as mere 'German intrigues', but could they be so conveniently dismissed?

So much about his brother—his views, his sense of entitlement, his hunger for status and money—was consistent with the content of the German telegrams. Now his brother's selfish, possibly traitorous, behaviour appeared to be caught on record for all time. 'The Duke was considering making a public statement disassociating himself from the present English policy and breaking with his brother,' German Ambassador Stohrer had written in 1940.[21] Even more repugnant was the idea of his brother waiting as a compliant 'king across the water' ready 'for any personal sacrifice' once bombing brought the British

34

copy sent Sir O Sargant
The Harvey
German Dept.

Win/45/22

[Cypher]   P R I S E C

FROM WASHINGTON TO FOREIGN OFFICE.

Earl of Halifax.   D. 11.47 a.m. 13th October, 1945.
No. 6827.
                                R. 5.00 p.m. 13th October, 1945.
13th October, 1945.

                              - - - - -

IMPORTANT.

DEDIP.

TOP SECRET.

        My immediately preceding telegram.

        You will see that in the course of their reply regarding the
general use of these German archives, the State Department have
also answered our particular representations on the subject of the
papers relating to the Duke of Windsor, dealt with in correspondence
ending with your telegram 9972. The proposal in this latter
telegram was put to them immediately on receipt so that they had
time to consider it before making their present reply.

        2. In handing Balfour this aide mémoire Atcheson was at
pains to explain that the inability of the State Department to
meet out wish that the microfilm in question in their possession
should be destroyed arose from the explicit provisions to the
contrary in the relevant act of Congress.

        3. He was also at pains to reiterate the assurance conveyed
in the last sentence of the aide mémoire that the State
Department were resolved to ensure that the documents about the
Duke were withheld from any publicity.

        4. Incidentally it appears from the aide mémoire that
State Department are still unaware that the original documents
about the Duke are no longer at Marburg.

O.T.P.

Cypher from the Earl of Halifax in Washington on 13 October 1945 warning
the British Foreign Office that the US State Department was unable to destroy
their microfilm copy of the Duke's incriminating Marburg file (PARA 2) and 'are
still unaware' that the British had removed the original from Germany (PARA 4)
(THE NATIONAL ARCHIVES)

to the negotiating table.[22] The Duke 'had agreed upon a code word' with his Portuguese host, Santo, 'on receipt of which he would immediately come back over'.[23] Sitting in his palace still bearing the scars of war, everything was cast in a new light. If he and his family had perished in the Battle of Britain or been forced to abdicate, would his brother have been conveniently waiting in the wings as a pro-Nazi prospective monarch? At a time when he had needed his loyalty most, was David prepared to act as traitor not only towards his country but to his own brother?

That summer, Balmoral did not bring its usual soothing relief from the strain. The king was still plagued by the contents of the duke's Marburg file in the autumn.[24] The very existence of the German file put the king in an acute predicament. He wished to protect his brother, but could not act in an undemocratic way or against the advice of his ministers. He knew the duke had sailed from America on 15 September. It would not be long before his brother returned with all his familiar demands. The duke was keen to meet in October. But the prospect of such an encounter was fraught with unknown undercurrents.

George VI was a principled man. He had a record of even-handedness when dealing with suspected quislings. When all around had declaimed the King of Belgium and Prince Paul of Yugoslavia, George VI had investigated, considered the evidence, and taken a measured line rather than joining the chorus of condemnation. In both cases he had taken the trouble to understand the pressures they were under that had led them to take a decision damaging to Allied interests.

But when it came to his brother, from the king's point of view, there was little that could be said in his defence. The Duke of Windsor was only ever under pressures of his own making. Each new betrayal was brought on by decisions that he had made and flaws in his own character. Over the years the duke appeared to have courted situations that deepened the conflict, all with a view to regaining status for his wife's glory and vanity. He had wasted energy maintaining past grievances and declined to show any insight or remorse. The German telegrams underlined the consequences of all this most painfully. The king's actions suggest that he really believed the duke had crossed the line. The Marburg file implied that his brother had contemplated the ultimate betrayal. For all the king's hard work, in his eyes once again the good name of the monarchy was held hostage to his brother's appalling behaviour. Behind the scenes the king took the lead in determining the family's united attitude. He told his mother on 23 September, 'we must take the line that he cannot live here'.[25]

When the brothers did meet on 5 October any hopes the duke entertained for a full reconciliation did not last long. Queen Mary joined them, possibly to help Bertie establish a firm and united family position. Unaware of the problem of the telegrams, David waited for his moment until after dinner before he raised the issue so essential to his peace of mind. He spoke of his wife. Would his mother receive her?

There was a silence that went on just too long. It was a silence that filled the room, swollen with the hurt that had divided the family since the abdication. The king described it as 'a stony silence'.

It allowed for all concerned to reflect on the essential question. A son was asking to come home, to be once again accepted with his wife. Immeasurable time seemed to pass before Queen Mary could bring herself to answer. 'She replied that she could never do so,' recorded the king, 'as nothing has happened to alter the circumstances which had led to his abdication.' She spoke in such a way that 'he could see this was final'.[26]

The following day the king met the duke and backed up his mother's strong emotional response with arguments. The king would not yield to the duke's demands. The duke's return to England to create a permanent home with Wallis was unwelcome.[27] Just how much the king revealed of the new predicament raised by the German telegrams is not clear. It seems likely that he hinted at enough to make his brother understand the damaging way his actions in 1940 might be construed and this lent weight to the family view that this was not the time for the ex-king to push his old demands for Wallis. The king did not raise his voice or lose his calm. And if David was shocked or angry that just when there was a chance of returning to his old life, captured German documents should be held against him—there is no record of it. The issues between them were discussed 'very thoroughly and quietly', the king wrote in his diary.[28] A certain polite and frosty distance separated them palpably. They were now strangers to each other, brothers in name only.

The duke bowed to his brother's wishes. That he gave in so readily after years of longing to return suggests he recognised the dangers of the incriminating file. 'While . . . I was sorry when your answer was in the affirmative to my question as to whether my taking up residence in Britain would be an embarrassment to you, I can see your point of view and am therefore prepared to put your feelings before my own in this matter . . . ' the duke conceded on 18 October.[29]

Churchill did continue to find time for the duke—perhaps out of respect for the monarchy, perhaps because he understood, better than most, the world that the duke had come from and the pain of his giddying fall from grace.

In November Churchill once again raised the hope that the duke might be able to take a diplomatic post 'with some undefined connection to the British Embassy' in Washington.[30] The king, too, championed the idea but none the less it foundered on an unsympathetic response in both Washington and London, where new Labour ministers were quick to spot obstacles to creating a post with special status for the duke. The diplomatic Walter Monckton was summoned once more to inform the duke that the king 'can do no more than I have done'.[31]

The duke could not quite believe it was all over. It was hard to accept that the doors to the palaces which he had taken for granted as a child were no longer open to him. He brooded on his predicament. He chided George VI that the most he had ever been offered was a position in 'a third class British colony' and now it was not clear whether he would be offered anything at all.

His rootlessness continued as he waited for the opportunity that never came while his wife busied herself in post-war Paris reviving their court in miniature around them, entertaining with candles in place of electricity, her numerous staff in attendance and still in royal livery. They were still waiting in the spring when they moved back to their villa at La Croë in the south of France. Wallis realised that the king and queen preferred them to make a permanent home in America without a specially created post, but she confessed to her aunt, 'I dread facing up to the press once again in that country.'[32]

The duke found it hard to accept that his pro-Nazi views had been misplaced. He maintained that 'if Hitler had been differently handled, war might have been avoided', a conviction which became an unshakeable point of faith with him.[33] One *Times* correspondent, Frank Giles, interviewing him years later, was shocked to find the duke's views were 'bilious and distorted'. The duke told Giles, 'There'd have been *no* war if Eden hadn't mishandled Mussolini. It was all his fault . . . Together of course with Roosevelt and the Jews.'[34] The duke also held to the conviction that he might have affected the course of history. 'Whether or not I could have prevented World War II had I remained king is an imponderable,' he later said to the writer Gerald Hamilton.[35]

The ex-king also found it hard to adjust to permanent exile. His beloved former home, Fort Belvedere, near Windsor Castle, was still untenanted. It occurred to him he might be able to enjoy it for at least part of the year. But the palace remained silent on the question of its use. The duke had one last try in 1946 to be reunited with his homeland. Without a hint of rancour he asked if he might return to England after his death, a question designed to add to his brother's discomfort. He set out his wishes to be buried at Fort Belvedere.

This did draw a response from the palace. An architect was consulted and designs were soon being drafted for a mausoleum in the grounds of Fort Belvedere. The ex-king could return home on his death.

Hamburg in June 1945 was a shell of a city. The obliterating firestorm of the Allies' Operation Gomorrah had seen to that. Gone was the grandeur of the handsome blocks of period houses and civic buildings, to be replaced with the chaos and misery of post-war Germany. But out in the suburbs there was a lodging house still standing run by a woman tough enough to have survived the transformation of her city. In early May, without asking any questions, she took in a new lodger, a quiet, unkempt man who rarely left his room and listened carefully to the radio.

The man had not taken the poison that was hidden on his body. Instead he began writing 'to the leaders of the British Empire' what he saw as Hitler's last message. 'I do not know if you wish to hear the political testament of a deceased man . . . ' Ribbentrop began in a grovelling account that bore all the hallmarks of delusion. 'I could imagine that its contents might be adapted to heal wounds . . . [and] . . . help bring about a better future for all people . . . ' He, Germany's Foreign Minister, was not in charge of creating German foreign policy, he declared. This was dictated by Hitler, for whom his fanatical devotion was undimmed. 'English-German collaboration has to his last hour always remained the political creed of the Fuhrer . . . '[36]

Ribbentrop's forays from his room, in dark glasses, his hat pulled over his face, were sufficiently infrequent that he did not know his image was posted in public places. The Allies had no intention of letting such a high-ranking Nazi slip through the net. So it was with some excitement that a Lieutenant Jimmy Adam at the local British headquarters received a tip-off in mid-June concerning the whereabouts of the last senior Nazi still on the run. He hurried to the lodging house. The door opened to reveal a startled landlady in her nightclothes who professed to know nothing. But it was not long before Adam's NCOs produced Germany's Foreign Minister, still in his pyjamas, and looking so haggard as to be almost unrecognisable. To Adam's surprise, when this excellent news was reported to senior officers there was a problem. The Americans had also just arrested a 'Ribbentrop'. How many Ribbentrops were there? The confusion was quickly dispatched by Ribbentrop's own sister who identified the dishevelled man in Hamburg as her brother.

Within weeks, Ribbentrop, now warily reunited with Hermann Goering, Dr Ley and other surviving members of the Nazi leadership, was flown across Germany to Nuremberg. From the plane windows he was forced to confront the reality of his foreign policy. Even Nuremberg, once the stage for the grandiose dreams and rallies of a 1,000-year Reich immortalised in such films as *Triumph of the Will*, was reduced to a pile of rubble save for the courthouse and jail, still standing by a stroke of serendipity. The flags of the Allies flew where gigantic Nazi banners had once hung and off-duty American soldiers fooled around in the remains of the great stadium.

The wheels of post-war justice turned slowly but, in time, the Nuremberg trials disposed of Ribbentrop and other Nazi leaders. Two of those who had proudly shown off Nazi Germany to the Windsors nine years previously committed suicide in October 1946 before their death sentences could be carried out. Hermann Goering managed to obtain cyanide that was smuggled into his cell.[37] Dr Robert Ley ended his life hanging from a toilet pipe using strips ripped from a towel.[38]

Following their deaths, it fell to Ribbentrop to be the first Nazi leader to be led to the execution chamber in Nuremberg jail. The man who had allegedly courted the mistress of the Prince of Wales with seventeen carnations and tried to buy the loyalty of the ex-king of England with 50 million Swiss francs was found guilty of war crimes and crimes against humanity. The court found that he had played 'an important part in Hitler's "final solution" of the Jewish question', he had 'assisted in criminal policies particularly those involving the extermination of the Jews' and his collaboration with Hitler in such crimes 'was wholehearted'.[39] On 16 November 1946, his hands in manacles, he walked up thirteen steps to the execution platform. The hangman adjusted the rope and pulled the lever. Ribbentrop dropped through the trap. Fate had one more cruel twist in store. The hanging was bungled and some witnesses claim it took him nearly twenty minutes to die.

Rudolf Hess was transferred from British custody to Nuremberg where he too was tried as a war criminal despite concerns about his mental health.[40] Following a verdict of life imprisonment, Prisoner No. 7 spent years alone in Spandau Prison in Germany, his mind increasingly disturbed. Appeals by his lawyer to release him on humanitarian grounds were turned down by the Soviets, whose unfailing suspicion that he knew the Nazis were about to invade the Soviet Union in 1941 ensured he would never be freed.

Despite two years in a Nazi concentration camp and the brutal treatment endured by his wife, Prince Philipp of Hesse faced a post-war world where he was categorised as No. 53 on the list of most wanted Nazis.[41] He was moved from camp to camp, often summoned to give evidence in the trials of others. During his incarceration, rough justice was meted out to the Hesse family. The Americans gave them just four hours to leave their imposing castle at Schloss Friedrichshof, the seat of family pride and security. Looting began on a small scale but it was not long before the family's fabled jewellery collection also vanished, stolen from a concealed chamber in their cellar by members of the American guard. Prince Philipp's surviving brothers, Prince Wolfgang and Prince Richard, went through a denazification court and were released within a couple of years. But the court reached a tougher verdict for Prince Philipp as 'an offender' in Category II with stiff penalties and fines that would strip him of 30 per cent of his property as well as other assets. This was reduced on appeal to Category III, or 'lesser offender', and eventually to Category IV, 'fellow traveller', but by now legal costs on top of the penalties had significantly reduced his estate.[42]

The Hesses were not the only German descendants of Queen Victoria to be caught up in the denazification process. The illustrious House of Saxe-Coburg, of which Queen Victoria's husband, Prince Albert, was the most famous member, also fell under suspicion. Charles Edward, Duke of Saxe-Coburg, who had first spied on the new king, Edward VIII, in 1936, had continued to represent the Nazi party throughout the war and his sons had fought on the German side.[43] His confidential reports 'Only for the Fuhrer and Party Member v. Ribbentrop', briefing them on Edward VIII's views, were among the captured German documents which finally reached the hands of 'C', Sir Stewart Menzies.[44] Saxe-Coburg was imprisoned by the Americans and his atonement payment left him impoverished after the war with most of his property confiscated.

The net to catch potential war criminals was cast ever wider in this fevered atmosphere, the press in hot pursuit of prospective villains without waiting for the legal process. Opening the *Sunday Times* on 3 March 1946 from the comfort of Coppins, Marina was alarmed to read her brother-in-law was branded a war criminal who must be brought to justice.[45] A campaign ran in the press demanding that Prince Paul be transported from South Africa to face trial at Nuremberg.[46] The fact that the Soviets had gained control of his country, branded him an 'enemy of the state' and seized his homes did nothing to redeem him in British eyes. Prince Paul hoped that the strengthening grip of communism in his country would vindicate his earlier pro-Nazi stance and he would no longer be regarded as a traitor in England. But the campaign against him and Olga reached such intensity in 1946 that they began to fear for the safety of their children at school in Johannesburg.

The traditional royal policy of strengthening dynastic power through marriage exemplified by Queen Victoria continued to trap her descendants in the tumult of post-war Europe. Many of those who were not separated from their sovereignties by the actions of the Nazis, or the post-war justice that followed, found they were unable to hold on in the face of the relentless Soviet advance. As Soviet interests mounted across Yugoslavia, Bulgaria, Hungary, Romania, Poland and East Germany, people began to refer to a great divide in Europe between an Eastern *bloc* and a Western *bloc*.

Churchill expressed the fears of many in a famous speech in Fulton, Missouri, in March 1946 when he referred to the Kremlin's desire for 'the indefinite expansion of their power and doctrine'. George VI was full of admiration for the speech; 'the whole world has been waiting for a statesman-like statement', he wrote.[47] He welcomed Mr and Mrs Churchill when they returned from America, invariably finding it a relief 'to have a friend to talk to for a change'.[48] The two men were soon engrossed in mulling over the problems facing the country. For the king, Stalin's angry tirade against Churchill 'showed he had a guilty conscience'.[49]

But the all-powerful Stalin was not interested in the views of kings: they were yesterday's men and swiftly dispatched from the Eastern *bloc*. King Michael of Romania, the great-great-grandson of Queen Victoria who had taken on the Fascists in a coup towards the end of the war, faced the Communists in post-war Romania. His palace surrounded, he was forced at gunpoint to sign his own abdication papers in 1948—the last monarch to leave Eastern Europe as the iron curtain fell.[50]

Churchill did try to ward off communist influence in Greece and establish stability. Marina was able to bring her mother to meet the king for tea in the summer of 1945. Princess Nicholas had survived the German occupation of her country with great resilience and 'unmolested', the king noted.[51] But Greece was racked with internal divisions and George II of Greece did not return to his homeland until September 1946 after a referendum. The country was in economic turmoil and the grip of civil war. The strain was too great and he died within the year.

But there was one great-grandson of Queen Victoria who managed to escape the traumas of Fascism, Communism and the process of denazification that had devastated so many of his relations or stripped them of their wealth. Protected by the intriguing machinations of British officialdom, his misdemeanours had so far failed to come to light. In a wonderfully British desire to protect national interests, safeguard the monarchy and avoid 'embarrassment', there was a sustained effort to suppress the Duke of Windsor's Marburg file. Declassified documents show the great lengths British officials went to—and how they almost got away with it, but for a card index.

Firstly an exchange of telegrams in the State Department in Washington in March 1947 reveals that Ernest Bevin had failed to secure American agreement to destroy their copy of the duke's file and, two years on, was still seeking to do so.

'Bevin [British Foreign Minister] says the only other copy was destroyed by the Foreign Office, and asks that we destroy ours to avoid the possibility of a leak of great embarrassment to Windsor's brother [George VI],' wrote the US Secretary of State, General George Marshall, to Dean Acheson in the State Department in March 1947. 'Please attend to this for me and reply for my eyes only.'[52]

So why would the Americans not oblige their British ally and destroy the Washington copy of the duke's Marburg file? The US Secretary of State set out the reasons in 1945: it would be 'unlawful' to sanction returning the copy to the British government or to destroy the passages in question 'without Congressional authorisation and attendant publicity'.[53] Two years on and Bevin reported to Attlee on 30 June 1947 that the American authorities remained 'uncomfortable about the whole question . . . They feel that withdrawal of the file at the instance of one of the Governments concerned in the work of editing constitutes a dangerous precedent.'[54]

Secondly—and potentially even more embarrassing—Bevin alerted the prime minister to the fact that there was a real risk that the British government would be caught out trying to destroy the evidence—by something as simple as the document index. The French were also now participants in the Allied archive project in Germany and had access to the master files. They were likely to raise questions 'and may well have noted from the German card indices this gap in the files of the former German State Secretary', Bevin wrote. The index of original documents in Germany could betray the British government's determined efforts to destroy the evidence. Embarrassment was piling upon embarrassment.[55]

Attlee and Bevin concluded that the original of the duke's Marburg file still held in London must therefore be returned to Germany if requested. If publication became inevitable, there was just the outstanding question of whether the duke should be told. Atlee thought it 'dangerous to forewarn the Duke since that would probably lead him to put out precautionary stories by way of defending himself and these might in turn provoke a leakage'.[56] But a few months later Bevin wrote to Prime Minister Attlee to inform him that agreement had been reached with George VI 'that the papers should be returned to the archives in Berlin on demand . . . ' At the king's request, his brother should have warning 'shortly before the actual publication takes place'.[57]

And so the master version of the duke's file went back to Berlin, an unexploded bomb from the war, the countdown to publication ticking away at the leisurely pace of Allied officialdom.

Meanwhile the doughty Gloucesters were upholding all things decent and British in Australia, embracing extremes of weather, combating a large array of animals, some dangerous, some poisonous, with whom the Australians shared their country, unfailing in their 'old world' charm even if the night's lodgings were less than lordly. With magnificent stamina, they flew to three state capitals on the day that the Pacific war finally ended and the fast pace continued as the duke endeavoured to visit all major cities across the country. Post-war Australia was delightfully rural and 'ramshackle' in the duchess's eyes; its towns distant outposts in a vast landscape dominated by sheep stations; sheep and cattle making their presence felt even in the cities. The king's brother received a generous welcome everywhere; flags were tied to gateposts lining their routes in the country; large cheering crowds in the towns. Even in the most far-flung islands, people 'call themselves English and are *very proud of it*', the duchess observed (her italics). She was astonished to find 'a tremendous veneration for Queen Victoria' on Norfolk Island, 1,000 miles out in the Pacific, an isolated spot once thought suitable to place the descendants of the mutineers of the *Bounty*. With tremendous reverence, some of the inhabitants showed her lovingly preserved sewing cases their forebears had received from Queen Victoria almost a hundred years previously.[58]

The Gloucesters were determined to live up to the expectations upon them. As a young mother, the duchess found this posed various challenges, starting with the flights. 'I always set off in a state of some trepidation,' she noted. 'Once or twice we were caught in frightening storms, engines were known to fail, tyres to burst.'[59] The hot climate brought out swarms of biting sandflies near Darwin, crocodiles in the drinking water at Elsie Station, and on one occasion the children were alarmed to spot a leech burrowing through their father's trousers. The soaring temperatures of over 100 degrees got the better of each member of the family; the duchess once fainted after prolonged standing in the heat. Even successfully navigating these hazards, the duchess found she could not entirely count on the diplomatic skills of the younger members of the family.

To her great concern at one gathering of local dignitaries, she found her oldest son, Prince William, giving one of the guests a piece of his mind. 'You're too
fat,' he announced rudely to a generously proportioned guest, who, to the duchess's huge relief, was equally generous in spirit. The Gloucesters found they loved
the wide landscapes, the outdoor climate and the informality of the people and
were reluctant to leave when the king asked the duke to return to Britain to
act as Regent once again.[60] The king was gratified to learn from the Australian
prime minister that his younger brother, of whom so little had been expected at
the outset, was 'very popular in Australia and will be missed'.[61] None the less,
he was planning a tour in South Africa in 1947 and, while abroad, wanted his
trusted brother representing the Crown in Britain.

The king's imperial tour aimed to help build goodwill at a time of dramatic
shifts in the empire. Anti-colonial movements demanded change and British
rule in India was drawing to a close. The king's South African tour also marked
a deeply personal transition. He knew that Princess Elizabeth wished to marry
Prince Philip and it could be the last chance to be together as a family. The 'We
Four' that had sustained him and provided a strong emotional background to
his life was changing. How could he sustain such a loss and never show it?
He wanted to hold on to it for a little bit longer. 'I was so anxious for you to
come to South Africa,' he told Princess Elizabeth later. 'Our family, us four,
the "Royal Family" must remain together with additions of course, at suitable
moments!!'[62]

The king's high hopes for the family tour evaporated almost as soon as they
left in February 1947, when extreme bad weather brought hardship to many
at home and there was criticism of the his absence. Snow lay on the streets for
three months. Fuel continued to be in short supply. There were power cuts.
Even the stores in Oxford Street relied on candlelight. Meagre wartime food
rations were still imposed. George VI felt torn and fretful about being out of
the country at such a time.

The unremitting glare from the sun, the unendurable African heat, the wildly
enthusiastic crowds and the overbearing police presence proved too much for
the king, who was tired and desperate for some peace. But day after day, the
many functions he attended allowed no respite. Everywhere, the people were
desperate to see their king and emperor who increasingly looked a small and
insignificant figure, imprisoned by the multitudes under burning African skies.
His break in the sun, meant to be a holiday, was becoming an ordeal. Now, the
flashes of temper and impatience, never easy to control, were impossible to conceal. The king's extreme tension could not be hidden from journalists, despite

Queen Elizabeth's soothing presence. 'This tour is being very strenuous as I feared it would be & doubly hard for Bertie who feels he should be at home,' the queen confided to Queen Mary. Even the queen's resilience was put to the test. 'I am rather gaga and tired,' she told her niece. 'It is a curious thing how driving through streets full of eager people seems to draw life out of one.'[63]

Tired or not, the king was determined to take advantage of his South African tour to visit Prince Paul and Olga. The Foreign Office advised against it, but the king would not be stopped. This may, in part, have reflected his feelings for his brother, the Duke of Kent, who had always valued his friendship with Prince Paul and his wife. But also the king believed that Prince Paul was wrongly blamed for the outcome in Yugoslavia and wanted to signal these views publicly. Marina was touched to receive a letter from the queen describing their visit. 'It is sweet of you to write the way you do, so full of heart,' she responded.[64] For her relatives, battling depression and malaria after six years' exile in Africa, the king's trust in them proved to be a turning point which paved their way for a return to European society.[65] But the excessive strains of the South African tour also proved to be a turning point for the king. By the time he arrived back in London he had lost seventeen pounds in weight and seemed visibly diminished.[66]

The sun was setting fast on the empire and across the world British influence waned. Burma concluded negotiations for independence in January 1947. India would follow soon afterwards. Britain's diminishing power was symbolically reflected in changes to the king's titles. From August 1947 George VI was no longer entitled to be called 'Emperor of India'. Queen Mary, whose long life had spanned the life of the British Indian Empire, duly took note of a letter she received from the king on 18 August 1947 signed simply *George R* not G.R.I. It was, she said, 'the first time Bertie wrote me a letter with the *I* for Emperor of India left out. Very sad.'[67] The British flag which had not been lowered at the residency in Lucknow since the Indian mutiny of 1857 was presented to the king, a symbol of the British Empire in India—'that bright jewel' handed to his great-grandmother, Queen Victoria—now reduced to a historical specimen in the collection at Windsor. After lengthy consultation the king's title changed to simply: 'Head of the Commonwealth'.

The king's fading health too was in full view of the world as news cameras were permitted in to Westminster Abbey for the marriage of his daughter on 20 November 1947. Some 200 million people listened to the radio broadcast and millions more flocked to cinemas to see the newsreel. Even in Berlin the picture houses were packed for days with crowds wanting to glimpse the fairy

tale of British royal pageantry that had somehow emerged unscathed from the
unrelenting horrors of war. There was a hunger for a 'flash of colour on the hard
road we have to travel', Churchill predicted correctly. All the glamorous ritual
of the British royal family managed to light up the drabness of the post-war
world.

Behind the scenes, last-minute preparations were not without mishap. The
moment had come for Princess Elizabeth to leave the palace when she suddenly
realised she was not wearing her pearls, a gift from her father. She was determined to have them with her as she walked down the aisle. Her private secretary, Jock Colville, came to her rescue. There might just be time, he calculated.
'I rushed along the corridor. I galloped down the Grand Staircase and into the
main Quadrangle of Buckingham Palace . . . I ran towards a large Royal Daim-
ler. "To St James's Palace," I cried.' But before he could commandeer the car, a
distinguished-looking gentleman 'ablaze with Orders and Decorations' inter-
vened. '"You seem to be in a hurry, young man. By all means have my car but
do let me get out first."' It was Uncle Charles of Norway who quickly grasped
the princess's urgent dilemma.[68]

Wearing her father's necklace and looking radiant, Elizabeth made her
entrance into the ancient abbey in a dress that had taken 3,000 clothes coupons
and bore 10,000 pearls. Some 2,000 guests were waiting, among them one of
the largest gatherings of royalty since the time of Queen Victoria.[69] All eyes
were on the silk-clad figure as she walked down the long nave. There was an
awareness that history was being made; all the ritual of a royal wedding in this
building so alive with past spectacle. Princess Marina, who had helped to facilitate the match with private meetings at Coppins between her young cousin,
Prince Philip, and her niece, Princess Elizabeth, was delighted.[70] The Duke and
Duchess of Gloucester were waiting in some trepidation as Prince William was
to hold the long train of her dress as a page.[71] From across Europe they came
drawn to this great royal reunion, like times of old. Many were direct descendants of Queen Victoria, such as King Michael of Romania, Queen Victoria
Eugenie of Spain and Queen Ingrid of Sweden; others were related by marriage,
such as Uncle Charles.

Despite the resplendent guests in their uniforms, jewels and medals, when
the familiar silhouette of Winston Churchill appeared in the doorway, the
entire congregation rose to acknowledge their respect. It was a day of heightened emotion and it proved impossible for the king to hide his feelings. 'I was
so proud of you and thrilled at having you so close to me on our long walk in
Westminster Abbey,' he told Princess Elizabeth later. 'But when I handed your

hand to the Archbishop I felt that I had lost something very precious . . . '[72] In a private moment, as they signed the register in St Edward's Chapel, the king could no longer hold back his tears.

The Duke and Duchess of Windsor were absent from the great event, spurned like the groom's German relations. The duke took Wallis for a long holiday in America to avoid the humiliation. But they missed nothing as they watched the newsreels later. For the duke his royal connection might just as well have been erased as though it had never existed. Painfully he saw the ascendancy of his Mountbatten cousins over him. The royal couple retired to the house of Earl Mountbatten in Hampshire when it was all over.

The marriage marked a transition in which the king was gradually eclipsed. His daughter's successful emergence into the limelight continued as she and her good-looking husband represented the future. The king had more than fulfilled the role to which he had been called so unwillingly a decade earlier, but at a very high price. As the queen had feared at the outset, the effort seemed to be visibly destroying him. By the New Year of 1948 he was suffering from severe pain in his feet and debilitating cramps in both legs. The pain was urgent and could not be ignored, but the king did ignore it, pressing on with his engagements. Many months elapsed in which the king found he could help his circulation and control his symptoms by banging his leg against the desk during prolonged periods of sitting. It was October before he sought the advice of his doctors.

The medical experts reached a worrying conclusion. The king was suffering from such severe obstruction in blood vessels to his feet and legs that he was in danger of developing gangrene. The doctors believed amputation was almost inevitable. A press release issued on 23 November referred to the 'strain of the last twelve years', which had affected the king's 'resistance to physical fatigue'.[73] The most likely cause of the marked inflammation and clotting in his circulatory system at a relatively young age was tobacco. The physical cost of the unremitting stress of the war years combined with heavy smoking was becoming apparent.

Faced with the prospect of radical surgery, the king at last submitted to becoming an invalid and tried to reduce his smoking. Over the winter months progress was slow. The situation was fraught with unknowns. The thought that the king could lose a leg or possibly both legs, confined to a wheelchair, was too awful to contemplate. But by March 1949 the surgeons judged it safe to carry out an operation to relieve the circulatory conditions in his leg by severing a nerve in the lower spine that controlled blood flow. Anxious crowds gathered outside Buckingham Palace. After a long wait eventually the news broke. The king's condition was 'satisfactory', declared the London press, news that was soon echoed around the world.[74] There was a reprieve.

Letters from the Windsors' friend, Kenneth de Courcy, to Wallis appear to indicate that the Windsors were watching the king's declining health closely and still scheming to find a way back into royal circles. 'The king faces the fearful tragedy of losing first one leg then the other,' de Courcy alerted the duchess on 13 May 1949. 'Those around him [the king] will gain greater and greater power. I may tell you most confidentially that a Regency has already been discussed and it seems likely enough that presently [a Regent] will be appointed . . . ' De Courcy noted the Mountbattens' unstoppable rise. To counter Lord Mountbatten's influence, he advised the Windsors to buy an estate in England. 'The Duke could . . . be a decisive influence for good—making it impossible for the Mountbattens to become the decisive political and social influence upon the Regency and the future Monarch . . . '[75]

But to return to England without an HRH for his wife was an insurmountable stumbling block for the duke. Despite the fact that his brother was very ill and he knew the issue distressed him, the duke decided to request an HRH for Wallis one more time. He first tackled the Lord Chancellor, William Jowitt, and then Clement Attlee: in both cases without success. Sensing the hand of the king in their unhelpful response, Windsor took his appeal to George VI himself. The king put off the meeting and it was winter before the brothers met.

The duke did not appear to take account of the signs of his brother's deteriorating health although it was obvious that the king was ill. It showed in his appearance. He was a shell of a man, gaunt and without vitality, his high cheekbones even more chiselled out from the hollowed face. But the duke saw only that cold, dull individual, once a brother, clinging like a miser to the keys that would unlock all the fortunate charms that came from being of royal birth. The king was surrounded by everything that once was his: the palace, the court, the courtiers, the all-enveloping, unassailable, untouchable stature of British monarchy. This was what he had been born to and his brother had not only taken it away but failed to share any part of it, even something as tiny as an 'HRH'. In a passionate appeal the duke gave vent to his feelings.

The king's responses are shown by a letter he wrote on 16 December. The capitals and italics highlight his strength of feeling about the abdication thirteen years on. The trauma of the abdication had shaped his life, Bertie explained. The duke had repeatedly failed to acknowledge the 'ghastly VOID' his selfish exit had caused, a decision that was 'your *own*'. How could his brother possibly claim that the present position was an insult to his wife, reasoned the king, when, as a duchess, Wallis had been bestowed 'the highest rank in the English peerage'? If she were to receive an HRH now, 'there is no reason why she should not have become Queen in 1937. It would not make sense of the past . . . ' There would never be an HRH for Wallis. The brothers had reached an unbreachable impasse.[76]

Over the following months, the duke lost hope of ever winning the coveted place within royal circles that meant so much to him. He gave the impression of being destroyed from within by his brother's unbending decision on this issue. He had no power to give Wallis what she really wanted: the trappings of royalty, the HRH, the dazzling, glittering stardom at the centre of the royal fold. All his efforts to secure this for her over twelve years of marriage had only served to push it further out of reach. In the late 1940s, Wallis took her revenge.

The handsome Jimmy Donahue, the 35-year-old playboy heir to the Woolworth fortune, became the constant companion of the Duchess of Windsor at this time. De Courcy had advised Windsor to do everything he could to avoid 'play boy propaganda'. But now his wife was courting the very worst of headlines. Wallis and Jimmy went everywhere together, utterly absorbed in each other. The duchess bloomed like a Hollywood star. The duke was visibly diminished. Pictures of her slim figure shown off to best effect in stunning dresses as she flaunted her millionaire boy toy in nightclubs appeared in the press for all to see. Even cynical New Yorkers were shocked to see her flirting with the playboy heir in a Manhattan nightclub on the night of Queen Mary's funeral.

The great romance of all time was now fooling no one. It had collected a fatal extra dimension: a man who was younger, taller, richer and more fun. The Duke of Windsor could not bring himself to pull out of this embarrassing threesome. He too enjoyed his wife's lover's money and his need for the security Wallis gave him obliged him to accept it on any terms. Such was the reduced currency of the Windsors that nothing was off limits. Journalists who had politely averted their gaze to the antics of the playboy Prince of Wales in the 1920s adopted a no-holds-barred approach to the shamed ex-king of 1950.

Gossip-column inches filled with sordid speculation of their sex life. 'She married a king and screwed a Queen,' according to one. In others, her alleged boredom with the 'smothering' and 'needy' ex-king was paraded. From foot fetishes to bedroom fantasies in which the duke was subjugated to a dominant Wallis, or alleged threesomes with the dime-store heir: there was nothing to protect him as he was trashed by crude comments in the gutter press. Everyone knew the former Edward VIII's romantic declaration of love, and abandonment of the greatest throne there is, had been for nothing. The *Mirror* summed up the perspective from Fleet Street. 'The Duke and Duchess thing is now a front.'[77]

Did the ex-king finally glimpse what others had seen all along? His wife was not in love with him and possibly never had been? She was behaving without any consideration for him and in a way that could only demolish him still further in public life. There were rumours she was even prepared to leave him, drawn as she was like a moth to the flame of the Woolworth wealth which was lavished on her. As her collection of furs and jewels grew ever more resplendent, so did her undisguised devotion to Jimmy. The ex-king had given up his throne for a woman whose passion was for wealth and money, not for himself. She no longer even took the trouble to disguise it. Such was her dominance over him, he was obliged to tag along in this threesome, courting the vacuous existence his wife pursued, paying homage to her and her playboy until the small hours and beyond, to the point of exhaustion. She had complete control.

The duke's turmoil did not go unwitnessed. He could not sleep, he could not concentrate and was quite prepared to abandon his contribution to his memoirs being drafted in the summer of 1950 by an editor at *Life* magazine, Charles Murphy. His wife had escaped to New York with Jimmy while the memoirs were completed. Rumours of her scandalous behaviour quickly reached him and he set off to New York in hot pursuit, ghost-writer in tow. Charles Murphy later claimed that the duke was in such a state he feared the ex-king might commit suicide and ensured he was not out on deck alone, according to the writer, Christopher Wilson.[78] The shallowness of their existence had deadened all hope. If in 1936 by abdicating he had imagined himself escaping an unacceptable yoke, he must by now have come to realise he had escaped nothing. The duke was doomed, tied to this woman he could not live without, condemned to trail forlornly after her till the day of his death. Images of the ex-king at this time cannot conceal the air of loss that seemed to pervade his features. 'He looked such a sad figure,' observed one friend.[79] He invariably had 'a sad and anxious expression,' said another.

The king and the ex-king each had a hand in the destruction of the other. In Buckingham Palace, Queen Elizabeth watched helplessly as the king failed to regain his vigour. In her heart she blamed his brother for the abdication. Physically, her husband was a broken man; gaunt and thin—'walking with death', in Churchill's words. Even in his enfeebled state, the king still felt the burden of each new shocking crisis. There were fears that the Korean War in 1950, between the communist North supported by Chinese troops, and the South, supported by US, British and Commonwealth troops would trigger the start of a Third World War.

In appreciation of the loyalty of the Duke of Gloucester, the king bestowed on him the title Great Master of the Order of the Bath, a British Order of Chivalry originally inspired by medieval customs for creating a knight. Such an honour carried with it the indefinable aura from centuries past associated with only the most worthy of men. The ceremony in Westminster Abbey on 24 May 1951 was a great accolade for the Duke of Gloucester; there had only been seven Great Masters since 1725. With due solemnity, the king's sword, which he in turn had received from their father, was given to his brother.

The king's desire to thank his brother turned into an ordeal. Onlookers saw their increasingly frail sovereign struggling to hide the signs of serious illness. A debilitating cough and a soaring temperature clearly had the better of him. It was hoped the summer break at Balmoral would sort things out but his cough persisted. Even the crystal air of the Highland moors failed to provide their customary tonic. The king could not throw off his infection. Reluctantly he returned to London in September for a series of tests, hopeful that his doctors would sort things out. But the news was not good. The king learned that his bronchial tubes were 'blocked' and he required an urgent operation to remove his left lung.

The king viewed the prospect of enduring further surgery as 'hell'. There was a risk of a fatal blood clot developing. There was also a danger that, in removing the 'blockage', nerves to the larynx might also need to be severed, making him unable to speak. Then there were the risks invariably associated with major surgery. Only Elizabeth knew what he did not, that the 'blockage' was in fact a cancerous tumour.

Just before the operation the king ordered three brace of grouse to be sent to the Duke of Windsor: the brother he could no longer talk to. Reconciliation seemed impossible but surely this gesture would rise above mere words. They were brothers still, even if they had nothing to give each other. There might never be a reconciliation, but should anything happen, he wished to end their relationship on a thoughtful gesture.[80]

Churchill was dismayed at the news of the king's operation. He guessed the illness was cancer and later confided to Lascelles that, on 23 September, the morning of the procedure, 'I did a thing . . . that I haven't done for many years—I went down on my knees by my bedside & prayed.'[81]

There was indeed a reprieve. The operation was successful. The king was still making good progress in October 1951 when Churchill was re-elected as prime minister. A great deal had passed since the two men had first worked together in the spring of 1940. Reunited on the evening of 26 October in Buckingham Palace, both men bore the scars of their journey.

As he entered, Churchill was unmistakably an old man, his 76-year-old frame slightly stooped, his famous features no longer so well defined in a stance of defiance, but softer, the lines deeper and merging with the folds of his skin, his eyes more hollowed. He had recovered from a stroke and was excited to be back in Downing Street. As for the king, he seemed immortal. He thought he had survived the risk of blood clots, amputation and the removal of a lung and felt optimistic he was on the road to recovery. He was delighted to welcome back his old friend. They discussed the road ahead together; two wise frail men, both nearer death than they knew: a marriage of true minds.

The king insisted on making the effort to give his customary Christmas Day speech to the nation. Perhaps he wanted to feel that everything was back to normal. For those who advised against it, he had one reply: 'I want to speak to my people myself.' The one concession he was prepared to make to meet the queen's anxious concerns was to prerecord the speech.

'I myself have every cause for deep thankfulness,' he said. He praised his doctors and expressed his gratitude for all the many messages of support from across the Commonwealth and the Empire. 'I thank you now from all my heart . . . ' Although the speech was pre-recorded, his words seemed to be extracted with extraordinary difficulty, his voice sometimes reduced to a husky whisper. For his listeners, the broadcast revealed all too plainly the heavy personal price the king had paid. 'I trust that you yourselves realise how greatly your prayers and good wishes have helped and are helping me in my recovery . . . '[82]

At the end of January the king went to Heathrow to wave goodbye to Princess Elizabeth and Prince Philip. They were setting off on a 30,000-mile tour, including Australia and New Zealand, that would take them away for five months. It was the king's first major public appearance since his operation and a large crowd gathered. Churchill, too, arrived in his bowler hat and white scarf against the icy wind. The king emerged from the plane, trying to keep up a polite conversation with the head of BOAC, while clearly wanting to maintain contact with his daughter; wanting that one last reassuring smile that would have to last him five months. He caught a glimpse of her from the tarmac: a face at the window as the plane moved away. The king showed no sign of emotion except in his eyes, as though he knew he had just seen his daughter for the very last time.[83]

The following week at Sandringham he recovered his spirits and seemed in better health. By 5 February he felt strong enough to organise a shoot, and after a satisfying day out in the sun, he enjoyed dining with his wife and youngest daughter, as they had always done when it was 'We Four'. His complete recovery was helped by such days. But later that night, alone, he died peacefully in his sleep. He was found the next morning by his valet.[84]

Prime Minister Winston Churchill was visibly upset when he was informed in Downing Street. It was 'the worst' of news, he said, scattering his papers in disarray. 'Our Chief is dead.'[85]

A little later Jock Colville found him 'sitting alone with tears in his eyes, looking straight ahead of him and reading neither his official papers nor his newspapers. I had not realised how much the King meant to him.' His valet reported that privately he broke down completely.[86] Something precious was lost: a deep mutual understanding gone. Churchill had lost his king; and more than a king, a friend. A man whose spirit he could admire, a man more like a brother; and he mourned him as though for a brother.

Across the country, cars stopped in the streets and people were weeping as they stood to mark the solemn moment when they heard of the king's death. Flags were adjusted to fly at half mast; cinemas, restaurants and theatres closed their doors; the BBC took its programmes off air. A growing crowd of mourners gathered outside Buckingham Palace, dark shapes hunched against perishing cold and rain.

Churchill was still tearful the next day when he drove from the airport after greeting the new Queen Elizabeth II. The two men had travelled an immense journey together, the one physically weakened by old age, the other held back by intrinsic flaws that made him ill-suited for the burden he was obliged to shoulder: but it had fallen to them to lead the country in its fight for survival. That long journey was now over. And as the convoy of black cars made the short trip back to London, Churchill tried to find the right words as he dictated a draft speech. His eulogy to George VI, broadcast on the BBC that evening, was widely reported as one of the most moving speeches he had made.

'My friends, when the death of the King was announced to us yesterday morning, there struck a deep and solemn note in our lives which, as it resounded far and wide, stilled the clatter and traffic of 20th century life in many lands, and made countless millions of human beings pause and look around them. A new sense of values for the time being took possession of human minds, and mortal existence presented itself to so many at the same moment in its serenity and its sorrow, in its splendour and in its pain, in its fortitude, and in its suffering. The King was greatly loved by all his peoples. He was respected as a man and a Prince far beyond the many realms over which he reigned. The simple dignity of his life, his manly virtues, his sense of duty—alike as ruler and servant of the vast spheres and communities for which he bore responsibility—his

gay charm and happy nature, his example as husband and father in his own
family circle, his courage in peace or war, all these were aspects of his character
which won the glint of admiration, now here, now there, from the innumerable
eyes whose gaze falls upon the Throne . . . We thought of him, so faithful in his
study and discharge of State affairs, so strong in his devotion to the enduring
honour of our country, so self-restrained in his judgments of men and affairs,
so uplifted above the clash of party politics, yet so attentive to them, so wise
and shrewd in judging between what matters and what does not. All this we
saw and admired, his conduct on the Throne may be a model and a guide to
constitutional sovereigns throughout the world today, and also in future generations . . . '[87]

The king's coffin was taken from Wolferton Station to London and thousands gathered silently along the line to say their own farewell as his train
passed. 'The King lived through every minute of this struggle with a heart that
never quavered and a spirit undaunted,' Churchill addressed the House. 'I who
saw him often, knew how keenly, with all his full knowledge and understanding of what was happening, he felt personally the ups and down of this terrific
struggle and how he longed to fight it, arms in hand, himself . . . '

The next day, George VI's coffin lay in state in the darkened Westminster
Hall, while people waited in a queue that stretched 4 miles for one last chance
to show what their king meant to them. Churchill laid a wreath of white flowers on the coffin. On the card he had found two more words for the king,
words that carried a world of meaning: 'For Valour'. In Churchill's mind he was
honouring the king's courage by awarding him posthumously the two simple
words that symbolise the ultimate bravery: the Victoria Cross.

EPILOGUE

....

I n summer of 1953 Prime Minister Churchill was critically ill but there was an important matter pressing on his mind. 'I had a sudden stroke which as it developed completely paralysed my left side and affected my speech,' he confided to his friend Ike, now President Eisenhower, on 1 July, adding, 'I have not told anybody these details which are for your eye alone.' Surprisingly, despite such a life-threatening condition, he was still troubled about the Duke of Windsor's Marburg file. But this was Churchill. Something as minor as a major stroke was not going to deter him from protecting England's glorious royal tradition, in spite of the fact that the paralysis made it harder for his cigar to make contact with his mouth, amongst other, more perilous difficulties. The wretched Marburg files were not going to flit around a world avid for sleazy gossip. Nothing must stain the great heritage. 'I am venturing to send you some papers about the Duke of Windsor which I hope you will find time to consider . . . ' Churchill wrote to Ike.[1]

Churchill appeared to be making one last attempt to destroy the Duke's Marburg papers. His correspondence with Eisenhower shows that both the world leaders, eight years on from the discovery of the German telegrams, still hoped to suppress the incriminating file on the Duke of Windsor. 'My purpose in writing this letter is to ask you to exert your power to prevent their publication,' Churchill wrote to Eisenhower on 27 June. 'The historical importance of the episode is negligible,' he reasoned and appealed to Ike's 'sense of justice and chivalry . . . I hope you will join with me and the French government who I am also approaching, in refusing to allow the official publication of the telegrams or their revelation to anybody outside the secret circles.' Eisenhower replied on 2 July to say that he was 'completely astonished' to learn that copies of the file had been made. He thought the matter was closed in 1945 when the American ambassador and a member of his intelligence staff examined the documents and were agreed 'that there was no possible value to them'.[2]

But in the 1950s, even Churchill could not stop the eventual publication of the duke's Marburg file. Plans were made to publish the papers in 1957 under the suitably unexciting title of *Documents on German Foreign Policy, Volume X, Series D*.[3] Finally, in accordance with George VI's wishes, Windsor himself was warned of their publication and given a chance to see the documents and prepare his response.[4]

The duke at last saw, with perhaps an unwelcome clarity, the course he had taken in 1940 when it looked as though England might be defeated. Even to an unprejudiced eye his behaviour appeared treacherous, with the voluminous correspondence between Ribbentrop and his Nazi agents apparently confirming his involvement. It was there for all to see in black and white: even Churchill knew of these German telegrams illustrating just how the duke might be able to profit from his country's defeat. Later, when he was outraged at the lack of a prestigious job and the continued withholding of an HRH for Wallis, the duke had blamed his brother: his brother who knew exactly what the telegrams indicated he had been planning in 1940 . . . and said nothing.

For years Windsor had seen his brother as the key perpetrator of an unreasonable prejudice against him. He had complained bitterly that the king's attitude lay behind what he saw as the studied insults and humiliations that were heaped upon him. But far from being his implacable enemy, his brother had done his best to protect him from the trauma of publication as long as he could. Did Windsor pause to consider what impact these documents might have had on his sensitive younger brother at the time? Was there a moment when he reflected on his last meeting with his brother and realised what the king knew? The Duke of Windsor was not a man prone to flashes of insight, but if he did feel any regret or remorse there was nothing he could do. It was too late for atonement now. His brother's tomb lay in the Royal Vault at Windsor.

Both the government and the Duke of Windsor released statements denying the claims in the German telegrams. Windsor's breezy rebuttal printed in *The Times* acknowledged that pro-Nazi sympathisers did try to persuade him to delay in Europe and not go to the Bahamas but he insisted that he treated the suggestion 'with the contempt that it deserved'. The German telegrams, he declared, were 'in part complete fabrications' and 'in part gross distortions of the truth . . . '[5]

While these denials were accepted at the time, the case has since mounted against the Duke of Windsor. British intelligence demonstrates the collaboration between the Windsors and the Nazis over their possessions in the summer of 1940 and raises serious concerns about communications of greater significance, as summarised by Edward Tamm for the FBI (Chapters 7 and 8). Foreign Office, FBI and other sources show that the duke's views in the German telegrams were also forcefully expressed to his Allied associates, including diplomats, businessmen and journalists (Chapters 7 to 9). His actions prompted sufficient concern that President Roosevelt and J. Edgar Hoover in America and Churchill and 'C' in Britain followed his case closely between 1940 and 1942 (Chapter 8). Equally telling is the duke's own behaviour. It is hard to put any other interpretation on the Windsors' erratic course through Europe in 1940 other than that, far from feeling loyalty to Britain, they thought of themselves as free agents in a time of great uncertainty and were looking for the best deal. A far more plausible interpretation of the duke's Marburg file is that the German agents *did* report what Windsor said, and Windsor was indeed prepared to act as a quisling or worse, playing for time to see whether it was the Germans or the British who gained the upper hand that summer. This interpretation also makes more sense of the coldness of the palace towards him over many years: there was good reason for George VI's attitude.

Most historians stop short of using the word 'traitor' to describe the Duke of Windsor. The German telegrams are second-hand accounts of what he is alleged to have said. Nothing has been published in Windsor's own hand to prove beyond doubt his support for the German plot. But did such written evidence once exist? There are some hints in the German records of additional material that has never seen the light of day. On 15 August 1940 the German Minister in Portugal reported that the duke's former host, Ricardo Santo, 'has just received a telegram from the Duke in Bermuda asking him to send a communication as soon as action was advisable'.[6] Such a telegram from Windsor himself to Santo would be a key piece of evidence incriminating the duke but the original has never surfaced. There are indications of the duke's involvement with the kaiser during the war but this too does not appear in the published Marburg file.[7] It is possible that some of the original material was never found or that the Germans themselves destroyed records during the war that could be damaging to Windsor, in case this jeopardised his usefulness later (it is noticeable that a transcript of Windsor's conversation with Hitler in 1937 has never surfaced). Alternatively, is it possible that there was once written evidence of the duke's complicity in the Marburg file and this has not survived the careful attentions of the record-keepers over the years?

There were further secrets that many historians believe Churchill and the palace went to some lengths to conceal. A great deal of speculation has centred on the purpose of Blunt and Morshead's mission into post-war Germany.

Historians have pointed out that years later, when Anthony Blunt was inter-viewed after his identification as a Soviet spy, he was not permitted to discuss his German post-war activities.[8] MI5 officer Peter Wright, who interrogated Blunt in 1965, alleges that the palace blocked this line of questioning.[9] The epi-sode remains veiled in secrecy but the enduring mystery lends weight to the view that the official line of a hapless duke exploited by Nazi intrigues is, to say the least, not very convincing.

While the Duke of Windsor's reputation has not improved with time, intriguingly some of his associates have been at least partially vindicated. Axel Wenner-Gren campaigned to clear his name after the war and became heavily involved in philanthropic ventures. He was welcomed at the White House in 1949 for the inauguration of Harry Truman. A Swedish study in 1979 concluded his blacklisting was 'a miscarriage of justice' prompted by the scale of his busi-ness interests rather than direct evidence that he acted for the Nazis during the war.[10] Meanwhile an investigation into Charles Bedaux under Charles de Gaulle's government in 1944 concluded that the French entrepreneur actively sought to harm German interests in France and he was posthumously awarded the *Légion d'honneur*. His case remains controversial, with new studies high-lighting his links to covert German initiatives.[11] In America many of the FBI papers covering his case are still not available.

The files concerning Charles Edward, Duke of Saxe-Coburg, are also not fully disclosed. Sarah Bradford refers to two Saxe-Coburg denazification files that were closed when she wrote her biography, *George VI*, in 1989.[12] One of these files has since been declassified and highlights potential royal family interests after the war in confiscated Saxe-Coburg property which included 'a number of forests, castles, hotels, inns, dwellings etc'.[13] In Soviet East Ger-many, Saxe-Coburg's assets were liquidated, but in the West, the Property Con-trol Branch in the Allied Commission for Germany faced a baffling headache. Saxe-Coburg's assets had been turned into a Family Foundation in February 1928; many of its members were listed as none other than the British royal fam-ily. Officials were concerned over whether such property could be 'confiscated' by the Allies. It will be 'for His Majesty and other members of the Royal Fam-ily to decide when the facts are accurately known how far they do want to claim whatever legal rights they have', wrote Sir Ulick Alexander, Keeper of the Privy Purse, on 3 December 1946.[14] The matter was classified presumably because it highlighted the closeness of the link between the British royal family and the disgraced Saxe-Coburg duke at the time of the denazification trials.

The second file on Saxe-Coburg is still unavailable.[15] It is catalogued at the National Archives in Kew, but the archivists could not trace it and believed it must still be at the Foreign Office. However, the Foreign Office was also unable to locate the file. At the National Archives, staff eventually tracked down a box with the correct file number—FO 120/1176—in their off-site storage in Cheshire. But curiously when it was opened, the box was empty and there remained only a note: 'Temporarily Retained.'

The archives on the Duke of Kent add to the mystery. The flight plan filed by the pilot, Frank Goyen, on the day of his death and the secret report of the Court of Inquiry cannot be found in the Royal Archives, the Public Record Office or the RAF archives and would explain much about his doomed flight. A number of conspiracy theories have been put forward over the years to explain the crash (a link to the case of Rudolf Hess or an intelligence plot to kill Kent). Many of these theories assume that Iceland was not the true destination, but the Royal Archives provided the records of Kent's private secretary showing his extensive travel arrangements for Iceland, with nothing to indicate a last-minute change of plan (Chapter 10). The most likely source of the enduring rumours about the mission is wartime counter-intelligence and foreign intelligence—especially Soviet intelligence given the high level of concern about Hess. The Kent family themselves had no further documents to shed light on the Hess affair or Kent's tragic accident and it seems plausible that continuing sensitivities about Kent's playboy years have led to the incompleteness of the records in his case.

The sensitivity of the missing papers and the number of documents that have gone astray do raise intriguing questions. There is doubtless more to be revealed. It is almost as if the spirit of Churchill was keeping an all-seeing eye across the decades over the record keeping itself, like some knight of old guarding the precious grail to ensure no scurrilous secrets ease their way out into the modern world which might not understand that fusing of the nation in a time of need under a monarch for the people.

But surely even Churchill could only take great pleasure in the eventual outcome for the British monarchy. When George VI died, he fretted about having to deal with his daughter, the new Queen Elizabeth. 'She was only a child,' Churchill famously declared. But both her grandfather and father had marked the future queen from an early age as extraordinarily well suited to the demanding role that Edward VIII had preferred not to take on and that George VI had reluctantly done so. Queen Elizabeth gave her first Christmas speech in 1952 at the age of twenty-six. Her ease at public speaking, in contrast to the heavy toll it exacted from her father, perhaps helped to change Churchill's mind. There have been more than sixty Christmas speeches since and the queen, despite the controversial actions of her uncle, has become Britain's second-longest-serving monarch and the enduring symbol of democratic stability that Churchill wished for, and that was thrown away so lightly in 1936.

NOTES

....

George VI's unpublished eleven-volume diary written between 1939–47 is held in the Royal Archives in Windsor Castle, (RA GVI/PRIV/DIARY). For ease of reference it is abbreviated below as George VI's War Diary.

Prologue
1. *The Memoirs of HRH The Duke of Windsor*, p. 10
2. Ibid., p. 72
3. James Pope-Hennessy, *Queen Mary*, p. 395
4. Countess of Airlie, in Ellis (ed.), *Thatched with Gold*, p. 113
5. Kirsty McLeod, *Battle Royal*, p. 21

Chapter 1: Circumstances Without Parallel
1. *The Memoirs of HRH The Duke of Windsor*, p. 237
2. Christopher Warwick, *George and Marina*, p. 103
3. The Duke of York's Abdication Chronicle, 3–11 December 1936, cited in John Wheeler-Bennett, *King George VI*, p. 286
4. *The Memoirs of HRH The Duke of Windsor*, p. 407
5. James Pope-Hennessy, *Queen Mary*, p. 579
6. Ibid., pp. 574–5
7. *Daily Mirror*, 5 December 1936
8. Noble Frankland, *Prince Henry*, p. 132
9. *The Memoirs of HRH The Duke of Windsor*, p. 335
10. Christopher Warwick, *George and Marina*, p. 62
11. Lord Birkenhead, *Walter Monckton*, p. 150
12. The Duke of York's Abdication Chronicle, 8 December 1936
13. *Daily Mirror*, 10 December 1936
14. John Wheeler-Bennett, *King George VI*, p. 212
15. The Duke of York's Abdication Chronicle, 11 December 1936
16. *Daily Mirror*, 'The King decides: Abdication Plans', 10 December 1936
17. *The Memoirs of HRH The Duke of Windsor*, pp. 354 and 370
18. Osbert Sitwell, *Rat Week*, p. 53
19. *The Memoirs of HRH The Duke of Windsor*, p. 258
20. Ibid., p. 255
21. Ibid., p. 331
22. Ibid., p. 343
23. Philip Ziegler, *King Edward VIII*, p. 274

24. TNA PREM 1/457 Note by the secretary, p. 3

25. The Duchess of Windsor, *The Heart Has Its Reasons*, p. 186

26. *The Memoirs of HRH The Duke of Windsor*, p. 400

27. TNA CAB 127/157 Sir Horace Wilson, p. 45

28. Robert Rhodes James (ed.), *The Diaries of Sir Henry Channon*, p. 206

29. TNA CAB 127/157 Sir Horace Wilson, p. 29

30. *Daily Mirror*, 7 December 1936

31. Ibid.

32. *Daily Mirror*, 4 December 1936

33. *Daily Mirror*, 5 December 1936

34. *The Memoirs of HRH The Duke of Windsor*, p. 382

35. Duff Cooper diary, cited in Philip Ziegler, *King Edward VIII*, p. 275

36. Roy Jenkins, *Churchill*, pp. 500–1

37. Ibid., p. 502

38. TNA CAB 127/157 Captain T.L. Dugdale notes of 8.12.36, Annex V, p. 3

39. Ibid.

40. Ibid.

41. Audrey Whiting, *The Kents*, pp. 90–1

42. *The Times*, 12 June 1935

43. Sarah Bradford, *George VI*, p. 215

44. *Tatler*, 30 May 1934

45. George VI to the prime minister, 30 December 1936, cited in John Wheeler-Bennett, *King George VI*, p. 297

46. George VI refers to the Duchess of Windsor as 'she' in his War Diary e.g. 3 July, 6 and 7 July, 1940

47. TNA CAB 301/101 Letter to Sir Thomas Gardiner, 5 December 1936

48. TNA CAB 127/157 Annex V, p. 7

49. Ibid., p. 9

50. Ibid., p. 8

51. Ibid., p. 9

52. The Duke of York's Abdication Chronicle, cited in John Wheeler-Bennett, *King George VI*, p. 287

53. The Duke of York to Sir Godfrey Thomas, 25 November 1936, cited in John Wheeler-Bennett, Ibid., p. 283

54. House of Commons debate, 11 December 1936

55. Duchess of York to Queen Mary, 17 November 1936, cited in William Shawcross, *Queen Elizabeth*, p. 373

56. *The Memoirs of HRH The Duke of Windsor*, p. 407

57. *Daily Mirror*, 11 December 1936

58. TNA CAB 21/4100/1 Hansard, 10 December 1936, pp. 2,204–5

59. FBI HQ 94-4-6650 Memorandum from L.L. Laughlin to Mr D. Ladd, 29 September 1942

60. Osbert Sitwell, *Rat Week*, p. 35

61. Patrick Howarth, *George VI*, p. 62

62. Osbert Sitwell, *Rat Week*, p. 36

63. *The Memoirs of HRH The Duke of Windsor*, p. 409

64. Ibid., p. 413

65. *The Memoirs of HRH The Duke of Windsor*, p. 414

66. *Daily Mirror*, 14 December 1936, p. 15

67. John Wheeler-Bennett, *King George VI*, pp. 293–4

68. Osbert Sitwell, *Rat Week*, p. 76

69. Mark Logue and Peter Conradi, *The King's Speech*, p. 116

70. Cosmo Lang, Abdication Broadcast, 13 December 1936

Chapter 2: A Very Full Heart

1. *Daily Express*, 2 January 1937, front page

2. *News Review*, 7 January 1937

3. 'Royal English Family Agog over Duke's Escapades', *Reading Eagle*, 7 January 1937

4. *News Review*, 7 January 1937

5. Christopher Warwick, *George and Marina*, p. 69

6. Michael Thornton, 'How Predatory Noël Coward Tried to Seduce Me . . . ', *Daily Mail*, 9 November 2007

7. Christopher Warwick, *George and Marina*, p. 71

8. Kenneth Young (ed.), *The Diaries of Sir Robert B. Lockhart*, Volume 1, 1915–38, p. 215

9. Christopher Warwick, *George and Marina*, p. 70

10. Douglas Fairbanks, Jr., *A Hell of a War*, p. 34

11. Maury Paul, 'Cholly Knickerbocker Says', *New York Journal-American*, February 1936

12. American *Vogue*, 15 September 1936

13. Prince George to Betty Lawson-Johnston, Private Collection, Letter 10, undated, 'Wednesday'

14. Prince George to Betty Lawson-Johnston, Private Collection, Letter 7, undated, 'Thursday'

15. Sophia Watson, *Marina*, pp. 94–5

16. Neil Balfour and Sally Mackay, *Paul of Yugoslavia*, p. 67

17. Robert Rhodes James (ed.), *The Diaries of Sir Henry Channon*

18. Christopher Warwick, *George and Marina*, pp. 55–7

19. Prince George to Betty Lawson-Johnston, Private Collection, Letter 12, 4 September 1934

20. Prince George to Betty Lawson-Johnston, Private Collection, Letter 14, undated, 'Sunday'

21. James Wentworth Day, *HRH Princess Marina, Duchess of Kent*, pp. 93–4

22. Robert Rhodes James (ed.), *The Diaries of Sir Henry Channon*, 6 May 1934–5, p. 32

23. Douglas Fairbanks, Junior, *A Hell of a War*, p. 158

24. *Tasmanian Advocate*, 19 March 1946

25. The Duchess of Windsor, *The Heart Has Its Reasons*, p. 204

26. Ibid., p. 206

27. *The Times*, 30 November 1934

28. 'Activities of Duke Disclosed', *Berkeley Daily Gazette*, 7 January 1937

29. 'Australians' Affair with a Future King', *Daily Telegraph*, 27 January 2014, p. 5

30. Prince Albert to Mabell, Countess of Airlie, in Jennifer Ellis (ed.), *Thatched with Gold*, p. 168

31. Osbert Sitwell, *Rat Week*, p. 41

32. Prince George to Prince Paul, cited in Sophia Watson, *Marina*, p. 148

33. Kenneth Young (ed.), *The Diaries of Sir Robert B. Lockhart*, Volume 1, 1915–38

34. Noble Frankland, *Prince Henry*, p. 27

35. Ibid.

36. Ibid., p. 43

37. Audrey Whiting, *The Kents*, p. 22

38. 'Garter Mission. Stately Ceremony in Tokyo. The Emperor and the Duke', *The Times*, 3 May 1929, p. 12

39. 'Emperor of Ethiopia Scenes at Addis Ababa', *The Times*, 3 November 1930, p. 12

40. *The Memoirs of Princess Alice*, pp. 103–5

41. Ibid., p. 104

42. Noble Frankland, *Prince Henry*, p. 103

43. Clive Turnbull, in the *Melbourne Herald*, 18 October 1934

44. Noble Frankland, *Prince Henry*, p. 119

45. Michael Bloch (ed.), *Wallis and Edward Letters 1931–1937*, p. 276, Wallis to Edward, 14 December 1936

46. Ibid., p. 288, Wallis to Edward, 3 January 1937

47. TNA MEPO 10/35

48. *The Memoirs of HRH The Duke of Windsor*, p. 355

49. Death threats cited in the *Daily Mirror*, 5 December 1936

50. Cosmo Lang, Abdication Broadcast, 13 December 1936

51. Osbert Sitwell, *Rat Week*, p. 54

52. Wallis to Betty Lawson-Johnston from Château de Cande, 16 March 1937, Private Collection

53. Wallis to Betty Lawson-Johnston from Château de Cande, Easter Sunday 1937, Private Collection

54. Churchill Archives, CHAR 2/300/9 Winston Churchill to the Duke of Windsor, 24 March 1937

55. Winston Churchill to Neville Chamberlain, 24 March 1937, cited in Sarah Bradford, *George VI*, p. 311

56. Churchill Archives, CHAR 2/300/35 Winston Churchill to George VI, 30 April 1937

57. Chamberlain Papers, NC 18/1/1001, Neville to Hilda Chamberlain, 10 April 1937

58. Michael Bloch (ed.), *Wallis and Edward Letters 1931–1937*, p. 279

59. Cecil Beaton, *The Wandering Years*, April 1937, pp. 305–6

60. 'The Duke of Kent in Vienna', *The Times*, 25 February 1937, p. 14

61. 'Reception by Lady Astor', *New York Times*, 27 February 1937

62. John Wheeler-Bennett, *King George VI*, p. 309

63. *Sunday Chronicle*, 9 May 1937

64. Mark Logue and Peter Conradi, *The King's Speech*, p. 133

65. Sarah Bradford, *George VI*, p. 279

66. John Wheeler-Bennett, *King George VI*, p. 311

67. 'The King's Memorandum of the Coronation', cited in John Wheeler-Bennett, *King George VI*, p. 312

68. Robert Rhodes James (ed.), *The Diaries of Sir Henry Channon*, 12 May 1937, p. 124

69. *Beyond Belief*, 'Religion and the Coronation', BBC Radio 4, 27 May 2013

70. 'The King's Memorandum of the Coronation', cited in John Wheeler-Bennett, *King George VI*, pp. 312–13

71. Sarah Bradford, *George VI*, p. 280

72. 'The King's Memorandum of the Coronation', cited in John Wheeler-Bennett, *King George VI*, p. 312

73. The Duchess of Windsor, *The Heart Has Its Reasons*, p. 298

74. Jim Christy, *The Price of Power*, pp. 149–50

75. TNA CAB 23/88/1 Volume LV, pp. 208–10

76. Cecil Beaton, *The Wandering Years*, April 1937, pp. 308–11

77. Frances Donaldson, *Edward VIII, The Road to Abdication*, p. 171

78. Hugo Vickers, *The Unexpurgated Beaton Diaries*, p. 199

79. Jim Christy, *The Price of Power*, p. 153

80. The Duchess of Windsor to Betty Lawson-Johnston from Schloss Wasserleonburg, dated 'July Thursd—', Private Collection

81. The Duchess of Windsor to Betty Lawson-Johnston from Schloss Wasserleonburg, dated 'Thursday the 12th', Private Collection

82. Frances Donaldson, *Edward VIII, The Road to Abdication*, p. 165

83. Anne Sebba, *That Woman*, pp. 212–13

84. Jim Christy, *The Price of Power*, pp. 154–5

85. Ibid., pp. 156–61

86. Michael Thornton, *Royal Feud*, p. 168

Chapter 3: Enmity and Fear

1. Winston Churchill, *The Second World War*, Volume 1, p. 55

2. Roy Jenkins, *Churchill*, p. 511

3. John Wheeler-Bennett, *King George VI*, pp. 318–19

4. Duchess of Windsor to Betty Lawson-Johnston from Hotel Le Meurice, September 30th, Private Collection

5. Duchess of Windsor to Betty Lawson-Johnston, Saturday 27th 1937, Private Collection

6. Charles Higham, *Trading with the Enemy*, p. 180

7. Jim Christy, *The Price of Power*, p. 164

8. Unsigned memorandum, dated January 1936, in *Documents on German Foreign Policy 1918–45*, Series C, Volume IV, No. 531, p. 1,062

9. Ibid., pp. 1,062–4

10. Letter from Leopold von Hoesch to the Foreign Ministry, 12 April 1935, in *Documents on German Foreign Policy*, Series C, Volume V, No. 27, p. 49

11. Ibid., 21 January 1935, No. 510, p. 1,025

12. Minute from Dr Stutterheim, London correspondent of *Berliner Tageblatt*, to Herr Paul Scheffer, 18 March 1936, *Documents on German Foreign Policy*, Series C, Volume V, No. 147, p. 193

13. Jonathan Petropoulos, *Royals and the Reich*, p. 206

14. 'The Duke of Windsor's Arrival in Berlin', *The Times*, 11 October 1937, p. 13

15. 'Herr von Ribbentrop's Dinner', *The Times*, 13 October 1937, p. 13

16. The Duchess of Windsor, *The Heart Has Its Reasons*, p. 308

17. 'The Duke and Duchess of Windsor at Krupps', *The Times*, 16 October 1937, p. 11, and William Teeling, 'Nazi School for Nordic Knights', *New York Times*, 22 May 1938

18. Goebbels diary, cited in Gerwin Strobl, *The Germanic Isle*, pp. 109–10

19. Churchill Archives, CHAR 2/300/56 Winston Churchill to the Duke of Windsor, 28 October 1937

20. Jim Christy, *The Price of Power*, pp. 169–73

21. *New York Times*, 4 November 1937

22. Jim Christy, *The Price of Power*, p. 181

23. Duchess of Windsor to Betty Lawson-Johnston, dated Saturday 27th 1937, Private Collection

24. Betty Lawson-Johnston to the Duchess of Windsor, 30 December 1937, Private Collection

25. *The Memoirs of Princess Alice*, p. 115

26. 'The Duke and Duchess of Kent', *The Times*, 6 January 1935, p. 12, and 7 August 1936, p. 10, and 22 February 1937, p. 14

27. 'The Duke and Duchess of Kent', *The Times*, 30 July 1937, p. 30

28. 'Private View', *The Times*, 26 May 1937, p. 19, and 'The Duke and Duchess of Kent', *The Times*, 7 August 1936, p. 10

29. Jonathan Petropoulos, *Royals and the Reich*, p. 66

30. Ibid., p. 4

31. David Irving, *Goering*, p. 127

32. Sarah Bradford, *George VI*, p. 340

33. Goebbels diaries, cited in Gerwin Strobl, *The Germanic Isle*, p. 118

34. 'Austria Surrenders to Force', *The Times*, 12 March 1938, p. 12

35. Ibid.

36. Robert Rhodes James (ed.), *The Diaries of Sir Henry Channon*, p. 155

37. 'German-Czech Tension', *The Times*, 23 May 1938, p. 14

38. Andrew Roberts, *'The Holy Fox'*, p. 102

39. John Wheeler-Bennett, *King George VI*, p. 343

40. Robert Rhodes James (ed.), *The Diaries of Sir Henry Channon*, p. 166

41. 'Britain Warns Germany', *Daily Mail*, 10 September 1938

42. George VI to Queen Mary, 27 September 1938, cited in John Wheeler-Bennett, *King George VI*, p. 352

43. Robert Rhodes James (ed.), *The Diaries of Sir Henry Channon*, pp. 170–2

44. 'Ovation in London', *The Times*, 1 October 1938, p. 12

45. Noble Frankland, *Prince Henry*, p. 137

46. *The Memoirs of Princess Alice*, p. 116

47. Lord Birkenhead, *Walter Monckton*, p. 169

48. Noel Gallaway, 'Life for the Windsors Grows Complex', *New York Times*, 22 January 1939, p. 94

49. TNA PREM 1/467 George VI to Chamberlain, 14 December 1938

50. 'Nazi Attack on Jews. Orgy of Hitler Youth', *The Times*, 11 November 1938, p. 14

51. 'The German Press and the Jews', *The Times*, 9 November 1938, p. 13

52. Martin Gilbert, *Winston S. Churchill*, Volume 5, p. 972

53. Churchill's Bodyguard, DVD, Episode 2

54. Walter Thompson, *Beside the Bulldog*, pp. 14–15

55. Duke of Kent to Betty Lawson-Johnston, telegram, 1 January 1938, Private Collection

56. Sophia Watson, *Marina*, p. 157

57. 'Death of Prince Nicholas', *The Times*, 9 February 1938, p. 12

58. TNA FO 371/22381 Letter from Southern Dept to the Chancery, Budapest, 14 July 1938

59. Jonathan Petropoulos, *Royals and the Reich*, p. 186

60. Robert Rhodes James (ed.), *The Diaries of Sir Henry Channon*, p. 179

61. 'The Fate of the Czechs', *The Times*, 16 March 1939, p. 8

62. Duke of Kent to Betty Lawson-Johnston, dated 16th April, Private Collection

63. Sarah Bradford, George VI, pp. 374–5

64. 'Friends to Honor Duke', *New York Times*, 7 January 1939

65. 'Windsor is Hailed as Envoy of Peace', *New York Times*, 21 January 1939, p. 18

66. Michael Bloch, *The Secret File of the Duke of Windsor*, Appendix III, pp. 313–14

67. 'Historic Broadcasts of 1939', *New York Times*, 31 December 1939, p. 96

68. RA GVI/PRIV/RF/08/01A Kent to George VI, 16 May 1939

69. RA GVI/PRIV/RF/06/01-30 Gloucester to George VI, 16 May 1939

70. John Wheeler-Bennett, *King George VI*, pp. 390–1

71. TNA FO 371/23780 Oliver Harvey to Sir Noel Charles, 16 June 1939

72. Ibid.

73. Jonathan Petropoulos, *Royals and the Reich*, p. 193

74. Robert Rhodes James (ed.), *The Diaries of Sir Henry Channon*, p. 207

75. Roy Jenkins, *Churchill*, p. 545

76. Churchill to Clementine Churchill, cited in Mary Soames (ed.), *Speaking for Themselves*, p. 451

77. Walter Thompson, *Beside the Bulldog*, pp. 13–15

78. *Churchill's Bodyguard*, DVD, Episode 2

79. Jonathan Petropoulos, *Royals and the Reich*, p. 194

80. John Wheeler-Bennett, *King George VI*, p. 401

81. Robert Rhodes James (ed.), *The Diaries of Sir Henry Channon*, p. 209

82. 'Home News', *The Times*, 28–31 August 1939

83. Noble Frankland, *Prince Henry*, p. 140

84. 'The King at the Abbey', *The Times*, 28 August 1939, p. 7

85. 'The Duke of Windsor Begs Italy's King to Intervene', *New York Times*, 31 August 1939, p. 1

86. Lord Birkenhead, *Walter Monckton*, p. 170

87. Michael Thornton, *Royal Feud*, p. 191

88. Dina Wells Hood, *Working for the Windsors*, p. 143

89. Robert Rhodes James (ed.), *The Diaries of Sir Henry Channon*, p. 211

Chapter 4: In This Grave Hour

1. Winston Churchill, *The Second World War*, Volume 1, pp. 346–7

2. William Shawcross, *Queen Elizabeth*, p. 486

3. Robert Rhodes James (ed.), *The Diaries of Sir Henry Channon*, pp. 212–13

4. Diary note, Queen Elizabeth, 4 September 1939, in William Shawcross (ed.), *Counting One's Blessings*, p. 276

5. Mark Logue and Peter Conradi, *The King's Speech*, p. 166

6. Diary note, Queen Elizabeth, 4 September 1939, in William Shawcross (ed.), *Counting One's Blessings*, p. 276

7. George VI's War Diary, Volume I, 3 September 1939

8. Diary note, Queen Elizabeth, 4 September 1939, in William Shawcross (ed.), *Counting One's Blessings*, p. 276

9. George VI's War Diary, Volume I, 3 September 1939

10. Diary note, Queen Elizabeth, in William Shawcross (ed.), *Counting One's Blessings*, p. 276

11. John Wheeler-Bennett, *King George VI*, pp. 410–12

12. George VI's War Diary, Volume I, 4 September 1939

13. Randolph Churchill and Martin Gilbert, *The Churchill War Papers*, Volume 1, p. 187

14. Winston Churchill, *The Second World War*, Volume 1, p. 320

15. Otto Dietrich, *The Hitler I Knew*, p. 47, cited in Michael Bloch, *Ribbentrop*, p. 262

16. Sir Nevile Henderson, *Failure of a Mission*, 1940, p. 110

17. *The Memoirs of Princess Alice*, p. 119

18. RA HDGH/Diary/2/14 September/Tours of Army Units France: 14 September 1939–2 May 1940. *Note*: diary thought to be by Gloucester's equerry, Captain Howard Kerr

19. Duke of Gloucester to his wife, cited in Noble Frankland, *Prince Henry*, p. 141

20. RA HDGH/Diary/2/14 September/Tours of Army Units France: 14 September 1939–2 May 1940

21. RA HDG/PRIV Gloucester to Queen Mary, 27 September 1939

22. RA GVI/PRIV/RF/06/04 Gloucester in France to George VI, 19 September 1939, and RA GVI/PRIV/RF/06/06 Gloucester to George VI, 6 October 1939

23. RA HDG/PRIV George VI to Gloucester, 25 September 1939

24. RA GVI/PRIV/RF/06/04 Gloucester in France to George VI, 19 September 1939

25. RA GVI/PRIV/RF/08/04 Kent to George VI from Rosyth, 7 September 1939

26. RA GVI/PRIV/RF/08/06 Kent to George VI from Rosyth, 7 September 1939

27. Robert Rhodes James (ed.), *The Diaries of Sir Henry Channon*, p. 218

28. RA GVI/PRIV/RF/08/04 Kent to George VI from Rosyth, 7 September 1939

29. RA GVI/PRIV/RF/08/06 Kent to George VI from Pitlever House, Fife, 7 October 1939

30. RA GVI/PRIV/RF/08/07 Kent to George VI from Rosyth, 25 October 1939

31. Duke of Kent to Betty Lawson-Johnston, 22 September 1939, Private Collection

32. The Duchess of Windsor, *The Heart Has Its Reasons*, p. 329

33. Metcalfe Papers, cited in Philip Ziegler, *King Edward VIII*, p. 347

34. 'With a Smile and a Song', *Daily Mirror*, 12 September 1939

35. George VI's War Diary, Volume I, 14 September 1939

36. 'Topics of the Times', *New York Times*, 14 September 1939, p. 18

37. George VI's War Diary, Volume I, 14 September 1939

38. The duke's preference for Wales is stated in The Duchess of Windsor, *The Heart Has Its Reasons*, p. 326

39. The private papers of Hore-Belisha, cited in Philip Ziegler, *King Edward VIII*, p. 349

40. Peter Padfield, *Hess, Hitler & Churchill*, pp. 57–8

41. Anthony Cave Brown, *"C", The Secret Life of Sir Stewart Menzies*, p. 271

42. RA QM/PRIV/CC12/112 George VI to Queen Mary, 24 September 1939

43. George VI's War Diary, Volume I, 16 September 1939

44. Kirsty McLeod, *Battle Royal*, p. 229

45. Duke of Kent to Betty Lawson-Johnston from Admiralty House, North Queensferry, 22 September 1939, Private Collection

46. RA QM/PRIV/CC12/111 George VI to Queen Mary, 6 September 1939

47. Ibid.

48. George VI's War Diary, Volume I, 24 September 1939

49. Ibid.

50. Duke of Kent to Betty Lawson-Johnston from Admiralty House, North Queensferry, 22 September 1939, Private Collection

51. Robert Rhodes James (ed.), *The Diaries of Sir Henry Channon*, p. 220

52. George VI's War Diary, Volume I, 6–8 September 1939

53. RA QM/PRIV/CC12/112 George VI to Queen Mary, 24 September 1939

54. Michael Bloch, *The Secret File of the Duke of Windsor*, pp. 148–9

55. RA GVI/PRIV/RF/06/07 Gloucester to George VI, 12 October 1939

56. RA GVI/PRIV/RF/06/09 Gloucester to George VI, 19 October 1939

57. RA HDG/PRIV George VI to Gloucester, 27 October 1939

58. Duke of Windsor to Churchill, 14 November 1939, Chartwell Archives, Char 19/2A/89-90

59. Winston Churchill, *The Second World War*, Volume I, p. 320

60. Churchill to Duke of Windsor, 17 November 1939, Chartwell Archives, Char 19/2A/84-86

61. Anthony Cave Brown, *"C", The Secret Life of Sir Stewart Menzies*, pp. 198 and 273

62. Peter Allen, *The Crown and the Swastika*, p. 128

63. Zech-Burkersroda to Weizsäcker, 27 January 1940, in *Documents on German Foreign Policy*, Series D, Volume VIII, No. 580, p. 713

64. George VI's War Diary, Volume I, 29 September 1939

65. Michael Bloch, *Ribbentrop*, p. 266

66. George VI's War Diary, Volume I, 2 October 1939

67. George VI's War Diary, Volume I, 28 October 1939

68. George VI's War Diary Volume I, 7 November 1939

69. Robert Rhodes James (ed.), *The Diaries of Sir Henry Channon*, p. 225

70. Sophia Watson, *Marina*, p. 166

71. John Wheeler-Bennett, *King George VI*, pp. 429–30

72. RA GVI/PRIV/RF/06/14 Gloucester to George VI, Letter undated: circa 26–31 December 1939

73. RA HDG/PRIV George VI to Gloucester, 3 January 1940

74. RA HDG/PRIV Queen Mary to Gloucester, 6 January 1940

75. Noble Frankland, *Prince Henry*, p. 147

Chapter 5: Into the Unknown

1. RA GVI/PRIV/RF/08/10 Duke of Kent to George VI, 6 January 1940

2. Ibid.

3. 'The Fighting Finns', *The Times*, 4 January 1940, p. 7

4. Philip S. Jowett and Brent Snodgrass, *Finland at War 1939–45*, pp. 43–5

5. 'The Fighting Finns', *The Times*, 4 January 1940, p. 7

6. Peter Padfield, *Hess, Hitler & Churchill*, p. 6

7. Charles Peake to Oliver Harvey, 26 January 1940, cited in Lord Birkenhead, *Walter Monckton*, p. 371

8. Zech-Burkersroda to Weizsäcker, 27 January 1940, in *Documents on German Foreign Policy*, Series D, Volume VIII, No. 580, p. 713

9. Minister Zech to State Secretary Weizsäcker, 10 February 1940, in *Documents on German Foreign Policy*, Series D, Volume VIII, No. 621, p. 785

10. State Secretary Weizsäcker to Minister Zech, 2 March 1940, in *Documents on German Foreign Policy*, Series D, Volume VIII, No. 648, p. 837

11. RA GVI/PRIV/RF/06/18 Gloucester to George VI, 21 February 1940

12. Noble Frankland, *Prince Henry*, p. 149

13. RA HDG/PRIV George VI to Gloucester, 9 March 1940

14. RA GVI/PRIV/RF/06/20 Gloucester to George VI, 2 April 1940

15. Noble Frankland, *Prince Henry*, p. 151

16. Duke of Kent Engagement Diary, held in St James Palace, 17 November 1939

17. Sophia Watson, *Marina*, p. 164

18. 'Appointment of Royal Duchesses', *The Times*, 13 March 1940, p. 8

19. 'The Duchess of Kent with W.R.N.S', *The Times*, 23 October 1940

20. George VI's War Diary, Volume II, 12 March 1940

21. George VI's War Diary, Volume II, 13 March 1940

22. George VI's War Diary, Volume II, 18 March 1940

23. *The Times*, 12 April 1940

24. George VI's War Diary, Volume II, 16–17 March 1940

25. Cartier Archives Paris. The flamingo brooch was commissioned on 4 March 1940. The date of collection is not known but it is estimated that it took over a month to make due to the skill involved.

26. George VI's War Diary, Volume II, 9 April 1940

27. Ibid.

28. Michael Bloch, *Ribbentrop*, p. 277

29. William L. Shirer, *The Challenge of Scandinavia*

30. George VI's War Diary, Volume II, 12 April 1940

31. Noble Frankland, *Prince Henry*, p. 151

32. George VI's War Diary, Volume II, 27–28 April 1940

33. George VI's War Diary, Volume II, 30 April 1940

34. Winston Churchill, *The Second World War*, Volume 1, p. 520

35. George VI's War Diary, Volume II, 9 May 1940

36. William Shawcross, *Queen Elizabeth*, p. 507

37. George VI's War Diary, Volume II, 9 May 1940

38. Winston Churchill, *The Second World War*, Volume 2, pp. 25–31

39. Noble Frankland, *Prince Henry*, p. 152

40. George VI's War Diary, Volume II, 10 May 1940

41. Roy Jenkins, *Churchill*, p. 584

42. Walter Thompson, *Beside the Bulldog*, p. 21

43. *The Diaries of Sir Robert Bruce Lockhart, 1939–65*, p. 748, cited in Michael Thornton, *Royal Feud*, p. 200

44. Robert Rhodes James (ed.), *The Diaries of Sir Henry Channon*, p. 250

45. Winston Churchill, *The Second World War*, Volume 1, p. 525

46. George VI's War Diary, Volume II, 10 May 1940

47. Winston Churchill, *The Second World War*, Volume 1, p. 527

48. George VI's War Diary, Volume II, 11 May 1940

49. RA GVI/PRIV/RF/06/22 Gloucester to George VI, 15 May 1940

50. Robert Rhodes James (ed.), *The Diaries of Sir Henry Channon*, p. 257

51. George VI's War Diary, Volume II, 13 May 1940

52. Ibid.

53. *The Memoirs of Princess Alice*, p. 122

54. George VI's War Diary, Volume II, 13 May 1940

55. RA GVI/PRIV/RF/06/22 Gloucester to George VI, 15 May 1940

56. Winston Churchill, *The Second World War*, Volume 2, p. 36

57. George VI's War Diary, Volume II, 14 May 1940

58. Winston Churchill, *The Second World War*, Volume 2, p. 38

59. Ibid., p. 39

60. RA GVI/PRIV/RF/06/22 Gloucester to George VI, 15 May 1940

61. Noble Frankland, *Prince Henry*, p. 154

Chapter 6: The Decisive Struggle

1. George VI's War Diary, Volume III, 12 September 1940
2. George VI's War Diary, Volume II, 16 May 1940
3. Winston Churchill, *The Second World War*, Volume 2, p. 40
4. Ibid., pp. 42–3
5. Ibid., p. 46
6. George VI's War Diary, Volume II, 16 May 1940
7. Ibid., 15 and 16 May
8. Noble Frankland, *Prince Henry*, p. 154
9. RA HDG/PRIV Gloucester to Queen Mary, 21 May 1940
10. RA HDG/PRIV Queen Mary to Gloucester, 22 May 1940
11. RA QM/PRIV/CC12/124 George VI to Queen Mary, 21 May 1940
12. Winston Churchill, *The Second World War*, Volume 2, p. 52
13. Ibid., p. 53
14. Sophia Watson, *Marina*, p. 169
15. Duke of Kent Engagement Diary, 20 May 1940
16. 'The Duke of Kent: Special Welfare Duties in RAF', *The Times*, 27 April 1940
17. RA GDKH/ENGT/A02, 1940
18. Duke of Kent Engagement Diary, 30 and 31 May
19. George VI's War Diary, Volume II, 22 May 1940
20. Ibid.
21. Philip Ziegler, *King Edward VIII*, p. 358
22. John Wheeler-Bennett, *King George VI*, p. 449
23. George VI's War Diary, Volume II, 24 May 1940
24. Ibid.
25. George VI's War Diary, Volume II, 23 May 1940
26. Winston Churchill, *The Second World War*, Volume 2, pp. 49–50
27. Mark Logue and Peter Conradi, *The King's Speech*, p. 175
28. John Wheeler-Bennett, *King George VI*, p. 450
29. George VI's War Diary, Volume II, 24 May 1940
30. Sarah Bradford, *George VI*, p. 419
31. George VI's War Diary, Volume II, 21–22 May 1940
32. Winston Churchill, *The Second World War*, Volume 2, p. 72
33. Ibid., p. 73
34. George VI's War Diary, Volume II, 26–28 May 1940
35. Hugh Sebag-Montefiore, *Dunkirk: Fight to the Last Man*, p. 254
36. Winston Churchill, *The Second World War*, Volume 2, p. 87
37. Metcalfe Papers, cited in Philip Ziegler, *King Edward VIII*, p. 359
38. Ibid., p. 358
39. Antony Beevor, *The Second World War*, pp. 108–10
40. Andrew Roberts, 'The Holy Fox', p. 221
41. Winston Churchill, *The Second World War*, Volume 2, p. 84
42. Ibid., p. 79
43. George VI's War Diary, Volume II, 28 May 1940
44. Ibid.
45. Roy Jenkins, *Churchill*, p. 608

46. Michael Bloch, *The Secret File of the Duke of Windsor*, p. 155

47. Michael Thornton, *Royal Feud*, p. 202

48. Duchess of Windsor to her Aunt Bessie on 11 June 1940, in Michael Bloch, *Operation Willi*, p. 43

49. FBI HQ 65–31113 Memorandum from Edward Tamm to J. Edgar Hoover, 13 September 1940

50. Winston Churchill, *The Second World War*, Volume 2, pp. 88–9

51. George VI's War Diary, Volume II, 29 May 1940

52. Winston Churchill, *The Second World War*, Volume 2, p. 88

53. George VI's War Diary, Volume II, 31 May 1940

54. Elizabeth Longford, *The Queen Mother*, p. 79

55. Winston Churchill, *The Second World War*, Volume 2, p.95

56. George VI's War Diary, Volume II, 1 June 1940

57. Ibid., 1 June 1940

58. Ibid., 3 June 1940

59. Ibid., 4 June 1940

60. Winston Churchill, *The Second World War*, Volume 2, pp. 103–4

61. George VI's War Diary, Volume II, 4 June 1940

62. 'The King with his Troops', *The Times*, 6 June 1940, p. 4

63. George VI's War Diary, Volume II, 10 June 1940

64. Ibid.

65. Ibid., 12 June 1940

66. Robert Rhodes James (ed.), *The Diaries of Sir Henry Channon*, p. 255

67. George VI's War Diary, Volume II, 18 June 1940

68. Andrew Roberts, *'The Holy Fox'*, pp. 231–3

69. Winston Churchill, *The Second World War*, Volume 2, pp. 198–9

70. TNA FO 800/326/183 Lord Halifax to British Consulates-General at Nice, Bordeaux and Marseilles, 19 June 1940

Chapter 7: Treachery

1. Italian newspaper reports and radio summarised in 'The Duke of Windsor and Wife in Spain', *New York Times*, 21 June 1940, p. 9

2. Il Messaggero, 20 June 1940

3. 'The Duke of Windsor and Wife in Spain', *New York Times*, 21 June 1940, p. 9

4. Churchill Archives, CHAR 20/9A/2, Telegram from Duke of Windsor to Prime Minister, 21 June 1940

5. Churchill Archives, CHAR 20/9A/3, Telegram from Prime Minister to British Ambassador, Madrid, for Duke of Windsor, 22 June 1940

6. Telegram from the Ambassador in Spain, Eberhard von Stohrer, to German Foreign Ministry, 23 June 1940, *Documents on German Foreign Policy*, Series D, Volume X, No. 2, p. 2

7. Antony Beevor, *The Second World War*, p. 120

8. Telegram from the Ambassador in Spain, Eberhard von Stohrer, to German Foreign Ministry, 23 June 1940, *Documents on German Foreign Policy*, Series D, Volume X, No. 2, p. 2

9. Telegram from Ribbentrop to the Embassy in Spain, 24 June 1940, *Documents on German Foreign Policy*, Series D, Volume X, No. 9, p. 9

10. Churchill Archives, CHAR 20/9A-B,12 Duke of Windsor to Churchill, 27 June 1940

11. Philip Ziegler, *King Edward VIII*, p. 364

12. FRUS 1940/III Weddell to Secretary of State, 2 July 1940

13. Stohrer to Ribbentrop, 2 July 1940, *Documents on German Foreign Policy*, Series D, Volume X, No. 86, p. 96

14. George VI's War Diary, Volume II, 22, 23 and 25 June 1940

15. Winston Churchill, *The Second World War*, Volume 2, p. 152

16. George Orwell, cited in Patrick Bishop, *Battle of Britain*, p. 51

17. John Wheeler-Bennett, *King George VI*, p. 461

18. George VI's War Diary, Volume II, 26 June 1940

19. George VI refers to 'Cousin Wilhelmina' in a letter to his mother, 21 May 1940, RA QM/PRIV/CC12/124

20. William Shawcross, *Queen Elizabeth*, pp. 517–18

21. Sarah Bradford, *George VI*, p. 424

22. John Wheeler-Bennett, *King George VI*, p. 464

23. George VI's War Diary, Volume II, 21 June 1940

24. William Shawcross, *Queen Elizabeth*, p. 513

25. George VI's War Diary, Volume II, 9 June 1940

26. Winston Churchill, *The Second World War*, Volume 2, p. 226

27. Patrick Bishop, *Battle of Britain*, p. 65

28. *The Memoirs of Princess Alice*, pp. 122–3

29. TNA AIR 2/5452

30. Patrick Bishop, *Battle of Britain*, p. 49

31. Antony Beevor, *The Second World War*, p. 129

32. RA GDKH/ENGT/A07/18 Duke of Kent War Records, 18 September 1940, from unknown writer, probably the Duke's Private Secretary, to Group Captain F.C. Halahan

33. Winston Churchill, *The Second World War*, Volume 2, p. 197

34. Sarah Bradford, *George VI*, p. 413

35. Robert Rhodes James (ed.), *The Diaries of Sir Henry Channon*, 25 June 1940, p. 259

36. Clementine Churchill to Winston Churchill, 27 June 1940, cited in Mary Soames (ed.), *Speaking for Themselves*, p. 454

37. Winston Churchill, *The Second World War*, Volume 2, p. 201

38. Ibid., pp. 236 and 239

39. 'Portugal's Day of Celebration', *The Times*, 5 June 1940, and 'The Duke of Kent in Lisbon', *The Times*, 26 June–3 July 1940, pp. 5 and 6

40. Winston Churchill, *The Second World War*, Volume 2, p. 206

41. Ibid., p. 211

42. William Shawcross, *Queen Elizabeth*, p. 513

43. The Duchess of Windsor, *The Heart Has Its Reasons*, pp. 339–40

44. 'Windsors Dine with Fascist', *New York Times*, 1 July 1940, p. 9

45. Foreign Minister's Secretariat to Foreign Ministry, 30 June 1940, Documents on German Foreign Policy, Series D, Volume X, No. 66, p. 68

46. Michael Bloch, *Operation Willi*, p. 59

47. Churchill Archives, CHAR 20/9A-B,12 Duke of Windsor to Churchill, 27 June 1940

48. Martin Gilbert, *Finest Hour*, p. 614

49. George VI's War Diary, 3 July 1940

50. Churchill Archives, CHAR 20/9A-B,12 Churchill to Duke of Windsor, 28 June 1940

51. Churchill Archives, CHAR 20/9A-B,32 Churchill to Duke of Windsor, 4 July 1940

52. Philip Ziegler, King Edward VIII, p. 368

53. TNA FO/1093/23 Letter to Sir Alexander Cadogan, 7 July 1940

54. George VI's War Diary, Volume II, 10 July 1940

55. Patrick Bishop, *Battle of Britain*, pp. 75–7

56. Telegram from Minister in Lisbon to Ribbentrop cited in a telegram from Ribbentrop to Embassy in Spain, 11 July 1940, *Documents on German Foreign Policy*, Series D, Volume X, No. 152, p. 187

57. Ibid.

58. Michael Bloch, *Operation Willi*, p. 112

59. TNA FO 1093/23 C/5023 Telegram to Cadogan, 26 September 1940

60. TNA FO 1093/23 C/4720 Telegram to Cadogan, 19 July 1940

61. TNA FO 1093/23 Sgt D. Morton for Prime Minister, 4 August 1940

62. Goebbels diary, 1 October 1940, *Germanic Isle*

63. Winston Churchill, *The Second World War*, Volume 2, p. 229

64. Gazetta del Popolo, 22 July 1940

65. 'Plenipotentiary Cabinet for Britain Urged on King by Windsor, says Italian Newspaper', *New York Times*, 23 July 1940, p. 3

66. TNA FO 371/24813 Telegram No. 567 from Mr Vereker, Helsingfors, to Foreign Office, 22 July 1940

67. TNA FO 371/24813 Telegram No. 361 from Foreign Office, 24 July 1940

68. Winston Churchill, *The Second World War*, Volume 2, p. 230

69. Hugh Trevor-Roper, Rudolf Hess: The Incorrigible Intruder, cited in David Stafford (ed.), *Flight from Reality*, p. 157

70. William Shawcross, *Queen Elizabeth*, p. 510

71. The Ambassador in Spain to the Foreign Ministry, 23 July 1940, *Documents on German Foreign Policy*, Series D, Volume X, No. 211, p. 277

72. Walter Schellenberg, *The Schellenberg Memoirs*, pp. 121–31

73. Stohrer for the Foreign Minister, 25 July 1940, *Documents on German Foreign Policy*, Series D, Volume X, No. 224, p. 290

74. Stohrer for the Foreign Minister, 26 July 1940, *Documents on German Foreign Policy*, Series D, Volume X, No. 235, p. 317

75. Ibid., fn 3, p. 315 refers to a subsequent telegram from Stohrer dated 26 July 1940 re the Windsors' Spanish visa

76. Ibid., p. 318

77. Winston Churchill, *The Second World War*, Volume 2, pp. 237–8

78. Lord Birkenhead, *Walter Monckton*, p. 179

79. Huene to Ribbentrop, 2 August 1940, *Documents on German Foreign Policy*, Series D, Volume X, No. 277, pp. 398–401

80. Schellenberg to Foreign Minister, 30 July 1940, *Documents on German Foreign Policy*, Series D, Volume X, No. 254, p. 363

81. Michael Bloch, *Operation Willi*, p. 193

82. Lord Birkenhead, *Walter Monckton*, p. 180

83. Ribbentrop to Legation in Portugal, 31 July 1940, *Documents on German Foreign Policy*, Series D, Volume X, No. 265, pp. 378–9

84. Huene to Ribbentrop, 2 August 1940, *Documents on German Foreign Policy*, Series D, Volume X, No. 276, pp. 397–8

85. Huene to Ribbentrop, 2 August 1940, *Documents on German Foreign Policy*, Series D, Volume X, No. 277, p. 400

86. Walter Schellenberg, *The Schellenberg Memoirs*

87. James Douglas Hamilton, 'Hess and the Haushofers', in David Stafford (ed.), *Flight from Reality*, pp. 82–3

88. *Documents on German Foreign Policy*, Series D, Volume XI, pp. 78–81

89. TNA KV 2/1684 Letter from Albrecht Haushofer to the Duke of Hamilton, 23 September 1940

Chapter 8: There Will Always Be an England

1. Winston Churchill, *The Second World War*, Volume 2, p. 284

2. TNA AIR 2/5452 The Duke of Kent: A Year's Work with the RAF

3. Winston Churchill, *The Second World War*, Volume 2, p. 285

4. *Daily Express*, 16 August 1940

5. James Ismay, *The Memoirs of General Lord Ismay*, p. 182

6. George VI's War Diary, Volume III, 6 September 1940

7. *Pittsburgh Post Gazette*, 26 August 1942

8. Patrick Bishop, *Battle of Britain*, pp. 265–6

9. Winston Churchill, *The Second World War*, Volume 2, p. 283

10. George VI's War Diary, Volume III, 9 and 10 September 1940

11. RA QM/PRIV/CC12/134 George VI to Queen Mary, 11 September 1940

12. George VI's War Diary, Volume III, 13 September 1940

13. Ibid.

14. George VI's War Diary, Volume III, 19 September 1940

15. Sarah Bradford, George VI, p. 429, and Peter Allen, *The Crown and the Swastika*, p. 170

16. RA QM/PRIV/CC12/133 George VI to Queen Mary, 28 August 1940

17. Sarah Bradford, *George VI*, p. 432

18. George VI's War Diary, Volume III, 10 September 1940

19. John Wheeler-Bennett, *King George VI*, p. 470

20. Ibid., p. 473

21. 'Bahamian Natives Hail the Windsors', *New York Times*, 24 August 1940

22. 'Windsors on Way to the Bahamas', *New York Times*, 16 August 1940, p. 5

23. Michael Bloch, *The Secret File of the Duke of Windsor*, p. 174

24. Wallis Simpson to Betty Lawson-Johnston, 19 October 1940, Private Collection

25. Ibid.

26. Draft of unsent letter from Duke of Windsor to Churchill, cited in Michael Bloch, *The Secret File of the Duke of Windsor*, p. 178

27. Orjan Lindroth, 'The True Story of Axel Wenner-Gren', *Swedish Press*, January 2006

28. FBI HQ 65-31113 Letter to General Watson, Secretary to the President, from Hoover's office, 13 September 1940

29. FBI HQ 65-31113 Memorandum from Edward A. Tamm to J. Edgar Hoover, 13 September 1940

30. Ibid.

31. *The Life of Axel Wenner-Gren in Reality and Myth: a Symposium on Axel Wenner-Gren*, The Wenner-Gren Centre, Stockholm, May 2012, pp. 20–1

32. Orjan Lindroth, 'The True Story of Axel Wenner-Gren', *Swedish Press*, January 2006

33. FBI HQ 65–31113 Memorandum from Edward A. Tamm to J. Edgar Hoover, 13 September 1940

34. *Palm Beach Daily News*, 18 March 1940, p. 2

35. FBI HQ 65-31113 Letter to the FBI, 8 November 1940

36. FBI HQ 65-31113 Memorandum re Axel Wenner-Gren, 21 January 1941

37. FBI HQ 65-31113 Memorandum for the Director, 2 May 1941

38. FBI HQ 65-31113 Memorandum for Mr Tolson from an unnamed classifier, 19 October 1940

39. George VI's War Diary, Volume III, 7 and 8 September 1940

40. John Wheeler-Bennett, *King George VI*, pp. 488–9

41. George VI's War Diary, Volume III, 5–6 and 7 October 1940

42. Ibid., 12–13 October 1940

43. Ibid., 15 October 1940

44. Ibid., 22 October 1940

45. Ibid., 18 October 1940

46. Sophia Watson, *Marina*, p. 169

47. John Wheeler-Bennett, *George VI*, p. 492

48. Ibid.

49. RA QM/PRIV/CC12/143 George VI to Queen Mary, 18 November 1940

50. George VI's War Diary, Volume III, 16 November 1940

51. TNA FO 1093/23 Cypher Telegram, Colonial Office to Windsor, 11 December 1940

52. TNA FO 1093/23 'C' to Henry Hopkinson, 14 December 1940

53. TNA FO 1093/23/ Cypher telegram, Duke of Windsor to Colonial Office, 19 December 1940

54. TNA FO 1093/23 K.E. Robinson to Henry Hopkinson, 26 December 1940

55. TNA FO 371/2619

56. TNA FO 1093/23 'C' to Henry Hopkinson, 17 March 1941

57. TNA FO 371/2619 Halifax to Churchill

58. Michael Bloch, *The Secret File of the Duke of Windsor*, p. 187

59. TNA FO/371/2619

60. Wallis Simpson to Betty Lawson-Johnston, 2 April 1941, Private Collection

61. Henry Ashby Turner, Jr., *General Motors and the Nazis*, p. 153

62. Charles Higham, *Trading with the Enemy*, pp. 171–2

63. Henry Ashby Turner, Jr., *General Motors and the Nazis*, p. 124

64. 'Windsor in Yacht Mishap', *New York Times*, 4 April 1941, p. 4

65. FBI HQ 65-31113 Memorandum for the Director, 16 April 1941

66. Ibid.

67. FBI HQ 65-31113 Memorandum from J. Edgar Hoover to the Attorney General, 17 April 1941

68. FBI HQ 65-31113 Letter from A.A. Berle to Attorney General, 18 April 1941

69. FBI HQ 65-31113 Memorandum from E.A. Tamm for Hoover, 19 April 1941

70. FBI HQ 65-31113 Memorandum for Hoover, 24 April 1941

71. Life, March 1939

72. FBI HQ 65-31113 Memorandums, 21–23 April 1941

73. Orjan Lindroth, 'The True Story of Axel Wenner-Gren', *Swedish Press*, January 2006

74. FBI HQ 65-31113 Memorandum for Mr Tolson and Mr Tamm from Hoover, 18 April 1941

75. TNA FO 1093/23 Counter-espionage report from 'C' to Henry Hopkinson, 29 May 1941

76. Ibid.

77. Letter from Norman Whitehouse to 'Darling', 12 April 1941

78. TNA KV2/1684 Memorandum, dated 21 November 1940

79. TNA KV2/1684 Memorandum from W.G. White to Major Robertson, 13 January 1941

80. Letter to the Editor from Clydesdale (Duke of Hamilton), *The Times*, 6 October 1939, p. 9

81. TNA KV2/1684 W.G. White to Major Robertson, 13 January 1941

82. TNA KV2/1684 Major Robertson to Air Ministry, 20 January 1941

83. TNA KV2/1684 Statement of Wing Commander, The Duke of Hamilton, 11 March 1941

84. Letter from Albrecht Haushofer to Duke of Hamilton, 16 July 1939, cited in David Stafford (ed.), *Flight from Reality*, p. 81

85. TNA KV2/1684 Statement of Wing Commander, The Duke of Hamilton, 11 March 1941

86. TNA KV2/1684 Major T.A. Robertson to Air Commodore Boyle, 7 April 1941

87. TNA KV2/1684 Boyle to T.A.R., 9 April 1941

88. George VI's War Diary, Volume IV, 14 January 1941

89. RA QM/ PRI/CC12/154 George VI to Queen Mary, 24 February 1941

90. George VI's War Diary, Volume IV, 7 February 1941

91. RA QM/PRIV/CC12/154 George VI to Queen Mary, 24 February 1941

92. RA QM/PRIV/CC12/156 George VI to Queen Mary, 27 February 1941

93. George VI's War Diary, Volume IV, 9 February 1941

94. RA QM/PRIV/CC12/138 George VI to Queen Mary, 14 October 1940

95. George VI's War Diary, Volume IV, 25 March 1941

96. Robert Rhodes James (ed.), *The Diaries of Sir Henry Channon*, 24 November 1940, p. 276

97. Neil Balfour and Sally Mackay, *Paul of Yugoslavia*, pp. 226–7

98. George VI's War Diary, Volume IV, 24 February 1941, and John Wheeler-Bennett, *King George VI*, p. 497

99. Robert Rhodes James (ed.), *The Diaries of Sir Henry Channon*, 25 March 1941, p. 296

100. Ibid., 24 March 1941, p. 295

101. Ibid., 27 March 1941, p. 297

102. Neil Balfour and Sally Mackay, *Paul of Yugoslavia*, pp. 249–50

103. Robert Rhodes James (ed.), *The Diaries of Sir Henry Channon*, 30 March 1941, p. 297

104. Sophia Watson, *Marina*, p. 173

105. Stella King, *Princess Marina*, p. 165

Chapter 9: Ever Widening Conflict

1. TNA FO 1093/1 Duke of Hamilton statement, 11 May 1941

2. *Daily Record*, 12 May 1941

3. Lothar Kettenacker, 'Mishandling a Spectacular Event', in David Stafford (ed.), *Flight from Reality*, p. 22

4. TNA FO 1093/1 Duke of Hamilton statement, 11 May 1941

5. Ibid.

6. Ibid.

7. Winston Churchill, *The Second World War*, Volume 3, p. 43

8. John Erickson, 'Rudolf Hess: A Post-Soviet Postscript', in David Stafford (ed.), *Flight from Reality*, p. 39

9. George VI's War Diary, Volume IV, 13 May 1941

10. Ibid., 10, 11 and 12 May 1941

11. Ibid., 13 May 1941

12. Winston Churchill, *The Second World War*, Volume 3, p. 44

13. Lothar Kettenacker, 'Mishandling a Spectacular Event', in David Stafford (ed.), *Flight from Reality*, p. 28

14. Winston Churchill, *The Second World War*, Volume 3, p. 43

15. George VI's War Diary, Volume IV, 16 May 1941

16. TNA AIR 19/564 Sir Archibald Sinclair's statement in the House, 22 May 1941

17. John Erickson, 'Rudolf Hess: A Post-Soviet Postscript', in David Stafford (ed.), *Flight from Reality*, pp. 40–4

18. Lynn Picknett, Clive Prince and Stephen Prior, *Double Standards*, p. 414–40

19. Hugh Trevor-Roper, 'Hess the Incorrigible Intruder', in David Stafford (ed.), *Flight from Reality*, pp. 155–6

20. *Documents on German Foreign Policy*, Series D, Volume XI, pp. 15, 16 and 78–81

21. Ibid., and also Hamilton identified as best contact is set out in Albrecht Haushofer's statement to Hitler on 12 May 1941 after Hess's flight, 'English Connections and the Possibility of their Employment', in TNA KV2/1685

22. TNA KV 2/1684 Correspondence between Major Robertson and the Air Ministry, January–April 1941, concerning Hess's letter to Hamilton

23. Hugh Trevor-Roper, 'Hess the Incorrigible Intruder', in David Stafford (ed.), *Flight from Reality*, pp. 155–6

24. Manuscript Simon 88, Special Collections, Bodleian Library, 'Interview of "Jonathan," i.e., Rudolf Hess, by "Dr Guthrie," i.e., Sir John Simon', on 9 June 1941

25. TNA FO 1093/12 Minutes to Cadogan from Colonel M. Rees 19 August 1941

26. TNA KV 2/1685 Albrecht Haushofer's statement to Hitler, 12 May 1941, 'English Connections and the Possibility of their Employment'

27. FBI HQ 65-31113-26 J. Edgar Hoover to Adolf A. Berle, 22 April 1942

28. George VI's War Diary, Volume IV, 22 June 1941

29. *The Memoirs of Princess Alice*, p. 125

30. George VI's War Diary, Volume IV, 24 June 1941

31. Roosevelt to George VI, 1 May 1940, cited in John Wheeler-Bennett, *King George VI*, p. 510

32. George VI to Roosevelt, 3 June 1941, cited in John Wheeler-Bennett, *King George VI*, pp. 525–6

33. RA GVI/PRIV/RF/08/11 Duke of Kent to George VI, 7 August 1941

34. Ibid.

35. Ibid.

36. TNA AIR 2/5452

37. William Shawcross, *Queen Elizabeth*, p. 539

38. Winston Churchill, *The Second World War*, Volume 3, p. 384

39. Roy Jenkins, *Churchill*, p. 665

40. RA GVI/PRIV/RF/08 12 Duke of Kent to George VI, 20 August 1941

41. *Sydney Morning Herald*, 24 August 1941

42. RA GVI/PRIV/RF/08/14 Duke of Kent to George VI, 30 August 1941

43. Christopher Warwick, *George and Marina*, p. 120

44. RA GVI/PRIV/RF/08/14 Duke of Kent to George VI, 30 August 1941

45. Duke of Kent to Betty Lawson-Johnston, Letter 11, Private Collection, 9 September 1941

46. George VI's War Diary, Volume V, 8 July 1941

47. RA GVI/PRIV/RF/08/14 Duke of Kent to George VI, 30 August 1941

48. Duchess of Windsor to Betty Lawson-Johnston, Private Collection, 19 September 1941

49. 'Roosevelt Host to the Windsors Today', *New York Times*, 28 October 1941

50. Ibid.

51. Ibid.

52. TNA FO 1093/23 Viscount Halifax to Lord Moyne, 26 June 1941

53. TNA FO 1093/23 Letter to Sir Alexander Cadogan, 19 September 1941

54. TNA FO 1093/23 Appendix to Report 166, Summary of Herman Rogers's interview with the Bermuda Censorship Authorities

55. Ibid.

56. Ibid.

57. Charles Glass, Americans in Paris, p. 200, and Jim Christy, The Price of Power, p. 121

58. William Shawcross, Queen Elizabeth, p. 541

59. George VI's War Diary, Volume V, 6, 7 and 8 December 1941

60. Ibid.

61. Ibid., 9 December 1941

62. William Shawcross, Queen Elizabeth, p. 542

63. George VI's War Diary, Volume V, 10 December 1941

64. Churchill Archives, CHAR 20/20, George VI to Winston Churchill, 10 December 1941

65. John Wheeler-Bennett, King George VI, p. 533

66. RA QM/PRIV/CC12/175 George VI to Queen Mary, 21 September 1941

67. Robert Rhodes James (ed.), The Diaries of Sir Henry Channon, 18 December 1941, p. 315

68. Winston Churchill, The Second World War, Volume 3, p. 594

69. RA QM/PRIV/CC12180 George VI to Queen Mary, 17 December 1941

70. King's speech 1941, cited in John Wheeler-Bennett, King George VI, p. 534

71. 'The King is Still in London', Bert Ambrose Orchestra, words by Roma Hunter

Chapter 10: It's My Brother

1. George VI's War Diary, Volume V, 24–31 January 1942

2. Ibid., 2, 3 and 10 February 1942

3. Winston Churchill, The Second World War, Volume 4

4. George VI's War Diary, Volume V, 13, 14–16 February 1942

5. 'After Singapore', Daily Mirror, 16 February 1942

6. 'WE CAN LOSE', Daily Mirror, 13 February 1942

7. 'Churchill's Broadcast', Daily Mail, 13 February 1942

8. RA QM/PRIV/CC12/6 George VI to Queen Mary, 16 February 1942

9. William Shawcross, Queen Elizabeth, p. 546

10. George VI's War Diary, Volume V, 14–16 February 1942

11. Ibid., 17 February 1942

12. Robert Rhodes James (ed.), The Diaries of Sir Henry Channon, p. 323

13. George VI's War Diary, Volume V, 24 February 1942

14. George VI's War Diary, Volume V, 28 February 1942

15. John Wheeler-Bennett, King George VI, p. 774

16. RA HDGH/DIARY/1/08

17. RA HDG/PRIV Queen Mary to Gloucester, 8 June 1941

18. RA HDG/PRIV Gloucester to Queen Mary, 6 January 1942

19. RA HDG/PRIV George VI to Gloucester, 12 March 1942

20. Noble Frankland, Prince Henry, p. 162

21. Charles A. Jellison, Besieged: The World War II Ordeal of Malta, pp. 137–8

22. 'Duke of Gloucester in Cairo', The Times, 18 April 1942, p.4

23. 'Duke of Gloucester in the Desert', *The Times*, 5 May 1942

24. 'Persian Friendship for Britain', *The Times*, 21 May 1942, p. 3

25. RA GVI/PRIV/RF/06/27 Gloucester to George VI, 3 June 1942

26. Robert Rhodes James (ed.), *The Diaries of Sir Henry Channon*, 25 March 1942, p. 325

27. RA QM/PRI/CC13/7 George VI to Queen Mary, 10 March 1942

28. RA HDG/PRIV Gloucester to Queen Mary, 27 May 1942

29. RA GVI/PRIV/RF/06/27 Gloucester to George VI, 3 June 1942

30. 'The King's Message of Good Cheer', *The Times*, 13 June 1942, p. 4

31. *The Times*, 13, 18, 20, 21 and 23 June 1942

32. Professor David Reynolds, *World War Two: 1942 and Hitler's Soft Underbelly*, BBC4, 30 April 2013

33. Robert Rhodes James (ed.), *The Diaries of Sir Henry Channon*, 21–30 June 1942, pp. 332–3

34. Ibid., 1 July 1942, p. 334

35. RA QM/PRIV/CC13/19 George VI to Queen Mary, 6 July 1942

36. FBI HQ65-3113 Letter to J. Edgar Hoover, 1942

37. M.E. Paz, *Strategy, Security and Spies*, p. 192

38. Letter from Commander Perkins to US Naval Intelligence, Washington, 11 February 1942, in NARA/NND 883021/SIS Intelligence Reports/29 November 1941–31 March 1942

39. *Reality and Myth: A Symposium on Axel Wenner-Gren*, p. 22

40. 'Windsor's Friend Among those on Blacklist', *Evening Independent*, 15 January 1942, p. 11

41. Letter from Commander Perkins to US Naval Intelligence, Washington, 11 February 1942, in NARA/NND 883021/SIS Intelligence Reports/29 November 1941–31 March 1942

42. Ibid.

43. 'Windsor's Friend Among those on Blacklist', *Evening Independent*, 15 January 1942, p. 11

44. Letter from Commander Perkins to US Naval Intelligence, Washington, 11 February 1942, in NARA/NND 883021/SIS Intelligence Reports/29 November 1941–31 March 1942

45. Letter from Wallace B. Phillips to Commander Perkins, 18 February 1942 in NARA/NND 883021/SIS Intelligence Reports/29 November 1941–31 March 1942

46. Report of S. Pinkney Tuck, chargé d'affaires, US Embassy, France, 23 July 1942, cited in Jim Christy, *The Price of Power*, p. 247

47. TNA FO 1093/23 Foreign Office report on German approaches to Duke of Windsor, 23 April 1941

48. Jim Christy, *The Price of Power*, p. 236

49. FBI HQ65-3113 Letter to J. Edgar Hoover, 22 July 1942

50. FBI HQ65-3113 Letter to J. Edgar Hoover, 2 March 1942

51. Christopher Warwick, *George and Marina*, p. 123

52. John Wheeler-Bennett, *King George VI*, p. 547

53. RA GDKH/ENGT/A40 Alexander Hardinge to John Lowther, 14 March 1941

54. RA GDKH/ENGT/B43 John Lowther to the Chief Constable of the Isle of Wight, 21 August 1942

55. RA GDHK/ENGT/B43 John Lowther to the ARP Controller in Newport, 21 August 1942

56. RA GDKH/PRIV19 John Lowther to V.G. Lawford, FO, 31 July 1942

57. Ibid.

58. RA GDKH/PRIV19 John Lowther to the War Office, War Transport and Passport Office on 11, 15 and 19 August 1942

59. RA GDKH/PRIV/19 John Lowther to Commander Campbell, 22 August 1942

60. 'The Duke of Gloucester's Farewell', *The Times*, 18 July 1942

61. *The Memoirs of Princess Alice*, p. 127

62. Noble Frankland, *Prince Henry*, p. 171

63. *The Memoirs of Princess Alice*, p. 128

64. Sophia Watson, *Marina*, p. 180

65. Wentworth Day, *HRH Princess Marina*, p. 125

66. 'The Tragedy at Eagle's Rock', *Scotsman*, 24 August 1985, p. 2

67. George VI to Edwina Mountbatten, cited in Sophia Watson, *Marina*, p. 181

68. RA GVI/PRIV/RF/08/18 Duke of Kent to George VI, 22 August 1942

69. Graham Payn and Sheridan Morley (eds.), *The Noël Coward Diaries*, 29 August 1942, p. 17

70. Telegram, Duchess of Kent to Betty Lawson-Johnston, Private Collection, 17 September 1942

71. Duchess of Kent to Betty Lawson-Johnston, Private Collection, 12 September 1942

72. George VI's War Diary, Volume VI, 18–21 September 1942

73. RA QM/PRIV/CC13/27 George VI to Queen Mary, 22 October 1942

74. RA QM/PRIV/CC13/30 George VI to Queen Mary, 4 December 1942

75. 'The Tragedy at Eagle's Rock', *Scotsman*, 24 August 1985, p. 2

76. Ibid.

77. Christopher Warwick, *George and Marina*, p. 126

78. Lynn Picknett, Clive Prince and Stephen Prior, *Double Standards*, pp. 406–7

79. Statement of Sir Archibald Sinclair to House of Commons on 7 October 1942, Hansard

80. TNA AIR 2/16973 Statement of Dr Kennedy on 29 August 1942

81. TNA FO 371/26376 Memorandum of T.K. Roberts of conversation between President Benes and General Sikorski

82. Huene to Ribbentrop, 5 December 1942, cited in 'The Tragedy at Eagle's Rock', *Scotsman*, 24 August 1985, p. 2

83. Lynn Picknett, Clive Prince and Stephen Prior, *Double Standards*, p. 434

84. Jonathan Petropoulos, *Royals and the Reich*, pp. 154 and 278

85. Colin Simpson, David Leitch and Philip Knightley, 'Blunt was an Emissary for George VI', *Sunday Times*, 5 November 1979

86. George VI's War Diary, Volume VI, 30 August 1942

87. Ibid.

88. Mrs Roosevelt's diary of trip to Great Britain October–November 1942, cited in John Wheeler-Bennett, *King George VI*, p. 550

89. Antony Beevor, *The Second World War*, pp. 377–8

90. Max Hastings, *Finest Years*, p. 338

91. Antony Beevor, *The Second World War*, p. 378

92. George VI's War Diary, Volume VII, 3 November 1942

93. John Wheeler-Bennett, *King George VI*, p. 553

94. George VI's War Diary, Volume VII, 4 November 1942

95. Martin Gilbert, *Road to Victory*, pp. 249–51

96. Mark Logue and Peter Conradi, *The King's Speech*, p. 184

97. George VI to Lionel Logue, 26 December 1942, cited in ibid., p. 185

Chapter 11: Tested as Never Before in Our History

1. John Wheeler-Bennett, *King George VI*, p. 585

2. Pathé, *Liberation of Stalingrad*, 1943

3. Robert Rhodes James (ed.), *The Diaries of Sir Henry Channon*, 16 February 1943, p. 351

4. RA QM/PRIV/CC13/38 George VI to Queen Mary, 1 February 1943

5. George VI's War Diary, Volume VII, 16 February 1943

6. RA QM/PRIV/CC13/42 George VI to Queen Mary, 28 February 1943

7. RA QM/PRIV/CC13/43 George VI to Queen Mary, 10 March 1943

8. Martin Gilbert, *Road to Victory*, pp. 357–8

9. RA QM/PRIV/CC13/40 George VI to Queen Mary, 22 February 1943

10. TNA FO 371/37627 Churchill to Colonial Minister, 12 February 1943

11. Robert Rhodes James (ed.), *The Diaries of Sir Henry Channon*, 19 May 1943, pp. 358–9

12. Duff Hart-Davis (ed.), *The Diaries of Sir Alan Lascelles*, p. 129

13. *The Times*, 15 May 1943, p. 1

14. *The Times* editorial, 18 May 1943

15. RA QM/PRIV/CC13/56 George VI to Queen Mary, 28 June 1943

16. George VI's War Diary, Volume VII, 20 June 1943

17. RA QM/PRIV/CC13/56 George VI to Queen Mary, 28 June 1943

18. British Pathé, *Malta Welcomes the King*, June 1943

19. Ibid.

20. John Wheeler-Bennett, *King George VI*, p. 578

21. James Owen, *A Serpent in Eden*, p. 6

22. Robert Rhodes James (ed.), *The Diaries of Sir Henry Channon*, 22 July 1943, p. 372

23. William Boyd, 'The Real Life Murder Case Behind Any Human Heart', *Guardian*, 13 November 2010

24. James Owen, *A Serpent in Eden*, p. 87

25. 'Bedaux Legendary as Mystery Man', *New York Times*, 20 February 1944, p. 28

26. 'Windsors in Miami on Way to Capital', *New York Times*, 29 May 1942, p. 14

27. 'Bahamas Blacklist Wenner-Gren Firms', *New York Times*, 3 February 1943, p. 7

28. 'General Foods, in Bahamas Deal, Gets Seized Wenner-Gren Plant', *New York Times*, 19 July 1942, p. 1

29. 'Bedaux Legendary as Mystery Man', *New York Times*, 20 February 1944, p. 28

30. FBI 65-HQ-33604 Memorandum from J. Edgar Hoover, 1943

31. Ibid.

32. Jim Christy, *The Price of Power*, p. 288

33. FBI 65-HQ-33604 Memorandum from J. Edgar Hoover, 1943

34. Ibid.

35. FBI 62-62736-1126, No 3965 Bedaux's Censorship Report

36. Charles Glass, *Americans in Paris*, p. 337

37. 'Bedaux, Mystery Man, Facing Treason Charges, Kills himself Here', *Miami Daily News*, 19 February 1944

38. 'Windsor's Cleric and Wife Held for Deportation Trial', *Washington Post*, 8 May 1943

39. Memo from A.A. Berle to British Embassy in Washington, NA (US) 811.711/4039

40. Philip Ziegler, *King Edward VIII*, p. 421

41. Letter drafted from Windsor to George VI, in Michael Bloch, *The Secret File of the Duke of Windsor*, pp. 202–3

42. Ibid.

43. Jonathan Petropoulos, *Royals and the Reich*, p. 290

44. Ray Moseley, *Mussolini: The Last 600 Days of Il Duce*

45. Jonathan Petropoulos, *Royals and the Reich*, pp. 296–7

46. Philip Eade, *Young Prince Philip*, p. 164

47. Jonathan Petropoulos, *Royals and the Reich*, p. 293

48. William Shawcross, *Queen Elizabeth*, p. 574

49. 'Comin' in on a Wing and a Prayer', Harold Adamson and Jimmie McHugh, 1943

50. *The Memoirs of Princess Alice*, p. 128

51. Ibid., pp. 131–2

52. RA QM/PRIV/CC13/63 George VI to Queen Mary, 8 September 1943

53. Noble Frankland, *Prince Henry*, p. 176

54. RA QM/PRIV/CC13/67 George VI to Queen Mary, 14 October 1943

55. *The Memoirs of Princess Alice*, p. 134

56. George VI's War Diary, Volume VIII, 21 December 1943

57. Ibid., 2 November 1943

58. Ibid., 15 December 1943

59. Philip Eade, *Young Prince Philip*, p. 153

60. William Shawcross, *Queen Elizabeth*, p. 578

61. George VI's War Diary, Volume VIII, 7 March 1944

62. Ibid., 18 January 1944

63. Antony Beevor, *The Second World War*, p. 568

64. Military Records, K.H. Cadbury, cited in J. Crosfield, *The Cadbury Family*

Chapter 12: Something More Than Courage

1. George VI's War Diary, Volume VIII, 3 February 1944

2. Winston Churchill, *The Second World War*, Volume 6, p. 5

3. John Wheeler-Bennett, *King George VI*, p. 600

4. David Eisenhower, *Eisenhower at War, 1943–45*, p. 234

5. Walter Thompson, *Beside the Bulldog*, p. 125

6. Roy Jenkins, *Churchill*, p. 743

7. George VI's War Diary, Volume VIII, 30 May 1944

8. Duff Hart-Davis (ed.), *The Diaries of Sir Alan Lascelles*, p. 226

9. John Wheeler-Bennett, *King George VI*, p. 602

10. George VI's War Diary, Volume IX, 1 June 1944

11. John Wheeler-Bennett, *King George VI*, p. 607

12. George VI's War Diary, Volume IX, 2 June 1944

13. Walter Thompson, *Beside the Bulldog*, pp.125–6

14. Duff Hart-Davis (ed.), *The Diaries of Sir Alan Lascelles*, p. 230

15. George VI's War Diary, Volume IX, 4–5 June 1944

16. Winston Churchill, *The Second World War*, Volume 6, pp. 4–5

17. Duff Hart-Davis (ed.), *The Diaries of Sir Alan Lascelles*, p. 230

18. RA QM/PRIV/CC13/90 George VI to Queen Mary, 10 June 1944

19. Mark Logue and Peter Conradi, *The King's Speech*, p. 195

20. John Wheeler-Bennett, *King George VI*, p. 607

21. Duchess of Windsor to her Aunt Bessie, 6 February and 5 April 1944, cited in Michael Bloch, *The Secret File of the Duke of Windsor*, p. 211

22. Helen Worden, 'The Duchess of Windsor', *American Mercury*, June 1944, pp. 675–81

23. Ibid., pp. 678–9

24. Ibid., pp. 680–1

25. FBI HQ65-31113, E.E. Conroy to J. Edgar Hoover, 1 August 1944

26. Ibid.

27. Ibid.

28. Michael Bloch, *The Secret File of the Duke of Windsor*, p. 212

29. Philip Ziegler, *King Edward VIII*, p. 422

30. RA QM/PRIV/CC13/100 and 102 George VI to Queen Mary, 12 and 20 September 1944

31. Letter from Duke of Windsor to Roy Howard, cited in Michael Bloch, *The Secret File of the Duke of Windsor*, p. 214

32. Duff Hart-Davis (ed.), *The Diaries of Sir Alan Lascelles*, 30 May 1944, pp. 222–3

33. Ibid., p. 224

34. Duchess of Kent to Betty Lawson-Johnston, 18 November 1944, Private Collection

35. Max Hastings, *Finest Years*, pp. 516–18

36. Duchess of Kent to Betty Lawson-Johnston, 18 November 1944, Private Collection

37. RA QM/PRIV/CC13/119 George VI to Queen Mary, 25 March 1945

38. Neil Balfour and Sally Mackay, *Paul of Yugoslavia*, p. 295

39. Sophia Watson, *Marina*, pp. 202–3

40. Robert Rhodes James (ed.), *The Diaries of Sir Henry Channon*, 19 November 1944, p. 380

41. British Pathé, *Home Guard 'Stand Down' Parade*, December 1944

42. Noble Frankland, *Prince Henry*, p. 179

43. *The Memoirs of Princess Alice*, p. 135

44. RA HDG/PRIV Duke of Gloucester to Queen Mary, 28 December 1944

45. *The Memoirs of Princess Alice*, p. 137

46. Ibid., p. 141

47. Noble Frankland, *Prince Henry*, p. 189

48. Mark Logue and Peter Conradi, *The King's Speech*, p. 200

49. Ibid., p. 201

50. RA QM/PRIV/CC13/122 George VI to Queen Mary, 23 April 1945

51. George VI's War Diary, Volume X, 13 April 1945

52. William Shawcross, *Queen Elizabeth*, p. 589

53. Laurence Rees, *Auschwitz: The Nazis and the Final Solution*, BBC TV, 2005

54. General Dwight Eisenhower on 12 April after his first visit to a camp

55. George VI's War Diary, Volume X, 19–22 April 1945

56. RA QM/PRIV/CC13/122 George VI to Queen Mary, 23 April 1945

57. Jonathan Petropoulos, *Royals and the Reich*, p. 296

58. Ibid., p. 302

59. Traudl Junge, 'Interview with Hitler's Secretary', *The World at War*, Thames, Disc 8

60. Michael Bloch, *Ribbentrop*, p. 432

61. William Shawcross, *Queen Elizabeth*, p. 591

62. John Wheeler-Bennett, *King George VI*, p. 627

63. RA HDG/PRIV George VI to Duke of Gloucester, 29 May 1945

64. Philip Ziegler, *London at War*, pp. 323–8

65. Robert Rhodes James (ed.), *The Diaries of Sir Henry Channon*, 8 May 1945, pp. 405–6

66. Mark Logue and Peter Conradi, *The King's Speech*, p. 207

67. Queen Elizabeth interview with BBC War Correspondent, Godfrey Talbot, 8 May 1985

68. Michael Vickery to his mother on 8 May 1945, posted by Patrick Vickery

69. RA HDG/PRIV Queen Mary to Duke of Gloucester, 10 May 1945

70. The King's Speech, Victory in Europe Day, Tuesday 8 May 1945

71. Graham Payn and Sheridan Morley (eds.), *The Noël Coward Diaries*, Tuesday 8 May: Victory in Europe Day, p. 29

Chapter 13: For Valour

1. Winston Churchill, *The Second World War*, Volume 6, pp. 512–13
2. RA HDG/PRIV George VI to Duke of Gloucester, 29 May 1945
3. George VI's Diary, Volume X, 18–20 May 1945
4. Ibid., 21–22 May 1945
5. Ibid., 25 July 1945
6. RA HDG/PRIV George VI to Duke of Gloucester, 29 May 1945
7. George VI's Diary, Volume X, 14 and 29 June 1945
8. Jonathan Petropoulos, *Royals and the Reich*, pp. 337–9
9. John Costello, *Mask of Treachery*, pp. 404–6
10. Jonathan Petropoulos, *Royals and the Reich*, pp. 339–40
11. George VI's Diary, Volume X, 26 July 1945
12. Ibid.
13. George VI to Winston Churchill, 31 July 1945
14. John Wheeler-Bennett, *King George VI*, p. 650
15. George VI's Diary, Volume X, 28 July 1945
16. Churchill to Attlee, 26 August 1945, cited in Philip Ziegler, *King Edward VIII*, p. 472
17. TNA FO 800/521 Ernest Bevin to Clement Attlee, 13 August 1945
18. Ibid.
19. TNA FO 800/521 Earl of Halifax to FO, 13 October 1945
20. TNA FO 800/521 Memorandum, 'The Windsor Papers', Ernest Bevin to Prime Minister, 30 June 1947
21. *Documents on German Foreign Policy*, Series D, No. 211, p. 277
22. *Documents on German Foreign Policy*, Series D, No. 276, p. 398
23. Ibid.
24. Cadogan diary, 25 October 1945, cited in Sarah Bradford, *George VI*, p. 563
25. George VI to Queen Mary, 23 September 1945, cited in Philip Ziegler, *King Edward VIII*, p. 430
26. George VI's Diary, Volume XI, 5 October 1945
27. Ibid., 6 October 1945
28. Ibid.
29. Michael Bloch, *The Secret File of the Duke of Windsor*, p. 218
30. George VI's Diary, Volume XI, 22 November 1945
31. Ibid., 6 December 1945
32. Michael Bloch, *The Secret File of the Duke of Windsor*, p. 229
33. Duke of Windsor to John Balfour, cited in Philip Ziegler, *King Edward VIII*, p. 428
34. Frank Giles, *Sunday Times*, p. 131
35. Duke of Windsor to Gerald Hamilton, cited in 'Duke Mused, If Still King Could I Have Halted Hitler?', *The Times*, 13 December 2013
36. Michael Bloch, *Ribbentrop*, pp. 430–1
37. Ian Kershaw, *Hitler: A Biography*, p. 964
38. Gitta Sereny, *Albert Speer: His Battle with Truth*, p. 573
39. *Nazi Conspiracy and Aggression*: Opinion and Judgement Volume, US Government 1947, pp. 115–16
40. Ibid., pp. 111–13
41. Lynn Picknett, Clive Prince, Stephen Prior and Robert Brydon, *War of the Windsors*, p. 195
42. Jonathan Petropoulos, *Royals and the Reich*, pp. 334–6

43. *Documents on German Foreign Policy*, Series C, Volume IV, No. 531

44. Anthony Cave Brown, *"C", The Secret Life of Sir Stewart Menzies*, p. 180

45. *Sunday Times*, 3 March 1946

46. Neil Balfour and Sally Mackay, *Paul of Yugoslavia*, p. 295

47. George VI's Diary, Volume XI, 12 March 1946

48. Ibid., 22 November 1945

49. Ibid., 22–28 April 1946

50. Craig S. Smith, 'Romania's King without a Throne outlives Foes and Setbacks', *New York Times*, 27 January 2007

51. George VI's Diary, Volume X, 16 June 1945

52. NA (US) Diplomatic Branch, 841.001/3–1547 George Marshall to Dean Acheson, 15 March 1947, cited in Sarah Bradford, *George VI*, p. 565

53. TNA FO 800/521 Earl of Halifax to Foreign Office, 15 October 1945

54. TNA FO 800/521 Memorandum, 'The Windsor Papers', Ernest Bevin to Prime Minister, 30 June 1947

55. Ibid.

56. Meeting between Attlee and Bevin on 28 February 1947, cited in TNA FO 800/521, Memorandum, 'The Windsor Papers', Ernest Bevin to Prime Minister, 30 June 1947

57. TNA FO 800/521 Ernest Bevin to Clement Attlee, 31 July 1947

58. *The Memoirs of Princess Alice*, p. 154

59. Ibid.

60. Ibid., p. 156

61. George VI's Diary, Volume XI, 22–28 April 1946

62. John Wheeler-Bennett, *King George VI*, p. 755

63. William Shawcross, *Queen Elizabeth*, p. 619

64. Ibid., p. 621

65. Neil Balfour and Sally Mackay, *Paul of Yugoslavia*, p. 297

66. John Wheeler-Bennett, *King George VI*, p. 762

67. Ibid., p. 716

68. John Colville, *Footprints in Time: Memories*, pp. 219–20

69. Philip Eade, *Young Prince Philip*, p. 202

70. Sophia Watson, *Marina*, p. 200

71. *The Memoirs of Princess Alice*, p. 164

72. John Wheeler-Bennett, *King George VI*, p. 755

73. Medical Bulletin released 23 November 1948

74. 'King's Operation: Condition Entirely Satisfactory', *Mail*, Adelaide, 12 March 1949, p. 1, and *Sunday Herald*, Sydney, 13 March 1949

75. Christopher Wilson, 'Revealed: the Duke and Duchess of Windsor's Secret Plot', *Daily Telegraph*, 22 November 2009

76. George VI to the Duke of Windsor, 16 December 1949, cited in Philip Ziegler, *King Edward VIII*, p. 457

77. Christopher Wilson, *Dancing with the Devil*, p. 163

78. Ibid., p. 164

79. Anne Sebba, *That Woman*, p. 270

80. John Wheeler-Bennett, *King George VI*, p. 789

81. William Shawcross, *Queen Elizabeth*, p. 647

82. George VI's Christmas Broadcast, 1951

83. BBC Newsreel, King and Queen see Royal Departure, 1 February 1952

84. John Wheeler-Bennett, *King George VI*, p. 803

85. Sarah Bradford, George VI, p. 608, from Bradford's interview with Sir Edward Ford.

86. John Colville, *The Fringes of Power: Downing Street Diaries*, p. 640

87. Churchill Archives, Winston Churchill's eulogy to George VI, 7 February 1952

Epilogue

1. TNA PREM 11/1074 Churchill to Eisenhower, 1 July 1953

2. Parliamentary Archives, BBK/G/6/20, Churchill to Eisenhower, 27 June 1953, and Eisenhower to Churchill, 2 July 1953

3. *Documents on German Foreign Policy*, Volume X, Series D

4. TNA FO 800/521 Letter from Ernest Bevin to Clement Attlee, 31 July 1947, confirms that the duke will be permitted to see German telegrams before their publication

5. 'German War Time Plot Revealed and Answered', *The Times*, 1 August 1957, p. 8

6. Footnote in *Documents on German Foreign Policy*, Series D, Volume X, No. 276 Huene to Ribbentrop, 2 August 1940, p. 398 refers to the Duke's telegram

7. Anthony Cave Brown, *"C", The Secret Life of Sir Stewart Menzies*, pp. 273 and 198, and John Wheeler-Bennett, cited in Sarah Bradford, *George VI*, p. 565

8. John Costello, *Mask of Treachery*, p. 405

9. Peter Wright, *Spycatcher*, p. 283

10. Leif Leifland, *Svartlistningen av Axel Wenner-Gren*

11. Adrian O'Sullivan, *German Covert Initiatives and British Intelligence in Persia 1939–45*

12. Sarah Bradford, *George VI*, p. 562

13. TNA FO 1049/596 Correspondence relating to the confiscation of Foundation Property of the Family of the Duke of Saxe-Coburg and Gotha

14. TNA FO 1049/596 Sir Ulick Alexander to Major J.P. Henniker at the FO, 3 December 1946

15. TNA FO120/1176 'British Royal Family interest in the Saxe-Coburg Gotha estates in Austria' (classified)

SELECT BIBLIOGRAPHY

Allen, Peter, *The Crown and the Swastika, Hitler, Hess and the Duke of Windsor*, Robert Hale, London, 1983

Balfour, Neil and Sally Mackay, *Paul of Yugoslavia, Britain's Maligned Friend*, Hamish Hamilton, London, 1980

Beaken, Robert, *Cosmo Lang, Archbishop in War and Crisis*, Tauris & Co, London, 2012

Beaton, Cecil, *The Wandering Years, Diaries 1922–1939*, Weidenfeld & Nicolson, London, 1961

Beevor, Antony, *The Second World War*, Weidenfeld & Nicolson, London, 2012

Birkenhead, Lord, *Walter Monckton, The Life of Viscount Monckton of Brenchley*, Weidenfeld & Nicolson, London, 1969

Bishop, Patrick, *Battle of Britain*, Quercus, London, 2009

Bloch, Michael, *The Secret File of the Duke of Windsor*, Little, Brown Book Group, London, 1988

———*Ribbentrop*, Little, Brown Book Group, London, 1992

———(ed.), *Wallis and Edward Letters 1931–1937: The Intimate Correspondence of the Duke and Duchess of Windsor*, Simon & Schuster, New York, 1986

Boyle, Peter G. (ed.), *The Churchill Eisenhower Correspondence 1953–1955*, University of North Carolina Press, North Carolina, 1990

Bradford, Sarah, *George VI*, Penguin, London, 1989

Brown, Anthony Cave, *"C," The Secret Life of Sir Stewart Menzies, Spymaster to Winston Churchill*, Macmillan, New York, 1987

Chisholm, Anne and Michael Davie, *Beaverbrook, A Life*, Hutchinson, London, 1992

Christy, Jim, *The Price of Power, A Biography of Charles Eugene Bedaux*, Doubleday, Toronto, Canada, 1984

Churchill, Winston S., *The Second World War: The Gathering Storm*, Volume 1, Cassell & Co., 1948

———*The Second World War: Their Finest Hour*, Volume 2, Cassell & Co., 1949

———*The Second World War: The Grand Alliance*, Volume 3, Cassell & Co., 1950

———*The Second World War: Triumph and Tragedy*, Volume 6, Cassell & Co., 1954

Colville, Sir John, *The Fringes of Power: Downing Street Diaries 1939–55*, Weidenfeld & Nicolson, London, 1983

Costello, John, *Mask of Treachery, Spies, Lies, & Betrayal*, Warner Books, New York, 1988

Documents on German Foreign Policy 1918–45: Series C, Volumes IV, V and VI; Series D, Volumes VII, VIII & X; HMSO, 1956

Donaldson, Frances, *Edward VIII, The Road to Abdication*, Weidenfeld & Nicolson, London, 1974

————*King George VI and Queen Elizabeth*, Weidenfeld & Nicolson, London, 1977

Eade, Philip, *Young Prince Philip, His Turbulent Early Life*, HarperCollins, London, 2012

Eisenhower, David, *Eisenhower at War, 1943–45*, Random House, London, 1986

Ellis, Jennifer (ed.), *Thatched with Gold, The Memoirs of Mabell Countess of Airlie*, Hutchinson, London, 1962

Fairbanks, Douglas, Jr., *A Hell of a War*, St Martin's Press, New York, 1993

Gilbert, Martin, *Finest Hour, Winston S. Churchill*, Volume VI, 1939–1941, Heinemann, London, 1983

————*Road to Victory, Winston S. Churchill*, Volume VII, 1941–1945, Heinemann, London, 1986

Giles, Frank, *Sundry Times, Autobiography*, John Murray, London, 1986

Glass, Charles, *Americans in Paris, Life and Death under Nazi Occupation, 1940–44*, HarperCollins, London, 2009

Gloucester, HRH The Duchess of, *The Memoirs of Princess Alice, Duchess of Gloucester*, William Collins, London, 1983

Hart-Davis, Duff (ed.), *King's Counsellor, Abdication and War: The Diaries of Sir Alan Lascelles*, Weidenfeld & Nicolson, London, 2006

Hastings, Max, *Finest Years, Churchill as Warlord, 1940–45*, HarperCollins, London, 2009

Hibbert, Christopher, *Edward VII: The Last Victorian King*, Palgrave Macmillan, New York, 2007

Hickman, Tom, *Churchill's Bodyguard, The Authorised Biography of Walter H. Thompson*, Headline, London, 2005

Higham, Charles, *Mrs Simpson, Secret Lives of the Duchess of Windsor*, Pan Books, London, 2005

————*Trading with the Enemy*, Robert Hale, London, 1983

Howarth, Patrick, *George VI*, Hutchinson, London, 1987

Ismay, James, *The Memoirs of General Lord Ismay*, Heinemann, London, 1960

James, Robert Rhodes (ed.), *Chips, The Diaries of Sir Henry Channon*, Weidenfeld & Nicolson, London, 1967

Jenkins, Roy, *Churchill*, Macmillan, London, 2001

Johnson, Paul, *Churchill*, Penguin, New York, 2009

Judd, Denis, *King George VI*, Michael Joseph, London, 1982

King, Stella, *Princess Marina, Her Life and Times*, Cassell, London, 1969

Leifland, Leif, *Svartlistningen av Axel Wenner-Gren*, Askelin & Hagglund, Stockholm, 1979

Lindroth, Orjan, *The True Story of Axel Wenner-Gren*, The Swedish Press, Stockholm, 2006

Lockhart, Sir Robert Bruce, *The Diaries of Sir Robert Bruce Lockhart, 1915–1938*, ed. Kenneth Young, Macmillan, London, 1973

Logue, Mark and Peter Conradi, *The King's Speech, How One Man Saved the British Monarchy*, Quercus, London, 2010

Longford, Elizabeth, *The Queen Mother*, HarperCollins, London, 1981

McLeod, Kirsty, *Battle Royal*, Robinson, London, 1999

Noble Frankland, Anthony, *Prince Henry Duke of Gloucester*, Weidenfeld & Nicolson, London, 1980

Owen, James, *A Serpent in Eden*, Little, Brown & Co., London, 2005

Padfield, Peter, *Hess, Hitler & Churchill, The Real Turning Point of the Second World War*, Faber and Faber, London, 2013

Payn, Graham and Sheridan Morley (eds), *The Noël Coward Diaries*, Little, Brown & Co., Boston, 1982

Petropoulos, Jonathan, *Royals and the Reich, The Princes von Hessen in Nazi Germany*, Oxford University Press, New York, 2006

Picknett, Lynn, Clive Prince and Stephen Prior, *Double Standards, The Rudolf Hess Cover-up*, Little, Brown & Co., 2001

Pope-Hennessy, James, *Queen Mary*, George Allen and Unwin, London, 1959

Roberts, Andrew, '*The Holy Fox*', *A Biography of Lord Halifax*, Weidenfeld & Nicolson, London, 1991

Schellenberg, Walter, *The Schellenberg Memoirs*, trans. L. Hagen, Deutsch, London, 1956

———(ed.), *Counting One's Blessings, The Selected Letters of Queen Elizabeth, the Queen Mother*, Macmillan, London, 2012

Sebag-Montefiore, Hugh, *Dunkirk: Fight to the Last Man*, Penguin, London, 2006

Sebba, Anne, *That Woman, The Life of Wallis Simpson, Duchess of Windsor*, St Martin's Press, New York, 2012

Shawcross, William, *Queen Elizabeth, The Queen Mother, The Official Biography*, Macmillan, London, 2009

Sitwell, Osbert, *Rat Week: An Essay on the Abdication*, Michael Joseph, London, 1986

Soames, Mary (ed.), *Speaking for Themselves, The Personal Letters of Winston and Clementine Churchill*, Doubleday, London, 1998

Stafford, David (ed.), *Flight from Reality, Rudolf Hess and his Mission to Scotland, 1941*, Random House, London, 2002

Strobl, Gerwin, *The Germanic Isle*, Cambridge University Press, Cambridge, 2000

Taylor, Fred (ed.), *The Goebbels Diaries 1939–1941*, Hamish Hamilton, London, 1982

Thompson, Walter, *Beside the Bulldog: The Intimate Memoirs of Churchill's Bodyguard*, Apollo Publishing, London, 2003

Thornton, Michael, *Royal Feud, The Queen Mother and the Duchess of Windsor*, Pan Books, London, 1985

Turner, Henry Ashby, Jr., *General Motors and the Nazis, The Struggle for Control of Opel, Europe's Biggest Carmaker*, Yale University Press, Newhaven, 2005

Vickers, Hugo (ed.), *The Unexpurgated Beaton Diaries*, Weidenfeld & Nicolson, London, 2003

Warwick, Christopher, *George and Marina, The Duke and Duchess of Kent*, Weidenfeld and Nicolson, London, 1988

Watson, Sophia, *Marina, The Story of a Princess*, Weidenfeld & Nicolson, London, 1994

Wenner-Gren, Axel, *Call to Reason, An Appeal to Common Sense*, Farrar & Rinehart, New York, 1938

Wentworth Day, James, *HRH Princess Marina, Duchess of Kent*, Robert Hale, London, 1962

Wheeler-Bennett, John, *King George VI, His Life and Reign*, Macmillan, London, 1958

———*Friends, Enemies and Sovereigns*, Macmillan, London, 1976

Whiting, Audrey, *The Kents, A Royal Family*, Hutchinson, London, 1985

Windsor, HRH The Duke of, *A King's Story, The Memoirs of HRH The Duke of Windsor*, Cassell, 1951

Windsor, The Duchess of, *The Heart Has Its Reasons*, Michael Joseph, London, 1958

Wright, Peter, with Paul Greengrass, *Spycatcher*, Dell Publishing, New York, 1987

Young, Kenneth (ed.), *The Diaries of Sir Robert B. Lockhart 1915–1938*, St. Martin's Press, New York, 1973

Ziegler, Philip, *King Edward VIII, A Biography*, Alfred A. Knopf, New York, 1991

———*London at War, 1939–1945*, Mandarin, London, 1986

ACKNOWLEDGEMENTS

I would like to express my gratitude to Her Majesty Queen Elizabeth II for her gracious permission to read the war-time records of her father and her uncles at the Royal Archives at Windsor. George VI's personal chronicle of the Second World War in his eleven-volume War Diary brought the times vividly to life, along with the private correspondence between the king, his brothers and Queen Mary. I am most indebted to the senior archivist, Pamela Clark, and the team at the royal archives for their generous assistance with my research over many weeks. In addition, Nicholas Marden, Private Secretary to HRH The Duke of Kent, and Alistair Todd, Private Secretary to HRH The Duke of Gloucester and Alistair Wood, Gloucester's former Private Secretary, provided valued support for the project.

This book could not have been completed without expert advice from historians working in the field. I would like to thank Gary Sheffield, Professor of War Studies, University of Wolverhampton, for reading the manuscript and for his thoughtful insights and patience with innumerable queries. I am also grateful to David Stafford, Emeritus Professor of History, Edinburgh University, author of *Flight from Reality, Rudolf Hess and His Mission to Scotland 1941* (2002), for his comments on the Hess episode and Jonathan Petropoulos, Professor of European History, Claremont McKenna College, California, author of *Royals and the Reich* (2006), for guidance on the German princes.

Thanks are due to many others for their specialist expertise: Gill Bennett, Official Historian, Foreign Office; Major General Charles Ramsay; Allen Packwood, Director Churchill Archives, Cambridge; Christopher Martin, Head of Development, Historic Royal Palaces; Deirdre Murphy, Curator, Kensington Palace; Lisa Heighway, Historic Photographs, Royal Collection Trust; Elizabeth Scott, Exhibitions Manager for the Cabinet War Rooms; Heather Johnson, National Museum of the Royal Navy, Portsmouth; Theresa Sear, Dover Castle, English Heritage; Carine Lachevre, Musée de l'Armée, Paris; Dave

Shawyer, British Telecom Archives; and numerous others who helped with queries along the way. Any remaining errors are my own.

In researching this story I am most grateful to the staff in a number of public archives including the National Archives at Kew, the Churchill Archives Centre, the Bodleian, the British Library, the former newspaper library at Colindale, the Cartier Archive and others. This project benefitted immensely from the investigative skills of my researchers. I am particularly indebted to Alison Ray, PhD candidate, University College London, for her searches in the public archives and her attention to detail which led to new records and sources. I would also like to thank Shamim Gammage, PhD candidate Oxford University, for his proficiency in finding his way through the American sources and the FBI archives. Research meetings were always a great pleasure and the book could not have been completed in its current form without their excellent input.

In piecing together the narrative, I owe much to previous authors of this period. I would like to thank Philip Ziegler, author of *King Edward VIII* (1991), and Sarah Bradford, author of *George VI* (1989), for their generous assistance with my queries. Thanks are due to Michael Bloch who worked with the Duchess of Windsor's lawyer, Maitre Suzanne Blum, to bring to light many documents that have informed his studies, notably *The Secret File of the Duke of Windsor* (1988), and to the Little, Brown Book Group for permission to cite extracts. Thank you, too, to the following copyright holders: The Orion Publishing Group and St Martin's Press for permission to quote from Wallis's honeymoon letters to her second husband cited in Anne Sebba's *That Woman: The Life of Wallis Simpson, Duchess of Windsor*; Rupert Crew Ltd, Orion, and the literary executor of the late Sir Cecil Beaton to quote from Beaton's diaries; Sheil Land Associates Ltd for permission to cite extracts from *Chips: The Diaries of Sir Henry Channon* edited by Robert Rhodes James; Alan Brodie and NC Aventales AG for *The Noel Coward Diaries*; William Shawcross; Mark Logue and Peter Conradi; *The New York Times*, *The Times*, *Daily Mail*, *Daily Mirror and Express Newspapers*; lines from 'The King is Still in London', words by Roma Hunter © *Copyright Chester Music Limited trading as Dash Music Co. Limited, all rights reserved, international copyright secured, used by permission of Music Sales Limited;* lines from 'Comin' in on a Wing and a Prayer', words and music by Jimmy McHugh and Harold Adamson © Copyright 1943 EMI United Partnership Limited, all rights reserved, international copyright secured and used by permission of Music Sales Limited. Rights for the Extended Term of Copyright in the U.S. Assigned to Cotton Club Publishing (administered by Universal-MCA Music Publishing, a Division of Universal Studios Inc.) and Harold Adamson Music (Administered by the Songwriters Guild Of America), all rights reserved and used by permission of Alfred Music.

In New York it has been a great pleasure to work once more with Clive Priddle, publisher at PublicAffairs, who helped to inspire the project in the first place and also provided access to many newly discovered letters between Betty Lawson-Johnston and members of the royal family. These provided fresh insights on the narrative from the outset and encouraged me to take on such an ambitious venture. Thank you, too, to Melissa Veronesi at PublicAffairs for her guidance during the book's US production and to Melissa Raymond. In London it has been a delight to work with Bill Swainson, Senior Commissioning Editor at Bloomsbury, London, and I appreciated his expert editorial view throughout the project. I feel most indebted to Anna Simpson at Bloomsbury for managing each phase of production and to Sarah-Jane Forder for her thoughtful copyedit. The project would never have happened without Gordon Wise at Curtis Brown and I have benefitted enormously from his wise overview during the years of writing.

Lastly heartfelt thanks to friends and family whose loyal support helped me to reach the final full stop. Thank you so much to Pete and Jo and particularly to Julia Lilley, whose help and encouragement made this book possible.

INDEX

Deborah Cadbury is a writer, award-winning documentary producer for the BBC, the author of seven books, and a relative of the famous Quaker family that gave their name to one of the world's most famous brands of chocolate. She lives in London.

PublicAffairs is a publishing house founded in 1997. It is a tribute to the standards, values, and flair of three persons who have served as mentors to countless reporters, writers, editors, and book people of all kinds, including me.

I. F. STONE, proprietor of *I. F. Stone's Weekly*, combined a commitment to the First Amendment with entrepreneurial zeal and reporting skill and became one of the great independent journalists in American history. At the age of eighty, Izzy published *The Trial of Socrates*, which was a national bestseller. He wrote the book after he taught himself ancient Greek.

BENJAMIN C. BRADLEE was for nearly thirty years the charismatic editorial leader of *The Washington Post*. It was Ben who gave the *Post* the range and courage to pursue such historic issues as Watergate. He supported his reporters with a tenacity that made them fearless and it is no accident that so many became authors of influential, best-selling books.

ROBERT L. BERNSTEIN, the chief executive of Random House for more than a quarter century, guided one of the nation's premier publishing houses. Bob was personally responsible for many books of political dissent and argument that challenged tyranny around the globe. He is also the founder and longtime chair of Human Rights Watch, one of the most respected human rights organizations in the world.

·   ·   ·

For fifty years, the banner of Public Affairs Press was carried by its owner Morris B. Schnapper, who published Gandhi, Nasser, Toynbee, Truman, and about 1,500 other authors. In 1983, Schnapper was described by *The Washington Post* as "a redoubtable gadfly." His legacy will endure in the books to come.

Peter Osnos, *Founder and Editor-at-Large*